T0396784

Endorsements

> **❝**

Human Resource is our most precious asset. Progressive HR enhances human capital. Regressive HR depresses it.

HR practitioners are entrusted with heavy responsibility. They must equip themselves with the knowledge and skills so that they could multiply the human capital under their care.

This HR management series is timely. It is written in the Singapore context guided by our local employment laws and tripartite guidelines and standards. I commend the authors for their endeavour to produce such a first.

Lim Swee Say
Former Minister for Manpower
Former Secretary General, National Trades Union Congress

Human Resource is a critical enabler. Good or bad HR can mean the difference between an organisation succeeding or failing. At the individual level, HR impacts an employee's job fulfilment and quality of work life. This is particularly important with a changing workforce profile made up of more professionals, managers and executives.

This HR series is a useful compendium of HR fundamentals and lessons drawn from real-life cases. The authors have distilled lessons from their decades of HR practice and poured their insights into it. Overall, a useful and practical guide for any HR practitioner and a laudable contribution to the HR community in Singapore.

Patrick Tay Teck Guan
Assistant Secretary-General, National Trades Union Congress

This is an outstanding Human Resource book series which comprehensively covers everything HR professionals need to know to get the people management function right. It is specifically tailored for the HR practitioner in Singapore as it navigates through all the employment statutes and tripartite guidelines and standards unique to Singapore.

One of my favourite aspects of this book series is the thorough treatment of special areas like retrenchment, retirement and re-employment which are complex and employers must pay particular attention to. The authors provide readers with a clear understanding of the legal requirements and obligations an employer must meet.

Another standout is the spotlight on HR's role in managing and uplifting our lower-wage and vulnerable workers and the importance of ensuring equal opportunity and inclusivity at the workplace.

HR practitioners who want to practise fair and decent HR for their organisations should have this HR book series as an essential toolkit.

Zainal Sapari
Assistant-Director General, National Trades Union Congress
Chairman, Tripartite Clusters for Cleaning, Security and Landscape Industries (2012–2023)
Member, Tripartite Workgroup on Lower-Wage Workers

HR practitioners play a pivotal role in helping organisations succeed, by managing and developing people. Not an easy task. We deal with people. HR practitioners are also people, so there is often no guaranteed outcome. To succeed, HR practitioners cannot just opine and emote. They must add knowledge and expertise. To get things right or close to right, HR must at the very least be legally compliant. Further, HR must provide policies and practices that are technically and conceptually sound. The onus is on HR practitioners to equip themselves with the essential knowledge on HR management. To do less is simply unprofessional.

This HR series gives a comprehensive treatment of the full range of HR topics. Most valuable are the real-life cases that offer good learning points from successes as well as mistakes. The authors have unreservedly poured their extensive knowledge and deep insights into the book series. With this valuable resource in their hands, HR learners and aspiring practitioners can learn, level up and step up.

Lim Suet Wun
Former Group Chief Operating Officer, IHH Healthcare
Former Group Chief Executive Officer, National Healthcare Group

---

I was a colleague of Jacqueline Chin, and am an admirer of her deep expertise in the fundamentals of HR and HR legal framework. I am glad she has taken pains to co-author this practical series to share her knowledge with aspiring HR practitioners and learners. A series written by HR practitioners for fellow HR practitioners. I have no doubt it will make a significant contribution to HR practice in Singapore.

Ng Lang
Chief Executive, Land Transport Authority

Having worked with Oun Hean for several years on a few human capital projects, I have experienced and learnt from him firsthand his deep knowledge, extensive experience and critical insights in human capital management. These have now been comprehensively and systematically documented in this series of books. These books are a must-have for all bosses and managers who are involved in managing and developing people.

Ervin Kua
Director, Easmed Asia Pte Ltd

This series is very useful as a guide and advisory to small business owners who may not have practical working experience in Human Resource but find themselves facing day-to-day challenges in this area. The breadth and depth of knowledge shared are very comprehensive, giving business owners different perspectives to explore and determine which practices best suit their industry and business. I believe this series will well equip and build much confidence in business owners and HR practitioners to make better decisions in HR.

Jessica Lim
Director, The Plattering Co

The series, Human Resource Management in Singapore, is easily the most comprehensive and leading treatment of HRM/employee relations in Singapore. It covers an extensive range of Human Resource topics in both the legal and practical aspects. Issues are candidly addressed from the perspectives of the government, employers, unions and employees. Complicated Human Resource management issues and problems are systematically analysed and clearly explained so that any HR practitioner, regardless of experience, will benefit. This series, the first in Singapore, will be an insightful guide for any person who has to deal with people management and employee relations matters.

Associate Professor David Wan
Head, Master of Human Capital Management Programme
Singapore University of Social Sciences

Human Resource management is complicated as it deals with people. The numerous functions and dimensions in managing and developing human capital are closely connected. It is challenging to master these functions and at the same time integrate them coherently and holistically in a dynamic context. This series will uniquely help Human Resource practitioners in their professional career as it covers all the relevant human capital topics with considerable emphasis and practical pointers. Students doing Human Resource management modules will also find this series tremendously helpful in their learning journey.

Irene Chu
Course Chair, School of Business
Singapore Polytechnic

This is an outstanding series. Human Resource management topics have been extensively covered. Many Human Resource management concepts, frameworks, processes and practices have been meticulously examined and clearly explained. Many real-life examples have been shared. The inclusion of some iconic court cases has further deepened the treatment of the topics. Without doubt, HR practitioners of all levels will find this series invaluable. The breadth and depth of all the chapters reflect the extensive and solid experience of Oun Hean and Jacqueline.

Kee Chia Choon
Director, Singapore National Employers Federation

Human Resource Management — The Complete Guide is poised to raise the standard of Human Resource management in Singapore. This publication is a remarkable achievement. Given the importance of human capital management and development in Singapore, this series of books comes in timely to help organisations manage and develop our people effectively. All Human Resource practitioners and organisations will find this Guide an indispensable asset.

Yeo Meng Hin
A Strong Advocate of Human Capital

Human Resource is a multi-faceted people function. Because HR deals with people, it is not easy to do HR well. I have benefitted immensely from Jacqueline's coaching and mentoring in the early days of my HR career. She has the ability to explain concepts in a most cogent and lucid manner, demystifying complexity so that it is easy to understand and apply. Her deep HR knowledge, wealth of experience and incisive insights now captured in this HR book series will surely stand to benefit HR students, newbies and practitioners who look to strengthen their grounding and gain confidence in HR practice.

Elena Leaw
Executive Director, Human Resource
in a financial institution

Series on Human Resource Management

Human Resource Management in Singapore

The Complete Guide

Series on Human Resource Management

Print ISSN: 2972-421X
Online ISSN: 2972-4228

Series Editors: Oun Hean Loh
Jacqueline Suet Peck Chin

Published

Human Resource Management in Singapore — The Complete Guide
Volume A: Employment Management
by Oun Hean Loh and Jacqueline Suet Peck Chin

Human Resource Management in Singapore — The Complete Guide
Volume B: Work and Remuneration
by Oun Hean Loh and Jacqueline Suet Peck Chin

Human Resource Management in Singapore — The Complete Guide
Volume C: Employee Benefits
by Oun Hean Loh and Jacqueline Suet Peck Chin

Human Resource Management in Singapore — The Complete Guide
Volume D: Performance and Development
by Oun Hean Loh and Jacqueline Suet Peck Chin

Human Resource Management in Singapore — The Complete Guide
Volume E: Employee Conduct and Relations
by Oun Hean Loh and Jacqueline Suet Peck Chin

Series on Human Resource Management

Human Resource Management in Singapore

The Complete Guide

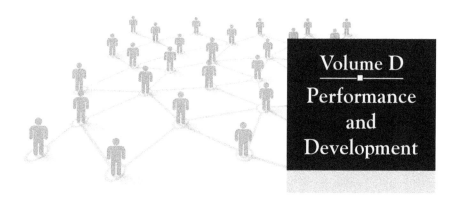

Volume D
Performance
and
Development

Oun Hean Loh | Jacqueline Suet Peck Chin

World Scientific

NEW JERSEY • LONDON • SINGAPORE • BEIJING • SHANGHAI • TAIPEI • CHENNAI

Published by

World Scientific Publishing Co. Pte. Ltd.

5 Toh Tuck Link, Singapore 596224

USA office: 27 Warren Street, Suite 401-402, Hackensack, NJ 07601

UK office: 57 Shelton Street, Covent Garden, London WC2H 9HE

Library of Congress Cataloging-in-Publication Data

Names: Loh, Oun Hean, author. | Chin, Jacqueline Suet Peck, author.

Title: Human resource management in Singapore : the complete guide.
    Volume A, Employment management / Oun Hean Loh, Jacqueline Suet Peck Chin.

Description: New Jersey : World Scientific, [2025] | Series: Series on human resource management,
    2972-421X | Includes bibliographical references.

Identifiers: LCCN 2023028674 | ISBN 9789811277016 (hardcover : volume A) |
    ISBN 9789811277023 (ebook : volume A) | ISBN 9789811277030 (ebook other : volume A) |
    ISBN 9789811279423 (hardcover : volume B) | ISBN 9789811279430 (ebook : volume B) |
    ISBN 9789811279447 (ebook other : volume B) | ISBN 9789811280849 (hardcover : volume C) |
    ISBN 9789811280856 (ebook : volume C) | ISBN 9789811280863 (ebook other : volume C)

Subjects: LCSH: Personnel management--Singapore.

Classification: LCC HF5549.2.S56 L65 2025 | DDC 658.30095957--dc23/eng/20230727

LC record available at https://lccn.loc.gov/2023028674

British Library Cataloguing-in-Publication Data

A catalogue record for this book is available from the British Library.

Volume D: Performance and Development

ISBN 9789811284168 (hardcover)

ISBN 9789811284175 (ebook for institutions)

ISBN 9789811284182 (ebook for individuals)

For any available supplementary material, please visit
https://www.worldscientific.com/worldscibooks/10.1142/13620#t=suppl

Desk Editors: Murali Appadurai/Pui Yee Lum

Typeset by Stallion Press
Email: enquiries@stallionpress.com

About the Authors

 **Loh Oun Hean** is a highly experienced Human Resource and Industrial Relations leader, whose career spanned over 30 years with key appointments in Singapore's Ministry of Manpower, Maybank, Singapore Airlines and Deloitte Southeast Asia. Following his corporate appointments, he has been providing consulting, advisory and training services on human resource and general management to numerous organisations.

He has extensive, both strategic and hands-on, experience in HR management, job analysis and evaluation, job grading and salary structure, performance management systems, wage reform, profit-sharing bonus schemes, flexible benefits scheme, competency framework design and organisational restructuring.

His in-depth involvement in industrial relations is recognisable, having negotiated with trade unions, reviewed labour legislation and practices, conciliated and resolved industrial disputes, managed and presented arbitration cases, dealt with disciplinary issues, as well as having conducted numerous wage negotiations, industrial relations and labour legislation courses.

Oun Hean graduated from the University of Melbourne and London School of Economics. He had served in the Industrial Relations Panel of the Singapore National Employers Federation and Employer Panel of the Industrial Arbitration Court.

He single-handedly wrote the book "Industrial Relations in Singapore — Practice and Perspective" which was published by World Scientific Publishing in June 2018.

Jacqueline Chin Suet Peck is a senior Human Resource leader whose 30-year career spanned both the public and private sectors, with key appointments in RHB Bank, International Enterprise Singapore, National Healthcare Group, National Trades Union Congress and the Public Service Division, Singapore Civil Service.

Her HR expertise spans the full spectrum of HR domains: manpower planning, salary and benefits design, performance management, training and development, competency framework design, talent management and succession planning, industrial relations, disciplinary management, expatriate compensation, HR information systems and organisational development.

Jacqueline had developed HR systems and capabilities for the entire employee value chain. As an architect of HR, she had built whole-of-enterprise HR information systems, laid HR foundation for several corporations to enable organisational growth, authored HR policies and standards and rationalised HR practices to support strategic alignment, and steered critical HR transitions through re-organisations and mergers and acquisitions.

Jacqueline had served in the HR Manpower, Skills and Training Council, the HR Sectoral Tripartite Committee, the National HR Professional Certification Taskforce, as judge for the Singapore Human Resources Institute HR Awards, and as senior assessor of the Institute for Human Resource Professionals for the HR certification examination. She also lectured in employment relations and rewards management.

Jacqueline graduated from the National University of Singapore and had attended the Columbia Business School and Wharton School of the University of Pennsylvania.

Contents

Overview of Performance Management Framework

Focus of this Chapter

This chapter introduces the topic of performance management: guiding, managing and motivating employees to perform and deliver results for the organisation. We examine the importance of performance management in helping organisations safeguard and enhance their performance and effectiveness.

Given the importance and complexity of performance management which has various aspects touching on people, we plan to cover them in detail, chapter by chapter. This chapter provides an overview and appreciation of the key concepts, processes, terms and tools used in performance management. The following chapters cover the different aspects of performance management in detail:

- Chapter D2 "Performance Planning and Goals Setting"
  Requires an employee to plan ahead and sets the stage for how his performance will be measured. Challenges in crafting performance goals and determining performance standards are examined.

- Chapter D3 "Performance Feedback and Coaching"
  Describes how an employee should be informed of his performance and be guided to help him achieve the best performance outcomes.

- Chapter D4 "Performance Appraisal"
  Describes how performance appraisal is carried out and the challenges involved.

- Chapter D5 "Performance Moderation"
  Describes how performance moderation is done to enhance consistency and fairness. Methodologies used are explained and challenges shared.

- Chapter D6 "Dealing with Weak Performers"
  Discusses the causes of weak performance and the ways and structured protocol to manage weak performers.

- Chapter D7 "Performance Management and Industrial Relations"
  Examines the industrial relations dimension of performance management and the involvement of unions in representing their members on performance issues. The focus is on rank-and-file employees and junior executives who are more likely to be represented by unions.

- Chapter D8 "Performance Management: The Challenges, Realities and Alternatives"
  Integrates the discussion on the different aspects of performance management, summarises the challenges and realities involved and examines the critical success factors in making performance management effective. The chapter also explores how performance management should be done differently and whether performance evaluation and performance development conversations should be fundamentally and optically separated.

Most organisations have hitherto paid less attention to performance management for the rank-and-file employees. Chapters D1 to D6 focus on performance management for professionals and executives; practices for rank-and-file employees are only covered in Chapter D7 as we discuss the industrial relations aspect of performance management. Practices and nuances specific to small and medium enterprises are broached in Chapter D8 as we wrap up the discussion on performance management.

We advise readers to first read Chapter D1 "Overview of Performance Management Framework" before proceeding with other chapters on performance management in this Volume.

Performance Management: The What and Why

What is Performance?

D1.1   What is performance to the employee and employer may mean different things. To most employees, being punctual in reporting to work and diligently doing one's best at work may well be "performance". The employee may feel that he has already met his side of the bargain in the employment relationship. However, to the employer, it may be insufficient (even if it is the employee's best) if it falls short of the organisation's requirements or expectations. Perspective and expectations matter.

D1.2   In an employment relationship, arguably it is the employer's expectations that count. The employer is the party that pays the goodies (the salary, bonus, incentives and other rewards, including a job promotion to enable one to earn more) and is accountable for the success or failure of the organisation; therefore, the employer gets to set the requirements (or expectations) for the employee to fulfil. The magnitude of expectation imposed on an employee depends on the job level and remuneration package of the employee, as well as the attitude and generosity or mercenariness of the employer, among other factors.

> Performance
> = Employer's requirements (expectations) of an employee to deliver at work

D1.3   While the employer supposedly has the discretion to set the performance requirements/expectations, this must be done with reasonableness. To achieve the best outcome, the aspirations and needs of the employee should also be factored into the equation, where possible. If the organisational objectives align with the personal objectives of the employee, the latter will be more motivated and committed. The reality is that an employee can simply quit if he feels that the employer's requirements/expectations are set too high and not commensurate with the reward that he is getting for his employment, or his personal objectives are not met. If an employee chooses to stay on, he may just cruise along or hide below the radar.

What is Performance Management?

D1.4   As to how an employer's requirements/expectations are specified, these can take various forms; some are quantitative, while others, qualitative. Once the employer has set his requirements/expectations, the next step is to manage the employee's performance. To manage performance requires the measurement or assessment of performance. As the saying goes: *That which is not measured will not be managed.* However, a huge challenge lies in that not all aspects of work can be meaningfully and quantitatively measured. Many aspects of performance and output can only be assessed qualitatively and (subjective) judgment comes in.

D1.5 Given that work and performance have many dimensions, there may be more than one set of measurement metrics. Also, even in measuring what is measurable, how well an employee is said to perform is relative to the expectations set. If the expectations are set "wrongly" (that is, too lenient or too strict), then the conclusion on the performance/success will be off the mark. More are discussed in the later part of this chapter and Chapter D2 "Performance Planning and Goals Setting".

Importance and Purpose of Performance Management

D1.6 Managing people effectively is a major challenge in all organisations. How effectively an organisation manages and develops its human capital can create a competitive advantage for the organisation. With money, it is easy for an organisation to acquire the hardware. However, money alone cannot buy a thriving performance culture staffed with committed, competent and effective performers.

D1.7 Employees are an organisation's people assets. Organisations spend time and money to acquire, maintain and sustain their people assets. As with all kinds of assets, organisations expect and need to get a "return". It is a fair concept. That return from people assets is to reap the best performance possible from employees. This is where performance management comes in. Performance management is the means to get employees to perform effectively and sustainably.

D1.8 Effective performance management increases employees' motivation and commitment because most employees look for meaningful work and opportunities to contribute, excel and progress, apart from remuneration and a conducive work environment.

D1.9 *Why measure and manage performance?*
An organisation embarking on performance management must be clear about its purpose for doing so. What will performance management achieve for the organisation? How will performance management support organisational success? And employee success? In a nutshell, we have the following:

(a) Organisations need to communicate what matters to organisational success and employees need to know how they can individually and meaningfully contribute to that.

(b) Organisations need to know how employees are performing so that they and their employees can sustain their efforts or take further or different measures to deliver results, compete and grow.

(c) Organisations need to identify and distinguish their better performers from the average and weak performers, so as to make informed decisions on rewards, such as bonuses, increments, incentives and promotions.

(d) Employees, too, need to know how they are faring and understand what is expected of them to earn a good bonus and a salary raise, grow professionally and advance in career.

D1.10 Performance management must serve the above purposes which can be further expanded into specific objectives as shown below. When objectives are clear, then only can the organisation be deliberate in designing its performance management framework to align with its objectives.

Objectives of Performance Management	Essential Features of Performance Management Framework
1. To inform the employee of the organisation's expectations of him.	Incorporate goals setting and agreement on performance standards.
2. To regularly monitor the employee's performance and his progress in meeting the expectations of him.	Set the frequency for periodic performance feedback and review.
3. To continually guide the employee to improve his performance and close gaps (if any).	Incorporate performance feedback, training and coaching, and performance counselling (if necessary).
4. To encourage upward and downward communication and allow the employee to surface any obstacles to his performance.	Incorporate a two-way communication channel and feedback mechanism.

5. To appraise and inform the employee on how much his performance has met, or exceeded, or not met expectations.	Use a rating scale to indicate the level of performance achievement. Enforce a critical conversation between the reporting officer and the employee to discuss the performance results and the way forward.
6. To reward the employee for his performance or deprive him for under-performance.	Link performance results to the organisation's rewards system (such as bonus, increment and promotion).
7. To manage weak performers to get them to improve.	Incorporate a Performance Improvement Plan (PIP) to "rehab" an employee to satisfactory performance, and if the employee fails, to manage him out.

D1.11   Performance management must serve the organisation's interests, that is, to align employees' effort with the organisational objectives, and to get employees to deliver what the organisation wants or needs. It does not make sense if an organisation puts in great effort to recruit very good employees and does a poor job in managing them to deliver results. Likewise, it is pointless for an organisation to pay well for its employees but is undemanding on their contribution.

D1.12   Performance management cannot be operated as a standalone people management process. For performance management to produce meaningful outcomes for the organisation, it must be fully aligned and integrated with other human capital initiatives and programs, such as employee rewards, training and development, staff deployment, talent management and succession planning. Without such supporting human capital initiatives, performance management will be purely "academic" or even moot. In essence, performance management is a means (or tool), not an end in itself. If there are no consequences for poor performance (say, no impact on an employee's rewards or development), it will not matter to an employee how he is performing or assessed to be performing, and it will not matter how robust or sophisticated the performance management framework is. What really matters is how an employee's performance result will be closely and directly linked to other aspects of his employment – his salary and bonus, promotion, training and developmental opportunities, as well as the continuance of his employment. More is discussed under the section "Applications of Performance Appraisal Results" in the later part of this chapter.

D1.13   Given that performance management is an essential alignment tool, it is relevant for all organisations, regardless of whether the organisation is a commercial enterprise or a non-profit entity. It should also apply to every employee, from the most junior worker to the chief executive officer. In practice, the performance management regime is usually more emphasised for professional, managerial and executive (PME) employees. Some organisations may even skip performance management for their rank-and-file employees, or do only a cursory version of it. The basis for such a variation in emphasis is the notion that PME employees have more room to exercise discretionary effort and their contribution can bring about a more significant impact to the organisation. Whereas for rank-and-file employees, they generally work under specific instructions and follow standard work protocol, and therefore they have much less autonomy and their discretionary effort is usually marginal. Whatever approach an organisation adopts with regard to applying emphasis on performance management, what is important is that the organisation must use performance management meaningfully (and smartly) to align employees' effort to serve the organisation's ends.

The Law and Tripartite Guidelines on Performance Management

D1.14   The employment laws in Singapore do not regulate performance management. Therefore, organisations have a freehand to design their own performance management frameworks, whether elaborate or otherwise.

D1.15   The Tripartite Guidelines on Fair Employment Practices mention that employers should adopt fair and objective appraisal systems with measurable standards for assessing job performance. The intention is to ensure that employers apply a merit-based system in treating and rewarding employees. Employers are also encouraged to conduct regular and constructive performance reviews to guide employees to enhance their performance. For good governance, performance reviews should be documented. The Tripartite Guidelines also recommend that an internal appeal process be established to deal with employees' concerns relating to performance appraisal. While the Tripartite Guidelines stipulate these principles to be followed, there are no specific standards or frameworks prescribed relating to performance management policies, processes and practices.

D1.16   Performance management comes under legal scrutiny only when an organisation terminates the service of an employee on account of poor performance. If the employee challenges the termination action and appeals to the Employment Claims Tribunals or the Minister for Manpower (in the case of an employee who is a union member working in a unionised organisation), the organisation will be asked to substantiate its performance assessment as the basis for its termination action. If the organisation cannot substantiate the employee's poor performance, the termination may be viewed as without just cause, and the organisation will risk being ordered to reinstate the employee or make compensation to the employee. The legal aspect of performance management and the implications on industrial relations are covered in Chapter D7 "Performance Management and Industrial Relations".

Terms Used in Performance Management

D1.17   Performance management is a complex people process. Organisations design their own frameworks/systems nuanced to their unique needs. Consequently so, there are a myriad of terminologies associated with performance management, some have been specifically "customised/created" by organisations to suit their own context. In the ensuing sections, we make an introduction of the common terms used in performance management and define them as used in this Volume. We broadly group the terms under (a) performance management processes, (b) performance management stakeholders, (c) performance measurement and (d) performance management architecture.

Performance Management Processes

D1.18   Performance management has many sequential processes which are repeated annually.

Performance Management
Performance management is the overarching framework comprising the following activities: (a) selecting performance goals, (b) setting performance

targets and expectations, (c) providing performance feedback and coaching, (d) appraising employees on their achievements and contributions and (e) arriving at a basis to reward good performance and manage weak performance. Performance management is a critical and integral component of the overall human capital management in an organisation. The other components include manpower planning, recruitment and staff deployment, salary and reward management, training and development, and employee engagement and relations.

Performance Planning
Performance planning, which takes place at the start of each performance management cycle or year, is a process of making plans, selecting performance goals, and setting expectations on what results employees should deliver as well as the types of competencies and behaviours that they should demonstrate in their work.

Performance Feedback
Performance feedback is providing the employee with information and observations related to his work and job performance behaviours. Through interacting with the employee at work and reviewing the work done by the employee, a reporting officer can form a view about the performance of the employee and the areas where due attention should be given to help the employee perform better.

Performance Coaching
Performance coaching is a process where the reporting officer (supervisor or line manager) acting as a coach or mentor guides, encourages and facilitates the employee to meet his performance goals and help him find solutions to work problems, learn, improve and grow.

Performance Counselling
Performance counselling is a special form of interaction where the reporting officer makes the employee become aware of his work performance and/or behaviour with the intention of getting him to rectify areas that are falling short of requirements. Performance counselling usually carries a degree of assertiveness. The employee is expected to cooperate by making effort to rectify and improve his performance and/or behaviour. If the employee does not make improvement, more serious actions are likely to follow.

Performance Review
While performance feedback and coaching are supposed to happen on a continual basis without a pre-fixed schedule, performance review is a

pre-determined and more formal session for the reporting officer to review the performance of the employee. This usually takes place at regular intervals (say, quarterly, half-yearly and at the end of the appraisal year). The formal sessions of review are documented as part of the assessment of the employee's work performance.

Performance Appraisal

Performance appraisal (or evaluation) is the formal assessment of an employee's performance against the work targets set and the required performance standards and competency-based behaviours. It is typically done at the end of the performance management cycle or appraisal year. The output of performance appraisal is the assignment of a performance rating for each employee. A performance rating is essentially a score or grade denoting the performance level of an employee for the appraisal year. A good rating means that the employee has performed well. Different organisations use different rating scales.

Performance Moderation

Performance moderation is a process to review and calibrate the performance ratings recommended by the reporting officers or appraisers so that there is consistency of standards applied across an entire department, division or the organisation. It is typically facilitated by Human Resource. In essence, it is to apply a common "ruler" to determine the final performance ratings for employees.

Performance Critical Conversation

Performance critical conversation is a one-on-one session between the reporting officer and the employee after completing the annual appraisal. The conversation covers the achievements and strengths of the employee, challenges faced, areas where he can improve and how he can learn and develop. The conversation may also cover the forward plan which provides inputs for the setting of performance goals for the next appraisal period.

Performance Improvement Plan

Performance improvement plan is a program or process designed to deal with weak performers systematically and sternly. The intention is to push them to level up their performance and attain a satisfactory level — what is commonly referred to as managing "up" an employee. If that fails, the

organisation may contractually terminate the employee's employment —
what is commonly referred to as managing "out" an employee.

Performance Management Stakeholders

D1.19   Several stakeholders are involved in performance management and
organisations have named them differently, differentiated by the roles that
they play. For clarity and consistency in usage in this Volume, we define and
use the following terms:

Reporting Officer
Reporting officer is simply the direct or immediate supervisor of an
employee. He is tasked to set (or co-set) performance goals for the employee
(or direct report), provide performance feedback and coaching and appraise
his performance and contributions.

Line Manager
Line manager may mean the reporting officer of an employee. It is also common
to generically label all managers who are in line functions as "line managers". For
clarity, "reporting officer" is used in this Volume to refer to the direct supervisor
of an employee (who may be of the rank of manager or in a more junior or senior
rank), while "line manager" denotes generically a managerial staff. Readers are
advised to look at the context when the term "line manager" is used.

Direct Report
Direct report is the direct subordinate of a reporting officer.

Counter-signing Officer
Counter-signing officer is usually the direct supervisor of the reporting officer
of a direct report. In performance appraisal, the "counter-signing officer"
reviews the appraisal (of the direct report) prepared by the reporting
officer and countersigns the appraisal. The counter-signing officer may concur,
disagree or modify the appraisal done by the reporting officer.

Primary Appraiser
Some organisations refer to the reporting officer as the "primary appraiser"
(or "primary evaluator"). We use the term "primary appraiser" only in a
situation where an employee is appraised by two appraisers, one being the
primary appraiser (also the primary reporting officer) and the other being
the secondary appraiser (also the secondary reporting officer).

Secondary Appraiser
Secondary appraiser (or evaluator) is another manager who appraises an employee. This happens when the employee has done work, assignments or projects for the secondary appraiser who may be from another department. Even when an employee reports equally (that is, 50-50) to two reporting officers, one of them will be designated as the primary reporting officer (or primary appraiser) and the other, the secondary reporting officer (or secondary appraiser).

Performance Moderation Committee
Performance moderation committee is a committee comprising a group of senior management staff whose mandate is to review the performance appraisal ratings of all the employees and adjust the ratings as necessary to ensure fairness and consistency in standards applied.

Performance Measurement

D1.20   Organisations use different terms such as Key Performance Indicators (KPIs), Key Result Areas (KRAs), Performance Objectives, Key Objectives, Work Targets and Objectives & Key Results (OKRs). While many may regard these terms as largely meaning the same, they do have some differences. In this Volume, we use the terms shown below:

Performance Goals
Performance goals are simply the objectives, results or targets that an employee is supposed to achieve or deliver in a particular year or appraisal period. The goals may relate to financials (revenue, cost and margin), quality (accuracy, defect rate and customer service), productivity (speed and efficiency), capabilities (effectiveness and impact), staff (engagement level and retention rate), risk management (corporate governance, controls and safety), etc.

Work Targets
In this Volume, the term "work targets" is used together with "performance goals". "Work targets" is more definitive as an end goal or level of performance to be achieved.

Performance Expectations
Performance expectations are essentially what the organisation or reporting officer expects the employee to deliver. Some organisations refer to them as performance standards. If they are quantitative and measurable, the term work targets may be used instead.

Balanced Scorecard (BSC)
Balanced scorecard is a measurement framework which integrates performance goals from four different dimensions, namely (a) financial, (b) customers, (c) processes and (d) learning/people. The intent is to achieve more holistic success for the organisation without compromising or neglecting any aspects of its critical pillars.

Performance Factors
Performance factors are elements that are viewed as important to an organisation and which are expected of employees. Performance factors that are typically used to measure individual performance are (a) results-based performance goals (or work targets), (b) competency-based behaviour standards and (c) core value-based behavioural attributes.

Competencies
A competency is an underlying characteristic or a capability of an individual employee that can predictably enable the employee to perform effectively in a job. A "characteristic" includes motives, traits and capabilities, while a "capability" includes knowledge, skills and aptitude. Simply put, competencies help an individual employee deliver superior performance.

Core Value-based Attributes
Core value-based attributes are those behaviours that relate to the core values of an organisation. Some organisations want their employees to be appraised on how well they have demonstrated the core values as a measure of values alignment.

Performance Management Architecture

D1.21   Performance management being a complicated process should have the necessary architecture to give it a logical structure as well as enable the process to be carried out systematically and efficiently. The following are the common terms used to describe the architecture:

Performance Management Framework
In this Volume, we use the term "performance management framework" to mean the entire performance management ecosystem comprising policies, processes, performance factors, measurement metrics, performance rating scale, tools (such as bell curve and forced ranking) and forms and documents.

Performance Management System

Performance management system is essentially a module of a human resource information system (HRIS) that handles performance management in a digital (online) mode. The system is primarily used to improve workflow relating to performance management, capture performance management-related data and house all the forms and documents. The more sophisticated system has functionalities on the analysis and presentation of dashboard data to facilitate management discussion and decision-making. A good performance management system is one which interfaces with the payroll system, training and development and talent management system to enable seamless data transfer, enhance work efficiency and improve speed in extracting employee data. Performance management system is not the focus of this Volume. To avoid confusion, we use the term "performance management framework" which encapsulates all performance management policies, processes, measurement metrics, tools, forms and documents. (Many organisations, however, use performance management system to mean performance management framework.)

Performance Management Cycle and Processes

D1.22   The performance management cycle consists of several essential steps that are done in sequential order on an annual basis. Please see the following flow chart which is a common process flow for most large organisations:

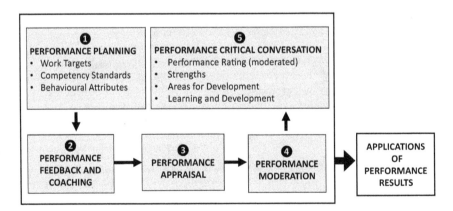

Performance Planning and Goals Setting

D1.23   Performance planning simply means to set out what is expected to be achieved or demonstrated on the job. This is one area that is often the most lacking in practice. Not every organisation does this. Even if its performance management framework purportedly specifies this step, it may be poorly enforced, leaving it much to the reporting officer and the employee (direct report) to do according to their preference. Some take performance planning seriously, while others only do a sketchy semblance of it, and there are yet others who do not do it at all.

D1.24   In a best practice scenario, the reporting officer together with the employee will jointly do performance planning to set expectations in three aspects: (a) results-based performance goals or work targets, (b) competency-based behavioural standards and (c) core value-based behavioural attributes. Details on performance planning and goals setting are covered in Chapter D2 "Performance Planning and Goals Setting".

Performance Feedback and Coaching

D1.25   Most organisations uphold the notion that performance feedback and coaching should be done on a continual ongoing basis throughout the appraisal year. That is the ideal scenario (or gold standard). The intention is to provide prompt feedback to employees regarding their progress and guide them steadily towards achieving their performance goals. If an employee is off the mark, no time is lost if the employee can be promptly alerted to close his gaps, change gear or step up the gear.

D1.26   In reality, it is difficult to enforce the gold standard. Most of the time, reporting officers and their direct reports are engrossed with work and under time pressure, tend to skip the feedback loop on how the employee is faring. Or the reporting officer may indicate in general how an employee is faring but has scant time to elaborate on how he can improve or enhance his performance, and no coaching is provided for it.

D1.27   Most organisations stipulate a requirement for mid-term review (some require quarterly reviews) in their performance management cycle. These are formal check-in sessions and are deemed to be the "minimal" even as ongoing and continual feedback and coaching may not be diligently followed.

D1.28   The real benefits of performance feedback and coaching depend a lot on how well such conversations are being conducted in practice. This is covered in Chapter D3 "Performance Feedback and Coaching".

Performance Appraisal

D1.29   The process of measuring or assessing an employee's performance is referred to as performance appraisal (or evaluation). Most organisations have taken due care to design and institutionalise performance appraisal so that the process (including the steps, protocols and formality) of appraising employees' performance can be consistent across the organisation. An organisation with the most rudimentary performance management framework usually has performance appraisal as the only component (that is, performance planning, feedback and coaching, the critical conversation and application of performance results are lacking or absent).

D1.30   Performance appraisal may come in various formats and with different features. Formats/features have evolved over the decades and are still evolving. Organisations will continue to experiment and adapt the way they handle performance appraisal, usually triggered by a change in leadership, organisational focus and people management philosophy, as well as a change in employee demographics (say, a shift from rank-and-file as majority to executives as majority). More are shared in Chapter D4 "Performance Appraisal".

Performance Moderation

D1.31   When a reporting officer gives his assessment of his employee's performance, it should be treated as a preliminary assessment. The next step is to let all preliminary assessments by reporting officers undergo a review and moderation process by the organisation's management.

D1.32   Moderation is the critical and final step in determining an employee's performance rating. The purpose of doing moderation is to allow all line heads (or senior management) to do cross-comparisons of all assessments done by the reporting officers (who report to them), so as to achieve as much consistency as possible in the standard of appraisal. Put simply, it is to calibrate to arrive at a common "ruler" so that no line managers/heads and reporting officers would be skewed in their assessments in either being too stringent or too lenient.

D1.33   Usually, the first round of moderation is done by the counter-signing officer (that is, the boss of the reporting officer of the employee), or the departmental/ line head. After which, these first-round moderated performance assessments (which are still treated as preliminary) will be submitted to the Human Resource (HR) department. HR will collate all the preliminary assessments and do a "thumb-through" to spot obvious inconsistencies or questionable patterns (such as an exceptionally large proportion of employees given high ratings).

D1.34   Following which HR would convene a cross-departmental or organisation-wide moderation exercise. The composition of the moderation panel, methods/protocols of doing moderation (or calibration) and the challenges and nuances involved are discussed in Chapter D5 "Performance Moderation".

D1.35   The typical process flow of performance appraisal and moderation is shown below:

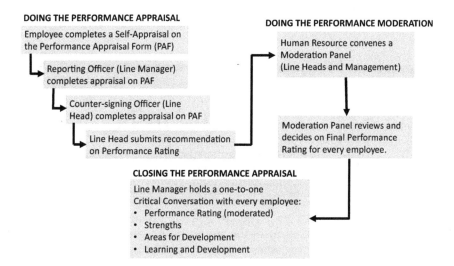

Performance Critical Conversation

D1.36   To have a proper closure to the performance appraisal exercise for the performance management cycle (or appraisal year), the reporting officer should hold a one-to-one critical conversation with the employee.

D1.37   The critical conversation should at least cover these aspects:

(a) the employee's final performance rating (after moderation);
(b) his strengths;
(c) his areas for development (or improvement); and
(d) learning and development plans for the employee (such as training opportunities, stretch assignments and postings to broaden exposure).

D1.38   The employee may also provide feedback to the reporting officer on the challenges that he faces (on the job or on the personal life front) so that the reporting officer can explore ways to provide resources and support to him where possible.

D1.39   The critical conversation should be employee-centric, as ultimately, the conversation is a wrap-up for the employee's performance for the entire appraisal year. It requires skill on the part of the reporting officer to hold a fruitful and meaningful performance-critical conversation. More are shared in Chapter D4 "Performance Appraisal".

Formats and Frequency of Performance Appraisal

Closed, Open and Semi-Closed/Semi-Open Appraisal

D1.40   In designing a performance management framework, the organisation must decide to what extent its employees should be involved in various performance management processes. "Involvement" may be in different degrees, as in being informed, consulted with and/or given permission to actively participate and co-own the process. The more an employee is involved (and co-owns the process), the more transparent the performance management becomes and creates greater buy-in.

D1.41   Potentially, an employee may participate in the following processes:

- Performance planning and goals setting
- Performance feedback and coaching
- Performance appraisal
- Performance critical conversation

D1.42   Generally, employees' involvement in performance management (and consequently the degree of transparency) is dependent on which model of appraisal the organisation has chosen to adopt – closed appraisal or open appraisal or semi-closed/semi-open appraisal. A comparison of these different models is summarised below:

Closed Performance Appraisal

(a) Typically, the organisation does not involve the employee in setting performance goals. The reporting officer sets the performance goals and expectations for the employee unilaterally (in some cases, the reporting officer may not even set any performance goals and expectations officially).

(b) At the end of the appraisal year, the reporting officer will review the employee's performance in confidence and submit his assessment to the management (or Human Resource).

(c) The reporting officer will not discuss the performance appraisal with the employee. The employee will also not be informed of his performance results.

Comments

The key feature of the Closed model is the minimal involvement of the employee. His input is not sought. Neither is he informed of the assessment of him. The Closed model does not garner buy-in from employees. The common complaint (or challenge) against this model is that it is shrouded in mystery and this alone creates doubt on the fairness and objectivity of the performance assessment.

Open Performance Appraisal

(a) At the start of the appraisal period, the reporting officer and the employee will jointly do performance planning and agree on the performance standards and expectations (such as work targets and competency-based behavioural standards).

(b) During the appraisal year, the reporting officer will monitor and review the employee's performance and give feedback and coaching to the employee.

(c) At the end of the appraisal year, the reporting officer will do an overall review and assess the employee's performance. The performance assessment will undergo moderation with the rest of the peer employees in the organisation.

(d) The reporting officer will hold a critical conversation with the employee to share the performance results (in terms of performance rating/band) and to address any feedback/concerns from the employee.

Comments

The key feature of the Open model is the high level of involvement of the employee. He is kept apprised from the start to the end of the process. This gives transparency and creates greater buy-in from employees.

Semi-Closed/Semi-Open Performance Appraisal

(a) This is the same as the Open model, except that some portions of the appraisal process are closed to the employee. The extent and which parts are closed are decided by the organisation.

(b) Typically, organisations will open the entire planning and appraisal process to the employee, <u>except</u> for the performance results (that is, Step (d) of the Open model). The employee will <u>not</u> be told of his final performance results (in terms of performance rating/band).

Comments
The intent behind closing the performance results from the employee is to avoid having employees obsess over their performance results. Rather, the emphasis is placed on getting employees involved in setting and co-owning their performance goals and also ensuring that they receive ongoing and continual feedback/coaching on how to enhance their performance. The employee will get a clue on his performance rating based on the feedback/coaching given to him as well as the amount of performance bonus and increment that he receives.

D1.43   The merits and demerits of the various models and the realities in practice and why often the model prescribed by an organisation may not be followed diligently are examined in Chapter D4 "Performance Appraisal".

Appraisal Period

D1.44   Organisations invariably conduct their performance management activities (which comprise performance planning, review, appraisal and moderation) on an annual basis. The period under appraisal is called the appraisal period, which is typically one year.

D1.45   The start and end of the appraisal period are usually aligned to the organisation's financial year. This is so that performance goals assigned to the employee for the appraisal period can be in sync with the organisation's corporate plan and annual budget for the financial year.

D1.46   All performance appraisals face an inherent challenge in keeping to the appraisal period. As the performance management cycle consists of several sequential steps, time is needed to complete all the steps. To get to the final performance results, first, the reporting officers and the departmental/line heads (as counter-signing officers) must complete all the appraisals of their employees and submit them to the management (or Human Resource).

The preliminary performance results are then moderated across all departments to ensure consistency in stringency, before arriving at the final performance results.

D1.47 The performance results will become the basis to decide on the performance-linked rewards for employees (including bonuses and increments, as well as promotions). To catch the timing of the bonus, increment and promotion exercises, often, the appraisal by the reporting officers must start even before the appraisal period is over, sometimes as early as 2–3 months before the end of the appraisal period (especially if the organisation has a large population of employees). Due to this, reporting officers have to appraise their employees over a "truncated" appraisal period and then "extrapolate" to the rest of the year. This is not ideal, but organisations generally live with it. An example is shown below:

Example

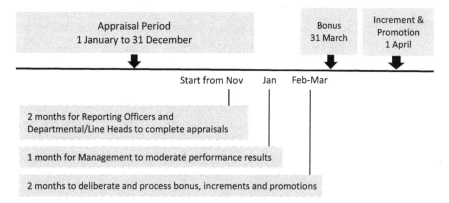

Frequency of Performance Review

D1.48 While the appraisal period is typically one year, the frequency of performance review can be more regular, usually half-yearly, and in some cases, quarterly. The rationale is simple. The objectives of performance management include monitoring the employee's progress in meeting the performance standards expected of him and helping him improve/enhance his performance, including closing gaps (if any). To meet these objectives, it would be insufficient to just review the employee's performance at the end of the appraisal period; it would be a missed opportunity for the employee to improve. The more frequent the performance review, the more opportunities for the employee to improve and the better chances that the employee will deliver the required performance.

D1.49   While the reporting officer should provide performance feedback/coaching on an ongoing basis to the employee throughout the appraisal year, these may not be formal sessions. Most organisations call for a mid-year review (some require quarterly reviews) in addition to the year-end review (which takes stock of the employee's performance for the entire appraisal year). Such mandated quarterly, mid-year and year-end reviews are regarded as formal sessions and the contents of the discussions must be documented in the employee's annual performance appraisal form. For example, in the mid-year review, if the original performance goals have been modified (say, due to changes in the operating environment or a shift in management direction), these should be duly documented to give clarity to the employee.

Tools for Assessing and Determining Performance

D1.50   Performance management is about managing, enabling and helping employees to deliver the best outcomes for the organisation while facilitating them to grow professionally. Managing people is essentially an art. However, when it comes to managing performance, many organisations try to put some science into it. For example, setting quantifiable and measurable goals, using a balanced scorecard, collecting data and evidence on how much the goals have been achieved, using a points system to assess the employee and deploying a bell curve to calibrate and moderate performance ratings. These methods are attempts to be quantitative (even mathematical) in arriving at an employee's performance assessment.

Performance Factors for Measuring Performance

D1.51   Performance factors are the organisation's requirements/expectations of an employee to deliver or fulfil. Performance factors can be in quantitative or qualitative terms.

D1.52   The common performance factors used to appraise an employee's performance are the following:

  (a) results-based performance goals (these are work targets);
  (b) competency-based behaviour standards (these are job competencies and work-related behaviours); and
  (c) core value-based behavioural attributes (these are behaviours related to the organisation's core values or non-negotiable work ethics).

Most organisations use a combination of results-based performance goals and competency-based behaviour standards to appraise their employees. More on performance factors are discussed in Chapter D2 "Performance Planning and Goals Setting".

Performance Rating Scale

D1.53   Performance results for employees are typically presented in rating scales or performance bands. They form the common ruler for an organisation to rate and compare the performance of its employees. How rating scales or performance bands are designed or defined is entirely up to the organisation. Rating scales can be constructed with 3-point, 4-point, 5-point or 6-point ratings. More details including the pros and cons of different rating scales are shared in Chapter D4 "Performance Appraisal".

Bell Curve and Forced Ranking

D1.54   In calibrating and determining the performance ratings of a large number of employees, many large organisations deploy statistical tools to guide them. The two common tools being used are the bell curve and forced ranking:

Bell Curve

D1.55   A bell curve (so named by way of its shape) is a normal distribution curve, which is a statistical tool. Premised on a social science theory that observes that human phenomena tend to distribute normally along a bell-shaped curve when measured using sufficiently large samples, many organisations use a bell curve to differentiate (or segregate) their employees in terms of relative performance. This involves comparing one employee against the others and lining up all employees from the strongest to the weakest. The employees are then slotted into bands along a bell curve. A quota (whatever percentage as decided by the organisation) is imposed on each band. An example of a bell curve is shown below.

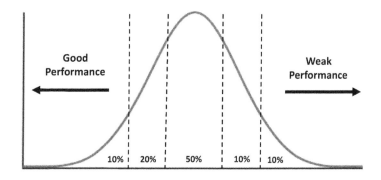

D1.56   The proportions (or quota) at the top and bottom ends are always smaller than the central portion. That is, it is presumed that for any group of employees (in sufficiently large numbers), the majority of them will have their performance falling in the middle, while a few employees will distinguish themselves away from this majority, either as exceptionally good performers or as weak performers.

D1.57   The primary purpose for organisations in using a bell curve is to differentiate the distribution of rewards. For example, the top 10% of performers should get the highest tier rewards, followed by the next 20%, then the middle 50%, and for the remaining bottom 20%, the rewards should be pared down or even forfeited. Some organisations also use the bell curve to calibrate or normalise the performance ratings of their employees. Details are covered in Chapter D5 "Performance Moderation".

Forced Ranking

D1.58   Forced ranking is a simple method to compare the performance of employees. While an employee's performance should be assessed against his own performance goals/standards or expectations, his performance can also be compared against other employees doing similar jobs in the same job grade. In practice and intuitively, a manager who has several direct reports will find it quite easy to identify the best (or best two) and the weakest one.

D1.59   Organisations usually use forced ranking in conjunction with the bell curve. In practice, a manager can simply use forced ranking to size up and rank his direct reports before assigning a performance rating to each of them. There are some challenges in using forced ranking, which are discussed in Chapter D5 "Performance Moderation".

Applications of Performance Appraisal Results

D1.60   For many organisations, the performance appraisal results of employees are critical inputs for several other employee programmes, namely:

(a) compensation and reward determination (such as bonus and increment);
(b) career planning and talent management (such as promotion and deployment);
(c) employee development (such as training and coaching); and
(d) employment decisions (such as renewal of contract and re-employment).

D1.61   Many organisations link employees' performance to salary and other monetary rewards (such as bonuses, increments and awards) as it is fair to distribute rewards based on merit and also allows the organisation to instil a performance-driven culture.

D1.62   Promotion of employees is part of an organisation's talent management. Invariably, an employee can be considered for promotion only if he has already shown consistent good performance in his current job role and has the potential and competencies to take on a bigger role or more complex assignments.

D1.63   As for the deployment of employees, the information gathered during the performance appraisal process regarding an employee's strengths as well as developmental needs are useful inputs when considering an employee for job postings. The job posting may either leverage on the employee's strengths and stretch him or give him a valuable opportunity to broaden his exposure to learn and develop. The transfer may also mean a better person-to-job fit for the employee.

D1.64   An employee's developmental needs surfaced from performance appraisal also enable the organisation to devise an individual development plan for the employee that covers training, coaching and other developmental activities. This is a critical aspect of performance management which unfortunately is quite often compromised because of the focus (or over-emphasis) on performance ratings. This is discussed further in Chapter D8 "Performance Management: The Challenges, Realities and Alternatives".

D1.65   Performance is a relevant factor for consideration in employment decisions that include the following:

(a) *Renewal of fixed-term contracts*
The organisation has the discretion to set the performance standard required for the renewal of contract. For example, if the organisation wants to be stringent in renewing contracts, it may stipulate a minimum of "Good" performance.

(b) *Re-employment*
The Retirement and Re-employment Act (RRA) requires an employee to have "Satisfactory" performance or better in order to qualify for re-employment. The Tripartite Guidelines provide additional pointers, stating that "satisfactory" performance refers to the *minimum level of performance* an employee is expected to meet and that in assessing an employee for re-employment, the employer should consider the employee's performance for the past 2–3 years and not only the most current or immediately preceding year.

D1.66   Where performance appraisal results are used as the main determinant factor that will materially and monetarily affect an employee, the performance appraisal exercise will be taken seriously by employees. In organisations that do not explicitly (and publicly say so) link rewards and career progression to an employee's performance, the performance management program may degenerate into a mere administrative routine. Line managers and employees will give only cursory attention to performance appraisal, and the performance appraisal results are often just filed away.

D1.67   On the other hand, over-emphasis on linking performance ratings to rewards may beget unhealthy and negative behaviours. Employees may take improper ways to manage the processes to get favourable ratings. Line managers may endeavour to set easy performance targets. Employees may also become overly individualistic in a highly competitive environment and compromise on teamwork. Staff development may take a backseat as employees tend to be less open in revealing their weaker areas. More are discussed in Chapter D2 "Performance Planning and Goals Setting", Chapter D4 "Performance Appraisal" and Chapter D8 "Performance Management: The Challenges, Realities and Alternatives".

Dealing with Weak Performers

D1.68   Performance management includes dealing with weak performers. If reporting officers proactively monitor and manage the performance of their employees and intervene promptly when the latter are not up to the mark, there should be a minimal number of weak performers. When an employee is quickly alerted and guided to help him address his performance gap(s), he should be back in the game. There will however be instances where an employee remains not up to the mark even after interventions. This should be reported, and the employee given counselling. The employee should be advised to reflect on the plausible reasons for his unsatisfactory performance and consider whether he is suitable for his current role or the organisation. The employee may request a transfer (if his basic work ethics are good) or opt to move on to another job.

D1.69   If the said employee stays on but continues to fare poorly, he should be put on the Performance Improvement Plan (PIP), which is commonly a component of the performance management framework in more established organisations. Under the PIP, the employee's shortcomings and unsatisfactory performance issues are discussed and he is required to commit to taking corrective actions to raise his performance to the required standard. If the employee fails to improve, his employment contract may be terminated. Details are covered in Chapter D6 "Dealing with Weak Performers".

Challenges of Performance Management

D1.70   Performance management is a vital function but not an easy one. It is a delicate and challenging management task that is influenced by many factors and dynamic in nature. It touches on people's emotions and egos and affects their pockets and careers. There are numerous challenges in making performance management work. Some of them are inherent in the nature of performance assessment (for example, subjectivity). Some are due to the way that organisations execute the various performance management processes and apply performance ratings in sensitive employee programs such as rewards management. We examine these challenges under the respective performance management processes in the ensuing chapters and also do a wrap-up in Chapter D8 "Performance Management: The Challenges, Realities and Alternatives".

Performance Management: The People Dimension

D1.71   To operationalise performance management, we need good policies, processes, tools and forms. These alone, however, do not guarantee a good outcome from performance management. Organisations can invest time and money to design sleek performance appraisal forms, spin a nice narrative on performance appraisal and build a state-of-the-art online performance management system and still reap less than satisfactory outcomes. Where organisations often fail is to pay attention to the people dimension of performance management. As the saying goes, a system is only as good as the people using it. The commitment and willingness of the people in the organisation in executing performance management activities and the sincerity (or ethos) with which they carry them out are critical success factors for performance management.

D1.72   The people dimension of performance management includes how the management, reporting officers, employees and Human Resource department view, execute and treat performance management. The following actions will have a definite impact on the effectiveness of performance management:

> (a) *How are performance goals and expectations set or communicated? To what extent are employees involved? Are the goals and expectations realistic and accepted by the employees?*
>
> (b) *How is performance feedback delivered? Is there honesty in the feedback shared? Is it done in good faith and with respect? How do the employees accept the feedback?*
>
> (c) *Is work progress being monitored and how? Is it done regularly and systematically?*
>
> (d) *How is learning taking place? In what ways are employees being supported, coached and mentored?*
>
> (e) *How is performance being appraised and moderated to arrive at the final performance ratings? Is the process fair and free from politics and personal agendas?*
>
> (f) *How is the final performance rating being communicated to the employee and disagreement being dealt with?*
>
> (g) *Are the performance conversations meaningful and do they focus on the past or future?*
>
> (h) *How is unsatisfactory performance being handled?*

D1.73   How employees and line managers go about doing the above actions is influenced by larger organisational forces that are at play. In Chapter D8 "Performance Management: The Challenges, Realities and Alternatives", we examine the following people dimensions:

- Focus and primary pursuits of the organisation
- Organisation culture and people management philosophy
- Relations between the reporting officer and the employee
- Reward philosophy and practices
- Attitude towards work discipline and performance in daily operations

D1.74   In the various chapters on performance management that follow, aspects of the people dimension are embedded in what we examine and share, and we highlight them to remind readers to pay attention to these people elements.

Performance Planning and Goals Setting

Focus of this Chapter

Chapter E1 provides an overview of performance management. This chapter focuses on performance planning, an important and challenging component of performance management that is done at the start of a calendar or financial year or performance management cycle. The contents of this chapter are more relevant to professionals, managers and executives, although the concepts and principles also apply to rank-and-file employees. Performance planning is generally practised by large and established organisations. Small and medium enterprises are not likely to do performance planning; even if they do, it is usually done in a much more simplified manner and not as systematic.

This chapter delves into the types of performance goals and how to set them. The quality of the goals as well as the determination of performance targets and standards are examined. Various challenges in setting performance goals are also discussed.

Performance Planning: The What and Why

D2.1   For an organisation to produce the best results, its various functional and operational units must work synchronously and synergistically. As employees man the functions/operations, they play a pivotal role in helping the organisation achieve success and excellence. Every employee in the organisation must do what he is tasked to do; he should perform well individually as well as collectively as a department or a team.

D2.2   *What is performance planning?*
Performance planning is the process whereby an organisation plans out for each employee what results are expected to be achieved (referred to as "performance goals") and/or what behaviours are expected to be demonstrated on the job (referred to as "competency-based behavioural standards"). The organisation then communicates these expectations upfront to the individual employee at the start of a performance cycle (also referred to as the appraisal period). We elaborate on performance goals and competency-based behavioural standards under the section "Performance Plan for the Individual Employee: The Components".

Performance Planning is Management by Objectives

D2.3   To provide a holistic understanding of performance planning, it is useful to highlight that performance planning is anchored on a management concept known as "Management by Objectives" (MBO) which was first put forth by management guru Peter Druker in 1955. He defined MBO as a management method that takes into consideration each individual employee's job responsibilities and at the same time guides all individual efforts collectively through a common direction of vision. The MBO concept was later further sharpened by John Humble, a businessman and management consultant who implemented MBO for many large organisations. He highlighted the elements of MBO as follows:

- With MBO, the assumption is that the employee wants to contribute to the organisation and develop himself;
- MBO seeks to achieve the organisation's goals — profit and growth;
- MBO integrates the goals and interests of the employee and the organisation; and
- All employees have 5 basic needs which can be fulfilled by a performance management framework that is based on MBO.

5 Basic Needs of Employees	Components of Performance Management Framework (per MBO concept)
Company agrees with me what is expected of me	Agreement on work scope, performance goals and expectations
Company gives me the opportunity to perform and contribute	Performance after agreement on scope and expectations
Company tells me how I am performing	Performance feedback and review
Company helps, guides and trains me to perform	Coaching and training
Company rewards me based on my contributions.	Recognition and rewards

D2.4   *Why is performance planning important for the organisation?*
Performance planning serves two primary purposes:

(a) *To achieve alignment and provide focus*
With performance planning, the organisation makes a deliberate and concerted effort to align its corporate goals with those of its operating units (divisions/departments), which in turn are translated to and cascaded down to individual employees as performance goals/expectations that they must fulfil. When goals are made clear, the employee can focus and prioritise his efforts. The alignment helps channel the efforts of employees towards producing what is of value to the organisation and thereby avoids distractions and/or misguided use of time and resources.

(b) *To provide clarity for performance management*
Performance planning communicates to the employee what is important to get done (and by reverse inference too, what is not), and to what level

(for example, the frequency, volume, intensity, speed, pace, quality and timing) expected of him. The employee is tasked to deliver these outcomes for the said appraisal period. When the goals are achieved, the employee is recognised and rewarded accordingly at the end of the appraisal period. This confers the perception of fairness and objectivity. Conversely, without any pre-set goals and other performance expectations, the organisation will not have a defensible basis to appraise the performance of its employees. Employees will perceive appraisal as largely an exercise of subjective judgment by their supervisors.

D2.5   Some organisations do not give sufficient attention to performance planning or even entirely dispense with it. Or it may be a case that while the organisation officially espouses performance planning, the enforcement is weak and much is left to the discretion of the line managers. With varying managerial styles, line managers will put varying emphasis on performance planning. Some may (wrongly) assume that their staff already know what is expected of them. Or some may even deliberately keep performance goals/ expectations vague, so as to leave room to adjust or manoeuvre a change. This easily leads to a misalignment of expectations and is often cited as the main basis of complaint (or defence) by an employee who is assigned an unfavourable performance rating. In all fairness, there is some validity to such a complaint. If performance goals/expectations have not been set out clearly through proper performance planning, the employee cannot be entirely and solely held accountable for missing the bull's eye. Something as important as directing and expending an organisation's valuable time and resources should not be left to chance for getting it right.

D2.6   Some smallish businesses can arguably do decently well without any detailed performance planning; say, only "broad strokes" of the organisational direction are articulated to their employees. Such businesses may have a simple business philosophy, which is to capture any business deals that come along that they believe they can fulfil and profit from. They do not do detailed (or systematic) corporate-level planning, much less planning at the individual employee level. The key is to remain agile to navigate the business volatilities, seize opportunities and maximise benefit to the organisation. For such fluidity to work, the caveat is that the organisation must have capable, versatile and dedicated employees who understand what is of value to the business and they are able to expend their efforts astutely in line with the broad business strategy/direction. They operate flexibly and yet at the same time are single-minded about serving the interests of the organisation.

D2.7   This modus operandi (of not doing performance planning), however, is not feasible for large and even medium-sized organisations. They have more employees whose roles are well-defined and compartmentalised. For such organisations to do well, they need their employees to collaborate; this requires pre-planning and coordination so that employees' efforts can be synchronised and optimised. Without pre-planning for the various departments/units and clear communication on performance goals/expectations cascaded down to the individual employees, employees' efforts may just go off-tangent. This is likely to result in inefficiency, wasted resources and in the worst case, chaos.

Performance Planning: The How and When

D2.8   By performance planning, it means that a performance plan is prepared for each individual employee in advance and communicated to him at the start of the performance cycle (also referred to as the appraisal period). The performance cycle is usually aligned to the organisation's financial year or the calendar year (whichever as defined by the organisation).

D2.9   *How is performance planning done?*
        Performance planning involves the systematic cascading down of corporate-level goals (usually put together and articulated as a corporate plan and supported by an annual budget) to all its operating units (divisions/departments). At the departmental level, the line heads/managers translate and break down their departmental plan/budget into performance goals for each individual employee.

Alignment Process

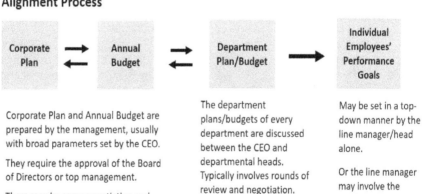

Corporate Plan and Annual Budget are prepared by the management, usually with broad parameters set by the CEO.

They require the approval of the Board of Directors or top management.

There may be some negotiation and adjustment typically on the key financials before the final approval.

The department plans/budgets of every department are discussed between the CEO and departmental heads. Typically involves rounds of review and negotiation.

These department plans/budgets support the organisation's Corporate Plan and Annual Budget.

May be set in a top-down manner by the line manager/head alone.

Or the line manager may involve the employee to co-set the performance goals, with some room to negotiate.

Corporate Plan and Departmental Plan

D2.10   Performance planning is contextual. How it is designed and executed varies depending on the set-up and complexity of the organisation. Generally, the larger the organisation and the more diverse the functions and roles of its employees, the more structured the performance planning.

D2.11   In small set-ups, performance planning may be a simple exercise where the department head articulates the overall goals and priorities of the department but without assigning individual performance goals to each individual employee. All team members are expected to work collectively towards the department's goals. At the end of the year, the department head will assess the performance/contribution of each individual employee and assign a performance rating as appropriate.

D2.12   For larger organisations, before the start of a financial year, the senior management will call for the preparation of an annual corporate plan (or business plan), which will be accompanied by a corresponding annual budget. The annual corporate plan essentially sets out what the organisation aims to achieve for the coming financial year, while the annual budget sets out the financial inputs (the costs and investment) and outputs (the revenue) if the corporate plan is materialised.

D2.13   To develop the annual corporate plan, every department must first propose its respective annual department plan/budget. A commercial corporation with several revenue-generating departments will require each of them to provide a revenue target and possibly one on profit margin as well. The departments are usually given some directions and broad planning parameters that reflect the expectations of the chief executive officer (CEO) or the board of directors (BOD) – for example, overall 10% revenue growth and no more than 5% increase in operating expenses. Such directions and planning parameters usually emanate from the strategic or long-term plan of the organisation, which is developed by the top management and endorsed by the BOD every few years.

D2.14   The proposed department plans/budgets go to the CEO for review and usually undergo a few rounds of reiteration before they are accepted. All department plans/budgets will be synthesised into the organisation's annual corporate plan and annual budget, which in turn will go to the BOD (or the equivalent) for approval.

D2.15   The approved annual corporate plan and annual budget, together with the department plans/budgets become the basis (or blueprint) to translate and break down into performance goals for individual employees.

From Corporate/Departmental Plan to Individual Plan

D2.16   Setting performance goals for individual employees involves two aspects:

(a) first, to select the type (or nature) of performance goals; and
(b) second, to calibrate the level for the said performance goals so selected.

	Example for Sales Executive	Example for HR Executive
Select the Performance Goal	Dollar value of sales	Recruitment efficiency
Calibrate the Performance Goal	Achieve $500,000 of sales revenue	Recruit within 2 months from approval of headcount fill.

D2.17   In many cases, the selection of performance goals (with regards to the type or nature) is usually decided by the management and assigned in a top-down manner. This is more efficient and can better ensure alignment between the performance goals of individual employees and the corporate plan. Most employees are also not sufficiently knowledgeable and confident in selecting the right performance goals.

D2.18   As for calibrating the level for the performance goals, it can be done in a top-down manner by the reporting officer or department head alone, or at times, the reporting officer may involve the employee in co-setting or calibrating the level for the performance goals. The advantage of co-setting is that it is seen as a fairer and more employee-centric approach as it allows the employee to highlight any relevant considerations to the reporting officer or department head who may otherwise not be aware of. Allowing employees to participate in the process also creates ownership and enhances commitment. The process is also developmental for the employee; he gets to understand the connection between his work and the corporate objectives, as well as identify the challenges and opportunities.

Planning at the Start of Appraisal Year

D2.19   Performance planning is purposed for the performance management of employees. The following flow chart shows the essential steps that are done in a sequential order for performance management. Performance planning is the first step in the performance management cycle.

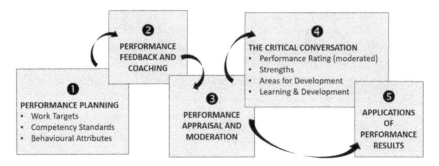

D2.20   Employees are typically appraised on an annual basis. As such, the appraisal period is typically one year. To manage an employee's performance in a transparent and timely manner, the organisation should set out and communicate the performance goals to the employee upfront at the start of the appraisal year.

D2.21   While it is important (and ideal) to complete performance planning for individual employees by the start of the appraisal year, in practice, there may be delay. To set individual performance goals, one would require the corporate plan, annual budget and department plan/budget to be ready, and often these get finalised mostly just in time before the start of the financial or appraisal year. The department heads require time to work out the performance goals of their individual employees. It is therefore not uncommon to find that by the time employees are informed of their performance goals, it may already be a few months well into the current appraisal year. To avoid such delays, organisations should be diligent in finalising their corporate plan and annual budget with sufficient lead time before the start of the new appraisal year.

D2.22   When performance goals of individual employees are worked out, some cases may require additional information and review (and hence further delay). For example, the employee's job may have evolved; hence an updated job description that captures the changes in key tasks and accountabilities will be useful (and even necessary). Other factors may include impending regulatory changes that impact the employee's work. Those in marketing and sales may await impending news of competitors, product manufacturers and/or principals before finalising their game plan. This is understandable because if performance goals are premised on the wrong assumptions, they become inaccurate or even meaningless.

D2.23 Often, it is not possible to wait for all the required information to be available or finalised before setting performance goals. If there are information gaps and it is impractical to delay finalising performance goals any further, the practical thing to do is to make reasonable assumptions and craft the performance goals, while highlighting those portions that require subsequent review once the missing information become available. For this reason, many organisations mandate a mid-year (or even quarterly) review of performance goals in their performance management framework. This way, it mitigates the risk of reporting officers or department heads neglecting to review and update performance goals and rendering them inaccurate, irrelevant or meaningless.

Performance Plan for the Individual Employee: The Components

D2.24 *What is a performance plan for the individual employee made up of?*
In most organisations, the annual performance plan for an employee comprises the following: (a) results-based performance goals and (b) competency-based behavioural standards. Some organisations add on a third component: (c) development plan for the employee.

Results-based Performance Goals

D2.25 Performance goals spell out the results that the employee must deliver. There can be various names for performance goals, such as key performance indicators (KPI), key result areas (KRA), work targets and the like. These terms are often used interchangeably, although there are some nuanced differences but this is not the focus of this chapter. For simplicity, we use the term "performance goals", and in some places, "work targets" especially if the performance goals are clearly quantitative.

D2.26 *Should performance goals be spelt out in quantitative or qualitative terms?*
Performance goals can specify results in either quantitative or qualitative terms.

Quantitative Performance Goals for Individual Employees (Examples)
Revenue of $xx million ◆ profit of $xx million ◆ xx number of units sold or produced ◆ number of customers/members served ◆ number of outreach programs organised ◆ customer satisfaction index ◆ number of employees recruited
Qualitative Performance Goals for Individual Employees (Examples)
To overhaul and enhance the learning management system for employees ◆ To develop the company's corporate website ◆ To develop an effective volunteer management program

D2.27   Performance goals that are quantitative make them measurable and hence allow for objective assessment. On the other hand, performance goals that are qualitative will require the reporting officer (appraiser) to assess and make a judgment on the significance, quality and impact of the work delivered, which, unavoidably, becomes more subjective. As far as possible, performance goals should preferably be quantitative and measurable; however, this can be a challenge, especially for support and administrative jobs. We elaborate more on this challenge under the section "Setting Performance Goals for Support and Administrative Roles".

D2.28   More than just measurable, ideally, performance goals should be crafted in a SMART manner – that is, Specific (S), Measurable (M), Attainable (A), Relevant (R) and Time-bound (T). Additionally, performance goals can be nuanced and targeted to achieve one or more of these purposes: (a) attain/ acquire, (b) preserve/sustain, (c) avoid/pre-empt and (d) discontinue/ eradicate. Performance goals may also be measured in terms of input (employee's effort) or outcomes (impact to the organisation). We delve into these aspects of performance goals under the section "Setting Performance Goals: Purposeful and SMART".

Competency-based Behavioural Standards

D2.29   Competency-based behavioural standards (sometimes simply called "competencies") spell out the work behaviours, traits and attributes that an employee must demonstrate at work.

D2.30   Competencies can be categorised into (a) core competencies, (b) leadership competencies and (c) functional/ technical competencies. As "competencies" is a broad topic, it is separately covered in Chapter D9 "Competency Frameworks". For a quick introduction, some examples are given below:

Core Competencies
Core competencies are applicable to all job families and all job levels. They are deemed critical by the organisation; all employees are required to demonstrate them at a proficiency level that is befitting their respective job levels and job roles.

Examples
Taking Ownership and Initiative. Problem-Solving. Result Focus. Pursuit of Excellence. Teamwork and Collaboration. Innovation. Adaptability. Resilience. Growth Mindset.

Leadership Competencies
Leadership competencies relate to managing, developing, motivating, aligning and inspiring people, as well as leading the organisation (or a functional area). They are applied to employees who are people managers and/or in leadership roles.

Examples
Critical Thinking. Strategic Vision. Foresight. Managing and Developing People. Leading and Inspiring.

Functional/Technical Competencies
Functional/technical competencies are specific to the job family or job role of the employee. They encompass the functional knowledge, technical skills, operational experience as well as aptitude requirements. Examples of some job families are given below:

Finance job family
Financial Budgeting. Cashflow Management. Accounts Preparation. Taxation. Treasury Management. Financial Governance and Risk Management.

Operations job family
Project Management. Resource Management. Work Scheduling. Contract Management. Workplace Safety. Business Continuity Planning.

Business Development and Marketing job family
Business Development and Sales. Customer Account Management. Branding and Product Marketing. Marketing Communications. Digital Marketing.

D2.31   Organisations should select those behavioural standards (or competencies) that suit their own operating context and which are aligned with their organisational core values. For example, an organisation that wants its employees to always think of growth and view situations (or challenges) as opportunities may choose "growth mindset" as one of its core competencies. For another organisation where it is critical for employees to work in synchrony to deliver results, it may choose "collaboration" as a core competency. A non-profit organisation with a social mission which relies on public funding may choose "service orientation" and "concern for governance" as its core competencies.

D2.32   Once the organisation has selected its competencies, the next step is to define each competency and describe it in observable and discernible behavioural terms (referred to as "behavioural markers") for different proficiency levels. An employee will be required to demonstrate a said competency at a specified proficiency level that is befitting his job level and job role (the more senior the job level/role, the higher the proficiency level expected of the employee). Please refer to Chapter D9 "Competency Frameworks" for more elaboration on competencies.

D2.33   During performance planning with the employee, the reporting officer must inform the employee about the competencies that he will be assessed on and at what proficiency level for each that he must meet. The behavioural markers for the specified proficiency level of each competency should be shared with the employee so that he is clear about what is expected of him.

Results-based Performance Goals versus Competency-based Behavioural Standards: Which of These are More Important?

D2.34   Both are equally important. They are inter-related in that an employee who demonstrates strong competency-based behavioural standards at work will likely also deliver strong results. Competencies are often regarded as a leading indicator of performance, that is, a predictor of the success or potential of the employee. But this correlation between competencies and results may sometimes be derailed by unforeseen or unusual circumstances.

D2.35   Some organisations only set results-based performance goals and appraise their employees solely on the achievement of results; competency-based behavioural standards play no part in the employee's appraisal. The reason may be that the organisation is concerned only with results (nothing else quite matters) or it may also be a case where the organisation has not put in place any competency framework to manage the performance of its employees.

D2.36 For organisations that have a competency framework in place, they would (and should) also want to appraise their employees' behaviours at work using the competency framework, for the plain reason that the competencies reflect what the organisations value and want to see in their employees. Chasing results is one thing; abiding by the organisation's core values should also be as important and not to be compromised. For example, if an employee delivers stellar results but shows lapses in his work behaviours (say, he is less than collaborative with his peers or he has taken high risks with scant regard for potential impact to the organisation), these factors should be taken into consideration in appraising him and ultimately rewarding him.

D2.37 Appraisal that is based only on either results alone or work behaviours alone is inadequate. We elaborate on the considerations in the table below:

If appraisal is based solely on **Results** (that is, achievement of **Performance Goals**)	Achievement of results often depends on external and other factors, which may be beyond the control of the employee. • Good results can sometimes be due to a confluence of favourable circumstances (not credited to the employee). This is the luck element. • Conversely, bad results may happen due to unforeseen circumstances (say, a change of law or adverse conditions in a foreign country) even when the employee makes all the right effort.
If appraisal is based solely on **Work Behaviours** (that is, demonstration of **Competency-based Behavioural Standards**)	It is not desirable to appraise an employee solely on work behaviours/competencies because the employee may not actually have delivered the required result (although generally employees who exhibit high competencies tend to produce better results, all else being equal). If an employee is rated highly on competencies but delivers poor results, it may be that wrong competencies have been chosen with weak correlation with the delivery of results. It may also be due to overly favourable assessment by the reporting officer on the employee's competency level. Another possibility is that the employee, though competent, may have focused on doing the wrong things.

D2.38   Competency-based behavioural standards are particularly important and necessary for support and administrative job roles. For these roles, it is often challenging to set quantitative results-based performance goals. Competencies and work behaviours therefore provide a fairly good basis to assess their effectiveness at work. However, when the appraisal of an employee leans heavily on competency-based behaviours, the downside is that being non-quantitative, it can be perceived as being subjective. We elaborate more on this challenge under the section "Setting Performance Goals for Support and Administrative Roles".

Development Plan for the Employee

D2.39   Progressive and enlightened organisations also require the line managers/heads to engage their employees on their development plans which should cover how to enhance their competencies, knowledge and skills and career development. A good starting point for the development plan is to draw salient points from the employee's preceding year's performance appraisal results. Development for the employee may entail stretch assignments and special projects, training opportunities (including coaching and mentoring), as well as possibly a job rotation or transfer. The objectives are to widen the employee's breadth of experience and/or deepen his domain expertise, stretch him beyond his comfort zone and/or expand his thinking and perspectives.

D2.40   In preparing the development plan, the employee and the reporting officer should refer to the behavioural markers of competencies as the goal posts to guide the employee to close current gaps or attain the next higher level of proficiency for the said competencies.

D2.41   Employees who are assessed to have high potential are likely to be given more attention in their career development. The senior management may be involved in planning their development and assessment to validate their potential for leadership roles. Reporting officers may have to work closely with Human Resource under the ambit of talent development program for high-potential staff. More details are shared in Chapter D14 "Talent Management and Succession Planning".

Setting Performance Goals: Purposeful and SMART

D2.42   Performance goals are important for guiding how employees perform their jobs. Hence, they must be set properly and meaningfully; otherwise, they can become superfluous or worse, a hindrance to effective performance. Reporting officers and line heads should not treat the setting of performance goals as an administrative routine (or even "chore") to be cursorily done and gotten over with.

D2.43   Performance goals may be viewed or categorised in several ways:

(a) First, they may be set to achieve any one or more of these purposes — attain/acquire, preserve/sustain, avoid/pre-empt and discontinue/eradicate.

(b) Second, performance goals may also be set to bring about any one or more of these improvements — cheaper, better, faster, safer and stronger.

(c) Third, performance goals may be based on either input (employee's effort) or outcomes (impact to the organisation) in terms of their measurement.

Purpose-driven Performance Goals

D2.44   Reporting officers and line heads may craft performance goals based on the purposes to be achieved. This provides focus and ensures that the performance goals are meaningful.

Purpose	Examples of Performance Goals (in abbreviated forms only to illustrate)
Attain/ Acquire	• Develop e-commerce marketing capabilities. • Secure 100 new customers. • Roll out a holistic HR information system.
Preserve/ Sustain	• Protect current market share. • Maintain staff engagement rate at not below 70%. • Ensure that response time to customer complaints must not exceed the standard of 1 working day.
Avoid/ Pre-empt	• Desist extending credit to first-time customers. • Improve financial governance to minimise regulatory lapses and audit issues. • Enhance measures to prevent potential complaints on workplace discrimination.

Discontinue/ Eradicate	• Convert the fixed bonus scheme to a performance-linked bonus scheme. • Discontinue product X by the end of financial year. • Eradicate the time lag between real-time inventory movement and the posting of inventory data into the inventory system.

Improvement-driven Performance Goals

D2.45　Performance goals may also be crafted with the aim of bringing about improvements in any one or more of the following aspects:

Improvement	Examples of Performance Goals (in abbreviated form only to illustrate)
Cheaper	Reduce the unit cost. Lower the cost of raw materials. Reduce the ratio of staff to customers. Reduce wastage.
Faster	Reduce the production cycle time. Cut waiting time to serve customers. Submit month-end reports to management 1 day earlier. Streamline and reduce the number of steps to raise procurement requisition.
Better	Improve the customer satisfaction index. Improve product features. Increase the employee engagement score. Improve the design of the corporate website to make navigation more user-friendly.
Safer	Improve the product design to reduce the risk of overheating. Enhance safety education and measures to reduce workplace accidents. Develop a 3-tiered checking protocol for the turn-on of engine propeller.
Stronger	Increase the company's market share. Expand the company's presence to Europe. Diversify the company's product and service offerings. Strengthen IT security controls to prevent cyberattacks. Improve employees' competency in teamwork and collaboration.

Input-based versus Outcome-based Performance Goals

D2.46   In setting performance goals, one must distinguish whether the goals are *input-based* or *outcome-based*. "Input" versus "Outcome" is not just semantics; they mean different things, as summarised below:

Input	• Inputs or efforts represent the actions/activities performed by employees aimed to bring about results desirable for the organisation. • Performance goals that are input-based stipulate the volume, scale or frequency of actions/activities to be performed by the employee.
Outcome	• Outcomes are the results that impact the interests, position and success of the organisation (may be financially or otherwise). • Performance goals that are outcome-based stipulate the level or scale of results that must be achieved by the employee.

Examples of Work Targets that are Input-based versus Outcome-based

Function/ Department	Input-based Performance Goal	Outcome-based Performance Goal
Membership Promotion	To hold at least 8 membership promotion events in 2025.	To achieve at least 600 new membership sign-ups in 2025.
Customer Service	To handle at least 800 customer enquiries per quarter.	To achieve a customer satisfaction score of at least 4/5.
Human Resource (Training)	To provide 600 digital literacy training places for employees in 2025.	To achieve 30% increase in digital literacy rate for employees (measured by a digital literacy test).

D2.47　In essence, inputs represent the employee's efforts (in terms of actions/ activities performed); whether they bring about the intended (or desired) positive impact to the organisation depends on how effective the actions/ activities are. If an employee puts in effort and yet fails to bring the intended/ desired impact, the likelihood is that the effort is misdirected or expended on insignificant or wrong areas, thus wasting time and resources.

D2.48　The danger of setting performance goals that measure only inputs without paying attention to outcomes is dubbed the "watermelon effect" – looks green (on target) on the outside but red (off target) on the inside. That is, on the surface, performance goals (that are input-based) may appear to be fine, but the organisation is not getting the results that matter.

Example of a Watermelon Effect in the Marketing Department

The marketing department has achieved all its performance goals (which are all input-based):
- Held 12 sales promotion events in retail outlets.
- Successfully launched 10 advertising campaigns over TV, radio and social media.

However, the company's market share has plummeted from 30% to 25% over the year (which is the business outcome). [Aside: one can also argue that without the events and campaigns, its market share could have nosedived to even lower, but it is not so straightforward to make the correlation. The key point is that achieving all the input-based performance goals is no cause for celebration if the organisation is suffering a setback.]

Example of a Watermelon Effect in the Customer Service Call Centre

The Customer Service Call Centre has reported a stellar increase in productivity:
- Number of incoming calls handled per officer has increased from 50 to 57 per day.
- Number of calls escalated to supervisors for resolution has reduced from 20% to 15%.

However, the customer satisfaction score for the Call Centre has headed south from 4/5 to 3.5/5 over the year.

D2.49　Outcome-based performance goals tend to encourage employees to look for effective solutions – do the right things and do them right. Input-based goals on the other hand tend to steer employees to focus on efficiency, which can be sub-optimal if the employee's actions/activities have not been correctly selected in the first place.

D2.50   Ideally, all performance goals should be expressed in the form of outcomes. One must also ensure that the outcomes are relevant and aligned with the strategy of the organisation. However, the reality is that while outcome-based performance goals are preferred, for many job roles, it can be challenging to craft such performance goals. One should not exclude an important or meaningful initiative simply because it cannot be crafted as an outcome-based measurable performance goal. Some jobs add a lot of value to the organisation, even if their value-add cannot be easily quantified and measured.

> Example
> A human resource manager puts in a lot of effort and undertakes initiatives to improve the quality of new hires. However, it is challenging to craft a performance goal that offers a way to measure the outcome quantitatively as it takes time for the new hires to contribute and manifest their good calibre.

> Example
> A company recently tarnished its reputation after a slip-up in releasing a batch of faulty products. The sales manager and his team subsequently made a lot of effort to engage customers to regain their trust. It is a challenge to quantify the immediate outcome of such effort as it takes some time for customers to show their trust in the company again.

D2.51   There are occasions when the outcome/impact may be affected by factors beyond the control of the employee. Outcome may not correspond with the great effort put in due to unfavourable circumstances and not because the effort is misdirected. The converse is also true; a good outcome may come about even if one has not put in commensurate effort.

D2.52   From the employee's perspective, input-based performance goals are "fairer". This is because outcomes can often be affected by environmental factors which may be beyond their control, whereas input-based performance goals largely depend on their commitment and diligence in executing them and less subject to environmental factors.

Is There a Way Out?

D2.53   Organisations prefer to measure goals based on outcomes, and logically so. Employees, on the other hand, prefer measurement by input, as this is more within their control. The way to get around this opposing tension is to have a balanced mix of both input-based and outcome-based performance goals where they best fit. If an outcome-based performance goal does not make sense, one can try to couch the performance goal as input-based in such a way that it becomes a good proxy for the desired outcome. While outcome-based performance goals that are relevant and meaningful are the ideal, an organisation cannot ignore or under-value genuine efforts that produce an output that cannot be easily quantified and measured. If a performance goal cannot be easily measured, one has to exercise judgment based on critical observation, logical deduction and good faith to make performance assessment as objective and fair as can be.

SMART Performance Goals

D2.54   In whichever way we classify performance goals, we should check that as much as possible, they meet the SMART criteria: (a) Specific, (b) Measurable, (c) Attainable, (d) Relevant and (e) Time-bound.

S	Specific	The goal must be specific and clear.
M	Measurable	The goal must be quantifiable (as far as possible). If it is qualitative, we should have a way or clear basis to evaluate.
A	Attainable	The goal (or target/standard) must be fair and realistic, and at the same time challenging.
R	Relevant	The goal must be relevant and matter to the organisation.
T	Time-bound	The goal must have a completion date, or a duration where the result is to be measured.

Brief Examples of SMART Goals
- Increase the sales volume ($ value) by 30% from new customer accounts by 31 December 2024.
- Achieve an overall customer satisfaction score of at least 4.2 (out of 5) in the customer survey 2024.
- Conduct recruitment expeditiously to fill vacancies (up to Manager grade) within 2 months from all approvals of headcount fills within 2024.
- Ensure delivery of goods to customers by the due delivery date in 99% of delivery orders in 2024.

We elaborate more regarding each of the SMART criteria.

Specific

D2.55   While it is not difficult to craft a performance goal to be specific, it is important to go into some detail and express the goal in precise terms and words so that there is no misunderstanding of intentions.

> Example: Performance Goals for a Sales Executive
> The performance goal should be specific on whether the measured result is based on all accounts/customers or only new accounts/customers. The sales executive may also be given other performance goals that cover sales margin and the size of customer accounts:
> - Achieve a total sales revenue of $xx in 2024 from both existing and new accounts.
> - Ensure that all sales deals have a minimum margin of xx%.
> - Attain at least 10 new customer accounts with a minimum sales order of $xx each in 2024.

> Example: Performance Goal for a Training Manager
> For a training manager, one may craft a performance goal as "Achieve an average of 35 training hours per employee for 2024." This statement appears specific. However, it should be refined to clarify what types of training programmes are to be included – for example, will courses of long duration (say, a 2-year diploma program sponsored by the company) be counted into the average training hours per employee?

Measurable

D2.56   This is the most difficult criterion to be met. Many important performance goals may not be easily measured. Notwithstanding, they must not be left out. One must accept that in performance appraisal, using judgment is inevitable. If a goal can only be qualitative (instead of quantitative), one will have to make sound and objective assessment using judgment. This is discussed in Chapter D4 "Performance Appraisal". On the converse, having measurable goals with quantitative targets does not guarantee objectivity, because in the first place, setting the target levels requires the use of judgment, which invariably comes with some subjectivity.

D2.57   Setting quantitative and measurable goals is the most challenging for support and administrative roles. Even when a quantitative metric is specified, it may entail huge efforts to gather the data. Where support/administrative services (such as human resource, finance, procurement and office facilities management) are provided to other employees, indeed, one way to measure the quality of service is to gather employees' (users') feedback. However, to do so for every support/administrative service rendered would certainly lead to survey fatigue and cause irk to employees. Feedback surveys should be used sparingly and appropriately, say, on the launch of a new system or the introduction of a new service. Even then, one should be circumspect in using employee feedback to measure the achievement of a performance goal. Employees' expectations may be unrealistic or insatiable.

> Example: Performance Goal of a Human Resource Manager
> A senior HR executive may be given a performance goal of, say, "Roll out a new HR information system by 31 December 2024". While timeliness for the system rollout is paramount, what about the quality? How holistic is the system in meeting the organisation's needs? How user-friendly is the system in enhancing employee experience?
>
> The challenge is in measuring these qualitative aspects. The organisation may conduct a survey with employees on their feedback on the new system and say, use 4/5 as the minimum "pass" score for the quality measurement of the system. However, how fair is it to use feedback score as a measurement of the performance goal? The system construct (that is, the extent of customisation) may have been limited by budget. Another factor to consider is whether the organisation has complex or legacy policies and procedures that complicate the system design. Employees may not take cognisance of these factors when they give their feedback.

D2.58   What is chosen to be measured will materially influence the behaviours of employees. It can be damaging to pick a "wrong" measurement metric simply because it can be measured easily.

> Example
> If a loan executive in a consumer bank has his performance measured solely by the total loan amount marketed, he will be driven to push for the numbers without regard to the quality of the loan deals. It is therefore highly advisable for an organisation to select the right metric or alternatively, to put in place meaningful safeguards to stamp out any undesirable behaviours or risks. For instance, the loan executive should be given another performance goal that measures loan quality so as to act as a counteracting force against the risk of bringing in many substandard loan deals.

D2.59   The strong proponents of measurable goals contend that only measurable goals are objective. This is ideal, but realistically, not always possible. If an outcome is qualitative rather than quantitative, one will have to exercise judgment in good faith and fairness – for instance, by comparing the "before" and "after" pictures after the employee has put in effort to make enhancements, or by benchmarking against the equivalent seen in other departments or industry competitors.

Attainable

D2.60   "Attainable" relates to calibrating a performance goal to an appropriate level – it should be reasonably achievable with diligent effort. It should require some stretch and not be simply "a walk in the park". Conversely, it should not be over-challenging to the extent that it is beyond fair expectations of the employee as if setting him up to fail.

D2.61   A fair way to calibrate a performance goal is to peg to the job grade/level (that is, seniority) of the employee.

> Example
> The organisation may set sales targets of $x for sales executives and $y for sales managers (where $y is higher than $x). It may even consider sub-levelling the sales targets, say, $x_1 and $x_2 and $y_1 and $y_2 based on the actual salary levels for the individual sales executives and sales managers respectively.

D2.62   Setting an attainable performance goal for an employee requires judgment and fairness. To complicate the matter further, often, one has to make assumptions (at times even with incomplete information) when exercising judgment.

> Example
> Using the sales executive/manager example, one has to ensure that $x and $y are indeed set at the correct levels. Say, if $x is set at $100,000, one may ask, why not $80,000 or $120,000? One has first to make assumptions on the business climate, consumer demand and competition to predict the realistic sales volume for the company before allocating the volume to the sales executives/managers.

D2.63   There are ways to facilitate better judgment in calibrating performance goals, including the following:

(a)   use recent past data as reference (provided that there is no major change in the conditions or circumstances that have impact on the performance result),

(b)   do actual simulations based on raw data and assumptions to derive a range of plausible scenarios (worst, best and realistic),

(c) consider the industry norm and

(d) use requirements imposed by the regulatory authorities (or example, deadlines for statutory reporting).

D2.64   Suffice to say, setting an attainable performance goal for an employee requires judgment and fairness as well as the application of acceptable parameters backed by data. We delve deeper into setting attainable performance goals under the section "Performance Expectations Level" in the later part of this chapter.

Relevant

D2.65   "Relevancy" refers to whether the performance goal is relevant and matters to the organisation. This requires one to go beyond just the superficial questioning; it entails deeper discernment on what outcomes really matter to the organisation.

> Example: Performance Goal for a Training Manager
> What is the value of having an impressive number of training hours/places per employee if the training has not been effective in improving the competencies of employees?

> Example: Performance Goal for a Sales Support Coordinator
> What is the value of handling a huge volume of sales inquiries if the actual number of sales leads generated and deals secured is disappointing in relation to the volume of enquiries?

> Example: Performance Goal of a Human Resource Executive
> Does it do any good to reduce the time to fill headcount vacancies if the quality of new hires is less than desired?

D2.66   In reality, in the quest to have measurable performance goals, some employees with the blessing of their reporting officers, inadvertently or otherwise, select measurable and attainable performance goals that are easy to measure but are of little real significance to the organisation. Organisations must guard against this.

Time-bound

D2.67   This is probably the easiest criterion to be satisfied. It is required because outcome is only meaningful if the time boundary is present. Most performance goals will simply use the appraisal period/year to define the time. Some performance goals may have a specific finishing point (for example, project X must be completed by 30 June 2025). Even for a long-term project that stretches beyond the appraisal period/year, one can put in a milestone check (with specific interim deliverables) that coincides with the end of the appraisal period.

Performance Expectations Level

D2.68   In setting a performance goal, one has to specify the expected level to be achieved. Put simply, after pinning down the "what" for an employee to do, the next thing is to specify the expected level (or standard) of results that he must achieve.

> Examples
> - Sales Executive: He must secure sales. What level of sales revenue must he achieve?
> - Production Executive: He is tasked to schedule and support production. How many production lines should he oversee?
> - Quality Control Manager: He is responsible for troubleshooting technical problems. What complexity level should he be expected to handle independently?

D2.69   The expected performance level/standard is essentially the "minimum" or "threshold" level, below which performance is taken to be unsatisfactory or unacceptable. In the case where an employee is given a stretch target, the intention and rationale should be made known to the employee and for the sake of fairness and transparency, both "threshold" and "stretch" components should be spelt out clearly.

D2.70   In setting performance expectation levels, one should take into account both the organisation's needs as well as the accountability that can be fairly expected from the individual employee.

Organisation-centric Factors	Employee-centric Factors
• Corporate objectives and strategies • Organisational culture • Agenda of senior leadership	• Job grade/level • Salary level • Capability level • Stretching the employee • Employee's overall work volume • Special circumstances • Preceding year's performance goals • Bargaining by Employee

Organisation-centric Factors

Corporate Objectives and Strategies

D2.71   Needless to say, the corporate objectives and strategies should be the most pertinent consideration. Indeed, they should govern and translate to the departments' and individual employees' performance goals and expectation levels. For example, if the organisation wants to achieve high growth for the coming year, it will not do if the departments' and employees' performance goals are set at "business-as-usual" expectation levels.

Organisational Culture

D2.72   Some organisations are aggressive in pursuing results and growth and have a highly competitive and driven work culture. They expect (and enforce) their employees to churn out higher output year after year; some even expect quantum leaps in one go. On the other hand, there are organisations with a more benign culture; they plan out graduated growth in a steady step-up manner.

Agenda of Senior Leadership

D2.73   There are times when a senior leader may pursue an agenda that affects the priorities of the organisation. For example, one may delay capital investment to shore up the financial indicators (such as Return on Capital Employed).

Another leader may opt to take things easy (not to take risks and rock the boat) if he is retiring soon or contemplating to quit.

Employee-centric Factors

Job Grade/Level

D2.74   Most organisations calibrate the level of performance expectations (that is, targets/standards to be met) pegged to the job grade/level (that is, seniority) of the employee. When an employee is promoted to a higher job grade/level, he is expected to take on a bigger role and be assigned higher performance targets/standards.

Salary Level

D2.75   The practice is varied in this aspect. Some organisations will consider the relativity (or differential) in salaries when assigning performance targets/ standards, while others will ignore the salary differentials if the said employees are in the same job grade and performing the same job.

Example

Say, 3 treasury dealers in a bank are performing the same job trading with the same forex instruments. While all 3 are in the same job grade, their basic salaries are different (due to commencing salaries and cumulated increments over the years).

	Organisation A	Organisation B
Employee A, job grade 5, salary $8,000	Revenue target $x	Same revenue target of $x for all 3 treasury dealers
Employee B, job grade 5, salary $10,000	Revenue target $y	
Employee C, job grade 5, salary $12,000	Revenue target $z	

(where $z > y > x$)

D2.76   On the surface, it appears fair to assign higher performance targets/standards to employees who are paid more (even if they are in the same job grade as their peers). This is acceptable for employees in job roles that are highly revenue-driven (for example, treasury dealers, financial advisors, as well as bankers in business development and sales roles). At the point of joining the organisation, these employees may request a certain remuneration package, and the organisation is willing to accede to their requests and thereon calibrate and assign performance (revenue) targets to them accordingly.

D2.77   For job roles which are not the key or substantial revenue earners, organisations generally do not peg the level of performance targets/standards to the employee's salary. To do so will be cumbersome and unwieldy: first, it would entail disclosing individual employees' salary information to all reporting officers, and this can be discomforting and untenable, and second, employees may argue that salary increments are earned as a reward for service loyalty and hence they may not be receptive to the notion of tying higher performance target to higher salary. Therefore, many organisations generally find it sufficient to just use job grade/level as the basis to determine the level of performance targets/standards.

Capability Level

D2.78   Logically, the overall (or total) performance targets of a department must be distributed amongst all its employees as individual performance targets. In distributing the targets, the principle should be to assign based on the seniority (job grade/level and at times including salary relativity) of the employees. This is the fairest way.

D2.79   *Should the level of performance targets/standards be set based on the capabilities of the individual employee? In other words, should a weak performer be given a discounted set of targets/standards?*
It is contentious to set targets/standards based on the capabilities of the individual employee. This is because the achievement of targets/standards will impact an employee's performance rating. In all performance-linked rewards schemes (such as bonus and increment), the quantum of payout is calibrated to the performance rating. To give discounted targets/standards to a weaker employee and then go about recognising him with a good performance rating (when he meets his discounted targets/standards) and reward him for it is an unwise thing to do. First, the weaker employee will become complacent and will not be spurred to put in extra effort to level up his performance. Second, the more capable employees will feel unfair

and unhappy and the organisation's reward policy will certainly come under fire.

D2.80   The correct way is to assign targets/standards based on the seniority (job grade/level) of the employees. Weak performers should not be accorded any discount. That said, in reality, if there are weak performers in the department and the line head is of the view that the weak performers are not likely to deliver the assigned targets, then it is only academic; the results are not going to happen. The weak performers failing to deliver will jeopardise the boat reaching the shore. The line head must therefore be astute and find other means to make up the shortfall for the department. The most practical way is to top up the performance targets of the more capable employees and assign these as "stretch" targets (we elaborate more on this under the sub-section "Stretching the Employee").

D2.81   The weak performer in delivering short of the normal target will have his performance rating, bonus and increment impacted (reduced), while the high performing employee should be rewarded commensurately based on how much he delivers his stretch target. This approach is fair and will be better received by employees, compared to the approach of assigning lower targets to weak performers and having them "celebrate" their success of delivering on target and be rewarded for doing so.

Stretching the Employee

D2.82   All performance targets should be set at a level that should be reasonably attainable with diligent effort. It is important to provide some challenge to the employee to energise and inspire him to push harder and higher. If an employee can deliver on his target just by merely cruising on the job, boredom may set in and more importantly, the employee will stagnate in his growth.

D2.83   The reality is that employees come with different levels of capability, hence what requires considerable effort for some (as in the case of average performers) may be "a piece of cake" for others (as in the case of high performers). In handling high performing and high potential employees, the reporting officer or line head should be deliberate in loading up on performance targets for them and assign as "stretch" targets. The said employee should be informed of the intention and rationale so that he will not view the stretch target as a form of unfairness. For the sake of fairness and transparency, the "normal" and "stretch" components of the target should be spelt out clearly so that the employee will not be unfairly assessed as failing in performance if, say, he meets or exceeds the normal component but misses the stretch component.

D2.84   While it is desirable to encourage the high performing and high potential employee to go for stretch goals, it must be reasonable and not be overly stretching to the extent that the employee becomes unduly stressed. There is a limit to continual stretching; the successive year-on-year increase cannot be sustained if the employee is already operating at a very high-performance level.

D2.85   In most organisations, the management and Human Resource will also have oversight of the high performing and high potential employees under the ambit of their talent management/development program. These select employees are often given additional assignments (such as cross-departmental special projects) over and above their normal work to stretch them and accelerate their growth. More are covered in Chapter D14 "Talent Management and Succession Planning".

Employee's Overall Work Volume

D2.86   The volume of work for an employee is an important consideration when setting performance goals. Reporting officers and line heads should take stock of the different work portfolios of their employees. For example, the employee may be multi-hatting, that is, he handles multiple portfolios reporting to more than just one reporting officer. For high performing and high potential employees, they may have been given special projects/ assignments by the management (or Human Resource) under the ambit of the organisation's talent management/development program. The primary reporting officer (or primary line head) for the said employee should take the responsibility of ensuring a fair and balanced performance load on the employee.

Special Circumstances

D2.87   An employee may encounter a special circumstance such as being on maternity leave, prolonged illness leave or no-pay leave. If the employee's impending absence from work is already known at the performance planning stage, the reporting officer or line head should take the absence period into account and adjust the performance targets accordingly.

D2.88   Another scenario is the employee's unfamiliarity with the job role or the organisation; he may be a new joiner or newly promoted or transferred. It is arguable whether he should be given a lower performance target. Most organisations think that it is fair to give them a grace period to settle in and hence will apply some leniency in setting performance targets. Other organisations may take another approach; rather than adjust the performance expectations level at the performance planning stage, they will instead apply some leniency during the appraisal at the end of the appraisal period. Where performance goals are quantitative, a new joiner who joins in the middle of an appraisal year should be given a pro-rated target.

D2.89   Having difficult personal issues (say, a family crisis) may be another scenario. Some organisations hold the view that personal matters are something that the employee has to handle himself and should not be allowed to affect the employee's accountability or obligations at work. On the other hand, there are organisations that are more employee-centric and empathetic and are willing to make some adjustments to the performance expectation level so as to give the employee some breathing space. That said, the usual caveats for taking this approach are: first, the employee must be committed and has good work ethics and second, the lower performance target is temporary (say, for one year only) and will eventually be re-adjusted to the norm level. It would be pointless if the organisation gives lenient treatment in perpetuity to an employee who is a persistent poor performer or has poor work ethics. For such cases, the organisation should remain strict and if the employee fails to deliver on his performance goals repeatedly, it is better off managing him out (please refer to Chapter D6 "Dealing with Weak Performers").

Preceding Year's Performance Goals

D2.90   When the job roles of an employee have not changed, it is tempting for the reporting officer or line head to adopt the preceding year's performance targets/standards without any change or at most with minor tweaking. This should not be the default mode. The reporting officer or line head should check whether the operating conditions have changed, such as (a) economic outlook, (b) competition landscape, (c) regulatory requirements, (d) organisation's focus and priorities including new projects and initiatives, (e) availability of resources including funding, (f) changes in staffing level and employee mix for the department and (g) lessons learnt from the preceding year. Any changes must be incorporated into the planning parameters for performance goals for the new appraisal year.

D2.91   The employee should also be made to embark on one or two new initiatives each year to provide him with opportunities to strengthen his competencies, broaden his exposure, enhance his adaptability and grow in resilience.

Bargaining by Employee

D2.92   Some employees may bargain for lower performance targets/standards, citing reasons such as (a) subordinates being new, thus requiring more supervision, (b) having many weak performers amongst the subordinates, (c) inadequate resources given and (d) poor cooperation from other departments.

D2.93   It is not wise to accede to such bargaining and lower the performance targets/ standards at the planning stage. Rather, if indeed any adverse circumstances that are beyond the control of the employee have taken place and provided that the employee has done his part in mitigating the adverse effects, the reporting officer or line head may then apply some leniency during the appraisal at the end of the appraisal period.

Number of Performance Goals and Weightages

Number of Performance Goals

D2.94   The key tasks of an employee should be found in his job description (JD), which should be regularly updated. Depending on the comprehensiveness and granularity, a JD may contain a long laundry list of tasks that the jobholder is supposed to undertake (please refer to Annex A2-1 of Volume A, Chapter A2 "Recruitment and Selection" for samples of JDs). There is no need to create a performance goal for every task listed in the JD. Many tasks (such as gathering information, preparing reports and coordination work) are "business-as-usual" activities that the employee must undertake on a routine basis. Some employees may feel the need to form performance goals for these to account for their efforts, but if these generate little impact to the organisation, they should not be included as performance goals so as not to dilute the employees' focus on more important objectives. Only the significant tasks in the JD or other significant assignments given to the employee that have impact need to be crafted into performance goals.

D2.95 *How many performance goals are sufficient?*
There is no hard and fast rule on the optimal number of performance goals. A reasonable range is 3 to 6 performance goals. Those in senior positions and who cover a broader range of functions or portfolios understandably have more performance goals, say, 6 to 8 performance goals.

D2.96 More performance goals will provide the breadth in capturing all significant areas and initiatives. However, focus is also important. Too many performance goals may overwhelm the employee and disperse his efforts and attention. Hence a balance between breadth and focus must be struck.

D2.97 *What happens when there are too few performance goals?*
If an employee has too few performance goals, it may mean that certain areas have been omitted or the performance goals may have been crafted in too broad a manner without enough specifics to funnel the employee's effort.

> Example
> A sales executive may be given one broad performance goal such as "Achieve a total top-line sales revenue of $1.5 million in 2025". He may like this because it gives him full flexibility in deciding what products to sell. He will be tempted to focus on products that are easy to sell instead of those that can generate better margin. If he is empowered to give discount (without reduction in his sales commission), he is likely to do so to garner more sales, and as a result, the margin will be eroded.
>
> Instead of having one broad performance goal, it may be expanded to a few to make them more effective in guiding efforts and driving behaviours:
>
> 1. Achieve a total top-line sales revenue of $1.5 million in 2025.
> 2. Secure at least $500,000 sales revenue from Product A (new and of high margin).
> 3. Achieve an average gross margin of 28%.

D2.98 *What happens when there are too many performance goals?*
If an employee has many performance goals, it may result in one or two goals being allocated a small weightage, say, 5% or even less. In this situation, the employee and his reporting officer should review whether it is worthwhile to retain the "micro" goals. One solution is to combine the "micro" goals if

they are related, into a bigger performance goal which can command, say, at least 10% weightage. This should only be done if the micro goals are worthwhile to be given due attention.

Weightages

D2.99   To help ensure that important performance goals are given the right attention, it is useful to assign different weightages to the goals. An example is given below for a sales manager:

Performance Goals for a Sales Manager	Weightages (%)
1. Achieve a total top-line sales revenue of $1.5 million (subject to meeting minimum margin).	40
2. Secure at least $500,000 sales revenue from Product A.	20
3. Sign on at least 10 new customers (minimum invoice of $15,000).	20
4. Ensure no more than $50,000 outstanding invoiced payment that exceeds 60 days (based on 12 month-end average).	10
5. Provide good customer service (to be assessed qualitatively based on attrition of customers, compliments/complaints and general feedback from customers).	10
Total	100

D2.100   Instead of assigning mathematical weightages, an organisation may describe relative weightages as, say, 3 levels of importance: High (H), Medium (M) and Low (L). If we apply this weightage method to the earlier example of performance goals for sales manager, it appears as follows:

Performance Goals for a Sales Manager	Importance
1. Achieve a total top-line sales revenue of $1.5 million (subject to meeting minimum margin).	H
2. Secure at least $500,000 sales revenue from Product A.	M

3. Sign on at least 10 new customers (minimum invoice of $15,000).	M
4. Ensure no more than $50,000 outstanding invoiced payment that exceeds 60 days (based on 12 month-end average).	L
5. Provide good customer service (to be assessed qualitatively based on attrition of customers, compliments/complaints and general feedback from customers).	L

D2.101 Weightages put on performance goals serve the following purposes:

(a) push the reporting officer or line head to analyse and reflect on priorities (on what matters more) and communicate these clearly to the employee;

(b) help the employee adjust his time and effort according to the priorities set out; and

(c) provide a more systematic and defensible basis for assessing how an employee has performed on an overall basis (see the following example).

> Example
> Employee X and Employee Y are in the same team and both have the same 3 performance goals with these weightages: A (80%), B (10%) and C (10%):
>
> - Employee X achieves goal A fully but falls short of goal B and goal C.
> - Employee Y achieves goal B and goal C fully but falls grossly short of goal A.
>
> Overall, Employee X should be assessed more favourably than Employee Y.

D2.102 Assigning weightages requires judgment. The weightages assigned need not be meticulously correct; they just need to be directionally correct. It suffices to signal to the employee the relative importance of the performance goals so that he is clear on the amount of effort and attention expected.

D2.103 If an employee remains in the same job role, the number of performance goals that he has may differ from year to year. Even if the employee has the same set of performance goals year after year, weightages can (and should) be adjusted to align with any change in focus, strategies and priorities of the department or the organisation. This reflects the dynamic nature of performance planning and goals setting.

Balanced Scorecard

D2.104   The Balanced Scorecard (BSC) was conceived by Robert S Kaplan and David P Norton in 1982. The BSC framework allows an organisation or a manager to look at the business from 4 important perspectives as follows:

> Customer
> *How do customers perceive the organisation? What would delight the customers?*
>
> Internal
> *What must the organisation excel at?*
>
> Innovation and Growth
> *How can the organisation improve its processes and quality and create more value?*
>
> Financial
> *How is the organisation faring in the eyes of its shareholders?*

D2.105   With the BSC framework, the organisation can integrate all its performance goals into a single report card. It helps avoid sub-optimisation of one performance goal in favour of another, as in the case of "contradictory" goals (see the elaboration in the box below). It enables the organisation's management to have sight of its performance goals categorised according to the critical areas (or perspectives), like how someone in the driver's seat can view from his dashboard. One can see more clearly how an action in one category may be done at the expense of another category (for example, acceding to customers' expectations may increase cost for the organisation). Having a clear vantage point of this will help the organisation navigate astutely to balance considerations and achieve the best overall outcome.

> **"Contradictory" Performance Goals**
> In a basket of performance goals, some may be "contradictory" in the way they impact the organisation.
>
> Examples
> • The quest for speed and efficiency may compromise the human aspect of customer service.

- The zealous pursuit of top-line revenue may mean reduction in profit margin and over-focus on easy-to-sell products.
- The unrelenting focus on short-term profits may persuade leaders to delay investing in projects/programs that do not generate immediate revenue.

One should not merely pursue one or two narrow performance goals at the expense of other equally relevant deliverables. The answer lies in striking a judicious balance and managing all performance goals collectively and holistically, considering both the short and long-term priorities of the organisation. This is where the balanced scorecard framework may be used.

D2.106 Invariably, the BSC will comprise a mix of financial and non-financial performance goals. It is an enlightened and prudent way for the organisation to guard against over-prioritising financial gains (especially short-term) at the expense of other aspects that affect its capability building and long-term survival. If profit is the dominant measurement of performance, the entire organisation (from management to line heads, managers and employees) may become too engrossed in chasing the revenue dollars and neglect the non-revenue generating activities, or worse, even withhold spending on capability-building (such as investment in operating systems, staff training and product innovation). Striking a judicious balance in priorities (financial versus non-financial and short-term versus long-term) is the aim of the BSC. Weightages may be assigned to each category of goals in the BSC to signify relative importance. We share two examples of BSC below:

Example
National Healthcare Group (NHG) uses a Balanced Scorecard (BSC) framework to measure the performance of its healthcare institutions. The BSC comprises performance indicators in 4 dimensions:

- Financial indicators (for example, Revenue, Budget Surplus)
- Customer indicators (for example, Patient Satisfaction Index)
- Process indicators (for example, Average Length of Stay for each Disease Class, Staff-to-Bed Ratio)
- Quality (for example, Critical Incidents Rate)

Each of the performance indicators is assigned a weightage. The composite of all the indicators gives the overall weighted score which is considered the overall performance of the healthcare institution. A corporate bonus matrix is developed where bonus payout is calibrated against a graduating scale of BSC overall weighted score.

> Example
>
> Maybank Singapore uses a Balanced Scorecard (BSC) framework to guide the setting of performance goals for its top executives. The BSC comprises performance indicators in 4 dimensions: (a) financial, (b) customers, (c) internal business process and (d) learning and growth.
>
> Each dimension has 1–2 performance goals. Each goal is assigned a weightage. The composite of all the indicators gives the overall weighted score which is considered the overall performance of the senior executive. The BSC reflects a balance between financial pursuit, capability building and customer relationship management.

D2.107   While the BSC can be quite easily implemented, it is however more suitable for employees in managerial and leadership roles who have a wider scope of accountabilities. For a non-revenue-generating executive, the financial goal can be represented by a cost target and customers can include internal customers. The BSC is still applicable even if only 3 (instead of 4) dimensions are considered.

Performance Goals for Rank-and-File Employees

D2.108   Most organisations generally do not invest a lot of time and effort in performance planning for individual rank-and-file employees. The reasons are as follows:

- First, tasks performed by rank-and-file employees tend to be narrowly and clearly defined, where the employees are mostly required to follow standard operating procedures with little room for variation and discretion; and

- Second, rank-and-file employees are less exposed to the larger issues and challenges of the organisation (such as capability building and growth priorities).

D2.109   Performance planning for rank-and-file employees tends to be simplified. Often, the reporting officer (supervisor) may articulate a set of standard performance goals and apply it uniformly to all the rank-and-file employees in the team who are performing the same job (say, all production operators). The communication may also not be done at the individual employee level.

It is common for the supervisor to do a briefing at a staff meeting and thereafter document it into the employees' performance appraisal forms, with an individual copy handed out to each employee for reference. So long as there is clarity in communicating the performance goals, the objective of performance planning is served for this group of employees.

Performance Goals for Support and Administrative Roles

D2.110   Setting performance goals for support/administrative roles is undoubtedly a challenge. The major obstacle is that one cannot easily quantify and measure the output and value-add of the support roles. There is some truth to it.

D2.111   The practical thing to do is identify and craft performance goals that can reasonably reflect the employee's output and value-add or impact to the organisation. The practical way is to use qualitative goals that come with reasonable measurement metric (say, based on observable incidents) supplemented by appraisal of competency-based behaviours. The goals, if not measurable, can still be crafted in a SART (specific, attainable, relevant and time-bound) manner.

D2.112   *Can performance goals be SMART for support/administrative roles?*
For support/administrative roles, very often, the quality of the service rendered is important. Care must therefore be taken to ensure that performance goals incorporate quality-related metrics. We illustrate with examples of performance goals where quality is an important measure.

Example of a SMART Goal for an Events Management Executive
Organise 10 community outreach events in 2024.

Is this goal adequate? What if the events are organised but the attendance is low? Or the feedback on the events is less than favourable?

The goal may be re-crafted as follows:
"Organise 10 community outreach events within the approved budget in 2024, and each event must have at least 100 participants and either generate positive feedback of 7/10 or higher, or a sign-up of at least 30 new memberships*"

*Note: The metric stated is just an example. The goal should incorporate whatever metric is a relevant measure of the impact on the organisation.

Example of a SMART Goal for an Administrative Executive
Prepare minutes of management meetings for management's review within 3 working days after the meetings.

Is this goal adequate? The quality aspect (which can make the goal more specific and relevant) is missing. What if the minutes are delivered promptly within the deadline but are of poor quality? How to specify the quality? Based on language correctness or style? How about the number and types of errors (or omissions) in the first draft, or the number of rounds of edit by the supervisor, or the finesse of the language?

The goal may be re-crafted as follows:
"Prepare minutes of management meetings for management's review within 3 working days after the meetings with not more than 10 material editorial/content changes and 2 rounds of edit to obtain management's approval of the minutes."

Note: This revised goal statement is not ideal but is reasonably acceptable given the fact that it is difficult to define and measure quality for minutes writing. (Often, the reporting officer may only be able to make a general comment after reviewing the minutes (*"yes, this is good"* or *"no, this is not up to standard"*).

Managing Deviations in Performance Planning

D2.113   All organisations want performance planning to be done and completed at the start of the appraisal year. In practice, performance planning is not always smooth and straightforward. Organisations must deal with possible changes in performance goals as well as off-cycle cases.

Review in the Middle of the Appraisal Year

D2.114   Some organisations require a mid-term review of performance goals. At the halfway mark of the appraisal period, the reporting officer and the employee must jointly review the performance goals agreed upon earlier. A mid-term review makes sense as it prompts the reporting officer and employee to pause and step back to take stock of the performance goals. Are there any changes to the goals? Have circumstances changed? How is the employee faring at this halfway mark? The value of having a mid-year review is obvious.

D2.115 If circumstances have changed (for example, work priorities have shifted, the assumptions used or the operating environment have changed, or the employee has been given new assignments), the performance goals should be revised and documented accordingly.

New Employees Joining during the Appraisal Year

D2.116 When a new employee joins service in the middle of the appraisal year, the organisation usually does not insist that he must have a full set of performance goals if his period of service in the appraisal year is short. Some organisations use 3 months while others use 6 months as a threshold to define "short". Generally, if the job grade/level is higher (correspondingly, the job is more complex), a higher threshold is used.

D2.117 For a new employee with, say, 6 months to contribute in the appraisal year, his performance targets should be adjusted (or pro-rated in the case of quantitative goals) to commensurate with the truncated appraisal period. For qualitative performance goals, the performance standard expected of him should perhaps also be moderated to take into account his unfamiliarity with his role. Most organisations tend to focus on observing and assessing new employees on competencies and general work ethics, with less emphasis on work volume or targets in their initial months of service.

Transfer Cases

D2.118 When an employee is transferred to a different position or department, his performance plan for that year must be reviewed. The timing of the transfer is material. If the employee is transferred near the end of the appraisal period (say, less than 3 months from the end of the appraisal period), for practical reasons, the organisation may waive the need for him to have a new set of performance goals for the remaining of that appraisal period.

D2.119 If the remaining of that appraisal year is, say, at least 3 months, the employee should be given a set of performance goals for his new position. The number of performance goals and the targets/standards expected must be adjusted correspondingly to take into account the length of the remaining appraisal period as well as the amount of time it should reasonably take the employee to familiarise with his new position.

Additional New Assignment/Project

D2.120　It is quite common for an employee to be given a new assignment/project after performance goals setting has been completed (for whatever reasons). If the new assignment/project is material, a performance goal on the said item should be added. This additional goal may be taken as a stretch goal, which is usually acceptable to an aspiring and motivated employee. Alternatively, the reporting officer may reduce the targets or expectations for the other performance goals accordingly. Where weightages have been assigned to the original set of goals, with the inclusion of a new goal, it would also be necessary to tweak the weightages.

D2.121　If the new assignment/project is injected very close to the end of the appraisal period, the employee and the reporting officer may concur not to add an additional performance goal in the current year. Instead, it will be taken into account in the following appraisal year. While it is important to account for changes and give due recognition to the employee, the question of practicability must be considered. In the final analysis, trust and fairness play a big part in performance management. An employee who willingly takes on a new assignment/project in addition to his existing set of performance goals reflects well on his work ethics and motivation, thus recognition may be accorded to him.

Administration of Performance Planning

The Role of Human Resource

D2.122　Functionally, Human Resource (HR) should be the overall owner and custodian of the performance management framework. HR's roles and responsibilities include the following:

(a) champion and oversee the design of the performance management framework and enforce its compliance;

(b) initiate, coordinate and administer the annual performance management exercise to ensure that the process is run smoothly and in a timely manner; and

(c) in some organisations (especially the smaller ones), may be expected to do quality check on the performance goals and targets/standards set and provide guidance and advisory to the line managers.

Documenting the Performance Plan

D2.123   Some line managers are not in the habit of doing performance planning "formally" with their employees. They may convey expectations in an informal manner to their employees in the course of reviewing their work or coaching and guiding them on the job, but these expectations may not be documented in any form. The line manager may think that such verbal exchanges and sharing should suffice, but the clarity of expectations may become contentious in the event that the employee is given an unfavourable performance rating at the end of the appraisal period. The employee may argue that the expectations are unclear or inconsistent, or that they have been changed, or that he did not perceive the expectations as being "official".

D2.124   The best practice is to do performance planning with the employee in a proper manner and document the performance goals (with targets/standards) in writing. Many organisations have taken due care to design their Performance Appraisal Form (PAF), usually in digital or e-form, to incorporate a section for the line manager and the employee to enter the agreed performance goals into the PAF. The employee is free to refer to the PAF at any time during the appraisal year for easy recall. Changes to the performance goals mid-way should also be documented.

Considerations and Challenges in Performance Planning

D2.125   Performance planning comes with some challenges. The common ones are discussed in this section. Organisations should find ways to mitigate them so that performance planning may fulfil its intended purposes of (a) achieving internal alignment and focus, and (b) providing clarity for managing the performance of employees.

Goals Too Narrow

D2.126   Under the pressure to set specific and measurable goals, the reporting officer and employee may inadvertently end up setting goals that are too specific and narrow. Narrow goals are usually easier to measure. The downside is that when an employee is too focused on narrowly defined performance goals, he may lose the bigger picture or ignore any initiatives that are not part of the measurable goals.

D2.127   If narrow goals cannot be dispensed with, the reporting officer and employee should include other relevant goals (even if they are non-quantifiable) so that the combined goals can, on a collective basis, be more holistic and better support the organisation's objectives and strategies. The concept of balanced scorecard should be applied.

Goals Not Relevant

D2.128   Reporting officers and employees are always reminded to make their performance goals SMART (specific, measurable, attainable, relevant and time-bound). Of the 5 criteria, "relevant" is the most critical, as an irrelevant goal is of no use.

D2.129   Performance goals set for an employee in an earlier year may become irrelevant if the organisation's strategy has since shifted or evolved. Sometimes, the goals are still retained because the reporting officer and employee fail to critically examine their relevance. Another possible reason is that the reporting officer and employee may have the inertia to change, preferring to cling on to "business-as-usual" and the familiar, especially if the said performance goals have existed for many years. They should have the resolve to drop goals that have ceased to be relevant.

D2.130   Often, the line head is the crucial second layer of check to ensure that the performance goals of employees are aligned with the department's, which in turn are aligned with the organisation's overall strategy and priorities. This responsibility cannot be taken lightly if the line head wants to see his department succeed in delivering results that meet the management's agenda.

Goals Compromising Other Critical Objectives

D2.131   In some instances, a goal is relevant but may compromise or contradict another equally important objective. Some examples are given below for illustration:

Performance Goals that are SMAT instead of SMART — Relevance is lost

Example (hypothetical)
School teachers are given a primary performance target based on the average national exam score for the subject taught to the students. The rating based on this measurement has a big impact on the teachers' increments and promotion prospects. The performance target may influence the teachers to focus on ways and teaching activities to make the students exam-smart. As a result, real learning may not take place.

> Example (hypothetical)
> The government has set aside $50 million to help small and medium-sized companies purchase human resource management software for them to improve their people management capabilities. A company needs to co-pay only 10% of the cost of the software. A team of government officers has been tasked to offer this to the targeted companies. The team will be assessed based on the number of companies that have taken up the offer. The team will invariably focus on quick wins – targeting financially stronger companies that are amenable to co-pay 10% to get any human resource management software. Furthermore, the team may "discourage" companies from getting a more comprehensive system, thereby taking up a bigger amount from the pool of funding. The team will want an end result that looks good in terms of the total number of companies that receive funding. The real impact and benefits to the companies may become secondary.

Goals Quantifiable but Challenging to Measure

D2.132 Some performance goals may be quantifiable and measurable, but they require a lot of effort to gather the data for measurement. Hence, it may not be worthwhile or practical to craft them as such. It is more pragmatic to find a proxy way (including substituting with qualitative goals) to assess the output or outcome.

D2.133 Quite often, the measurement metric may be crafted in such a "unique" or specific manner that the required data is not catered for in the organisation's existing information system. At times, it may also be that the data takes time to gather and may not come in time for performance appraisal.

> Example
> An organisation wants to use the improvement in the employee engagement score as a measurement metric for a particular performance goal. It takes time to do the employee engagement survey. Often, the survey is timed to take place at the time of the year when it is the best "off-peak" season for most departments. This may therefore not coincide with the performance appraisal cycle. Moreover, most organisations conduct employee engagement surveys bi-annually rather than annually to avoid survey fatigue and also to give the organisation sufficient time to follow up on the survey results to address issues (or pain points) surfaced before the next round of survey.

Shared Goals

D2.134 There are instances where all the members of the same team share one common set of performance goals. This happens when the team members perform different parts as well as cover for one another, thus making it not feasible or meaningful to draw lines and assign individual targets. Asking the employees to singularly focus on individual goals will disrupt teamwork and affect customer service. The team arrangement and dynamics should not be sacrificed simply to have individual performance goals. Performance management is a means, not an end. What matters is that the team is able to, through team-based performance goals, produce the intended outcomes.

D2.135 In this situation, the performance result should first be appraised at the team level and thereafter adjusted for individual team members based on the assessment by the reporting officer using perhaps qualitative measures and competency-based behaviours demonstrated by the individuals.

Balancing Goals

D2.136 Every organisation invariably has a portfolio of objectives, some of which are counteracting in nature. Logically, all organisations want to strive for success that is holistic and sustainable. Organisations therefore put in check-and-balance in their systems. This may include setting up departments to undertake a "control" or "policing" function. These control/policing departments are in turn given their own performance goals and targets/standards (such as to ensure high governance, low rate of delinquent accounts or low rate of exceptions to the rule). If these control/policing departments are over-exacting and uncompromising (so as to meet their own targets/standards), the other departments will feel that they are hindered in meeting their performance goals.

> Example
> If an internal auditor in the organisation is a perfectionist (or petty over trivial matters), the operating departments will protest (usually covertly) as they will have more checks to do and procedures to follow. The audit findings may also affect their performance ratings.

> **Example**
> In a commercial bank, if the credit control department is meticulous and demanding on the terms and conditions that potential borrowers must fulfil, the loan executives will face challenge in achieving their loan targets. Similarly, if the credit processing department is exacting and uncompromising on loan documentation, the loan executives will be frustrated with the delay in loan disbursement.

> **Example**
> Most line heads want autonomy in spending. They would also ask for more resources, especially if they do not need to pay for them (say, support/administrative services that are not charged directly to their own departments). Finance department has the unenviable task of controlling the budget and expenditure of the operating departments.

D2.137　These are real and common challenges that organisations must deal with. Those undertaking the control/policing functions are doing so to protect the interests of the organisation. However, if they are overzealous on issues of little significance, their drive for perfection will adversely affect the fulfilment of other corporate objectives. This is where a balanced scorecard is useful and also where the senior management must take oversight and exercise judicious balance and judgment.

Assumptions, Judgment and Contention

D2.138　Setting work targets involves looking at past data and doing extrapolations to the future year, scanning the operating environment, sizing up the competition and estimating business potential. Data about the operating landscape is usually incomplete and thus assumptions must be made. Even if data is available, it still requires making subjective judgment in applying it to the organisation. To make better assumptions and judgment, one must have a solid understanding of corporate objectives and astute knowledge of the operating environment.

D2.139　Depending on the comfort level between the employee and the reporting officer, sometimes, the employee may contend that the assumptions and judgment are "harsh" and bargain for a lower performance target/standard.

This is understandable since his performance rating depends on his achievement of targets/standards, and this will affect his monetary rewards.

D2.140   As no one can claim to be absolutely "precise" or "correct" in the targets/standards (since the setting of these requires making assumptions and judgment), it can leave much room for contention.

D2.141   To manage this challenge, reporting officers and line heads should use as much factual data as possible, including past results (taking into account changes in the operating parameters), achievements of the employee's peers as well as industry norms to guide the target setting. The organisation may also compute and consider the value-add (in terms of additional dollar value) derived from the work targets vis-a-vis the cost of remunerating the employee (although this approach is more suitable for sales personnel and traders).

D2.142   Ultimately, it boils down to trust and good faith. If the employee has trust in the reporting officer and management in being fair, he will be less inclined to quibble on the work targets or expectations. When the appraisal year comes to a close, he trusts that the reporting officer will look at not only the gap between the target and the actual result but also the efforts put in and any adverse factors that are beyond the control of the employee that have hindered his performance. Setting of performance goals cannot be divorced from performance appraisal; they are tightly coupled. This tricky problem is discussed again in Chapter D4 "Performance Appraisal".

Factors Beyond the Employee's Control

D2.143   At times, performance results may be laden with factors and events that are beyond the control of the employee. We do not work in a vacuum. Events outside the organisation and priorities and work practices of other departments and our colleagues affect our work. It is expected of the employee to navigate, influence, socialise and work with whoever and whatever factors that may affect the pursuit of his performance goals. His abilities to do so depend on his competencies and will be reflected in the outcomes. It is fair to say that the types and extent of challenges vary greatly and not all are always entirely within the employee's means to handle. Therefore, the reporting officer should take these factors into consideration and appraise the employee as fairly as possible.

<u>Example</u>
Staff resignation rate is often used as a performance indicator for the Head of Human Resource (HR). While HR initiatives have some impact on staff retention, employees resign for a myriad of reasons. Uncompetitive remuneration (the organisation cannot afford or is unwilling to pay more), poor workplace relations, toxic work culture and uninteresting work are among the many factors that can push employees out the door, not to mention the tight labour market and poaching by other employers. Most of these factors are largely beyond the control of the Head of HR.

Notwithstanding, the organisation can still set a staff resignation rate target based on past data as well as industry norms, tempered with the assessment of the operating environment. For example, the performance goal may be "To reduce staff resignation rate from 15% to 13%". The 2-percentage point reduction may be deemed to be within the influence and effort of the Head of HR under the envisaged operating environment. This is ultimately a judgment call.

Reference

1. "Balanced Scorecard", Harvard Business Review, January-February 1992

Performance Feedback and Coaching

Focus of this Chapter

Performance feedback and coaching are integral parts of performance management. Ideally, it should be a continual interaction between an employee and his reporting officer throughout the performance management cycle. However, even if this is mandated by the organisation, it is seldom done and difficult to enforce. Most organisations set a requirement for a formal performance feedback, review and coaching session usually at the mid-year mark as the "minimal".

This chapter highlights the importance of performance feedback and coaching and candidly discusses why this important interaction has been much neglected or done superficially. We offer pointers on how information can be gathered to form feedback and how feedback should be crafted and delivered. Preparing the reporting officers (or managers) for this function is crucial; they must see the value in it, have the right mindset and possess some fundamental skills to conduct it.

Purpose and Importance
of Performance Feedback and Coaching

What is Performance Feedback and Coaching?

D3.1   Performance feedback is providing the employee with information and observations related to his work. Through interacting with the employee at work and reviewing the work done by the employee, a reporting officer can form a view about the performance of the employee and the areas where due attention should be given to help the employee perform better.

D3.2   Performance coaching is a process where the reporting officer acting as a coach or mentor guides, encourages and facilitates the employee to meet his performance goals and help him find solutions to work problems, learn, improve and grow.

Why Do Performance Feedback and Coaching?

D3.3   The main purpose is to help employees sustain and improve their work performance. Feedback will make the employees aware of how they are faring. Coaching will help the employees reflect and explore better ways of doing things to enhance their performance. Generally, employees want feedback; they want to know that their efforts at work are on the right track, as it is frustrating to an employee if his efforts are misdirected and go down the drain. Most employees also aspire to improve and grow, instead of stagnating in their performance; coaching helps them improve and grow. In essence, performance feedback and coaching are as much a staff development function as it is a component of performance management process.

Performance Feedback and Coaching Should Be On-going

D3.4   For performance feedback and coaching to be effective and beneficial to the employee, it should be done on an on-going and regular basis. The reasons include the following:

(a) When feedback is given regularly (say, right after a work assignment is completed by the employee), it will be more specific. The recall of events is still fresh, and hence the employee will be less defensive. This makes it easier to get the message across and understood by the employee.

(b) Generally, when feedback is on-going and done with less proximity to the year-end performance rating season, it will be perceived as less threatening. Employees will be less anxious about whether the feedback will impact their performance ratings. In other words, the feedback will be more issue-centred than rating-centred. Employees will be better able to focus on the content of the feedback rather than the expected (or imaginary) "penalty" exacted on their performance ratings. They will be more forthcoming in acknowledging their performance gaps and focus on making improvements.

(c) Feedback given regularly and promptly (say, right after the completion of every work assignment or at every important milestone of a mega project) will serve to ensure that the employee is on the right track. If an employee is off the mark, no time is lost and the employee can be promptly alerted to close his gaps, change gear or step up momentum.

(d) When performance feedback is done on an on-going, regular and frequent basis (instead of giving feedback only once a year during the year-end performance appraisal), it reduces the aberrative effects of performance appraisal, such as the "halo", "horn" and "recency" effects. The year-end appraisal will be made easier and more objective, much like a consolidation (and closure) of what has been conversed throughout the year between the reporting officer and employee. This is further discussed in Chapter D4 "Performance Appraisal".

Other Benefits of Performance Feedback and Coaching

D3.5   Other than the primary objective of helping employees improve or enhance their work performance, providing feedback and coaching on a continual, regular and frequent basis has other positive effects, including the following:

(a) It encourages open communication, helps build trust and strengthens the working relationship between the reporting officer and employee.

(b) If employees have a positive experience of receiving performance feedback and coaching and have personally benefitted from it in growing professionally, they tend to "pay it back" in due course. When they themselves become people managers (reporting officers), they will feel confident and be genuine in offering performance feedback and coaching to their own direct reports. When this virtuous cycle repeats itself continually and across the board, a nurturing and positive performance culture will emerge and take hold within the organisation.

(c) Regular and prompt feedback will help the organisation identify weak performers as well as employees who are misfits for their job positions. Line managers can flag out these cases to the management (or Human

Resource) early so that the organisation can take appropriate counter-actions, such as requiring the weak performers to undergo a corrective plan and redeploying misfitted employees to other job positions.

D3.6 The year-end appraisal session is evaluative in nature and tends to be held in a solemn manner, therefore often putting both the employee and reporting officer in an uncomfortable position. During the performance appraisal conversation, the employee may be reluctant to volunteer information (such as his weak points) that may jeopardise his performance rating. The employee is often guarded and careful with what to say and not to say. In contrast, regular performance feedback can be done in a more spontaneous and informal manner. This puts both the employee and reporting officer in a more relaxed mood, thus paving the way for a more positive and candid conversation.

D3.7 Despite the usefulness of performance feedback and coaching, many reporting officers do not do it. While organisations may institute that performance feedback and coaching should be done regularly, in reality, it is difficult to enforce. And even if/when it happens, it may be more form than substance. There are many reasons (hovering on will, skills and resources) why this happens. The common ones are as follows:

(a) Doing performance feedback and coaching is much about commitment and practice. If a reporting officer does not believe in its usefulness and is not prepared to put in effort, true performance feedback and coaching will not happen. Even if done (to comply with the organisation's requirement), it will be more form than substance. It is regarded much as an administrative chore to be done and be over with.

(b) Some reporting officers may have the desire to do performance feedback and coaching, but lack the skills and therefore not comfortable with doing it. They may have been promoted from individual contributor roles and not adequately prepared when they transition into people managers. This causes inertia or a general avoidance to do performance feedback and coaching to their direct reports.

(c) Reporting officers themselves may not have experienced getting effective performance feedback and coaching from their own direct supervisors. They do not have a role model to follow. Since their own direct supervisors are laissez-faire in this aspect, they too follow suit.

(d) Reporting officers invariably claim (or rationalise) that they are too busy with day-to-day operations and firefighting. They cannot find time to pause and provide feedback and coaching. Or the reporting officer may indicate in general how an employee is faring, but has scant time to elaborate on how he can improve or enhance his performance, and no coaching is provided for it.

D3.8   Sometimes, the obstacle to having regular and effective performance feedback and coaching is the employees themselves. Not all employees appreciate the importance of getting feedback and coaching; some have the fear of knowing "unpleasant" things about themselves, preferring to avoid it instead. They rather second guess their own performance than receiving candid and honest feedback from their reporting officers.

Consequences of Not Doing Performance Feedback and Coaching

D3.9   If performance feedback and coaching are not done effectively, there will be adverse consequences impacting the employees, reporting officers and the organisation. The common ones include the following:

(a) Employees may produce the "wrong" work or sub-standard work, repeat the same mistakes and/or miss deadlines. It will require re-work and other interventions, which will sap the organisation's resources and affect work efficiency. Since reporting officers are overall accountable for the results of their direct reports, they too will be impacted in their performance assessment.

(b) Some employees may get frustrated and leave service because of the lack of performance feedback and coaching from their reporting officers (for many employees, having guidance/coaching from their reporting officers is an important motivational factor and a criterion for holding respect for their reporting officers). High staff attrition ensues; the organisation is adversely impacted and the reporting officer will be held accountable.

Organisational Practices in Performance Feedback and Coaching

Best, Undesirable and Common Practices

D3.10   Most organisations will have a performance management framework that requires the reporting officer to do a mid-term performance review and a year-end performance appraisal session. The framework is also likely to mention that reporting officers should provide continual and on-going performance feedback and coaching throughout the appraisal year. These requirements are considered generic and typical. In practice, however, the requirements prescribed by an organisation's performance management framework are seldom observed in full and enforcement is generally weak.

D3.11   We share the best practice scenario, as well as the undesirable and common practice scenarios that we have observed:

Best Practice Scenario

The organisation has a performance management framework that stipulates clearly what is expected of reporting officers and employees. The reporting officer jointly sets the performance goals with the employee at the start of the appraisal year and duly enters them into the performance appraisal form. All the performance goals are then collated at the departmental level, amalgamated as the department's targets/goals and submitted to the management for information/review as part of corporate planning for the new financial year.

The employee will receive on-going feedback on his performance from the reporting officer, together with guidance and coaching to help him sustain or improve his performance, including closing any gaps and/or correcting any misalignment vis-à-vis the performance goals set.

Such feedback and coaching sessions are done in an informal and ad hoc manner at any time, say, whenever the employee submits a piece of work for review or when the reporting officer observes an action or work behaviour of the employee that warrants a performance feedback conversation. During the feedback conversations, the employee is encouraged to surface any challenges that he may be facing and the reporting officer will provide guidance and help as necessary.

In addition to the on-going feedback and coaching, the reporting officer will dutifully conduct a formal mid-term review, and revise/update any changes to the performance goals. At the year-end appraisal, the reporting officer appraises the employee and conducts a critical conversation with the employee and documents the key points, together with the recommended rating, into the performance appraisal form.

Undesirable Practice Scenario

The organisation does not have a policy or framework on performance management. It only prescribes a performance appraisal form for use by the reporting officer. The reporting officer does not do any performance planning and goals setting with the employee.

Reporting officers are not told to provide feedback and coaching to their employees. Some take the initiative to do so since they depend on their employees' efforts to deliver team results which they are accountable for.

The reporting officer will do the year-end appraisal by filling up the performance appraisal form and entering a rating for each employee. Depending on the personal relationship between the reporting officer and the individual employee, he may or may not inform the employee of his rating. Generally, no feedback is given, or if given, is not specific enough for the employee to apply the feedback to make improvements to his performance. For example, a general response of "good" or "okay" or "no problem". After a while, employees come to accept that "no news is good news".

An employee will only be told about his mistakes or performance shortfall when a problem arises, such as a customer complaint, the loss of a key customer, failure to secure a deal, a hiccup in production or a workplace accident. Or when the organisation axes headcounts through termination or retrenchment, some employees will suddenly be told that their performance has not been good and have to be let go of.

Common Practice Scenario

The organisation has a decent performance management framework and performance appraisal form. Human Resource does its basic duty of announcing the start of the performance management cycle and calling upon reporting officers to set their performance goals. However, follow-through and enforcement are often weak. Some reporting officers comply while others don't and they are not being questioned. There is also no enforcement to enter the performance goals into the performance appraisal form. Neither is there a requirement to do a mid-term performance review.

> On performance feedback and coaching, most reporting officers know vaguely that they are supposed to do it. However, being busy in daily operations and fire-fighting, it is put as low priority, hence more often than not, employees will not receive any feedback or coaching until at the year-end appraisal, or when a critical (negative) incident happens.
>
> Reporting officers also may not have a habit of consciously observing how their individual employees are faring. If the team (or department) is not faring well in its results, the reporting officer (team or department manager) may raise some observations and issues during staff meetings but usually not specific on a one-on-one basis. The more conscientious reporting officers may hold feedback sessions with their direct reports on performance matters, but much depends on their individual managerial style.

Practice for Rank-and-File Employees

D3.12   Performance feedback and coaching are also relevant to rank-and-file employees as they too should strive to improve performance and develop.

D3.13   In unionised organisations, rank-and-file employees are represented by a union; when they have an issue regarding performance, they may seek union representation. For those who are due for statutory retirement and to be considered for re-employment, performance is a consideration. Therefore, it is important that weak/unsatisfactory performers be given feedback on their performance and provided with coaching and if there is no improvement, to be counselled. Not taking action is not the way because when the crunch comes for the organisation to take drastic action on the employee (say, not to offer re-employment), the organisation will not be on a high moral ground and will be challenged by the union.

Practice in Small and Medium Enterprises

D3.14   Small and medium enterprises (SMEs) have a lean workforce and their employees tend to do more multi-tasking. Therefore, every employee counts and must be fully competent in his job. If an employee slackens, it is important that he be given prompt feedback, coached and pushed to level up quickly.

D3.15   Many bosses and managers in SMEs tend to work and interact closely with their employees and are active in providing feedback, coaching and mentoring to them. These are usually done to deal with work problems on hand rather than purposefully to develop the employees per se or to observe the gold standard of performance management principles or practices. They do it simply because they need capable employees to run their operations. Training and coaching employees on the job is the practical thing to do since most SMEs do not have the budget to recruit ready-made talent from the market.

D3.16 Many SME bosses are resourceful, creative and tenacious in dealing with issues and problems, and as a result, employees benefitting from their coaching will pick up such valuable skills and emulate the positive traits.

Performance Interventions:
Helping Employees Perform, Improve and Grow

D3.17 Every reporting officer is accountable to his direct report in the following ways:

(a) that the direct report knows what needs to be done;
(b) that he is actually able/capable of doing the tasks; and
(c) that he does not face unnecessary obstacles in carrying out the tasks.

D3.18 For the reporting officer to fulfil the above accountabilities, he should regularly check in with his direct report to know how he is faring and guide him to deliver results:

- If an employee is faring well, the reporting officer must help him sustain it or even surpass it.

- If an employee is falling below the mark, the reporting officer must help him close the gaps and deliver up to the job requirement.

- As a manager of a team of employees, the reporting officer must synchronise and align his entire team's efforts to produce the best outcomes for the organisation, much like how an orchestra conductor pulls together all musicians to produce harmonious music.

D3.19 In a typical scenario, a reporting officer plays several/different roles at different times and to different employees to help his team perform, improve and grow. These roles include (a) teaching, (b) mentoring, (c) performance coaching, (d) counselling and (e) appraising. Let's regard all these roles as "performance interventions". The various performance interventions serve different purposes and have different characteristics. For clarity, we elaborate on them below:

Intervention	Purpose, Application and Characteristics
Teaching	**Purpose** Impart knowledge and skills. For example, teach an employee how to do a task or work assignment that is new to him. **Characteristics** • To teach, the reporting officer (Teacher) must be knowledgeable and skilled. • The employee (Student) lacks the knowledge and skills. • The Teacher speaks mostly. The Student asks questions and clarifies.
Mentoring	**Purpose** Share experiences and insights. Help the Mentee navigate. For example, help an employee familiarise with a new area (or social strata) of the organisation. May also include helping the employee plan and grow his career. **Characteristics** • To mentor, the reporting officer (Mentor) must be experienced and have walked the path before. • The employee (Mentee) lacks experience and direction in certain roles and areas. • The Mentor advises, guides and helps contextualise challenges and issues. Helps connect the Mentee with people/resources. • The Mentor speaks more. The Mentee seeks advice and clarifies.

Performance Coaching	**Purpose** Guide, advise and help an employee improve and sustain his performance. For example, after reviewing an employee's work and observing his work behaviours, the reporting officer guides the employee to reflect and find ways to overcome challenges, and explore how to do things better to achieve higher performance. **Characteristics** • To do performance coaching, the reporting officer (Manager-Coach) must be familiar with the work of the employee. • Done in the context of managing the performance of the employee, it normally centres on the performance goals that the employee must fulfil. • Usually ad hoc and impromptu but can also be pre-scheduled with planned conversation topics. • The Manager-Coach listens and uses questions to elicit information (say, on work challenges) from the employee and provides pointers/suggestions as appropriate. The employee is encouraged to reflect and take ownership in exploring and finding solutions. • May have some elements of mentoring (guidance and sharing of knowledge and experiences) depending on the needs of the employee.
Counselling	**Purpose** Resolve behavioural and/or performance misalignment. For example, a reporting officer makes an employee aware of the areas where his behaviour and/or performance is off the mark from the organisation's requirements, clarifies the requirements and monitors the employee in making the necessary improvements. **Characteristics** • To counsel, the reporting officer (Counsellor) acts as an enforcer of behavioural standards. • Helps employee rectify misaligned behaviours or performance. • Both the Counsellor and employee talk, listen, question and clarify, depending on the issues and context.

Appraising	**Purpose** Assess performance. For example, a reporting officer does the year-end appraisal and recommends a performance rating for the employee. **Characteristics** • To appraise, the reporting officer (Appraiser) performs the role of a supervisor in performance planning and appraisal. • Sets meaningful performance goals and expectations for the employee (Appraisee) to fulfil. • Evaluates and rates the employee's performance. • The Appraiser holds a critical conversation with the Appraisee at the year-end performance review to inform him about his performance results.

D3.20   Other than performance coaching that occurs between a reporting officer and an employee, there is another form of coaching known as executive coaching. Executive coaching is typically provided by a certified executive coach who is an external party. As executive coaching fees can be rather expensive, it is usually only found in large and established organisations and mostly provided only for senior management executives, while some may extend it to their high potential executives in mid-management who are being groomed to assume future key leadership positions. We do a brief touch on the salient features of executive coaching below:

Intervention	**Purpose, Application and Characteristics**
Executive Coaching	**Purpose** Enable self-discovery, encourage self-learning and empower personal actions. For example, an external executive coach or a senior management person (who is trained in executive coaching) guides a high potential employee to grow in self-awareness, navigate his career choices and take actions to actualise his aspirations. **Characteristics** • To do executive coaching, the Executive Coach (usually an external party) should be professionally certified and a trusted person whom the employee feels comfortable in being honest in revealing his weak spots and personal concerns.

> - Helps employee reflect and discover his own strengths, challenges and weak spots. Spurs, encourages and supports the employee to take ownership of his journey in self-discovery, learning, solutioning and execution.
> - The employee speaks mostly. The Executive Coach listens a lot and asks good questions to challenge and broaden the employee's perspectives.

D3.21 As to which performance intervention is used on an employee will depend on the profile and specific development needs of the employee. For example, for a new employee, the reporting officer will spend more time teaching and instructing. Whereas an experienced and high potential employee who has performed well and is being groomed for higher roles will be given more mentoring and coaching.

Heart-ware and Skills for Performance Feedback

D3.22 Most reporting officers (or line managers) are thrust into their people management role without any preparation. An employee may have been performing well as an individual contributor and become promoted to a managerial role to supervise a team of employees. Being an effective individual contributor is different from being a people manager. It requires a different set of skills and also mindset. Not many reporting officers are natural people managers.

D3.23 Managing people is a complicated task. Reporting officers must reckon with direct reports who come with different profiles, motivations and priorities. They would also have varied experiences with respect to receiving performance feedback and coaching. Some of them are more receptive while others may be more guarded or even negative.

D3.24 Often, reporting officers who are new in their managerial role rush to pick up people management skills on the fly, learn by doing and make some mistakes along the way. They may attend structured training programs to pick up technical pointers. They may also observe how their own bosses manage their staff and emulate the same style or behaviours. Unfortunately, not many bosses are good role models for performance feedback and coaching.

The Necessary Heart-ware

D3.25   While people management requires some degree of intellect, cognitive skills and common sense, these are not sufficient. Managing people goes beyond just "head-ware"; it also involves mindset and attitudes, which are all about "heart-ware". Very often, possessing the right heart-ware (or otherwise) determines whether a reporting officer will succeed as a good people manager, more so than head-ware.

D3.26   *What are these Heart-ware elements? What mindset and attitudes should a reporting officer possess?*

Pivot into Being a Team Leader
Reporting officers must shed the thinking and habit that they are individual contributors. While they may continue to be hands-on in doing certain tasks personally, they are supposed to lead and manage their team of direct reports to produce team results. They must recognise that for a team to fulfil its performance targets, it requires the collective competence and effort of all the team members.

Be Perceptive and Discerning in Using Performance Interventions
Reporting officers must know the various performance interventions that can be used, and be discerning about which one to adopt under what conditions in dealing with their direct reports. In other words, they need to give the "right" help. Giving "wrong" help or helping in the wrong way may backfire and produce adverse outcomes. For example, if a high performing employee will best benefit from mentoring to help him navigate and make his career decisions, it will be inappropriate (and frustrating to the employee) to shove hard advice or top-down instructions to him to choose or act in a certain way.

Have a Genuine Interest in Developing People
Admittedly for most reporting officers and managers, coaching and developing direct reports is seldom an act of altruism entirely. There will always be an element of self-interest. Since reporting officers and managers derive their performance results through their direct reports, it makes economic sense to coach and develop their direct reports to become competent and effective. That said, people are most inspired by leaders who coach and develop others out of a genuine interest in helping others grow and succeed. Without genuine interest, the coaching and development may be felt as a transactional activity – the reporting officer coaches so that the direct report learns and delivers the goods for the reporting officer. While this may seem sufficient, it does not have the multiplier and emotional effect of inspirational coaching and learning.

Be Secure and Confident about Self

Some reporting officers hold back on coaching and developing others as they feel insecure about their own abilities. They worry about their direct reports doing too well and may eventually surpass and replace them. In this respect, the organisation's management must unequivocally commit and demonstrate that they value managers who are effective in grooming their staff to succeed in higher roles.

The Necessary Skills

D3.27   To do well in performance feedback and coaching, reporting officers need to sharpen basic communication skills, such as (a) active listening, (b) reflective listening, (c) speaking to be understood and (d) asking the right questions. These may seem like basic (even ordinary) communication skills, but not everyone does it well.

D3.28   In addition to the above basic communication skills, giving performance feedback and coaching require techniques that go beyond what we ordinarily use in daily conversations and interactions. Some specific skills are required, including the following:

(a) how to couch and deliver feedback, what tonality to use;
(b) how to use body language to convey or augment one's intentions;
(c) how to deliver unpleasant feedback and deal with tough conversations;
(d) how to pick up and use relevant incidents, activities and behaviours that can give context to the feedback;
(e) how to handle objections and challenges to the feedback; and
(f) how to handle the emotional reactions from the employee, especially negative ones.

D3.29   For performance feedback to have substance, the reporting officer must be observant and situationally alert to the employee's work progress and behaviours. For example, if an employee misses a deadline to finish a task, the reporting officer should pay closer attention and perhaps start a conversation with the employee early. Likewise, if an employee is not producing the same quality of work that he normally produces, the reporting officer should check in with the employee early.

D3.30   For performance feedback to feel less threatening to the employees, a reporting officer should also make his employees feel safe to talk to him and raise issues. Most employees are conscious of rank and have reservations initiating a conversation with their reporting officers. Hence the ball is at the court of the reporting officer to send signals to his employees that they are welcome to approach him for a candid conversation.

Opportune Moments for Giving Performance Feedback

The Right Setting for Giving Feedback

D3.31   The following are suitable occasions that call for a conversation on performance feedback and coaching:

> (a) *Upon the review of a piece of written work (such as a report, meeting minutes and proposal paper)*
> The reporting officer can look at the employee's clarity of thought, creativity of ideas/solutions, cogency and articulation. It will be helpful to offer edits/comments on the piece of written work. A conscientious employee who is interested in learning and improving can learn a lot from the edits/comments. The reporting officer can also reinforce the learning by discussing the edits/comments with the employee.

> (b) *After the employee's participation in a meeting*
> The reporting officer can observe the employee's participation and value-add to the meeting. It is important, however, to be constructive in the feedback so as not to discourage the employee, otherwise he will become guarded and less willing to participate in meetings.

> (c) *Upon reviewing the progress of a project or after a project meeting*
> The reporting officer can assess the employee's ability to manage the project stakeholders, organising skill, and how meticulous and careful he is in meeting deadlines, keeping within budget as well as dealing with surprises along the way.

> (d) *When a critical incident happens or after dealing with a particular work issue or problem (for example, a customer complaint, a missed deadline, loss of sales, a proposal rejected by senior management or the employee fails to get a task done)*
> A critical incident or problem offers valuable lessons for the employee. The reporting officer should do a debrief with the employee and guide him in picking out the mistakes made, how to avoid the same mistakes in future as well as how to do scenario planning to be better prepared for contingencies.

(e) *When an employee requests advice or help, or raises an issue for discussion*
The reporting officer should ride on the occasion to provide performance feedback and coaching. In this scenario, the employee is most ready for advice and learning. Indeed, the reporting officer should always encourage the employee to take the initiative to seek out learning by soliciting advice and feedback without worrying about how he will be perceived (as say, incompetent or not confident).

(f) *When an employee expresses frustration or dissatisfaction with the job, or his mood or behaviour is different from normal*
It is an opportunity for the reporting officer to first show his concern, understand the underlying reasons for the employee's frustration or mood/behaviour change and thereafter to provide feedback and coaching.

D3.32   Besides catching the right occasion for feedback/coaching, it will be helpful to consider the right "setting" or "timing". That said, there is no such thing as a perfect setting/timing. However, there are some situations which are obviously not suitable for a feedback conversation – say, when an employee is emotionally charged or mentally depressed, if he is rushing for an assignment, or troubled over a personal or domestic matter. He will be distracted and less receptive to feedback. Needless to say, if the setting/timing is inappropriate, the feedback conversation will not be productive.

Giving Feedback on the Spot

D3.33   While a reporting officer may do performance feedback for an employee as scheduled sessions (that is, with time specially set aside to hold a conversation on performance matters), sometimes, a suitable moment presents itself for the reporting officer to give feedback to the employee instantaneously. For example, if the reporting officer observes that his employee is doing an excellent thing, he may instantaneously give a compliment or a pat on the shoulder. If the employee is caught making a mistake, the reporting officer may intercept and instantaneously give his feedback. The reporting officer may also take the opportunity to bundle the feedback with some impromptu coaching.

> Examples
> - "What you just proposed is an interesting new idea. Have you looked at the cost aspects?"
> - "You handled the customer's complaint well just now. You have solved the immediate problem. What can be done to prevent a recurrence of such customer complaints in the future?"
> - "The analysis in your proposal paper is sound and has depth. This proposal is going to the Board. Can you condense the presentation and improve the graphics to cater to the busy board members?"
> - The reporting officer observes that his employee is fumbling as he handles a difficult customer. He intervenes to calm the customer and do service recovery. The intervention by the reporting officer is itself immediate feedback to the employee. This incident calls for a deeper conversation (debrief) with the employee.

D3.34   Where the feedback is negative (say, the reporting officer catches the employee making a mistake), after the reporting officer has intercepted to resolve the mistake, it calls for a deeper conversation (debrief) with the employee. A debrief can be done on the spot only if there is nobody else around since it should be done in privacy. If there are other persons around, the reporting officer should arrange for another time to conduct the debrief.

D3.35   On-the-spot feedback is impactful because the incident (evidence) is right in front of both the employee and reporting officer, and the feedback is given in "real-time" as events unfold. The feedback conversation should be more easily remembered by the employee.

How to Provide Performance Feedback

D3.36   Giving performance feedback generally comprises the following steps, done in sequential order:

> ❶ Gather information to form the basis of the feedback.
> ❷ Craft the feedback statement or message.
> ❸ Deliver the feedback.
> ❹ Document the feedback and the agreed follow-up actions.
> ❺ Monitor and check in with the employee on the progress of the follow-up actions.

Gathering Information for Feedback

D3.37 To be able to provide performance feedback, the reporting officer must have meaningful information and observations regarding the employee's work performance and behaviours. These provide the basis (or evidence) for the performance feedback. Information and observations may be gathered in the following ways:

(a) *Review the employee's work assignments*

> Note the quality, quantity of output, speed of delivery and whether deadlines are met. Pick out special points. Very often, the employee's work (say, a report or proposal) can tell a lot about his level of knowledge and other generic competencies (such as command of language, articulation skills, critical/analytical thinking, clarity of thought, persuasive skills, creativity and imagination and how meticulous, systematic and organised the presentation of data, ideas and arguments). A report/proposal that is overladen with surfeit information with little or no analysis which is essentially a cut-and-paste job will score low for the employee. The insights gathered from reviewing the employee's work will provide excellent feedback and learning points for the employee.

(b) *Observe the employee's behaviour in work situations*

> Make a first-hand observation of the employee's behaviours in work situations to form a substantiated opinion or assessment. Note down any critical incidents that warrant a feedback conversation with the employee.

(c) *Pay attention to the employee's participation and contributions during meetings and discussions*

> Meetings and discussions are a good platform to assess an employee based on what they share and the questions they ask. Much like reviewing a piece of written work, the employee's participation and contributions at meetings/discussions will often show his knowledge and competencies. In addition, it also reveals the employee's verbal articulation skills and confidence as well as his ability to think and respond on the spot.

(d) Gather inputs from other parties for a holistic picture

> Many employees take care to say the "right" things or behave in the "right" way when they interact with their bosses. Some can be very astute in putting on a facade. For this reason, the reporting officer may consider getting feedback on the employee from other persons (such as peers, subordinates, customers and business partners) who interact or work with the employee. Such feedback will help provide a more holistic picture of the employee, which is useful for coaching. However, it is important for the reporting officer to be discerning about the accuracy or authenticity of such feedback. Ask for the feedback to be substantiated by evidence or corroborated by other accounts. If the feedback is not substantiated or corroborated, it may not be accurate or objective and may be based only on the perspective of the party giving the feedback, or worse, it may come with a hidden agenda. For example, if the feedback comes from a peer who cannot get along with the employee, he may give negative feedback in vengeance. The reporting officer should be astute and prudent to check whether the feedback is given in good faith.

D3.38   Invariably, reporting officers (managers) are often inundated with daily work pressures doing firefighting and meeting deadlines and may therefore not have the time and energy to make sufficient or frequent enough observations regarding their employee's work and behaviours. As a result, some noteworthy observations may be missed out as valuable feedback and learning opportunities for the employee. This is unfortunate but happens often enough. Reporting officers must bear in mind that as people managers, one cannot make light of the responsibility of giving performance feedback and coaching to employees. Hence no matter how busy, one must make the time to observe, give feedback and coach.

Crafting the Feedback Statement

D3.39   Feedback that is poorly crafted can backfire. The golden rule in crafting feedback is to focus on the employee's behaviours and not the person or his character per se. Feedback that is centred on the person or his character will usually be perceived as subjective, judgmental or even a personal attack. Whereas if feedback is directed at a person's behaviours and actions (and substantiated with evidence), the said party will find it difficult to be defensive and refute.

D3.40   We sometimes hold the notion that giving feedback to a person is to get him to change himself (his nature). However, the reality is that most of the time, we cannot change a person. The more realistic outcome to hope for is to get the person to desist in behaviours that are unacceptable at work. For example, a habitual latecomer who is pointed out by his reporting officer may make the effort to improve his punctuality at work, but in his personal/social life, he may still perpetuate his latecoming behaviour. Likewise, an employee who is loud and rude in his communication, after receiving feedback, may learn to correct his behaviour when he deals with customers and fellow colleagues, but he is likely to continue with his communication style in his personal/social circle.

D3.41   Since the aim is to change <u>behaviours</u> rather than the person (character) per se, it follows that the feedback given by the reporting officer to the employee should be targeted at his observable behaviours at work. Feedback should cite and focus on work incidents/outcomes that bear evidence of the employee's behaviour. The more specific, the better.

D3.42   It takes effort and practice to craft feedback that focusses on an employee's behaviours/actions. The tendency is to direct it at the person (or his character). Many reporting officers struggle with this. It is best that reporting officers pause to think through what behaviour needs to be changed vis-à-vis the organisation's requirement. For example, if an employee is a habitual latecomer, focus on his latercoming versus the organisation's requirement on punctuality. If an employee makes a lot of mistakes, focus on his high error rate versus the organisation's requirement on accuracy. Steer clear of remarks on personality or character. It pays for a reporting officer to first craft a feedback statement and review it to check for this aspect before conversing with the employee, rather than give feedback on impulse that is person-focused and inappropriate. To compare feedback that is focused on behaviour/actions versus feedback that is focused on the person/character, please refer to the section on "Common Mistakes in Giving Performance Feedback" in the later part of this chapter.

D3.43   *Should feedback be honestly crafted?*
     This is a very relevant question. How brutally honest should feedback be? In crafting the feedback statement, should the truth be sugar-coated? Generally, people tend to be uncomfortable with feedback, therefore, reporting officers may choose not to be totally honest in crafting and giving

feedback. Many use the "sandwich" method of wrapping negative feedback between two layers of positive feedback (hence the name "sandwich") to soothe the emotions of the employee. While the sandwich method is useful for this purpose, it may mute or dilute the negative feedback to the extent that it becomes lost on the employee.

> Example of Sandwich Method
> *You have received many good compliments from customers on your good sales service, well done! However, you have recently made a gross error in providing a sales quotation which the customer accepted, and since the company has to honour the sales, it has caused some loss to the company. That said, overall, your sales results are good and you are on track to meet your sales target, so keep up your sales efforts.*

D3.44   Many employees have a tendency to dread receiving feedback as they generally associate feedback with "bad news". Truth can be hurting; hence, one may avoid knowing the "truth" carried in feedback and apply "selective" hearing to filter out the bad news.

D3.45   For performance feedback to be effective, the reporting officer must ensure that no matter how the feedback is packaged (using sandwich or whatever method), the negative feedback must be clearly understood and acknowledged by the employee. Feelings may be hurt and emotions may be difficult, and yes, these must be handled delicately, but it is important for the feedback to get through for the employee's sake, as otherwise, he will miss the opportunity to improve.

Delivering Feedback

D3.46   Crafting the appropriate feedback statement is the first step. Next, the delivery of the feedback must also be done appropriately. Delivering performance feedback can be a sensitive and delicate act. Even if the intention is right and the statement is appropriate, a wrong way of delivery can spoil the matter. If the intention is perceived to be dubious or unhelpful, even well-crafted feedback will not bring about the intended result.

D3.47   For performance feedback/coaching to be delivered well, one should pay heed to the following aspects:

(a) *Give feedback purposefully.*
     Performance feedback and coaching must be purposeful. The desired outcome must be to help the employee improve, sustain or exceed his

current performance. It should not be treated as a casual or social conversation with no outcome expected.

(b) *Feedback must come with the right intention.*
There should not be any personal agenda shrouded in the feedback. For example, a reporting officer must not use performance feedback as a way of showing his personal dislike of the employee. When the intention is authentic and done in good faith, the employee can feel it and will be more receptive to the feedback.

(c) *Use a respectful and helpful tone. Project positive body language.*
In communication, the tone of voice conveys a lot about the authenticity and intention of the speaker. Likewise, body language should be positive, say, giving good eye contact and nodding to project a reassuring posture. As giving feedback is often a serious and/or sensitive matter, using the right tone and body language are particularly important. It should convey respect and care for the individual.

(d) *Should not be overly formal. Neither should it be too casual.*
The feedback/coaching session should be a two-way communication where the employee is at ease and feels comfortable enough to raise questions to clarify any doubts. If it is too formal (likened to attending a judging session), the employee will be guarded and what results is likely a one-way top-down communication by the reporting officer. Neither should the session be too social and casual to avoid it being taken lightly by the employee. Say, a conversation held in a rush over lunch in a crowded staff canteen is not likely to be taken seriously by the employee.

(e) *Use an appropriate physical setting.*
The feedback/coaching conversation should be conducted in privacy between the reporting officer and employee. Even if it is done in an open venue (say, an open office or shop floor), the conversation should be away from the earshot of other people.

(f) *Catch a good timing.*
A feedback session should be held only when both the reporting officer and employee are in a calm state of mind and are not distracted. If a particular work incident causes any one party to be emotionally charged, it is better for the reporting officer to set another time to provide the feedback rather than confront the employee on the spot. If the feedback is not urgent (as in it must be conveyed immediately), it is better to

advise the employee a few days ahead of holding a feedback conversation with him and specify the topic of the feedback (say, "to talk about your sales results" or "to talk about the project schedule"). This way, the employee will have some time to ponder over the issue to be discussed and it will make for a more productive feedback session.

(g) *Explain the impact of the employee's work behaviour.*
If the employee knows the impact and consequences of his action/ behaviour, he will be able to assess cognitively and more rationally, and as a result, will be more open to making changes. For example, if the employee realises that his frequent latecoming or tardiness at work causes delay, inconvenience and unnecessary time wasted by the team, it will weigh upon him to correct his behaviour.

(h) *Adopt a forward-looking focus. Ask for follow-up actions.*
While a feedback conversation must cite past work incidents as the basis of the feedback, it should not stay "stuck" in the past mode. The conversation should progress and turn its focus on the future – what the employee must do henceforth. Once the feedback has been acknowledged by the employee, the reporting officer should prompt for follow-up actions, for example, by asking the employee: "What do you propose to do from now?" It is better to get the employee to articulate what and how he intends to follow up to improve or change his work behaviour. This way, it will generate more ownership and commitment from him. The reporting officer may make some suggestions to guide the employee on his proposed follow-up actions; what is important is to get the employee to reflect, propose and commit. When the employee gives his agreement on the follow-up actions, it signals the closure of the feedback episode.

D3.48   In delivering feedback, there may be difficult situations where the reporting officer and employee do not see eye to eye. The employee may refute the information cited in the feedback. Or he may disagree over the follow-up action(s) required of him. When this occurs, it is better to pin down the points of differences, and what other sources of information may be helpful for resolving the differences, and set another session to revisit the feedback. This will give both parties time to review and reflect. At the second feedback session, based on the information/evidence (and taking into account any new items that surfaced), the reporting officer should make a firm stand and bring the feedback to a closure.

Documenting the Feedback

D3.49   The essence of feedback is to have a quality conversation with the employee regarding his performance. Documentation is not the goal per se. Hence, there is no need to go overboard to document the feedback conversation in detail. It suffices to just note down the key points of the feedback so that it serves as a reference for the year-end appraisal.

D3.50   The key points to capture are as follows: (a) the work behaviour or performance matter, (b) work incidents, data or information as the basis and (c) the follow-up actions agreed upon with the employee. In some organisations, such information may be entered into the performance appraisal form, especially if the form is in a digital format.

Monitoring the Progress of Follow-up

D3.51   The reporting officer should monitor the employee's progress on the follow-up actions and check in with the employee periodically until the matter is closed. The check-in will show that the feedback expectations are to be taken seriously. It also serves the purpose of checking whether the employee needs support and help; this way, the employee will feel encouraged and positive.

Common Mistakes in Giving Performance Feedback

D3.52   As giving performance feedback is a challenging and delicate conversation, one can expect a reporting officer to make some mistakes along the way. It takes effort to learn to provide performance feedback effectively. Knowing "how" is one thing; it takes practice to hone one's skills and gain confidence in giving performance feedback well to bring positive outcomes.

D3.53   Very often, "mistakes" can be very "situational" – that is, it depends on whether the content and message and the approach and setting for delivering the feedback are appropriate (or inappropriate) for a particular employee in a specific situation. In other words, feedback crafted in a certain way and delivered in a certain manner in a particular setting may well be appropriate for a particular employee in a specific situation, but yet may be inappropriate for another employee in another situation. For example, feedback crafted with a no-nonsense message and delivered in a direct manner to an employee who has a long trusting relationship with the reporting officer may work well, but the same feedback delivered to a new employee with a somewhat diffident and meek personality may be counter-productive.

D3.54   While some mistakes can be "situational", there are also ways of delivering feedback that are obviously below par whatever the context and regardless of the employee profile or the situation. Some common mistakes to steer clear of include the following:

(a) feedback that is directed at the person or his character/personality, rather than at the work incident or work-related behaviour;

(b) the feedback conversation focuses solely on the past without addressing how to move forward;

(c) the feedback carries comments that are judgmental, say, based on one's personal standards, values and beliefs;

(d) feedback that is too general, which is not helpful or actionable, and therefore has not much value to the employee;

(e) the message of the feedback is unclear or muted (at times this may be due to overapplying the "sandwich" technique to camouflage negative news);

(f) the feedback is delivered with negative emotions (such as anger, impatience, sarcasm, disrespect and belittling) and/or with inappropriate or hostile body language and tone (such as shouting);

(g) the feedback conversation is largely one-way from the reporting officer to the employee without giving the employee a chance to share his views; essentially the reporting officer "tells" instead of "communicates" with the employee; and

(h) the reporting officer hints to the employee that the feedback session is a mere administrative "requirement" and done to comply with the organisation's performance management policy and therefore should be done with and over quickly so as not to take away precious time.

D3.55   We show some examples of feedback that is directed at the person or his character/personality (which is inappropriate) and how the feedback can be re-crafted to direct at the work behaviour and with citing of work incidents (which is the correct way).

Feedback directed at the Person	Feedback directed at the Work Behaviour
You are sloppy.	• Your frequent latecoming is unacceptable. • Your work attire does not meet the company's standards. • You make too many mistakes and fail to check your work before submitting. This quality of work is unacceptable.
You are somebody who couldn't care less. Or You are irresponsible.	• The way you deal with work in terms of quality and meeting deadlines is not up to our expectations ... Here are the specifics ... (where quality failed and where deadlines were missed). • You are our department representative to attend the committee meeting. When you could not attend the meeting yesterday, you did not inform anyone and did not arrange for another colleague to cover for you. • It was your turn to do the collation of team report this month as set out in the team roster. You went on leave but held on to the report data and did not pass it over to the colleague who is covering for you.
You are unreliable.	• You missed several deadlines and this had caused problems to the project. This is unacceptable. • You mentioned twice that you would get the task done. We have yet to see the action. This is now a bottleneck to the team.
You cannot be trusted.	• You repeatedly gave your promise that you will not repeat the same action. Yesterday, we saw you do it again. • The information that you hold is confidential and embargoed before announcement. Yet you divulged it to colleagues in other departments.

You and your silly ideas.	• Your idea is quite different from the norm. You need to provide a basis or logic to support your idea, otherwise it will be difficult to gain acceptance.
You are simply too arrogant.	• Many of your colleagues have given feedback that they do not feel respected and comfortable with the way you talk and interact with them. For example …
You are selfish and individualistic.	• You have not shown cooperation to your team members. For example …

D3.56   As the primary purpose of giving feedback is to enable the employee to learn and improve, the feedback should therefore be both development-oriented and future-oriented; that is, the reporting officer should pin down with the employee on what he needs to do and improve going forward. While the reporting officer should cite past work incidents as the basis of the feedback and a critical learning point, it must not be the dominant (or sole) point of the feedback and coaching conversation. The following are some examples of feedback that are past-focused versus better versions that are development and future-oriented:

Feedback that is Past-focused	Feedback that is Development and Future-oriented
The mistakes that you made are serious. Make sure that you don't repeat them.	Your mistakes must be corrected. What can you do to avoid them? How will you do it differently? What steps?
Your recommendations have been rejected outright by the management. You have to do better than that.	The management did not accept your recommendations. How can we convince them better? Are there other alternative solutions to recommend? Can you think through and discuss?

You are abrasive and unprofessional. You are always like that and never change. This is you.	You already know the feedback about you being abrasive and unprofessional in the way you interact with customers and colleagues. How are you changing the way you interact? For example, in scenario A (describe) and scenario B (describe), how will you act and behave?
Customers complained again about your poor follow-up. You are still the same.	Customers told us that your follow-up was poor (cite the specifics). You need to tell me how you will deal differently with the same situations moving forward.

D3.57   One common mistake to avoid in giving feedback is being judgmental, that is, imposing one's personal standards, values and beliefs onto the employee. The correct way is to give feedback comparing the employee's work outcomes against the performance goals set, and the employee's work behaviours against the organisation's competency-based and core value-based behavioural attributes (please refer to Chapter D2 "Performance Planning and Goals Setting" for details on these performance requirements). In other words, it is the organisation's requirements that count and should form the basis for the feedback; the reporting officer's personal standards, values and beliefs are not relevant per se.

D3.58   Judgmental feedback often invokes negative reactions from the employee, which should be avoided. The following are some examples of judgmental feedback statements as well as the equivalent non-judgmental versions:

Feedback that is Judgmental	Feedback that is Non-judgmental and based on the Organisation's Requirements
I don't like the way you talk; I find it very unprofessional.	The company requires that all employees show respect to each other. Some colleagues have commented that they do not feel comfortable with your tone of voice and loudness.

Your work is sub-standard and not to my expectations.	Your report lacks the breadth of coverage and depth of analysis. It does not meet the quality expected of a manager. Take a look at similar reports submitted to the management by other managers.
Your approach appears silly; it makes no sense to me.	Your approach is quite different from what has been done in the past. Can you explain more about how your approach will bring the results that the company wants?

Performance Coaching and Executive Coaching

Performance Coaching

D3.59   Performance coaching is the type of coaching that is carried out by a reporting officer as part and parcel of performance management. The coaching is closely related to the performance feedback given to the employee, which is targeted at the work issues on hand. It serves to guide an employee to develop better competencies and aspire to higher performance in his job. The key characteristic is that while the reporting officer supports as a coach, the employee must take ownership of his own growth.

D3.60   In most situations, after giving performance feedback, it is constructive for the reporting officer to immediately follow on with coaching to deepen the employee's learning. On the other hand, there are also occasions when it is better to do the coaching on another occasion (not immediately), especially when the reporting officer feels that it is necessary for the employee to first do some reflection on his own. The employee should be asked to think about the learning points from the performance feedback and how he will apply them. The employee will then be better prepared to engage and assimilate the subsequent coaching given by the reporting officer.

D3.61   The beneficiary of performance coaching is not just the employee. Reporting officers and line managers also stand to benefit when they coach their employees. The benefits (or value proposition) for coaching employees include the following:

(a) Managers deliver results through their employees; it pays to have the employees competent in their jobs so that they are effective and efficient.

(b) When employees are effective and efficient in their jobs, the manager will need to spend less time managing them and thus have more time to focus on strategic matters (such as planning, innovation and achieving breakthroughs).

(c) When employees feel cared for and given the opportunity to grow in their careers, they will be more committed and motivated. There will be lower staff turnover and consequently less disruption to operations.

(d) Good people managers who develop their employees earn the respect of the employees they coach and this elevates their standing in the eyes of the employees and management. They become magnets for attracting and retaining good talent.

(e) In the bigger scheme of things, most managers and leaders would invariably have benefitted from coaching in their careers. It is therefore enlightened of them to pay it back by coaching and developing others to nurture the next generation of managers and leaders. Managers and leaders who are good people developers find fulfilment in doing so.

Executive Coaching

D3.62   Executive coaching is a more formal and structured form of coaching. The focus of executive coaching is to facilitate, nudge and challenge the employee to do self-discovery, find his own solutions and take ownership to initiate actions and change. The focus is not on routine workplace issues but on the deeper and more fundamental areas relating to the longer-term development of the employee. Executive coaching is normally carried out by persons who have been trained and certified as executive coaches.

D3.63   For executive coaching to be effective, the employee must be honest and open to reveal and discuss his "true self", including his weaknesses (and even fears, anxieties and insecurities) with the executive coach. Due to this characteristic of executive coaching, the reporting officer is not considered as suitable to be the executive coach for his direct report. The employee will be hesitant to reveal his weaknesses due to the worry that his performance rating and chances of promotion may be jeopardised. In view of this, executive coaching is almost always conducted by external certified executive coaches engaged by the organisation. The conversations between the executive coach and the employee are treated as confidential and not to be shared with any other persons, including the reporting officer, senior management and Human Resource of the organisation.

D3.64   As executive coaching fees can be rather expensive, it is usually only found in large and established organisations and mostly provided only for senior management executives and perhaps extended to high potential executives in mid-management who are being groomed for leadership positions.

D3.65   Another alternative practice adopted by some organisations is to train a selection of their people managers (for example, senior line managers, human resource managers and senior management executives) to become certified executive coaches. These internal executive coaches will take on coaching of employees who are not their direct reports (for example, a senior line manager from department A may coach a more junior executive from department B). With this approach, the cost of executive coaching will be more manageable and consequently, executive coaching can be made available to more employees in the organisation. This practice model is however not without its disadvantages or obstacles. Executive coaching is effective only if there is total assurance that confidentiality will be safeguarded and there is trust and rapport between the coach and the employee. In reality, the employee may have a lingering fear that the conversation with an internal executive coach may "leak" to his reporting officer or the management, or may be used "quietly" or "subtly" by Human Resource against him. To mitigate this problem, some organisations let their employees choose their own executive coaches (from amongst the internal panel of executive coaches), rather than for the organisation to assign an executive coach to the employee. Ultimately, the employee must have trust and feel "safe" with his coach.

Coaching Approach and Focus

D3.66   For performance coaching (done by the reporting officer), the focus is on work issues. The performance coaching will invariably be specific on driving better performance and behaviours from the employee: *How to improve? How to change behaviour? How to become more competent? How to overcome the work challenges? How to deliver better results?*

D3.67   Executive coaching on the other hand is concerned with the broader developmental needs of the employee. Executive coaching generally follows the 4-step GROW model which is elaborated below:

Step 1	**G**oal	Discuss and agree with the employee on the topic and objectives of the coaching conversation. For example, does the employee want to work on his career choices, say, how to pivot to another field of work? Or to work on resolving his anxieties or insecurities? Or to work on being a better leader?
Step 2	**R**eality	Ask the employee what his current reality (state) is. This is then used as the baseline (or starting point).
Step 3	**O**ptions	Explore the options to bridge the gap between the goal and the current reality.
Step 4	**W**ay Forward	Select the best or most pragmatic options and consider how to execute them, taking into account potential obstacles and resources required.

Coaching Skills

D3.68   Coaching skills are largely teachable. Coaching skills that are used extensively include the following: (a) building rapport, (b) showing interest, (c) active listening and (d) asking questions.

Building Rapport	Coaching requires good relations between the coach and the employee (coachee) as the foundation. If there is no rapport and trust between the two, the coaching conversation cannot go deep, and the two parties will avoid difficult or sensitive subjects. To build rapport, there must be mutual respect, authenticity and sincerity. There must be investment of time and effort to meet and talk, going beyond cursory conversation and pleasantry.
Showing Interest	To coach effectively, the coach must want to coach. He must be interested in seeing the coachee develop and grow. To show interest, the coach must demonstrate that through words, actions and body language. He must give time to the employee and show patience. During conversations, the coach must show that he is with the person through active listening, positive posture, right tone of voice and warmth.

Active Listening	The coach must listen actively to pick up the key points and the "whys" behind what the coachee is saying. He must also observe the non-verbal elements of the conversation (such as silence and emotions) to appreciate the true state of affairs of the coachee.
Asking Questions	Asking the right questions is crucial in enhancing understanding and leading the conversation towards issues and points that really matter and help reframe the issue thereby pointing to a solution or leading to an action. Questions can also bring the exchange to greater depth and wider exploration. Most importantly, asking good questions can trigger the coachee to think more deeply, analyse more critically and explore more intensely. This will help pull the coachee out of complacency (or stagnation) and lead him to growth.

D3.69   Other important and situationally appropriate skills and techniques that can be used (depending on the situation) to enhance the success of coaching include the following:

- Ask for views and suggestions instead of offering ready answers. This will encourage the coachee to be proactive.
- Prompt and nudge the coachee, instead of exerting pressure and coercion.
- Encourage the coachee to be proactive and take ownership of his own growth.
- Cheer the coachee on, give praise and support.
- Assure confidentiality to win and keep the trust of the coachee.

How Should Employees Treat Performance Feedback and Coaching?

D3.70   Performance feedback and coaching is not a one-way street. Regardless of how committed and enthusiastic the reporting officer is, the outcome of feedback and coaching will not be satisfactory if the employee does not see the value in it and do his part to make it work. *What should an employee do?*

(a) The employee should listen carefully and actively and ask questions to clarify.

(b) During the feedback and coaching session, the employee should participate actively by sharing his concerns and views. This makes for a constructive and productive two-way conversation to enhance mutual understanding.

(c) The employee must be open-minded and willing to consider embracing other views. If he is fixated on his thoughts and stubborn in his behaviour and becomes defensive despite the good intentions of the reporting officer, he will not learn.

(d) If the feedback is fair and given in good faith, the employee should accept the feedback and internalise the advice offered.

Role of Human Resource in Performance Feedback and Coaching

D3.71   Giving performance feedback and coaching is the responsibility of every line manager and reporting officer. This task cannot be "outsourced" to Human Resource. However, Human Resource can value-add by playing the following roles:

(a) define the requirements for performance feedback and coaching;

(b) arrange training of line managers in crafting feedback statements and giving performance feedback and coaching;

(c) communicate to employees on the importance of performance feedback and coaching so that they can imbibe feedback and coaching as a normal workplace practice; and

(d) monitor the performance feedback and coaching activities, update the management and enlist its help to remind reporting officers of the organisation's expectations in this respect and institutionalise performance feedback and coaching as part of the organisation's culture.

Linking Performance Feedback and Coaching to Performance Review

D3.72   *What is performance review?*
Performance review is a planned and formal conversation between the employee and his reporting officer on the employee's work performance. Many organisations require mid-term and year-end performance reviews to be conducted. However, while year-end performance review is mostly done (as this is required to assign a performance rating to the employee), the same cannot be said about the mid-term review. If enforcement is weak, many line managers take the mid-term review lightly and may even skip it entirely. This is not ideal but is common. Enforcement by the management (spelling it out as a clear expectation) is key.

D3.73   *How is performance feedback and coaching linked to performance review?*
If performance feedback and coaching have been done regularly and properly, there should not be any surprises at the mid-term and year-end performance reviews. The review sessions will serve more as a platform to consolidate and summarise the important feedback given by the reporting officer throughout the entire appraisal year and the follow-up actions duly taken by the employee. At the year-end review, the reporting officer will give an overall assessment of the employee's performance for the appraisal year. Since the overall assessment is merely a summary of the ongoing performance feedback throughout the year and should offer no surprises to the employee, both parties can devote more time to discuss the developmental needs of the employee and plan forward. More are covered in Chapter D4 "Performance Appraisal".

Performance Appraisal

Focus of this Chapter

In Chapter D1 "Overview of Performance Management Framework", we highlighted that performance management consists of several essential steps that are done in sequential order: (a) performance planning and goals setting, (b) performance feedback and coaching, (c) performance appraisal, (d) performance moderation, (e) performance critical conversation and (f) applications of performance results.

In this chapter, we discuss performance appraisal in detail. This is the most challenging process in performance management. Generally, both managers/appraisers and employees don't look forward to having it. This chapter candidly sheds light on this difficult function. We advise readers to first read Chapter D1 before proceeding with this chapter.

The What and Why of Performance Appraisal

What is Performance Appraisal?

D4.1   Performance appraisal is a formal assessment of an employee's performance, and it is a scheduled exercise that takes place at the end of the appraisal year. By "formal", it means that the employee will be officially assigned a performance rating, and it will be documented and become part and parcel of the employee's career record in the organisation.

D4.2   Performance appraisal is to be distinguished from the on-going performance feedback and coaching that an employee may receive from his reporting officer, which is usually done on an ad hoc and informal basis (this has been covered in Chapter D3 "Performance Feedback and Coaching"). The objective of giving feedback and coaching is for developmental reasons rather than for assessment/appraisal.

D4.3   Apart from year-end appraisal, some organisations also require their reporting officers to do quarterly or half-yearly check-ins with employees on their work progress; these check-ins are more commonly referred to as performance review (which is closer to performance feedback and coaching) rather than performance appraisal.

Why Do Performance Appraisal?

D4.4   Performance appraisal is done for the following purposes:

(a) to assess an employee and officially inform him on how he has fared in meeting the performance requirements and competency standards expected of him;

(b) to have a defensible basis for granting performance-linked rewards (such as bonuses, increments and other incentives) to an employee;

(c) to assess an employee's suitability and readiness for promotion to a higher job;

(d) for an employee on a fixed-term employment contract, to assess whether his performance renders him suitable for contract extension; and

(e) for an employee reaching the minimum statutory retirement age, to assess whether his performance qualifies him for re-employment.

Persons Doing Performance Appraisal

Self-Appraisal by Employee

D4.5   Some organisations institute self-appraisal by the employee as the start (first step) of the performance appraisal process. Even where self-appraisal is not part of the formal appraisal process, a reporting officer may on his own accord ask his employee to do a self-appraisal before he appraises the employee. This is usually done with these practicalities in mind – first, it saves the reporting officer from having to recall the work done by the employee in the past year, and second, the self-rating by the employee gives the reporting officer a "starting point" for the ensuing discussion with the employee on his performance.

Purposes/Benefits of Self-Appraisal

D4.6   The purposes (or benefits) for getting an employee to do a self-appraisal include the following:

(a) It gets the employee to pause and ponder over his performance requirements and to what extent he has met these requirements, as well as to take stock of his own strengths and weaknesses.

(b) The employee certainly has a better recall (than his reporting officer) of the work done and achievements made in the year that has just passed. While the information from the employee is likely to be more complete, the caveat is that his account may not be entirely accurate or objective (given his personal stake in the matter and perhaps also his narrower perspective).

(c) Self-appraisal allows the reporting officer to check whether the employee understands his performance requirements well enough. For example, if the employee is not faring well and yet gives himself a very favourable self-appraisal, it may indicate a lack of understanding of the performance requirements and/or a low appreciation of excellence. This should alert the reporting officer to spend more time re-orientating and re-aligning the employee to the performance requirements.

Challenges of Self-Appraisal

D4.7   While there are benefits in getting employees to do self-appraisal, there are also inherent challenges, including the following:

(a) If an employee mostly works in silo and has limited work interaction with other colleagues, he may tend to have a narrow or lop-sided view of his own performance and competencies, as he has few sources to draw comparisons from. This is especially so where higher order competencies (such as critical thinking and strategic visioning) are involved. If an employee is deficient in such higher order competencies, without any source of comparison from fellow colleagues, he may not be able to sufficiently appreciate the behavioural markers of these competences to do an accurate self-appraisal.

(b) It is a natural (survival) instinct for people to be self-preserving. Even if one is aware of one's mistakes and shortfalls, invariably, one will be able to find reasons to "justify" one's shortfalls. People tend to think they deserve better. The natural instinct for self-preservation (or self-protection) often leads one to justify a more favourable rating for oneself.

(c) Research studies also suggest that there are some behavioural or psychological traits that are common to weak performers.

> Some Research Findings (please refer to references at the end of the chapter)
> - The poorer the performer, the higher and more inaccurate the self-appraisal.
> - Incompetent performers are generally incapable of discerning the difference between good and bad performance.
> - Weak performers make wrong judgments and decisions but are often not aware of their deficiencies.

(d) If an employee overrates himself, it will bring the disagreement on the performance rating into the open. This may shift the attention and discussion of the employee and reporting officer unduly towards the rating to the extent of neglecting other important aspects of performance appraisal (for example, a discussion on the employee's developmental needs). The situation may even degenerate into a contentious bargaining on the performance rating.

(e) A reporting officer may advertently or inadvertently let his judgment be influenced by the employee's self-rating. The reporting officer may prefer to avoid the awkwardness of having a big disparity between the employee's self-rating and the rating that is to be assigned to the employee. He may choose to assign a rating that is within a "safe zone" (say, at most only one degree lower than the employee's self-rating). This compromises the accuracy and honesty in appraisal. The performance appraisal becomes more of a political exercise to keep peace.

D4.8   For the reasons elaborated above, some organisations dispense with self-appraisal by employees, with the general view that self-appraisals do not hold any value, as after all, it is ultimately the reporting officer's appraisal that counts and not the employee's.

D4.9   However, other than the practical benefits directly related to the act of performance appraisal, getting employees to do self-appraisal also holds another side benefit. It can usually offer some valuable insights into an employee's psyche, including his humility, confidence level and ambition. For instance, there are anecdotes of high performers giving themselves very harsh self-appraisals. For such cases, regular feedback and encouragement by the reporting officer will boost the employee's confidence and help him articulate his own standing. On the other hand, there are also employees who are highly competitive or overly obsessed with performance ratings that they intentionally inflate their own self-ratings in the hope of skewing the reporting officer to give a high rating. Such insights into an employee's psyche may come in useful in assessing his suitability for leadership roles.

D4.10   A better way may be to take the "middle road" – keep the self-appraisal but dispense with the employee giving himself a self-rating. In other words, at the start of the appraisal exercise, the reporting officer may ask the employee to list and quantify his contributions and achievements, as well as cite any challenges that he had encountered in delivering his results. These inputs may be entered into the performance appraisal form. The employee should however not be asked to give a rating for himself (the performance appraisal form should be designed without the self-rating feature). Such inputs from the employee will enable the reporting officer to have a more complete view of the employee's work and achievements and thereby do a more accurate appraisal. It will also facilitate a more constructive performance review conversation with the employee, focussing the discussion on evidence such as work incidents, results and work behaviours and going into learning points.

Primary Appraisers

D4.11   For some organisations, especially small and medium enterprises, performance appraisal for an employee may just be a simple exercise involving the employee's direct supervisor (the reporting officer) as the sole appraiser. On the other hand, some organisations, particularly the large and established ones, involve multiple appraisers with the intention of getting a more rounded and holistic appraisal of the employee. The multiple appraisers may comprise primary appraisers and secondary appraisers. We elaborate on what "primary" and "secondary" means.

D4.12   Primary appraisers are those appraisers who oversee their employees' main/primary job portfolios. There are usually two tiers of primary appraisers involved:

Reporting Officer (RO)

He is the direct/immediate supervisor of the employee. The RO is tasked with giving instructions to the employee to carry out work. The employee's work goes to the RO for review. The RO is expected to guide and coach the employee at work. The RO is accountable to his supervisor (the next higher level) for the work output/outcomes of the employee. The RO is responsible for appraising the performance of the employee.

Counter-signing Officer (CO)

He is the direct/immediate supervisor of the RO. Typically, as the CO, he also has some degree of work interaction with the employee. At times, the CO may even assign work directly to the employee, while keeping the RO in the loop. The CO is typically expected to review and sign off on the appraisal done by the RO on the employee. However, there can be exceptions. If the employee is in a small unit, the CO may be a senior management person in the organisation. For example, a Human Resource (HR) Executive reports to the Head of HR, who in turn reports directly to the Chief Executive Officer (CEO). In this case, although the CEO is the CO, it is not practical (or common) for him to review and sign off on the performance appraisal of the HR executive.

Secondary Appraisers

D4.13   A "secondary" appraiser is one who oversees an employee's secondary job portfolio. Some examples are given below:

Example
An employee may be assigned to handle another project (say, a stretch assignment) outside of his main/primary job portfolio. The supervisor for the project will be his secondary appraiser.

Example
An employee may straddle two departments, say, 70% in Department A and 30% in Department B. His RO and CO in Department A will be his primary appraisers, while his RO and CO in Department B will be his secondary appraisers.

> Example
> Some organisations (especially multinational corporations) practise matrix reporting for their senior executives, which is commonly referred to as functional (domain subject) reporting and staff (operational) reporting. A Marketing Director reports to the CEO of the Singapore branch (for staff reporting). He also reports to the Global Head of Marketing at the company's head office in London (for functional reporting). The staff head may be designated as the primary appraiser (commonly referred to as direct line reporting), while the functional head may be designated as the secondary appraiser (commonly referred to as dotted-line reporting). Or it may be the reverse. It all depends on the company's preference for its reporting structure.

D4.14   Most employees have only primary appraisers. Secondary appraisers generally apply to senior executives and employees who are high performing or high potential. These categories of employees are usually given secondary portfolios that are meant as stretch assignments to test them as well as to broaden their exposure and accelerate their learning curve. In a typical talent management programme for high performing and high potential employees, having multiple assessors will allow the organisation to gather more evidence to validate the employees' performance and potential.

D4.15   When an employee has two groups of appraisers (primary and secondary), his performance appraisal will be a co-ordinated and collective assessment done by both groups of appraisers. How this is done depends on the organisation's preference and design of the performance appraisal process:

- One approach is for the secondary appraiser to submit his appraisal of the employee to the primary appraiser and the latter will take the appraisal into account and consolidate and recommend an overall performance rating for the employee.

- Another approach is to arrive at the overall performance rating using the weightage method. Say, if the primary and secondary portfolios constitute 70% and 30% respectively, the overall performance rating may just be a simple weighed average of the two ratings.

Performance Appraisal Models

D4.16   Transparency in performance appraisal helps build trust and gives a perception of fairness around how employees are being assessed. It also heightens accountability on the part of the appraisers and reduces the likelihood of victimisation. Nobody likes a process that is shrouded in secrecy to dictate their rewards and career fate in the organisation.

D4.17   The degree of transparency present in performance management depends on two factors:

(a) the extent the employee is involved in the appraisal process and
(b) the extent the employee is informed about his appraisal results.

How (a) and (b) are incorporated into the performance appraisal process is dependent on which performance appraisal model the organisation has chosen to adopt – closed appraisal or open appraisal or semi-open/semi-closed appraisal.

Closed versus Open versus Semi-Open/Semi-Closed Appraisal

D4.18   A comparison of these different models is summarised below:

> **Closed Performance Appraisal**
>
> (a) The employee is not involved in setting performance goals. The reporting officer sets the performance goals and expectations for the employee unilaterally.
> (b) At the end of the appraisal year, the reporting officer will review the employee's performance in confidence and submit his recommended performance rating to the management (or Human Resource). The performance rating may undergo moderation by the management (if the organisation has this step) to determine the final performance rating for the employee.
> (c) The reporting officer will <u>not</u> discuss the performance appraisal with the employee. The employee will also <u>not</u> be informed of his final performance rating.
>
> Comments
> The key feature of a Closed model is the minimal involvement of the employee. There is no transparency in the Closed model. The common complaint against the Closed model is that it is shrouded in mystery and this alone creates doubt on the fairness and objectivity of the performance appraisal. There is low buy-in from employees.

The Closed model is mainly used by big organisations that employ employees in the thousands, especially if the organisations do not practise performance-linked increments or bonuses. Since the Closed model dispenses with the performance critical conversation between the reporting officer and employee, line managers have an easier (or less stressful) time. The performance appraisal process is kept simple and viewed largely as an administrative routine.

Many organisations including the Singapore civil service had used the Closed model up till the 1990s. As employees have become increasingly educated and sophisticated with the professionals, managers and executives (PMEs) growing in proportion, the Closed model has come under challenge. Linking rewards to performance ratings has also triggered the employees' desire (or demand) to have more transparency so that they can see if they have been given a fair appraisal. Few organisations now use the Closed model.

Open Performance Appraisal

(a) At the start of the appraisal year, the reporting officer and the employee will jointly do performance planning and agree on the performance goals and standards.
(b) At the end of the appraisal year, the reporting officer will review the employee's performance and submit his recommended performance rating to the management (or Human Resource). The performance rating may undergo moderation by the management (if the organisation has this step) to determine the final performance rating for the employee.
(c) The reporting officer will hold a performance critical conversation with the employee to inform him of his final performance rating (moderated/confirmed) and address any feedback/concerns from the employee. The conversation will then move on to discuss the employee's strengths, areas for development and the learning/development plans for him.

Comments
The key feature of an Open model is the high involvement of the employee from start to end of the appraisal process. This gives transparency. Generally, PME employees welcome the transparency while rank-and-file employees tend to be lukewarm about it.

The success of the Open model hinges a lot on the quality (and candour) of the critical conversation between the reporting officer and the employee. Some line managers get through the critical conversation in a cursory manner and merely inform the employee of his final performance rating. Many employees also do not insist on having a proper conversation, preferring to avoid the awkwardness of it.

While the Open model offers the highest degree of transparency, it is not without challenges. Some organisations experience their reporting officers spending a lot of (unproductive) time debating with their employees over performance ratings. This is especially so if the employee profile comprises highly competitive individuals. The debate can turn acrimonious and affect staff morale.

Semi-Open/Semi-Closed Performance Appraisal

This is the same as the Open model, except that the employee will not be informed of his final performance rating. He will also not be able to view his performance rating in the performance appraisal form.

<u>Comments</u>
The intent behind closing the performance ratings from employees is to avoid having employees obsess over their performance ratings and to dispense with reporting officers debating with employees on performance ratings. During the critical performance conversation, the employee is still given feedback on his performance – on the areas that he has done well and where he has room for improvement. The conversation just stops short of the final performance rating to spare the unnecessary debate and angst. Rather, the emphasis is on gleaning the learning points from the past year's performance and guiding the employee to focus on out-doing himself by improving on his performance year-on-year. The "exemption" from talking about performance rating may in fact help maintain a harmonious relationship between the reporting officer and the employee.

D4.19　In deciding whether to adopt a Closed, Open or Semi-Open/Semi-Closed model of performance appraisal, an organisation should consider its employee profile and organisation culture:

- If an organisation has many PMEs in its workforce, a Closed model will receive a lot of push back.

- If its line managers are not equipped and ready for handling open conversations on performance ratings and handling emotional reactions from employees, having an Open model will not be advisable. While transparency may sound desirable, it may backfire and bring about adverse outcomes, such as generating divisiveness among employees, higher incidence of staff grievances and even affecting staff morale if the managers do not have the essential people skills to handle it.

Performance Rating Scales

D4.20   Performance results for employees are typically presented in rating scales. How rating scales are designed or defined is entirely up to the organisation.

D4.21   Rating scales are commonly constructed with 3-point, 4-point, 5-point or 6-point ratings. We present some typical examples below:

6-point Rating Scales
Unsatisfactory – Marginal – Satisfactory – Good – Very Good – Excellent
Did Not Meet Expectations – Met Some Expectations – Met Most Expectations – Fully Met Expectations – Exceeded Expectations – Significantly Exceeded Expectations
5-point Rating Scales
1 – 2 – 3 – 4 – 5 or A – B – C – D – E
Poor – Unsatisfactory – Satisfactory – Good – Outstanding
Unsatisfactory – Satisfactory – Good – Very Good – Excellent
Poor – Below Average – Average – Very Good – Excellent
Unacceptable – Needs Improvement – Acceptable – Good – Excellent
Unsatisfactory – Needs Improvement – Meets Expectations – Exceeds Expectations – Far Exceeds Expectations
Did Not Meet Expectations – Met Some Expectations – Fully Met Expectations – Exceeded Expectations – Significantly Exceeded Expectations

Needs Significant Improvement – Needs Improvement – Meets Requirements – Exceeds Requirements – Significant Strength as Role Model
4-point Rating Scales
Needs Development – Consistently Meets Expectations – Sometimes Exceeds Expectations – Always Exceeds Expectations
Failed Expectations – Marginally Met Expectations – Fully Met Expectations – Exceeded Expectations
Low Performer – Developing Performer – Valued Performer – Top Performer
3-point Rating Scales
Poor – Good – Excellent
Failed Expectations – Met Expectations – Exceeded Expectations

D4.22   The 5-point scale is the most common rating scale. With an odd number, it may mean that the central point is neutral, that is, neither impressive nor negative. This leads to the challenge of "central tendency", that is, line managers tend to gravitate their employees to the middle of the scale. Very often, when a line manager gives a rating that is "very good" and above or "borderline" and below, he is asked to justify his assessment. Not all line managers are comfortable or confident in presenting or defending their viewpoints. A central rating is the least debatable and the least "cumbersome" for the line manager. One way to combat central tendency on a 5-point scale is to make the second point as "Meeting Expectations" or "Satisfactory", which will then leave more room to differentiate the higher performers. A finer differentiation of the higher performers is useful when it comes to differentiating which employee deserves more reward.

D4.23   Another way to eliminate the central tendency is to use a 4-point or 6-point scale. With an even number, the line manager has to pick a side, either the top half or the bottom half.

D4.24   Organisations should refrain from using just a numerical scale (1-2-3-4-5) or an alphabetical scale (A-B-C-D-E) without any description as to what the numeral or the alphabet means. Such simple numerical or alphabetical scales get a lot of pushbacks. Line managers cannot second-guess what constitutes a 4 versus a 5.

D4.25 In defining the descriptors for the ratings on the scale, organisations should not inflate or sugar-coat the descriptors. Using "Good" as a descriptor when in reality the employee is just performing satisfactorily (and nothing beyond) will send the wrong message and raise unrealistic expectations of rewards. If a "Good" employee is given only a modest bonus, he may become cynical. If "Satisfactory" or "Adequate" is sugar-coated and communicated as "Good", employees may be given a false sense of confidence if they consistently obtain "Good" ratings over several years. Then where is the organisation heading in the drive for excellence?

Sub-ratings

D4.26 In some organisations, what may have started off as a 4-point or 5-point scale slowly evolves into a rating scale with many more ratings, by creating "sub-ratings" within some ratings. Examples are given below:

Original Rating Scale	A		Outstanding	B		Good	C		Satisfactory	D	Unsatisfactory	E	Poor

Original Rating Scale	A Outstanding	B Good	C Satisfactory	D Unsatisfactory	E Poor
Bonus (months)	4	2.5	1	0.5	0

Variation 1	A+	A	A–	B+	B	B–	C+	C	C–	D	E
Bonus (months)	4.5	4	3.5	2.75	2.5	2.25	1.5	1	0.75	0.5	0

Variation 2	A	B	C+	C	C–	D	E
Bonus (months)	4	2.5	1.5	1	0.75	0.5	0

D4.27 Sub-ratings are most commonly created in the middle of the scale (at "Satisfactory"), the reason being that the middle rating is where the majority of employees fall. With a big number of employees, organisations may want to differentiate this group a bit more by identifying the top and bottom amongst them (the C+ and C–). The rewards will also be differentiated accordingly, as shown in the examples above.

D4.28 Likewise, at the higher ratings (A and B), some organisations create sub-ratings (the A+ and A– and B+ and B–). The fine differentiation may come in handy for talent management purposes. Say, the organisation may want to offer prestigious study awards and consider candidates only from amongst its top performers (say, at least B+).

Performance Appraisal Form

Design of Performance Appraisal Form

D4.29 The Performance Appraisal Form (PAF) serves to document the relevant personal information of the employee and the important points regarding the employee's performance that surface during the appraisal year.

D4.30 The PAF should incorporate these components and information:

<u>Appraisal Details</u>
(a) Appraisal Period
(b) Name of Employee
(c) Name of Reporting Officer (RO)
(d) Name of Counter-signing Officer (CO)

<u>Personal Particulars of the Employee</u>
(a) Job Designation
(b) Job Grade
(c) Date Joined and/or Years in Service
(d) Date of Appointment/Promotion into Current Job Grade and/or Years in Job Grade
These are relevant factors for the appraiser to take into account.

<u>Performance Factors</u>
Performance requirements may comprise the following:
(a) Performance Goals or Work Targets
(b) Competency Standards
(c) Core Value-based Behavioural Attributes

Rating Scale
A rating scale should be provided with clear descriptors.

Self-Appraisal (if this is part of the appraisal process)
The employee is asked to do self-appraisal on how he has fared against each of the performance factors.

Appraisal by RO
Next to the employee's self-appraisal (if there is) on each of the performance factors, the RO should indicate his appraisal. The PAF (the e-version) may likely have a built-in function to compute the overall weighted performance score (for example, the overall score may be based on 50% of the score on performance goals and 50% of the score on competency standards).

Inputs by Secondary Appraiser
A section should be provided to allow a secondary appraiser to provide his inputs. Usually, there is no need for the secondary appraiser to appraise the employee on each performance factor. The secondary appraiser can give inputs specific to the performance goals that the employee is accountable to him and perhaps provide some comments/observations on other performance factors. These will be taken and considered by the primary appraiser in arriving at the overall appraisal. In practice, the primary and secondary appraisers may have an off-line conversation to discuss about the performance of the employee. With that, the primary appraiser will do all the paperwork.

Overall Rating (preliminary by RO and CO)
The RO will recommend an overall rating, after taking into account inputs from the secondary appraiser (if any). The CO will review the overall rating; he may validate the rating, or he may adjust it higher or lower, taking into account the relative performance of other employees and ensuring consistency in stringency across his department. The overall rating given by the CO will override that given by the RO and is what is submitted to the management (or Human Resource) to undergo moderation across the entire organisation.

Final Performance Rating (after Moderation/Confirmation by Management)
The overall ratings of employees submitted by the respective line heads will be moderated by the management (or an appointed moderation panel). The overall ratings may be confirmed (that is, no change) or moderated (that is, adjusted higher or lower). The final performance ratings will then be entered into this section of the PAF (usually by Human Resource in the backend).

> **Strengths and Areas for Development**
> The employee should do self-appraisal on this (if this is part of the organisation's appraisal process). The RO should complete this section. The CO should also give his input.
>
> **Performance Critical Conversation**
> There should be a checklist for the critical conversation covering:
> (a) the employee's final performance rating (after moderation/confirmation)
> (b) the employee's strengths
> (c) the employee's areas for development or improvement
> (d) learning and development plans for the employee
> The RO and the employee can check off the above items and jointly sign off on the PAF. The sign-off indicates that the PAF is completed.

D4.31   There are many ways to design the PAF. The design will vary according to whether the organisation adopts a closed or open or semi-open/semi-closed appraisal model. Some organisations may not even have performance goals setting, while others may adopt a comprehensive format that comes with weightages for several performance factors. We elaborate on the variations in the ensuing sections.

PAF for Open Appraisal Model

D4.32   For the Open model, the employee will get to see the entire contents of the PAF, including the following:

- the RO's appraisal of him for each and all of the performance factors (that is, for each performance goal or work target, competency standard and behavioural attribute);
- the inputs given by the secondary appraiser;
- the final performance rating (after moderation/confirmation); and
- the RO's views on his strengths and areas for development.

D4.33   It is pertinent to highlight that even for an Open model, the overall ratings given separately by the RO and the CO (before moderation/confirmation) should <u>not</u> be visible to the employee. This is because these are deemed to be only preliminary ratings, which await moderation/confirmation by the management or the moderation panel. If the PAF is in e-copy, it should be designed in such a way that the preliminary ratings given by the RO and CO are hidden from the view of the employee and visible only to the RO, CO and Human Resource (who is usually the PAF system administrator).

The employee should only see his final performance rating (after moderation/confirmation). This is so as not to "confuse" the employee, in case the ratings given by the RO/CO are adjusted by the moderation panel.

D4.34 Unfortunately, some organisations knowingly or unknowingly allow the employee to view the preliminary ratings given by the RO and CO. Such a PAF design should be avoided. If the management or moderation panel adjusts the rating downwards, it will cause the employee to become cynical and disillusioned and perceive his RO/CO to be "powerless". If the relationship between the employee and RO is thick, the employee may direct his dissatisfaction towards the management. Some ROs may also play the political card and put the blame on the management for not appreciating the employee. Such sowing of discord is unhealthy and to be frowned upon. ROs/COs should be strongly reminded not to play the "nice guy" game and circumvent the PAF design (that masks the preliminary ratings) by verbally telling (or hinting to) their employees the more favourable preliminary ratings given by them.

PAF for Closed Appraisal Model

D4.35 For the Closed model, the employee will not get to see the PAF again after he has done his self-appraisal (if this is part of the organisation's appraisal process). He will be blocked from accessing the PAF. He cannot see the RO's appraisal of him for any of the performance factors, as well as the inputs given by the secondary appraisers (if any). He also cannot see his final performance rating (after moderation/confirmation).

D4.36 Notwithstanding a Closed model, most organisations still require their reporting officers to have a performance critical conversation with their employees to wrap up the appraisal year. However, the critical conversation will only touch on the employee's strengths and areas of development so that the RO can guide the employee to improve. The official protocol is not to disclose any information on the employee's rating. The spotlight of the conversation will solely be on the employee's developmental needs and not on the employee's rating. Notwithstanding, some ROs may informally and privately (outside of the organisation's official protocol) give hints to their employees on their ratings (especially if the rating is good).

PAF for Semi-Open/Semi-Closed Appraisal Model

D4.37 For a Semi-Open/Semi-Closed model, the employee is usually allowed to see the entire contents of the PAF, including the RO's appraisal of him for each and all of the performance factors, as well as the inputs given by the secondary appraisers (if any). This is so that he is made aware of how he has fared on his job. However, he will <u>not</u> see the overall ratings given by the RO and CO (before moderation/confirmation). He will also <u>not</u> see his final performance rating (after moderation/confirmation).

Differences in Transparency

D4.38   The differences in transparency (visibility) to employees for Closed, Open and Semi-Open/Semi-Closed models are summarised below:

	What Employee Can See in PAF		
	Closed	**Open**	**Semi-Open**
Appraisal by RO on all the performance factors	✘	✓	✓
Inputs by Secondary Appraiser (if applicable)	✘	✓	✓
RO's/CO's Inputs on Strengths and Areas for Development	✘	✓	✓
Overall (Preliminary) Ratings given by RO and CO	✘	✘	✘
Final Performance Rating (after Moderation/Confirmation)	✘	✓	✘

D4.39   Invariably, there can be many variations to the PAF design. A generic sample is provided in Annex D4-1. Organisations should adapt from this sample to suit their unique organisational context, as well as whether the organisation has chosen to adopt a Closed, Open or Semi-Open/Semi-Closed appraisal model, and whether it has incorporated self-appraisal.

Flow Sequence for Performance Appraisal Form

D4.40   In completing the PAF, the form flows through the various parties involved in appraising the employee and in recommending and deciding on his performance rating. A typical flow sequence of the PAF is shown below:

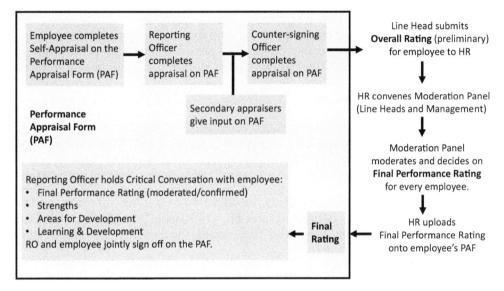

E-Performance Appraisal Form

D4.41   For most organisations, the PAF has gone from hard copy to e-copy. There are several advantages to having an e-copy, including the following:

(a) easier to store and retrieve;

(b) easier to route from the employee to the appraiser and from appraiser to appraiser;

(c) multiple appraisers can enter their inputs into the PAF concurrently (as opposed to sequentially in a hard copy);

(d) the e-system can collate inputs from multiple sources automatically, thus cutting down administrative work for Human Resource to collate and consolidate; and

(e) the preliminary overall ratings in the PAF that are recommended by ROs/COs for their employees can be "pumped" into a template that is suitable for presentation at the performance moderation session. After the moderation has been completed, the final ratings for employees can be "pumped" back to the PAF. Human Resource is usually the backend system administrator to do this "pumping" of e-data.

Default Performance Ratings

D4.42   Some organisations institute "default" performance ratings to specific categories of employees, usually arising from the employee having served too short a tenure during the appraisal period to allow a proper assessment of his performance. This is discussed in more detail in the ensuing sections.

Employees on Probation

D4.43   The common probation period for employees is 3 months for non-executive positions and 6 months for executives. The purpose of the probation period is to allow the organisation to have time to assess whether the employee is competent for the job that he is hired for and a suitable fit for the organisation.

D4.44   For employees who are still on probation, most organisations prefer to allow the probation assessment to carry on, and "exempt" the employee from the annual performance appraisal. This is so that there will not be any duplication in assessing the employee.

D4.45   When organisations waive the annual performance appraisal for employees on probation, the normal practice is to assign a default performance rating to these employees. The default rating is usually the middle rating that denotes "satisfactory", which is commonly a "C" rating (for a rating scale of A-B-C-D-E) or a "3" rating (for a rating scale of 1-2-3-4-5).

D4.46   In some instances, the organisation would give the default rating a special denotation, such as "C#" or "3#". The purpose of the special "#" denotation is to differentiate the default rating from the normal "C" or "3" rating given to employees who have undergone the annual appraisal and moderation exercise. The "#" denotation is useful for future reference when one views the employee's record some years later. For example, if the employee turns out to be an exceptionally good performer after he has passed his probation and earns, say, an "A" rating for his annual appraisal, it will not appear "incongruous" that he has jumped from a modest "C" rating to an "A" rating since the "C#" rating is a default one and not based on an assessment of his performance.

D4.47   Some organisations disqualify employees on probation from bonus payment, whereas some pay a pro-rated bonus for an incomplete year of service.

Where a pro-rated bonus is paid, the normal practice is to pro-rate using a base quantum tied to a "satisfactory" rating (which is normally a "C" or "3" rating).

Employees on Long Leave of Absence

D4.48   For employees who have been away on long leave of absence during the appraisal period (such as hospitalisation leave, maternity leave, or no-pay leave), they may have served too short a tenure during the appraisal period to allow a proper assessment of their performance. Most organisations require employees to serve a minimum of 6 months during the appraisal period before they can undergo annual appraisal to earn a performance rating.

D4.49   One may argue that an employee should still undergo appraisal for the short period (say, 5 months) that he has worked during the appraisal year to earn a performance rating. This view however can be challenged because it may not be fair to extrapolate the employee's performance for that short period to the entire appraisal period. For example, if an employee performs exceptionally well for 5 months (which warrants an "A" rating) and then goes on extended maternity leave for 7 months, one cannot assume that the employee would have sustained the exceptional performance for the entire 12 months had the employee not gone on leave. The reverse also applies; if an employee performs badly for 5 months, it does not necessarily mean that his performance would have remained poor over the entire 12 months had he not gone on leave.

D4.50   If an employee has served for less than "x" months during the appraisal period (whatever "x" as set by the organisation), the normal practice is to assign a default (middle) performance rating to the employee, which is a "C" rating (for a rating scale of A-B-C-D-E) or a "3" rating (for a rating scale of 1-2-3-4-5). Again, a special denotation such as "C#" or "3#" can be used to differentiate the default rating from the normal "C" or "3" rating. The "#" denotation is useful for future reference to indicate that the "C" or "3" rating arose out of a special circumstance. For example, if an employee is a high performer who consistently scores "A" rating and is given a "C#" rating for a particular year when he takes several months of leave away from work, it will not create askance in future when his performance record is being reviewed for career-related opportunities (such as a promotion or scholarship award).

Employees with Misconduct

D4.51   Some organisations impose a default adverse rating, say, a "D" rating (for a rating scale of A-B-C-D-E) or a "4" rating (for a rating scale of 1-2-3-4-5) for employees who have committed misconduct and been given a warning letter or any other more severe form of penalty. The purpose is to send a message of deterrence. However, it is debatable whether a default adverse rating is entirely fair. One may argue that if an employee has already been punished for the misconduct, he should not be penalised for another time unless his performance has been adversely affected arising from the misconduct. For example, if an employee has received a written warning for frequent latecoming (which is a form of poor discipline), his performance rating should not be deliberately pushed down to a default "D" or "4" rating if he has performed well in his job in spite of his frequent latecoming.

D4.52   Perhaps the way to approach the matter of appraising employees with misconduct is to go back to the fundamentals of performance appraisal – we should examine what an employee must fulfil for the organisation. Since every employee is given performance requirements (what we refer to as performance factors) to meet, it follows that every employee should be appraised based on how he has fulfilled them. Performance requirements may comprise (a) performance goals or work targets, (b) competency standards and (c) core value-based behavioural attributes. If an employee has committed misconduct, it would be fair to consider the extent of breach in performance requirements the misconduct represents. The weightage attached to each performance requirement will matter. An employee who has received a warning for being a habitual latecomer would have breached a core value-based behavioural attribute (that is, he has failed to demonstrate work discipline). Likewise, an employee who has received a warning related to a work safety rule or for being negligent at work has breached a competency standard. The question to ask is: *Taking all performance requirements as a whole, what weightage does the misconduct bear to the whole? The misconduct aside, how has the employee delivered on the other performance requirements (especially his work targets)?* By viewing the misconduct vis-à-vis the sum total of the employee's performance requirements, one may then decide what should be a fair performance rating for the employee.

Employees with High Sick Leave

D4.53   Some organisations institute a policy of capping an employee's performance rating if he incurs high Sick Leave. The cap may be a "C" rating (for a rating scale of A-B-C-D-E) or a "3" rating (for a rating scale of 1-2-3-4-5). This means that even if the employee delivers well or exceeds his performance requirements, the best rating he can earn is a "C" or "3" rating, which usually denotes average performance. This is controversial.

D4.54 Again we should go back to the fundamentals of performance appraisal. One should not confuse performance with Sick Leave consumption. Performance appraisal should strictly be based on an employee's performance and not on Sick Leave consumption per se. If, however, an employee's high Sick Leave has adversely impacted his performance or caused disruptions to operations and team work, then it is logical and defensible to give a lower performance rating to the employee. Indeed, frequent absence due to Sick Leave (or other types of leave taken on short notice) may affect an employee's reliability or dependability, and if these are important performance factors for the employee's job, then it is fair to appraise the employee accordingly for the undesirable impact. This is especially so if the employee's work output requires his physical presence at the workplace (for example, in frontline and customer-facing jobs).

D4.55 On the other hand, there are employees whose jobs are individual contributor roles and where physical presence is not a must. If absence on Sick Leave does not cause any operational disruption and the employee makes up for the loss in manhours (by using his personal time or working more efficiently and/or smarter) and delivers well on his work targets, he should not be penalised solely on account of his high Sick Leave.

Performance Critical Conversation

D4.56 To have a proper closure to the performance appraisal exercise, the reporting officer (RO) should hold a one-to-one critical conversation with the employee. This conversation should be employee-centric, as ultimately, it is a wrap-up and closure for the employee after he has put in one year's worth of work; he deserves to be given attention for it. The conversation should also be purposeful; at the end of the conversation, the employee must get an accurate picture of his performance and development needs. The conversation should not degenerate into an administrative "ritual" – something to be done and over with, only because the management expects it.

D4.57 The conversation must be done with sincerity and candour. The employee should be fully involved. For this reason, the conversation should be held in person, and if not possible (say, due to the RO and employee being located in different countries), a video conferencing meeting (with camera on) should be held. Conversations via a phone call or worse, via email will just not do. This is because it is important to reduce the "distance" between the RO and the employee when a critical conversation is held, and reading facial expressions and other body language is important to gauge how receptive the employee is to the conversation. Both parties must be fully present (both physically and mentally) for the conversation.

D4.58   The critical conversation should at least cover these areas of discussion:

(a) the employee's final performance rating (after moderation/confirmation);
(b) the employee's strengths;
(c) the employee's areas for development or improvement; and
(d) learning and development plans for the employee.

Final Performance Rating

D4.59   Most employees tend to focus their attention on the final performance rating. It may in fact be the piece of information the employees are only interested in. The RO must handle the communication of this information sensitively and professionally.

D4.60   The RO should inform the employee that the final performance rating has undergone moderation/confirmation by the management (or moderation panel). Explain what moderation means – to align the consistency of appraisal standards across the entire organisation.

D4.61   It is not a wise thing for the RO to disclose to the employee the preliminary ratings given by the RO/CO, especially if the final rating (after moderation) has been adjusted downwards. The right thing to do is for the RO to just reveal the final (moderated/confirmed) performance rating and not mention what was or would have been his own assessment of the employee.

D4.62   ROs should desist from playing the "nice guy" in telling the employee that he deserves a higher rating (as per the preliminary rating) or playing a political game criticising the management for not sufficiently recognising the employee. The management (or Human Resource) should remind ROs that how they handle this communication is a reflection of their objectivity and professionalism, and that should there be complaints surfacing from this conversation that reveal that ROs have acted unprofessionally (by disclosing preliminary ratings when it is uncalled for), they will be held accountable for it.

D4.63   Although employees invariably focus on their performance ratings, it is important that the conversation should not stagnate there. The RO should at the appropriate juncture steer the conversation to other equally important aspects of the employee's performance. For example, the RO can guide the employee to reflect on these points:

> (a) What lessons can be learnt from the past year? For example, what could have been done differently or better?
> (b) Were assumptions made at the start of the appraisal year on-the-mark or off-the-mark? How did that affect work targets? How can assumptions be derived more accurately in future?
> (c) What circumstances and/or environmental factors have impacted or impeded the employee's performance? Is there any way to pre-empt these and/or overcome these in future? What new challenges (if any) are expected in the coming year?

D4.64   By delving deeper into the context of the employee's performance (rather than just focusing on the rating), the RO and employee will be able to glean valuable insights and learning points, which can then be inputs for performance planning for the following year.

D4.65   At times, the RO and employee may disagree on the causes of unfavourable or favourable performance. If the performance is unfavourable, the employee may tend to attribute it to external or organisational factors as a way to excuse himself, while the RO may take the view that it is the employee's lack of effort. If the employee has done well, the reverse happens; he is more likely to claim full credit, while the RO may discount it on account of a favourable environment or too easy a target set for the employee. It is important for the RO to manage the conversation assertively and yet tactfully so that the discussion does not degenerate into a "blame" or "excuse" exercise.

Employee's Strengths

D4.66   The RO should highlight what the employee has done well during the appraisal year and the strengths that he has demonstrated. Such positive validation goes a long way to boost the employee's confidence and will put the employee in the right direction to sustain and build on his strengths.

D4.67   In discussing the employee's strengths, the RO should refer to the organisation's competency framework and the behavioural markers of the competencies as these serve as a useful goal post. Strengths are meaningful if they match the organisation's requirements. If strengths cannot be optimised to serve the organisation's purpose, they are not relevant.

Employee's Areas for Development or Improvement

D4.68 Generally, there are two likely scenarios that come with the discussion on weaknesses. Some employees may be very keen to know how he can improve. They are usually the good performers who are self-critical and feel the need to constantly keep up and push their competencies to the next level. On the other hand, there are also employees who are over-confident and may not welcome feedback on their shortcomings.

D4.69 Regardless of whether the employee is eager or uninterested when a discussion touches on these sensitive words – "improvement", "development", "shortcomings" and "gaps" – the conversation must be handled with care and sensitivity because people are naturally sensitive and feel vulnerable about these aspects of themselves. They may feel hurt and embarrassed and become defensive. Although a difficult conversation, the RO should not skim through the subject superficially. A cursory and politically convenient discussion will not do any good to the employee apart from not hurting his feelings. The feedback and comments should be centred on events, incidents and behaviours, and not on his character as a person.

D4.70 *Should the "sandwich" method be used to communicate to the employee about his weaknesses or gaps?*
The sandwich method delivers a negative message by wrapping it between two layers of positive messages (aka, good-bad-good layering). While this method soothes the listener, there is a risk that it may mute or dilute the negative message to the extent that it becomes lost. Many people have selective listening. One chooses to listen to what one wants to hear. An optimistic listener may go away hearing only the two positive messages. Likewise, a listener who is inclined to reject the negative message will focus on only the good part of the sandwich and discard the unpleasant part.

D4.71 However the message is packaged, the RO must ensure that the message gets across to the employee. Saying it sincerely but gently and saying it vaguely are not the same thing. For the employee's sake, he must hear, understand and acknowledge the negative feedback, as then only can he move on to making improvements. If employees are misinformed about their actual performance and competencies, they will lose the opportunity to improve, and this will eventually hurt them in the long term.

Learning and Development Plans for the Employee

D4.72   To address the employee's areas for development, the RO should consult with the line head and Human Resource on how these can be addressed through training and other developmental activities (such as job transfers and other assignments) and discuss these with the employee. The RO should also engage the employee to understand his career aspirations and priorities (and reservations/concerns, if any), and how they can be synced with the organisation's needs.

D4.73   Apart from training and developmental activities arranged by the organisation, there are actions that the RO can take on himself to help an employee learn and develop. These include the following:

(a) provide timely feedback and coaching to the employee;
(b) encourage and support the employee to pursue higher performance goals;
(c) provide the employee with stretch assignments;
(d) guide and coach the employee, engage him in work discussions, pose him questions to challenge him to think critically;
(e) provide exposure to the employee to broaden his perspectives (such as attending large-scale management meetings and events);
(f) widen the employee's network by introducing him to management executives and other external professional contacts; and
(g) share knowledge, experiences and insights with him.

Documentation and Closure

D4.74   When the performance critical conversation is completed, the RO and employee can both sign off on the PAF. With the sign-off, the PAF is taken as completed. The sign-off also officially closes the performance management exercise for that year. The whole cycle will repeat in the following year.

Challenges of Performance Appraisal

D4.75   As appraisal involves human judgment, numerous challenges surface, some of which are inherent in the nature of performance appraisal. The common challenges include the following:

Challenges that affect the Accuracy of Rating
(a) subjectivity, (b) personal bias and favouritism, (c) leniency bias and nice guy mentality, (d) central tendency, (e) recency effect and (f) halo and horn effects.

These challenges stem from human nature and affect judgment, and thus cause an appraiser to give an employee a performance rating that is higher or lower than he actually deserves.

Challenges that affect the Completeness of Appraisal
(a) equivalence and (b) discontinuity.

These challenges arise out of imperfect method or incomplete information, thus making it difficult to appraise and assign a fair rating to the employee.

Challenge of Wrong Performance Goals and/or Wrong Target Levels
First, the right performance goals (or work targets) must be selected. Second, the goals must be calibrated at the right target level. Getting any of these wrong will mean that the employee is appraised on the wrong basis or at the wrong level.

We discuss the challenges in more detail below.

Subjectivity

D4.76   The biggest complaint against performance appraisals is subjectivity. As humans are shaped by personal preferences, perspectives and experiences, each comes with his own "lens" or "ruler". What looks good to one may look terrible to another. A proposal written in a certain style may find favour with a reporting officer but not another. An idea that resonates with a reporting officer may not with another. An employee who is full of initiative to try new things may find favour with a reporting officer who is equally a maverick, but not so with another who prefers the stable status quo. This is not to say that the reporting officer is biased. The reporting officer may actually be appraising the employee in good faith, with no intention of bias. It is just that different people view things differently and value different things.

D4.77   *How to mitigate subjectivity?*
This is a difficult question. There is no magic pill to this. Appraisers should be reminded to make a conscious effort to view things from a broader and more balanced perspective and make judgment in good faith. But there is

since the central point is considered neutral and therefore the least optically visible and debatable. Especially in large organisations, due to the sheer number of employees' appraisals to be moderated upon and coupled with tight timelines, Human Resource and the moderation panel tend to skip debating on the names in the central performance rating.

D4.83   There are also other reasons why appraisers may hesitate to give ratings that are higher or lower than the central rating. The common reasons are as follows:

Avoiding giving the Top Rating to Best Performers

(a) The thinking is that there is always room for the employee to do even better, hence it is prudent to reserve the top rating for really exceptional or phenomenal performance.

(b) Some appraisers worry about raising the expectation of the employee to continue to receive the same top rating in subsequent years.

Avoiding giving the Bottom Rating to Poor Performers

(a) The appraiser recognises that the employee has contributed in some ways in spite of falling short on overall performance.

(b) The appraiser does not want to hurt the employee emotionally and psychologically, especially if the employee is a pleasant person.

(c) The appraiser is not comfortable or confident in dealing with any ensuing employee grievance or complaint from the union (if the employee is represented by a union).

D4.84   In some instances, the rigour of the performance moderation process also leads to an unintended effect in this respect. Invariably, moderation panels will seek clarifications from appraisers when the recommended ratings are "out of the norm" – that is, when an appraiser gives an exceptionally good or bad rating to an employee, he must be able to explain it. Understandably, this is the check-and-balance objective of the moderation panel. For a top rating, the panel wants to see supporting evidence. Likewise, for a bottom rating, the panel wants to ensure that there is no victimisation and that the organisation will be able to defend it in the event of a challenge by the employee or his union. Not all appraisers are comfortable or confident enough to defend their recommendations in front of the moderation panel, hence the result is that they will learn to refrain from giving a highly favourable or unfavourable rating even when it is warranted.

D4.85   *How to mitigate the central tendency?*
The moderation panel must exercise a judicial balance in handling the moderation process and not inadvertently "scare" appraisers away from

using the entire suite of ratings. Some organisations implement a ranking process, where employees (belonging to the same job grade) are ranked from top to bottom in terms of performance. The ranking order is decided by the panel members after deliberating on the inputs provided by the appraisers. This way, where the performance of the top-ranked employees substantially fits the description of the top rating, the rating is assigned accordingly. Likewise, the same approach is taken for the bottom-ranked employees.

D4.86   Another way to remove central tendency is for the organisation to consider using an even-number rating scale (that is, either a 4-point or 6-point rating scale) instead of an odd-number one (a 5-point rating scale). Even-number rating scales will force a choice, that is, the appraiser must pick a side, either the top half or bottom half of the rating scale. This way, there is a dividing line between the top half and bottom half of performers, and this facilitates decisions on performance-linked rewards and incentives.

Recency Effect

D4.87   Recency effect means that an appraiser tends to attach more significance to incidents that happened more recently than those that happened a longer time ago. Recency effect is often at play in performance appraisals. For example, when an employee does well in a piece of work towards the end of the appraisal period, the appraiser may mentally and disproportionately give it a higher weightage compared to other assignments that the employee has done in the earlier part of the appraisal period. The reverse may also happen. An employee who has been consistently producing good work but fumbles in one assignment towards the end of the appraisal period may negate all his earlier good work and bring down his rating disproportionately.

D4.88   *How to mitigate the recency effect?*
Reporting officers should be reminded that a fair way to appraise employees is to review the evidence of the employee's full body of work throughout the appraisal period, and not only on one or two isolated incidents. Having a list of clearly defined performance goals or work targets will also help, because a particular recent event may only pertain to one of the goals or targets. If the reporting officer cannot recall clearly the employee's full body of work for the entire appraisal period (this is understandable if he has a big team), he should ask the employee to list out and elaborate on the results/deliverables he has achieved.

Halo and Horn Effects

D4.89   By "halo" effect, it means that an appraiser is influenced by one distinctly positive aspect of a person and unconsciously extends it to other aspects of him. For example, if a reporting officer finds an employee to be very pleasant and helpful to colleagues, he unconsciously thinks well of the employee in all other aspects, to the extent that he may neglect seeking evidence to substantiate his opinion, and this leads to the employee being appraised favourably, even if he may not deserve to be so.

D4.90   The "horn" effect is the opposite. When an appraiser is influenced by one distinctly negative aspect of a person, he unconsciously extends it to other aspects of him. For example, if a reporting officer is put off by an employee's unkempt appearance, he will assume that the employee is sloppy, and nothing done by him will please the reporting officer.

D4.91   Whether unconsciously or otherwise, both halo and horn effects are played out to some degree in performance appraisals, as appraisers being humans, are emotive beings who are susceptible to making wrong assumptions.

D4.92   The phenomena of halo and horn effects are sometimes manifested arising from an occasional comment made by a senior management person on an employee. For example, a senior management person may remark that a particular employee has done a good job (say, the said employee followed up on a request promptly or went the extra mile to attend to the request). The favourable comment will confer a halo effect on the employee. The reporting officer of the employee will likely be influenced and give the employee a good rating to be "in sync" with the senior management person's opinion. The reverse also happens – an unfavourable comment from a senior management person will confer a horn effect on the employee and, in extreme cases, may cause the employee's career to stagnate in the organisation.

D4.93   *How to mitigate halo and horn effects?*
The way to mitigate the halo and horn effects is to insist on having evidence of the employee's work performance to support a reporting officer's assessment of the employee. This due diligence should be observed by the counter-signing officer (CO), and if not done, the moderation panel is the last gatekeeper. In reality, some COs may also be guilty of the halo and horn effects. Having measurable performance goals/targets for assessment will reduce the possibility of halo and horn effects seeping in.

Equivalence

D4.94   In any organisation, there is usually more than just one job family. The performance rating scale applies to all employees in the organisation, regardless of the job family. Therein lies the challenge to find "equivalence". How should one equate a finance executive's performance with, say, a marketing executive's performance and assign the same rating? Or a legal officer versus an engineer?

D4.95   *How to work around the challenge of finding equivalence?*
One way is for the performance moderation panel to review the performance of employees within the same or related job families as one homogeneous group so that it is easier to compare (or find equivalence) and thus make the appraisal of employees more meaningful. For example, a hotel company can review the performance of its employees in F&B jobs as one group, and likewise, the same is done for employees in housekeeping, security, sales and marketing, finance and administration, marcomms and front office (one job family at a time). The ratings of employees across all job families can then be "mechanically" combined. There is really no scientific basis for the practice of equivalence across different job families, that is, equating (or comparing) the performance of an employee in job family A to that of another employee in job family B.

D4.96   The challenge can also be mitigated if employees from different job families are assessed based on the same set of core competencies (or generic behavioural standards) that apply across all job families. The rating should also be based on the assessment of an employee's achievement of his own performance goals/targets.

Discontinuity

D4.97   Whenever an employee leaves service, the top priority is for him to do a proper handover of his outstanding tasks before his last day of service in order to minimise any potential disruption to the organisation's operations. If the employee leaving service is a manager, it is not always that he remembers (or is reminded) to complete the appraisal of his direct reports. When the appraisal is not done, the direct reports' performance will go unrecorded for that portion of the appraisal period. The problem is more pronounced if there are no clear and measurable performance goals or work targets set for the employee in the first place, and his appraisal is based mainly on non-quantifiable goals and/or competency-based behaviours.

The incoming new manager will start afresh to observe and assess his direct reports. This causes a discontinuity in appraisal. The problem can be quite widespread if the organisation faces high attrition at the managerial level.

D4.98   If there are only a few months left to the appraisal period when the new manager takes over, it is common to see the new manager refer to the previous year's performance ratings of his direct reports and then just give them the same rating for the transition year. The new manager will also usually take the prudent approach of postponing decisions on promotions for his direct reports for another year till he has more time to do his own assessment. When this happens, employees who are "due" for a promotion during the transition year will feel aggrieved.

D4.99   *How to mitigate discontinuity in appraisal?*
         The way to mitigate discontinuity in appraisal is for the organisation to enforce that all managers who leave service should diligently complete the appraisal of their direct reports for that portion of the appraisal period up till their last day of service. Human Resource should incorporate this requirement in the exit procedures for employees leaving service and do the gatekeeper role to enforce it. Additionally, setting specific and measurable (quantifiable) performance goals and work targets for all employees will minimise the discontinuity effect when there is a change of appraiser during the appraisal year.

Wrong Performance Goals or Wrong Target Levels

D4.100   For a reporting officer to set performance goals and work targets for an employee, he must have a good understanding of the employee's job role. It also requires astuteness and sound judgment. Performance goals setting must be done at the start of the appraisal year.

D4.101   There can be two dimensions of error with regard to setting performance goals or work targets:

         (a) *The performance goal is wrongly selected or crafted*
             To select the right performance goal, the important questions to ask are: What outcomes must the employee produce that will benefit or matter to the organisation? What does success look like? For example, if a marketing executive is tasked with organising sales promotion events throughout the year, is the attendance rate of the events a fair and only indicator of his achievement? What about the sales volume

generated from the events? If, say, the employee is only measured by the attendance rate at the events, and he scores well on this front, but the organisation barely benefits from any sales volume generated (say, because the invitees to the events were wrongly targeted), is he a good performer? If performance goals (and their measurement metrics) are wrongly selected for an employee, it means that the employee will be appraised on the wrong (or incomplete) basis.

(b) *The performance goal is set at the wrong level*
At times, the performance goal is correctly selected but may be set at the wrong level. Using the same example cited above, say, the marketing executive is measured on the attendance rate as well as the sales volume generated from the events. While the performance goals are holistic and correct, the next question is what level of target is fair to be imposed on the employee – Attendance of 200 or 500 sales leads? Sales volume of 100 or 200 units generated? The fixing of targets is subjective. It involves making assumptions on the operating context under which the employee is executing his work. It also involves taking into account the employee's job seniority level. All these require human judgment, and as a result, subjectivity creeps in. If the performance target is set wrongly (too high or too low), it means that the employee is either appraised too strictly or too leniently, and it makes the appraisal unfair.

D4.102 *How to avoid setting the wrong performance goals or setting at the wrong level?*
If the reporting officer has a good understanding of the employee's job role and the objectives of the organisation, it will reduce the incidence of setting the wrong performance goal. As for setting the performance target at the right level, if the reporting officer is aware that he is making a lot of assumptions when he sets the target for the employee, it will be prudent for him to include a caveat to review the target, say, 3 months into the appraisal year, and if necessary, re-adjust the level of target set. Re-adjustments at the mid-term review of the appraisal year also help. In reality, the possibility of making errors cannot be totally prevented because of the dynamic context under which jobs operate today; for example, environmental factors may change, organisation's objectives may shift, and how the employee's job is done may also evolve.

Appraisers Not Trained to Appraise

D4.103 Deciding on performance ratings accurately and fairly is a complicated and delicate task. To make matters worse, many appraisers may not be trained to do appraisal and how to determine performance ratings fairly. At the very least, appraisers need to be made aware of the challenges that affect judgment – subjectivity, personal bias and favouritism, leniency bias, central tendency, recency effect, halo and horn effects and the blind spots leading to setting the wrong performance goals and/or setting targets at the wrong levels – then only can they steer themselves away from these derailers. Training all managers on "performance appraisal 101" is useful (in fact essential), but it does not automatically turn managers into good appraisers.

D4.104   Appraisal skills can also be honed through guidance and mentoring. This is where the counter-signing officer (CO) comes in; he can guide the reporting officer (RO) if he observes that the RO is skewed in his appraisals out of ignorance of the pitfalls. That said, at times, the COs themselves are also not good appraisers.

Other Challenges and Mitigating Measures

SMART Performance Goals

D4.105   The important criteria for doing good performance appraisals are to reduce subjectivity and increase objectivity as much as possible. One way to raise objectivity is to set SMART performance goals that can be as clear and quantifiable as possible. SMART goals are (a) specific, (b) measurable, (c) attainable, (d) relevant and (e) time-bound. This has been covered in detail in Chapter D2 "Performance Planning and Goals Setting".

Clearly Described Behavioural Standards

D4.106   When employees are assessed on competency-based behaviours, the behaviours should be systematically and clearly described/specified in relation to the job levels of the employees. This is so that an appraiser can better relate these behavioural standards to what he has observed of the employee and can then appraise the employee more objectively, even though behaviours are not "quantifiable" per se. Competency-based behaviours are covered in detail in Chapter D9 "Competency Frameworks".

Tracking and Documenting Evidence of Employee's Performance

D4.107   Accurate performance appraisal is underpinned by information and evidence. Appraisers should observe, track, collect and document information on the employee's performance throughout the appraisal period. With the information, appraisal becomes more evidence-based. There will also be less room for recency and halo/horn effects to creep in, and also give the appraiser more confidence in making judicious judgment and less tendency to fall prey to personal bias, leniency and central tendency.

Rigour in Performance Moderation

D4.108 The rigour of performance moderation often makes a material difference to the quality of appraisal results. At moderation sessions, when an employee is assessed by his reporting officer (RO) to be a good/outstanding or weak/poor performer, this assessment should be cross-referenced and validated with other managers who have interacted with the said employee over work. The RO should also be asked to provide data points (or evidence) of the employee's work performance to justify the said performance rating. The more rigour is pursued at the moderation, the more disciplined and circumspect the ROs will be in assigning performance ratings.

D4.109 ROs should also be made to realise that if they have been found to be persistently non-judicious in assigning performance ratings, their credibility and reputation will be negatively viewed by the moderation panel members who are senior management staff.

Performance Appraisal in Small and Medium Enterprises

D4.110 The performance management framework, processes, forms, tools and practices described so far in this chapter are commonly found in large and established organisations. They have resources and capabilities to design and execute a comprehensive performance management framework.

D4.111 The situation in small and medium enterprises (SMEs) is likely to be quite different. SMEs may have very simple performance appraisal forms that list out a few performance goals or work targets for their employees. These may be set by the management without involving the employees, or even not communicated to the employees. Most SMEs also just do year-end performance appraisal without any mid-term review. There are SMEs that do not even go through the formality of performance appraisal; the boss (owner) may just informally discuss with his managers (direct reports) and then decide on how to reward the junior employees. As for the direct reports to the boss himself, he may give them feedback directly and decide unilaterally on how to reward them. There may not be the formality of assigning performance ratings to employees per se.

D4.112   The feasibility of such a simplified and informal way of handling performance appraisal in SMEs hinges on the close working relationships that prevail in SMEs. As the number of employees is small, SME bosses usually work closely with their employees and therefore have first-hand observations and information about their performance and are able to assess them.

D4.113   As SMEs grow in the number of employees, there will invariably be more layers added to the management hierarchy. The boss (owner) will not be able to retain a direct line of sight of his employees. Bigger SMEs will find a need to put in place a more structured performance appraisal protocol – one that is systematic and comes with sufficient rigour and governance to ensure the accuracy and fairness of appraisals.

Performance Appraisal for Rank-and-File Employees

D4.114   Performance appraisal policy and process should apply uniformly to all employees, that is, to both professional, managerial and executive employees (PMEs) and rank-and-file (RnF) employees alike. However, in practice, some organisations adopt a simplified process for their RnF employees for the following reasons:

(a) The jobs of RnF employees are usually clearly defined and follow standard operating procedures. Quite often, there is little room for the employees to display discretionary effort.

(b) The impact of RnF employees' performance to the organisation is lesser than that of PMEs, hence organisations are less inclined to spend as much management time on RnF employees' performance issues.

(c) RnF employees are more focussed on bread-and-butter issues (rewards) and less on career development, hence the objective of performance appraisal is more singular and less so on developmental needs.

D4.115   Notwithstanding the above, organisations should recognise that no matter how much the performance appraisal process is simplified for RnF employees, the sacrosanct criterion is fairness. The performance of RnF employees is an important factor for consideration in the following employment decisions:

(a) offer or non-offer of re-employment when an employee reaches statutory retirement age; and

(b) extension or non-extension of employment contract when the said contract expires.

D4.116 If the organisation decides unfavourably against the employee in employment decisions on account of performance, it must be able to substantiate that the employee's performance is unsatisfactory. In the event that an employee feels aggrieved, he may seek redress at the Employment Claims Tribunals. If the organisation is unionised, the union may represent its members and ask the organisation to show justification for its decisions. It is therefore pertinent and worthwhile for organisations to put in place a fair and systematic performance appraisal protocol for their RnF employees that will stand up to scrutiny.

Performance Appraisal for Special Employee Categories

Personal Assistants

D4.117 It is a common observation in most organisations that there is a particular category of employees who seem to be favoured in their performance ratings. These are the personal assistants, personal secretaries, executive secretaries or the equivalent (we refer to them as PAs in short) who serve and report to the top bosses in the organisations. Bosses tend to protect their PAs and want to keep them happy. Therefore, bosses often lobby for (or even insist on) top ratings (say, A or B+ or at least B) to be given to their PAs. In one actual case example, 100% of the PA population in the organisation (totalling about 15 of them) earned either A or B+ ratings.

D4.118 One must appreciate that bell curves (stipulating the quotas for each performance rating) are seldom cut by job families because it is often not practical to do so, given the diversity of job families in most organisations and there may be too few employees in some of the job families to apply a bell curve. Bell curves are therefore typically cut by job grades or by departments. Given this situation, the bosses would argue that there is no breach of any bell curve even as their PAs monopolise the top ratings. Bosses should take cognisance that in effect, the monopoly of top ratings by PAs is done at the expense of other employees and job families.

D4.119   It takes collective will from all bosses to rein in the intended or unintended skew in favouring PAs. Preferably, the top echelon bosses (say, Chairman, President or Chief Executive Officer) should set the example by giving fair performance ratings to their PAs and if a high rating is assigned, provide clear justifications for the PA's contributions. This will set the tone for other bosses (divisional/functional directors) to follow.

Personal Chauffeurs

D4.120   Some bosses are also inclined to give good ratings to their personal chauffeurs. If there are many personal chauffeurs in the organisation, the same approach as suggested for the PAs can be adopted to rein in the skew (if any).

Employees on Secondment

D4.121   For employees who are seconded to external organisations, since their work is performed at the host organisations, it follows that they will be appraised by their respective host organisations.

D4.122   If the host organisation uses a different performance rating scale from the employee's employing organisation (say, the host organisation uses a 5-point scale while the employing organisation uses a 6-point scale), the employee's performance rating given by the host organisation must be "mapped" back to an equivalent rating on the employing organisation's scale. Human Resource of the employing organisation must take due care to do this. The seconded employee will be accorded performance-linked rewards (such as bonus, increment and other incentives) based on the employing organisation's policies. Please refer to Volume A, Chapter A6 "Transfer and Secondment of Employees" for a more detailed discussion on the performance appraisal of seconded employees.

360-Degree Feedback or Reverse Appraisal

D4.123   Before we close off the chapter on performance appraisal, it is appropriate to discuss the use of 360-degree feedback. By "360-degree", it means that feedback is sought from multiple parties in the employee's work ecosystem –

his supervisor (upwards), peers (sideways) and subordinates (downwards). Typically, it involves 1 supervisor, 3–5 peers and all direct subordinates. The feedback is usually sought via a survey done individually with the parties involved.

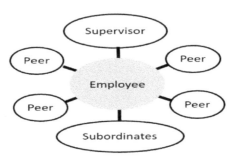

D4.124 The 360-degree feedback survey usually focuses on these attributes of the employee: (a) management style, (b) leadership effectiveness, (c) interpersonal skills and (d) collaboration. Basically, it gives an added dimension that goes beyond just the assessment done by the reporting officer which focuses on work targets and mostly cognitive competencies. For example, an employee who is very competent and a high performer may fare very well in cognitive and achievement-oriented competencies and delivering work targets, but he may be overly competitive and self-centred. Or a manager may behave professionally in front of his superiors but treat his subordinates harshly or unfairly or take all credit for his team's ideas and good work. The 360-degree survey may likely surface such behaviours or shortcomings.

Using 360-degree Feedback as Reverse Appraisal

D4.125 Some organisations have incorporated the 360-degree feedback as part of the performance appraisal for their employees, but this is not common. Essentially, the 360-degree feedback is used as a "reverse" appraisal, that is, subordinates get to appraise their supervisor. A negative report from the 360-degree feedback survey will materially affect the supervisor's overall and final performance rating, and ultimately, his rewards. The idea appears liberating (and even hip), as seemingly, it "equalises" the powers of both the supervisor and the subordinates. However, this practice must be viewed with extreme caution, for reasons elaborated below. [The authors do not recommend using 360-degree feedback as reverse appraisal.]

Concerns over Using 360-degree Feedback as Reverse Appraisal

D4.126   All 360-degree feedback surveys face an inherent challenge, which is, the conflict of interest. It exists when peers appraise one another and when subordinates appraise their supervisors. This has to do with the basic human instinct of protecting one's self-interest.

Conflict of Interest in Peer Appraisal

In a competitive work environment where peers are pitted one against the other for rewards, the objectivity of peer feedback may be questionable. Peers may view rewards as a zero-sum game; a good report for a fellow peer may put oneself further away from the pot of gold. As 360-degree feedback surveys are almost always done anonymously, the raters may be emboldened to rate subjectively. Generally, peer appraisal can only work in an environment where there is a high level of trust and sharing among peers, underpinned by a reward system that does not make it possible for employees to pit against one another. The other prerequisite is that the peers must be familiar with each other's domain of work.

Conflict of Interest in Appraisal by Subordinates

Conflict of interest also exists in subordinates giving feedback on their supervisors. If a supervisor enforces strict discipline and high standards on his team to drive results, subordinates who resist the high standards or resist changes pushed by the supervisor may feel tempted to lash back and give a bad report on the supervisor. Moreover, the subordinates will likely focus on the extent of help and "generosity" shown to them by their supervisors, instead of the supervisors' contributions towards the organisation's goals. In any case, the work (especially the quality aspect) of their supervisors is not readily visible to the subordinates.

Gaming

Separately, there are anecdotes of peers striking "deals" in private to give favourable (or stellar) feedback in reciprocity so that both will score a good survey report. Likewise, anecdotes of supervisors striking deals in reciprocity with say, a select few of their subordinates. These disturbances and gaming techniques that stem from a conflict of interest seriously compromise the authenticity of the feedback and defeat the objective of the feedback.

Using 360-degree Feedback for Developmental Purpose

D4.127   For those reasons stated above, most organisations will use the 360-degree feedback survey for the employees' developmental purposes only, and not for appraisal, or tie to any reward or penalty. The results of the 360-degree feedback are provided to the said employee only and meant to raise his self-awareness on how he is viewed by other stakeholders on his work-related attributes, including his management style, leadership effectiveness, interpersonal skills and collaboration. With enhanced self-awareness, the employee can be more mindful of his work behaviours and make effort to mitigate any shortcomings.

Administration of 360-degree Feedback

D4.128   Assuming that the 360-degree feedback is used for the employee's developmental purpose only, the survey results should therefore be kept confidential to him and not accessible by his supervisor, Human Resource and management or any other party who can influence his performance appraisal rating. To safeguard confidentiality, organisations would invariably engage an external consultant to administer the feedback survey.

D4.129   As the usefulness of the feedback survey hinges on the participants to give truthful responses, the survey results are compiled in aggregate form by the external consultant so that the individual responses will be masked. Often though, the said employee may be able to guess and match the responses to the respondents, especially if the number of survey respondents is small. However, since the feedback results will not affect his performance rating and rewards, the employee should not be unduly perturbed by negative responses. He should be encouraged to embrace the spirit of the 360-degree feedback, which is to enhance his self-awareness and enable him to work on improving his work behaviours.

Conclusion

D4.130   Performance appraisal is a necessary function. It provides the basis with which an organisation can recognise and reward its good performers. It also provides the organisation with the basis to confront its weak performers to get them to shore up.

D4.131   Performance appraisal is a difficult function fraught with challenges because the process involves human judgment from start to end. The results of appraisal also invoke human emotions, since they touch on rewards and recognition. Ultimately, organisations need to do their best to ensure that performance appraisals are done in good faith and fairness.

References

1.   M. Lombardo and R. Eichinger. "The Leadership Architect Norms and Vitality Report". Minneapolis, MN: Lominger, 2003. http://goliathecnext.com/coms2/gi_0199-720322/Knowledge-summary-series-360-degree.html
2.   D. Grote. "How to Be Good at Performance Appraisals". Harvard Business Review Press. Boston, Massachusetts, 2011
3.   J. Kruger and D. Dunning. "Unskilled and Unaware of It: How Difficulties in Recognising One's Own Incompetence Lead to Inflated Self-Assessment". Journal of Personality and Social Psychology, 77(6), 1999

Annex D4-1

Sample 1 of Performance Appraisal Form
(Open appraisal model and includes Self-appraisal by Employee)

Appraisal Period (from dd/mm/yyyy to dd/mm/yyyy)			
Name of Employee		Department	
Current Job Grade		Date Joined	
Current Job Title		Date to Current Grade	
Appraisers			
Name of Reporting Officer		Designation of RO	
Name of Counter-signing Officer		Designation of CO	
Name of Secondary Reporting Officer (if any)		Designation of Secondary RO	
Structure of Performance Appraisal Form			
There are 4 Parts in this form: **Part 1: Work Targets** **Part 2: Competency Standards** **Part 3: Overall Assessment** **Part 4: Critical Conversation Sign-Off**			
If the employee is in a multiple (matrix) reporting structure, the secondary Reporting Officer should complete a separate performance appraisal form. All parts of the form are to be completed.			

PART 1: WORK TARGETS

At the Start of the Appraisal Period
Reporting Officer and Employee to jointly set the work targets.
At the End of the Appraisal Period
Employee and Reporting Officer to state the extent to which the work targets have been achieved, using any of the 3 ratings:
Above Target (AT) or Met Target (MT) or Below Target (BT)

Description of Work Targets, Progress and Achievements	Self-Appraisal by Employee			Appraisal by Reporting Officer		
	AT	MT	BT	AT	MT	BT
	☐	☐	☐	☐	☐	☐
	☐	☐	☐	☐	☐	☐
	☐	☐	☐	☐	☐	☐
	☐	☐	☐	☐	☐	☐

PART 2: COMPETENCY STANDARDS

At the Start of the Appraisal Period
Reporting Officer and Employee to jointly confirm the expectations in competency standards in accordance with the organisation's Core Competency framework (HR will be able to advise).
Additionally, Reporting Officer and Employee to confirm the functional competency standards required for the job.
At the End of the Appraisal Period
Employee and Reporting Officer to state the extent to which the core and functional competency standards have been demonstrated, using any of the 3 ratings:

Role Model (RM): Consistently exceeds the behaviours expected for the competency
Proficient (P): Consistently demonstrates the behaviours expected for the competency
Needs Development (ND): Still developing the competency

Description of Competency Standard and Employee's Demonstration of Competency	Self-Appraisal by Employee			Appraisal by Reporting Officer		
	RM	P	ND	RM	P	ND
	☐	☐	☐	☐	☐	☐
	☐	☐	☐	☐	☐	☐
	☐	☐	☐	☐	☐	☐
	☐	☐	☐	☐	☐	☐
	☐	☐	☐	☐	☐	☐
	☐	☐	☐	☐	☐	☐
	☐	☐	☐	☐	☐	☐

PART 3: OVERALL ASSESSMENT

Employee's Feedback

Employee may provide reasons if he/she has not performed to expectations or has encountered any difficulties on the job. Employee may also provide feedback on his/her career path preferences, and how he/she wishes to learn and develop.

Reporting Officer's Feedback

<u>Employee's Strengths</u>

<u>Employee's Areas for Development</u>

<u>Career Development Plan for Employee for Next 12 months</u>

OVERALL RATING

Note that these are preliminary ratings and should not be visible to the employee. The employee should only see the Final Performance Rating after moderation/confirmation by the Moderation Panel (assuming an open appraisal model).

A: Outstanding contribution. Exceeds job requirements in many areas.
B: Major contribution. Fully meets job requirements and exceeds in some areas.
C: Good contribution. Meets job requirements.
D: Marginal contribution. Needs improvement in some areas of job requirements.
E: Unacceptable outcomes. Major shortcomings in several areas of job requirements.

Overall Rating by Reporting Officer	Overall Rating by Counter-signing Officer
A B C D E ☐ ☐ ☐ ☐ ☐	A B C D E ☐ ☐ ☐ ☐ ☐

FINAL PERFORMANCE RATING (AFTER MODERATION)

To be completed by Human Resource
(or uploaded via e-Appraisal system after moderation)

A   B   C   D   E

☐   ☐   ☐   ☐   ☐

PART 4: CRITICAL CONVERSATION SIGN-OFF

Reporting Officer has held a critical conversation with the Employee, covering these points:

- Employee's achievement of work targets
- Employee's achievement of competency standards
- Employee's strengths
- Employee's areas for development
- Learning and career development plans for Employee
- Final performance rating (after moderation) – assuming an open appraisal model

☐ Sign-off by Employee	☐ Sign-off by Reporting Officer
Date:	Date:

Note

In practice, there are numerous variations and designs. For example, there may not be any self-appraisal, there may be a mid-year review, the rating scale may be different, a weightage may be assigned to each work target, or a method may be prescribed for deriving the overall performance rating integrating the employee's performance in two areas (namely, work targets and competency standards), etc. Organisations should design their Performance Appraisal Forms to suit their own context and needs. Forms should not be overly designed with nice but unnecessary features. It is important to be practical and make the form easy for the employees and reporting officers to use.

Annex D4-2

Sample 2 of Performance Appraisal Form (Closed appraisal model and in simplified format)

Appraisal Period (from dd/mm/yyyy to dd/mm/yyyy)			
Name of Employee		Department	
Current Job Grade		Date Joined	
Current Job Title		Date to Current Grade	
Appraisers			
Name of Reporting Officer		Designation of RO	
Name of Counter-signing Officer		Designation of CO	
Name of Secondary Reporting Officer (if any)		Designation of Secondary RO	
Structure of Performance Appraisal Form			
There are 3 Parts in this form: **Part 1: Work Targets** **Part 2: Competency Standards** **Part 3: Overall Rating**			

PART 1: WORK TARGETS

Work Targets are set by the Reporting Officer.
At the end of the appraisal period, the Reporting Officer to state the extent to which the work targets have been achieved, using any of the 3 ratings:
Above Target (AT) or Met Target (MT) or Below Target (BT)

Description of Work Targets, Progress and Achievements	Appraisal by Reporting Officer		
	AT	MT	BT
	☐	☐	☐
	☐	☐	☐
	☐	☐	☐

PART 2: COMPETENCY STANDARDS

At the end of the appraisal period, the Reporting Officer to state the extent to which core competency standards have been demonstrated, using any of the 3 ratings:

Role Model (RM): Consistently exceeds the behaviours expected for the competency
Proficient (P): Consistently demonstrates the behaviours expected for the competency
Needs Development (ND): Still developing the competency

Description of Competency Standard and Employee's Demonstration of Competency	Appraisal by Reporting Officer		
	RM	P	ND
	☐	☐	☐
	☐	☐	☐
	☐	☐	☐
	☐	☐	☐

PART 3: OVERALL RATING

A: Outstanding contribution. Exceeds job requirements in many areas.
B: Major contribution. Fully meets job requirements and exceeds in some areas.
C: Good contribution. Meets job requirements.
D: Marginal contribution. Needs improvement in some areas of job requirements.
E: Unacceptable outcomes. Major shortcomings in several areas of job requirements.

Overall Rating by Reporting Officer					Overall Rating by Counter-signing Officer				
A	B	C	D	E	A	B	C	D	E
☐	☐	☐	☐	☐	☐	☐	☐	☐	☐

FINAL PERFORMANCE RATING (AFTER MODERATION)

To be completed by Human Resource
(or uploaded via e-Appraisal system after moderation)

A	B	C	D	E
☐	☐	☐	☐	☐

Performance Moderation

Focus of this Chapter

In Chapter D1 "Overview of Performance Management Framework", we highlighted that performance management consists of several essential steps that are done in sequential order: (a) performance planning and goals setting, (b) performance feedback and coaching, (c) performance appraisal, (d) performance moderation, (e) the performance critical conversation and (f) applications of performance results.

This chapter examines performance moderation in detail and brings readers through a typical moderation process. Performance moderation is essentially a check-and-balance process to improve the accuracy, consistency and fairness of appraisal, and therefore the rigour of pursuing it often makes a material difference to the quality of appraisal results. We advise readers to first read Chapter D1 before proceeding with this chapter.

The What and Why of Performance Moderation

D5.1   *What is Performance Moderation?*
        Performance moderation is a structured process whereby the organisation's management collectively reviews and normalises/moderates the preliminary assessments of employees given by line managers. At the end of moderation, every employee is assigned a final performance rating.

D5.2   *Why do Performance Moderation?*

The purpose of performance moderation is to do a cross-calibration across the organisation to arrive at a common "ruler" to give as much uniformity and consistency as possible in appraisal standards so that the final performance ratings assigned to employees are accurate and fair (as much as possible).

The cross-calibration (or moderation) is necessary because line managers have varying performance expectations; some are more demanding and discerning, while others are more lenient and accommodating. Additionally, the linkage between performance ratings and rewards for employees is an undercurrent that can affect the objectivity of line managers in appraising their employees. Performance moderation is the check-and-balance process to mitigate such skew in being either too stringent or too lenient. The mere provision of performance moderation as a must-have process in itself will educate and condition line managers to be more circumspect and objective in assigning performance ratings to their employees.

Performance Moderation: Practice in Large versus Small Organisations

D5.3   The performance moderation process can take various formats, which mostly depend on the size and hierarchical structure of the organisation. We first describe the typical format/process in large organisations. For small organisations, the format/process is usually much simplified. While the format/process of performance moderation differs between large and small organisations, the same objectives and principles should apply. Small organisations can take reference from the format/process used in large organisations and apply the underlying objectives/principles in whatever way practicable to suit their own context.

D5.4   In large organisations, after the Reporting Officer (RO) and Counter-signing Officer (CO) have completed the performance appraisals for their employees, the recommended Overall Rating for each employee is submitted (or routed via the e-appraisal form) to the organisation's management or Human Resource (HR). At this stage, the Overall Rating for the employee is only an interim rating. The next step is to undergo performance moderation, where the Overall Ratings of all employees are reviewed collectively across the organisation by the management/HR. The performance moderation process in large organisations can be quite formal and structured, which we elaborate in the later part of this chapter.

D5.5   In small organisations, the usual practice is that the Overall Ratings given by the ROs and COs (if there is this second layer of managers) will be collated by HR and tabled for review by the Chief Executive Officer (CEO) or Managing Director (MD) or owner/boss of the company. The CEO/MD/boss may request for 1 or 2 key management personnel to join him in a simple meeting session to review the Overall Ratings. HR will document any changes made to the Overall Ratings at the review session. While such a review format/process is simple (and even somewhat unstructured), so long as the review session aims to put in some consistency in appraisal standards, the purpose of performance moderation is served. In very small organisations where the boss/owner works closely with his employees, he alone may do performance appraisal and moderation rolled into one.

Moderation Participants and Roles

D5.6   In large organisations, HR is invariably tasked to convene a performance moderation panel and arrange the moderation sessions. For the moderations to be perceived to be conducted in a fair and transparent manner, care is usually taken in assembling the moderation panel to ensure that all stakeholders (that is, the division/line heads) are adequately represented. Other participants may also be invited as attendees to the moderation session. The roles (and rights) of the various participants of the moderation session (that is, panel members and attendees) should be clearly defined so that the moderation sessions can be conducted systematically and efficiently.

Moderation Panel

D5.7   The moderation panel typically comprises senior management representatives (for example, division/line heads), while the line managers will be attendees at the moderation sessions to present and "defend" their assessments.

D5.8   The size of the moderation panel should not be so large that the sessions become too unwieldy and difficult to manage. Typically, a panel size of about 20 members should be the maximum. A practical way to deal with a moderation panel that is too big is to break it up into 2 or 3 panels, with some common members (say, the CEO, Chief of HR and/or the Division

Head of Corporate Services) sitting on all the panels. The purpose is to have some common overview to connect all the separate panels. The construct of the panels will depend on the structure of the organisation. A possible permutation is to have one panel for employees in commercial roles (such as business/sales/marketing), another panel for employees in support or backroom roles (such as HR/IT/finance/planning/operations) and yet another panel for non-executive (that is, rank-and-file) employees, regardless of their job roles.

D5.9   The moderation panel usually comprises the following members:

(a) *Division/Line Heads*
These are line heads who oversee a sizeable number of employees in their respective departments. If there are too many line heads, then the division heads (one level up, who oversee the line heads) should sit on the panel instead, and the line heads will become the invited attendees to the moderation sessions.

(b) *Senior Management*
These are typically the top executive (Chief Executive Officer or Managing Director or President of the organisation) and his deputies.

D5.10   Every member of the moderation panel has a voice, that is, the member has a right to speak for or against a case. If voting is called, every member has the right to vote.

D5.11   For some organisations, the same moderation panel will preside over all the moderation sessions. However, in the case of large organisations where the number of employees is very big, the moderation sessions can be arranged in a "tiered" fashion, that is, moderations can first be done at the individual division level covering the different departments under each of the divisions, before culminating at a moderation session at the organisation-wide level. In this case, the moderation panels will be different for the different divisions.

Example

	Moderation Panel Members	Facilitator	Invited Attendees
Moderation for Division A	Division Head A (Chair) Department Heads of Division A (members)	HR Manager	Direct ROs in Division A
Moderation for Division B	Division Head B (Chair) Department Heads of Division B (members)	HR Manager	Direct ROs in Division B
Moderation for Division C	Division Head C (Chair) Department Heads of Division C (members)	HR Manager	Direct ROs in Division C
Final Moderation for Entire Organisation	Chief Executive Officer (Chair) Deputy CEOs (members) Division Heads A, B, C (members)	Chief of HR	Department Heads of Divisions A, B, C

In this example, it is assumed that the organisation has the following hierarchical structure: Organisation > Divisions > Departments. Each division oversees a few departments, and the divisions report directly to the CEO.

Moderation Chairperson

D5.12   The moderation chairperson is typically the most senior person on the panel. The role of the chairperson is to preside over the moderation session. If there is an impasse at the collective decision-making during the moderation session, the chairperson may be vested with making the final decision.

Process Facilitator

D5.13   The process facilitator is usually a Human Resource (HR) person. For the moderation sessions at division level, it is usually the HR business partner or the HR project lead for the performance management portfolio who will facilitate the process. At the final organisation-wide moderation session, it is typically facilitated by the HR Head or Chief HR Officer.

D5.14   Essentially, the process facilitator is the process owner. The process facilitator must undertake the duties as described below:

    (a) brief the moderation participants (panel members and the invited attendees) on the process and ground rules of the moderation session, including the sequence, the protocol to speak, the confidentiality requirements, etc.;

    (b) assist the chairperson in steering the moderation process, highlighting the areas that need closer scrutiny and review, monitoring the speed and progress of the moderation session, etc.;

    (c) manage the admission and exit of the invited attendees to the moderation session at the appropriate times; and

    (d) be the secretariat in charge of the presentation of information at the moderation session, as well as the documentation of the decisions taken at the session.

Invited Attendees

D5.15   Invited attendees are not considered as members of the moderation panel. They are the resource persons that the panel members will rely on to provide more information that will enable the panel members to make more informed decisions. For example, at the moderation session at division level, while the moderation panel will comprise the division head (as the chairperson) and the department heads (as the panel members), the Reporting Officers (ROs) of the employees whose ratings are being moderated upon will be the invited attendees. During the course of the session, the panel may call upon the relevant RO to present his case for the employee's rating.

D5.16   Invited attendees need not (and are in fact not allowed to) attend the entire moderation session. This is because performance ratings are confidential information and should be visible only to relevant parties. Once an invited attendee has presented or defended the cases under him, he should leave the moderation session. Moderation sessions are not meant to be open for "observers", so as to safeguard the confidentiality of the discussions. The process facilitator should ensure this discipline and manage the admission and exit of the invited attendees.

Tools of Moderation

D5.17   During the moderation process, appraisers will be asked to explain, substantiate and justify their recommendations on performance ratings for their employees. These will be articulated in words which often times may be understood or interpreted differently. An eloquent and persuasive appraiser may stand a better chance in convincing the moderation panel. This is not ideal. Hence, the use of assessment and moderation tools is essential. The bell curve and forced ranking are very commonly used.

Bell Curve

D5.18   Invariably, almost all moderation panels use a bell curve to manage the assignment of performance ratings to employees. However, there is considerable controversy and debate surrounding the use of the bell curve, or specifically, how the bell curve is used.

D5.19   A bell curve (by way of its shape) is a normal distribution curve, which is a statistical tool. It has a unique feature where the ends are always smaller than the central portion. When a bell curve is imposed on the performance ratings of employees, it means that the majority of employees will have their performance falling in the middle (the central portion), while a small minority of employees will distinguish themselves away from the majority, either as distinctly good performers, or as weak performers. How big the central portion is, and how small the top and bottom ends are, will be determined by the quota set by the organisation. The organisation is free to set the quota in any manner.

D5.20   Many organisations label the various portions of the bell curve according to the performance rating scale that it uses. For example, if the organisation uses a rating scale of A-B-C-D-E, the portions of the bell curve will be labelled as such accordingly. An example is shown below:

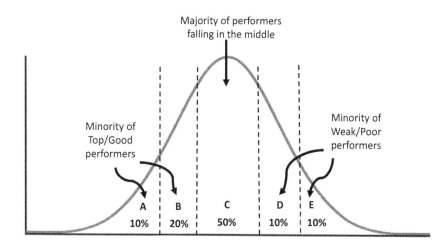

D5.21   The primary purpose for organisations to use a bell curve is to differentiate the distribution of rewards. For example, the top 10% of performers should get the highest tier rewards, followed by the next 20%, then the next 50%, and for the remaining bottom 20%, the rewards should be pared down or not be given.

D5.22   *How many bell curves should be used at the performance moderation?*
Sloting employees into a bell curve is done by cross-comparing (or force ranking) one employee against the others. To make comparisons meaningful, it would be logical to compare employees who belong to the same job grade/level. For example, a rank-and-file employee should be compared with other rank-and-file employees, a junior executive with other junior executives, and managers with managers. If the number of employees is too few for a certain job grade/level, two or more adjacent job grades/levels can be combined into one single bell curve. Generally, for any bell curve to be meaningful, there should be at least 10 employees, and preferably 20 or more.

Example

Job Grade	Appointment	Number of Employees	Bell Curve
JG 1	Admin Assistant I	10	Bell Curve (JG 1-2)
JG 2	Admin Assistant II	15	
JG 3	Executive	20	Bell Curve (JG 3-4)
JG 4	Senior Executive	8	
JG 5	Assistant Manager	5	Bell Curve (JG 5-6)
JG 6	Manager	10	

D5.23   Apart from imposing bell curves based on job grade/level, organisations will usually also call for a bell curve for every department/division, subject that the department/division has at least 10 employees, and preferably 20 or more. If the number of employees is too few for a certain department, two or more departments performing a similar or related function can be combined into a single bell curve. Alternatively, two or more departments reporting to the same department head may be combined into a single bell curve.

Example

Department/Division	Number of Employees	Bell Curve
Sales	35	Bell Curve (Sales)
Technical Sales Support	22	Bell Curve (Technical)
Product Promotion	8	Bell Curve (Promotion and Marketing)
Marketing Communication	6	
Supply Chain Management	6	Bell Curve (Operations)
Logistics & Operations	12	
Finance	9	Bell Curve (Corporate Services)
Legal	3	
Administration	7	
Human Resource	4	

D5.24   The purpose of having bell curves cut by both job grade/level and department/division is to ensure that the fairness and consistency of the bell curve distribution are observed in both dimensions – by job grade/level, as well as by department/division. In other words, the premise is that no particular job grade/level should monopolise or take a disproportionate share of the higher ratings, unless there are exceptional and valid reasons. Likewise, the same for any department/division. Some organisations also analyse the bell curve distributions cut by job families, especially for mission-critical ones (say, engineers who are spread across several job grades/levels and different departments in an engineering company, and likewise, doctors and nurses in a healthcare institution). The purpose is to give an additional dimension of oversight of how the ratings of such mission-critical job families have panned out after performance moderation.

Skewing the Bell Curve for a Particular Job Grade/Level or Job Family

D5.25   If any particular job grade/level or job family takes a disproportionate share of the higher ratings, the moderation panel must be convinced of a good reason to do so. The questions for the moderation panel to ask are: *How did this particular job grade/level contribute exceptionally well to the organisation compared to the other job grades/levels? For example, did employees in this particular job grade/level face the brunt of work challenges (say, an unforeseen crisis) in the past year? Did they make the most impact?* For example, during the Covid pandemic, doctors and nurses in healthcare institutions overcame immense challenges in providing patient care and would justify skewed bell curves for their exceptional contributions.

D5.26   It is relatively common to find organisations allowing a skewed bell curve for senior management executives (say, the direct reports of the CEO or those who are commonly referred to as C-1 executives). The skewed bell curve will provide a bigger quota of the higher (that is, A and B) ratings. The common "justification" (or argument) for giving such preferential treatment is that the organisation views the senior management executives as a very select pool of talent who are handpicked for their senior roles because they are deemed to be good, and if any one of them is not good, he would have been managed out early to minimise the adverse impact on the organisation. In essence, the premise is that a bell curve should only be imposed on a "random" population, and since the senior management executives are not a random population, they can be exempted from the bell curve. More on this is discussed in Chapter D8 "Performance Management: The Challenges, Realities and Alternatives".

Skewing the Bell Curve for a Particular Department/Division

D5.27   Likewise, the moderation panel should only make exceptions for high-performing departments/divisions to deviate from the bell curve. Evidence of the high performance (and high impact) must be presented to the moderation panel for review and endorsement. The questions for the moderation panel to ask are: *How exceptionally well did this particular department contribute compared to the other departments? Did this department deliver well above its performance targets? Were the performance targets realistically set? If it was a stellar performance, was it solely due to the employees' effort? Or was it attributed to the favourable environment or other external factors?*

D5.28   The converse should also be done. If a particular department/division has performed badly, the moderation panel may (or should) tweak the bell curve quota so that a smaller number of employees will qualify for the higher ratings.

Approval for Exceptions to the Bell Curve

D5.29   In order for there to be proper discipline in enforcing the bell curve, all deviations from the bell curve should require the approval of the top executive (that is, the Chief Executive Officer) at the final moderation stage.

Junior moderation panels (those that moderate on the appraisal results at the division/department levels) should not unilaterally allow such deviations.

Forced Ranking

D5.30 Forced ranking is essentially a process where employees are compared one against the others and then lined up from the strongest to the weakest. Forced ranking allows employees to be assessed and compared on relative terms. The comparison is a way of doing a sanity check on the assessments done by the appraisers. It also gives a more granular view of the relative assessments of the employees – for example, if 5 employees are rated as "A", who among them is the strongest? And if there are 50 employees rated as "C", who among them are the stronger ones and who are the borderline cases to watch out for?

D5.31 For forced ranking to be meaningful, it can only be applied to employees who belong to the same job grade/level. There is no meaning in force ranking (or comparing) employees who belong to different job grades/levels.

D5.32 After employees (of the same job grade/level) are force ranked, they are then slotted into the different portions of the bell curve, with the strongest going into the top rating, the weakest going into the bottom rating, and the rest of the employees going into the other ratings, complying with the quota set for each of the ratings.

D5.33 To do forced ranking, the collective evaluation by the moderation panel is required. The panel members will review the citations given by the Reporting Officers, probe for clarifications as necessary and do relative comparisons between employees. Panel members will also give their inputs on any employees with whom they have had direct work interactions. More about this process is elaborated under the section "Moderation Process".

D5.34 *Does forced ranking have to be done for every employee?*
Some organisations will do forced ranking on each and every employee in the respective bell curves for the job grades/levels. For example, if there is a bell curve imposed on 20 managers, these managers will be force ranked from 1 (the strongest) to 20 (the weakest). This is being thorough and meticulous. But it is very time-consuming and practical only if the employee population is small enough for the moderation panel to find it manageable. In large organisations where the number of employees in a job grade/level can run into the hundreds, it would be neither practical nor meaningful to force rank each and every employee for the following reasons:

(a) Forced ranking requires collective review, evaluation and inputs by the moderation panel. When the number of employees is large, it is unrealistic to expect the panel members to have enough cross-knowledge of the employees to rank one employee accurately above or below the other.

(b) Rewards for employees are tiered based on the final performance ratings of the employees. That is, rewards for employees rated as "A" will be higher than those rated as "B", which in turn will be higher than those rated as "C", and so on and so forth. There is little or marginal value in differentiating between a top "A" and a bottom "A" if rewards for all who are rated as "A" will be the same. This extends to other treatment for employees, such as talent management and developmental activities.

D5.35   For the reasons above, most large organisations with sizeable employee populations may choose to only scrutinise on the extreme "fringes" of each rating (for example, identify and rank the top 3 and bottom 3 for "A", top 3 and bottom 3 for "B" and top 3 and bottom 3 for "C"). By scrutinising on the "fringes", it would already allow sufficient sanity check on the rating standards. The other employees sitting safely in the "middle" of each rating (that is, a middle A, middle B and middle C) need not be force ranked. That said, some organisations, however, want to force rank their top employees (those rated as "A") to have a finer differentiation for this select group of talent. This usually happens when the organisation offers a limited number of special perks/benefits (such as a prestigious postgraduate scholarship) to only the most elite of its employees.

Moderation Process

D5.36   The objective of the performance moderation exercise is to calibrate and achieve a uniform appraisal standard (of stringency/leniency) across the entire organisation so that the final performance ratings assigned to employees are as accurate and fair as possible.

D5.37   In large organisations, the moderation session usually follows a certain protocol which is more or less the same, although there will be slight variations depending on the organisation's preference and/or its hierarchical structure. For small organisations, the moderation session (which is usually a simple review meeting comprising the CEO/MD, HR and a few key management personnel) is usually much less structured. The steps that we describe below for the moderation process pertain to large organisations:

Citation and Validation

D5.38   The overall ratings recommended by the respective line heads will be collated by Human Resource and presented at the moderation session. There are different ways to proceed. One way is to first focus on employees who have been given outlier ratings, that is, a rating either at the top or bottom end of the rating scale. Once that has been settled, the panel can next examine the other ratings sequentially, one rating at a time. The other way is to look at all the ratings, department by department sequentially. The panel should decide on its preferred sequence of moderation and Human Resource should flash out the cases in an orderly fashion for discussion.

D5.39   Whichever sequence is adopted, the Reporting Officers (ROs) of the employees may be called upon to give a citation of the employees' contributions to support their recommended ratings or defend or answer queries posed by panel members. The panel members are free to probe or seek more clarifications. In particular, attention should be paid to the following:

(a) the citation must highlight the employee's achievement of work targets in a quantitative manner, where possible. Focus should preferably be on outcomes, rather than on effort or activities;

(b) on competency standards, the citation should highlight how the employee has demonstrated the said competencies at work (perhaps through critical incidents and/or his specific work behaviours), and not just cite the employee's academic/professional/technical qualifications; and

(c) while positive attributes such as diligence, helpfulness, likeability, cheerfulness and humility are desirable and such information would give a more complete profile of the employee, these are not competencies per se and do not guarantee effectiveness in delivering work outcomes. Therefore, the moderation panel should not be unduly influenced or overly weigh in on an employee's rating solely on account of these general nice-to-have attributes.

D5.40   The rigour of moderation at the citation/validation stage often makes a material difference to the quality of appraisal results. Especially so for employees who are assigned ratings at the top and bottom ends of the rating scale by their respective ROs, the assessment must be supported by evidence and should also be cross-referenced and validated with other managers who have interacted with the said employees over work. The more rigour is pursued at this stage, the more disciplined and circumspect the ROs will be in assigning performance ratings to their employees. Conversely, if the moderation panel is laissez-faire over the validation process, the ROs will be emboldened and less disciplined in assigning ratings.

D5.41   ROs should also be made to realise that if they have been found to be persistently non-judicious in assigning performance ratings, their credibility and reputation will be negatively viewed by the moderation panel members who are senior management staff.

Benchmarks and Relative Comparisons

D5.42   To make the moderation process easier, one "trick" is to find benchmarks among the employees being moderated upon. For example, if there are 50 employees, the panel should attempt to identify which employees from amongst the 50 would be widely and clearly accepted as an "A" performer, a "B" performer and a "C" performer. These employees are those who are more widely known to the majority of panel members (say, they have served job stints in more than one division, or they have handled cross-divisional projects and therefore have work interactions with more than one division head).

D5.43   Once the benchmarks are established for "A", "B" and "C" performers, when the citations of the other employees are made, the moderation panel can, by relative comparison, decide for each employee one by one, whether he is the closest match with the "A", "B" or "C" benchmark. For employees who fall clearly below the "C" benchmark, they can be assigned as "D" or "E" performers, depending on how grave the shortfall in performance is.

Scrutinising the Top, Bottom and Fringe

D5.44   Once all employees have been slotted into "A", "B", "C", "D" and "E" ratings (using the benchmarks and relative comparison method), it will be useful for the moderation panel to scrutinise the names in each rating once again to do a final sanity check.

D5.45   The panel should focus their scrutiny on the names in the extreme "fringes" of each rating. For example, identify and rank the top 3 and bottom 3 names for "A", top 3 and bottom 3 names for "B" and top 3 and bottom 3 names for "C". If say, after the scrutiny, it is discovered that there is hardly any discernible difference between the bottom "A" performers and the top "B" performers, then the panel may want to review the ratings for these employees – some names may be moved one notch up or one notch down. Likewise, the same is to be done for the bottom "B" performers and the top "C" performers. This process is necessary for due diligence but is tedious and often challenging. At times, if it is "impossible" to adjust the ratings for any names and as a result, the bell curve quota is marginally exceeded, the moderation panel may decide to accept a slightly distorted bell curve.

D5.46   Special mention must be made here for the bottom performers, that is, those slotted into the "D" and "E" ratings. The moderation panel must satisfy itself that there is adequate data and evidence that point to the employee's unsatisfactory/weak performance and that there is no victimisation or personal bias on the part of the Reporting Officer or Counter-signing Officer. This is especially important in a unionised organisation. If the employee is represented by a union and challenges the adverse rating, the management must be able to defend the basis for the adverse rating. While it is prudent and imperative to ensure no victimisation, the moderation panel must also not send a wrong signal to the appraisers to be soft in dealing with poor/ weak performers. Fairness and honesty in appraisal are both crucial.

D5.47   A litmus test to an adverse rating is that it should not come as a "surprise" to the said employee. In other words, during the course of the appraisal year, the Reporting Officer should have already flagged out the employee's performance gaps and done performance counselling regularly (or repeatedly) with the employee and documented such incidents. The good practice is to forward such performance counselling records (for example, email correspondences to the employee) to Human Resource for documentation and filing. This evidence can be cited at the performance moderation session.

Managing Conflict of Interest

D5.48   During the moderation process, the moderation panel should be alerted to any potential conflict of interest that may arise. For example, if any employee being moderated upon is related in any way to a panel member by way of family ties, then the panel member concerned should be recused from participating in reviewing the said employee, including giving any comment or input. This is to avoid bias and safeguard the impartiality of the moderation panel. Family ties include spouse, child, parent, parent-in-law, son/daughter-in-law, sibling, brother/sister-in-law, cousin, uncle/aunt, nephew/niece, etc.

D5.49   Usually, Human Resource having the personal records of employees will be the party tasked to alert the panel of any potential conflict of interest. However, not all family relationships are captured or evident in the personal records of employees (for example, parent-in-law, sibling, uncle/aunt and nephew/niece). Therefore, the onus is on the respective panel members to do a self-declaration on any family relationship that will pose a conflict of interest.

Ways of Reaching Consensus

D5.50   At times, the moderation panel may reach an impasse in some cases, where views are divided. This is quite common since performance assessment involves human judgment, and unavoidably, there will always be some degree of subjectivity and differences in perspective. Organisations generally attempt to break the impasse and reach consensus by the methods elaborated below. Each method has its pros and cons:

(a) *Consensus by Debate*
This is likened to a "jury" process, where all jury members must collectively debate the merits (that is, hard evidence) of the case, and collectively arrive at a unanimous decision. This method is an attempt to be evidence-based and thorough; however, the process is time-consuming. In reality too, quite often, some panel members may go into fatigue over the debate and relegate their position and go along with the decision of others. Therefore, the consensus is only in appearance or form, rather than in substance.

(b) *Decision by Voting*
Some organisations use voting to break an impasse. This appears to be a practical approach but with a caveat. Voting should only be used after a thorough debate has been held on the merits of the case, and as a last resort to break an impasse. In other words, voting should be used sparingly. It would be unwise to use voting indiscriminately as a short-cut way or default method to make decisions. In one actual case example, an organisation used voting to decide on almost 90% of the cases. Voting without first knowing the facts of the case is just plainly blind voting. Blatant use of voting may also lead to "gaming" by panel members to mutually vote favourably for one another's cases.

(c) *Final Decision by Chairperson*
Some organisations would allow the chairperson of the panel to be vested with making the final decision to break any impasse. This is a practical approach. As a good practice, the chairperson should provide his reasons to the panel for deciding one way over the other. Human Resource (as the secretariat) should document the basis for reference.

D5.51   The quality of decisions at a moderation session hinges on the quality of debate by the panel to uncover evidence to support the assessment of an employee's performance. The panel chairperson and Human Resource (the process facilitator) should guide and encourage debate. However, at times, the panel chairperson may enter the debate too soon. His comment may sway the views of other panel members, especially those who want to please the chairperson. Or other panel members may just simply feel awkward or uncomfortable with contradicting the chairperson. Ideally, the chairperson should reveal his views only after hearing from the panel members and the matter has undergone some vigorous debate.

Challenges and Derailers of Performance Moderation

D5.52   Performance appraisal and moderation are essentially people processes. Very often, the success of performance appraisal and moderation is not about how efficient, systematic, comprehensive or meticulous the processes have been. Rather, the success hinges largely on the attitude, commitment and discipline of the people involved.

D5.53   Because performance appraisal and moderation are emotive processes, at times, there will be behaviours exhibited by the stakeholders (that is, the panel members and the appraisers) that can potentially and materially compromise or derail the outcomes of performance appraisal and moderation. These are discussed below:

Personal Agenda

D5.54   Some appraisers (the Reporting Officers, Counter-signing Officers and department/division heads) may harbour personal agenda other than just giving objective and honest inputs at the moderation session.

> Example
> A member of the moderation panel may want the employees in his own division to stand out above the employees in other divisions. At the moderation session, when asked for his inputs on other employees, the panel member (say, head of Division A) may deliberately give somewhat skewed or unfavourable comments on employees of the other divisions.

> **Example**
> At times, a panel member (say, head of Division A) may harbour personal grudges against an employee from another division for whatever reasons (say, bad chemistry, or perhaps the employee had previously refused a transfer to Division A, etc.). His inputs on the employee may be coloured by a personal agenda to discredit the employee.

> **Example**
> Two fellow panel members (say, heads of Division A and Division B) may have a less than cordial working relationship. Both division heads may consciously or subconsciously be unduly harsh or skewed in providing inputs on employees from the other division.

> **Example**
> One panel member (A) who is supportive of another panel member (B) may choose to keep silent or not to tell the truth when the performance of an employee under B is being scrutinised. The quid pro quo will come later for B to return a favour to A when the rating of an employee under A is being debated.

D5.55   Usually, the moderation panel would have to take all inputs in good faith when there is no alternative or disputing evidence from other panel members. In other words, the panel would not second-guess if any panel member was acting with a personal agenda. From experience, it is unfortunate to observe that such unbecoming behaviours do occur, as humans being humans, are emotive beings. The way to mitigate such derailers is for the panel to probe for specific details or evidence to support the input rather than just accept an opinion or a cursory narration offered, but it is difficult to entirely nullify the derailer.

Hotline to Top Management

D5.56   The purpose of performance moderation is to improve the consistency in appraisal standards across the organisation so that no line head would be skewed in his assessment by either being too stringent or too lenient. With the collective inputs provided and cross-validations done at the moderation sessions, another important goal of the moderation process is achieved, which is to make it transparent how the final performance ratings for employees are arrived at.

D5.57　At times, the moderation process may be derailed by what we call "hotline" or "side-bar" requests made to the top management to seek special concessions. For example, a panel member keen to protect the performance rating of his employee may approach the top management (say, the CEO or chairperson of the final moderation panel) to seal the deal privately. This is highly undesirable and compromises the integrity of the moderation process.

> Actual Case Example
> A panel member emailed the CEO to put forth her case, citing that the other panel members did not heed her explanation and that HR was not effective in facilitating the moderation session, calling it "chaotic" and "unproductive". The moderation session was chaired by the Deputy CEO. The email sought to reinstate the performance rating that she recommended for her officer, and to promote the said officer. The email was not copied to the Deputy CEO and HR. Fortunately, the CEO did not entertain the request and instead routed the email to Deputy CEO and HR for attention. Deputy CEO and HR provided a summary report on the discussion points and decision made at the moderation session. The CEO agreed with the decision and directed the said panel member to abide by the decision of the moderation panel.

D5.58　It is important for the top management to safeguard and protect the integrity of the moderation process and not undermine it in any way by entertaining "hotline" or "side-bar" requests. In short, the organisational culture and most importantly, the mandate of the top management (specifically the top person) to support the moderation process is critical for its success.

Conclusion

D5.59　Performance appraisal and moderation are people processes that involve multiple stakeholders. Unavoidably, these are also emotive processes where "competition" is involved amongst the line heads in securing the most favourable outcomes for their own employees. The discipline to insist on data and evidence is crucial. The moderation chairperson and the moderation process facilitator (that is, Human Resource) play pivotal roles in steering the moderation process to ensure objectivity and to reach collective decisions that are acceptable to all panel members. Ultimately too, the reasonableness and good faith of the panel members also play a big part in making or breaking the success of the moderation process.

Dealing with Weak Performers

Focus of this Chapter

This chapter focuses on how to deal with weak performers. It is useful for readers to go through the earlier chapters in this Volume, especially Chapter D1 "Overview of Performance Management Framework", Chapter D2 "Performance Planning and Goals Setting" and Chapter D4 "Performance Appraisal" before proceeding with this chapter.

Defining Weak Performance

D6.1   *What is "weak" performance?*
        Put simply, weak performance is performance that falls below a minimum level of performance required of the employee. And who specifies the minimum level? The employer. This is logical, since in an employment relationship, the employer is the party that pays salary, bonus, incentives and other rewards; therefore, it is a fair deal that the employer should hold the right to set requirements for the employee to fulfil. Once the minimum level of performance is set, any performance that falls below this minimum level is considered weak performance. The minimum level is sometimes also referred to as the "threshold" level.

Threshold or Minimum Performance

D6.2   How an organisation defines its threshold/minimum performance depends very much on how its performance rating scale is constructed; that is, whether a 3-point, 4-point, 5-point or other more tiered rating scale is used. It is common for the threshold/minimum performance to be set at the middle of the rating scale. However, this is not always the case; therefore, never presume this as a default. One should look carefully at the definitions/descriptors of each rating to conclude which rating on the rating scale represents the threshold/minimum performance. Ratings that fall above the threshold/minimum are favourable ratings, while ratings that fall below the threshold/minimum are adverse ratings. We use some examples of 3-point, 4-point and 5-point rating scales to illustrate.

Adverse Ratings		Threshold/ Minimum	Favourable Ratings		
Poor	Unsatisfactory	**Satisfactory**	Good	Outstanding	
	Unsatisfactory	**Satisfactory**	Good	Very Good	Excellent
Poor	Below Average	**Average**	Good	Excellent	
Unacceptable	Needs Improvement	**Acceptable**	Good	Excellent	
Unsatisfactory	Needs Improvement	**Meets Expectations**	Exceeds Expectations	Far Exceeds Expectations	
Did Not Meet Expectations	Met Some Expectations	**Fully Met Expectations**	Exceeded Expectations	Significantly Exceeded Expectations	
Needs Significant Improvement	Needs Improvement	**Meets Requirements**	Exceeds Requirements	Significant Strength	
	Needs Development	**Consistently Meets Expectations**	Sometimes Exceeds Expectations	Always Exceeds Expectations	

Failed Expectations	Marginally Met Expectations	**Fully Met Expectations**	Exceeded Expectations		
Low Performer	Marginal Performer	**Valued Performer**	Top Performer		
	Poor	**Good**	Excellent		
	Needs Development	**Proficient**	Role Model		
	Failed Expectations	**Met Expectations**	Exceeded Expectations		

D6.3   It is important for an organisation to pin down on its performance rating scale exactly which rating represents the threshold/minimum performance level. It is useful to embed this message clearly in its performance management policy and communicate it widely and consistently to all its employees. There should be no room for ambiguity. This is especially so if the descriptors for its performance rating scale are less than explicit. For example, some organisations are fond of using positive and fanciful descriptor labels for their rating scales (such as using labels like "Valued Performer" or "Consistent Performer" to mean Average/Satisfactory), perhaps to make their rating scales psychologically more palatable to their employees. Clarity on the threshold/minimum performance level is crucial because in managing employees' performance, the threshold/minimum is used as the basis (or reference point) that will trigger corrective or punitive actions (including termination of contract) on employees whose performance falls repeatedly below this level.

D6.4   Additionally, it is critical for the organisation to cascade downwards what the threshold/minimum performance level will translate into for the employees in their respective jobs. At the stage of performance planning and goals setting, every line manager must communicate clearly to his employees what the threshold/minimum performance (according to the job grade/level of the employee) translates into, in terms of (a) the work targets to be delivered, (b) the competency standards to be demonstrated on the job and (c) the behavioural attributes that must be upheld. The more clarity there is, the more effective it will be for the line manager to manage the performance of his team. Please refer to Chapter D2 "Performance Planning and Goals Setting" for more elaboration.

D6.5   *Must an employee satisfy <u>all</u> components of his performance requirements in order to be deemed as meeting the overall threshold/minimum performance level?*

The short answer to this question is No. However, sometimes, a failure in just one performance requirement alone, where it is a critical, core and non-negotiable one, will render the employee as failing to meet the overall threshold/minimum performance level. Whether an employee is taken as an "overall pass" or "overall fail" depends on the weightage of his shortfall area(s).

D6.6   Generally, employees are appraised on two sets of performance requirements: (a) result-based performance goals or work targets and (b) competency-based behavioural standards. In a typical case, the employee's work targets will comprise multiple items (not just one), where some are more important than others. Likewise, his set of competency standards will comprise a list of items, some may be more important than others. The reporting officer will assign quantitative weightage to each of the work targets and competency standards. At times, in lieu of quantitative weightage (expressed in numerical %), the reporting officer may instead classify the work targets and competency standards qualitatively in terms of level of importance.

D6.7   It is not uncommon that an employee may have done well or satisfactorily in all except one or two work targets. Some degree of discretion on the part of the reporting officer can and should be exercised. If the employee is deficient in one item but over-achieves in another item, the compensatory effect may allow him to have a decent overall rating. However, if a work target is core and non-negotiable (say, a teacher must deliver class lessons as per the prescribed course syllabus), then the non-fulfilment of that single work target may render the employee as an "overall fail". Or if a salesperson fails to meet his sales target, he will be taken as an "overall fail" since his primary/sole job function is to generate sales.

D6.8   It is also normal to expect that an employee may not score equally well in all his competency standards. Again, if the employee is deficient in one item, but over-achieves in another item, the compensatory effect may allow him to pass. That said, if an employee is deficient in a core, critical and non-negotiable competency (say, an engineer who fails in basic engineering knowledge, or a corporate communications executive who cannot write in proficient business language), then that single deficiency will be sufficient to render the employee as an "overall fail".

D6.9   Some organisations assign weightage and use mathematical scores to appraise their employees against each work target and competency standard. A total score will be derived for the work targets. Likewise for the competency standards. The two scores will then be combined on a weighted basis (say, 50-50 or 60-40, etc.) to derive the overall performance score and performance rating for the employee. A threshold/minimum score is set for the overall performance score – that is, if the employee scores above it, he is taken as an "overall pass", and if he scores below it, he is taken as an "overall fail".

Differentiating between Performance, Discipline and Grievance

D6.10   It is useful to pause here to remind that we need to differentiate between a weak-performing employee, an ill-disciplined employee and an aggrieved employee. This "confusion" in perspective is fairly common, perhaps because when organisations think about dealing with "difficult" employees, it usually revolves around any of these three aspects: (a) employees with weak performance, (b) employees committing misconduct and (c) employees lodging grievances/complaints against the organisation or their colleagues or reporting officers.

D6.11   An organisation must take caution not to draw any unsubstantiated correlation between an employee's performance and his discipline and grievance. It is important to appreciate that these three are distinctly different issues, and the methods or actions to deal with them are entirely different.

- For example, an employee who raises a grievance does not automatically signify that he is a weak performer. Even a good performer may raise a grievance. One should not presume that grievances are always borne out of performance-related reasons. It would be wrong to use performance counselling or other performance management actions to address grievances.

- Likewise, an employee who is a weak performer should not be treated as a delinquent who is out to create trouble. Performance and conduct are two separate issues. Weak performance, although undesirable, is not a misconduct. One should not presume that weak performance arises out of ill-discipline or bad conduct on the part of the employee. An employee who is exemplary in conduct may genuinely be deficient in performance, say, due to knowledge or skills gap or weak learning ability. It would be wrong to use disciplinary tools or actions to address performance issues.

D6.12   In some instances, however, there is the possibility that an employee may be both weak in performance as well as poor in conduct. It may be a case of one attribute leading to the other. For example, an employee who falls into weak performance may quickly lose his motivation and as frustration builds up, may take on an anti-organisation stance and engage in actions that harm the organisation's interest or do not conform to the organisation's prescribed behavioural standards. The reverse can also be true. An employee with poor conduct may lose his focus at work and eventually slip into underperformance. Whatever the case, the bottom line is that the organisation must base its assessment strictly on evidence of the employee's performance and conduct, and not make any presumption to couple the two attributes automatically.

D6.13   The manner to handle weak performance is discussed in this chapter. For the proper way to handle employee grievances, please refer to Volume E, Chapter E4 "Grievance Handling". And for the proper manner to handle bad conduct (or misconduct), please refer to Volume E, Chapter E7 "Disciplinary Framework for Misconduct".

Purpose and Importance of Managing Weak Performers

D6.14   The primary purpose of managing weak performers is to preserve or enhance the performance culture of the organisation. An organisation must send a clear message to its employees that weak performance cannot be tolerated or accommodated beyond a certain level or duration in the organisation. Weak performers should be managed "up" and if that fails, managed "out". Even when the organisation is doing well, it must not neglect the need to manage weak performance and take prompt and reasonable actions.

Manage Up or Out

D6.15   The best outcome in managing a weak performer is for the employee to level up his performance and attain a satisfactory level. This is what is commonly referred to as managing "up" an employee.

D6.16   However, not all cases will have a positive outcome. Some weak performers will fail to level up their performance despite efforts to help them improve.

In such circumstances, the organisation may have no option but to terminate the employee's employment. This is what is commonly referred to as managing "out" an employee.

D6.17 Basically, by managing a weak performer "up", and if that fails, "out", it will eliminate weak performance and not allow it to take hold within the organisation, as otherwise weak performance will exact a long-term cost to the organisation. This is elaborated below.

The Cost of Weak Performance

D6.18 Invariably, weak performance from employees will cause many adverse effects on the organisation. The longer weak performance persists in an organisation, the more ramifying the effects will be. These include the following:

(a) a decline in productivity for the organisation;
(b) a decline in staff morale, motivation and commitment of employees, affecting both weak and good performers;
(c) a degradation in service quality;
(d) the eventual fall in overall organisational performance and capability; and
(e) the long-term survival of the organisation being jeopardised if poor performance is pervasive.

D6.19 The above adverse effects will befall in an escalating manner like a disease slowly taking hold and bringing sickness to a body. A silent but steady killer of sorts. The initial effects may not be immediately felt, which is the reason why organisations may be complacent and show inertia in managing their weak performers. It is also common to find line managers wanting to be nice guys and avoid going through the arduous task of dealing with weak performers. If the organisation is complacent or too forgiving, some managers will take advantage to avoid or delay as much as possible in dealing with the weak performers. Some of these managers may leave their departments (transfer out) or organisation (retire or resign), thus leaving the unpleasant task to be handled by their successors. Imagine if most of the managers adopt the same attitude.

D6.20 If an organisation does not take proactive steps to address weak performance, the following events will unfold gradually but surely:

→ It will send the wrong message to its employees that it is acceptable to give sub-par performance.

→ This message will gradually take root in the organisational culture and will thwart other organisational initiatives to drive performance and excellence.

→ Employees who are good performers will become cynical and put off by the impunity enjoyed by underperforming colleagues and view them as free riders to the organisation's reward system.

→ High performers want to work with people whom they can respect and learn from and desire to immerse in an environment of excellence to feel adequately challenged and stimulated. An organisation that is nonchalant about performance and excellence will frustrate the high performers.

→ Without a culture of excellence, the organisation will find it difficult to attract and retain high performers.

→ Weak performers being less mobile in employment will show lower attrition, while high performers being more mobile will show higher attrition.

→ Over time, the population of weak performers will grow and will cause the organisation's overall performance to level down.

→ The weak performance culture will erode competitiveness and jeopardise the long-term survival of the organisation.

Causes of Weak Performance

D6.21   Weak performance may arise from a myriad of causes; some may be viewed as the employee's own accountability, while others not quite so, in that the organisation must also share the "blame" for bringing about the undesirable phenomenon of underperformance of employees. The plausible causes of weak performance are discussed below:

(a) *Job Mismatch*
An employee may be wrongly fitted into a job that is not suitable for him. It may be that the job requires a different personality from what the employee is, and/or a different set of competencies from what the employee possesses. Job mismatch can be quite a common occurrence

for new employees joining an organisation, especially so if the employee is a new entrant to the job market, or if he is a mid-career person making a career switch. He may not have enough self-awareness of his own intrinsic strengths and weaknesses, as well as likes and dislikes of job tasks. Organisations that do not describe a job accurately enough in their recruitment process compound the likelihood of job mismatch. Job mismatch does not only afflict new joiners; it may also occur when an organisation implements job transfers for its existing employees, without giving sufficient consideration as to whether the new job posting is suitable for the employee. With job mismatch, the result is often weak performance from the employee. Even if the employee puts in his best effort to stay afloat, over the long term, it will not be sustainable and will only lead to sub-optimal results.

(b) Cultural Misfit

At times, even if the job is suitable for a new joiner, the organisational culture may also make or break the performance of the employee. For example, an executive from the private sector may not adapt well to the working culture in the public service and this can materially affect his performance, even if he is fully competent for the job.

(c) Skill or Knowledge Obsolescence or Deficiency

In today's age and era, change is a constant at the workplace. Job processes are continually being automated and replaced by technology and digitalisation. Job skills and knowledge must evolve alongside. A lot of skills and knowledge that are relevant today will become obsolete. It is fair to say that organisations, while getting output from their employees, have a share of responsibility to retrain them to keep their skills and knowledge current and relevant to their jobs or trades. Employees must also embrace an attitude of wanting to learn and take ownership of upskilling and reskilling. The transition must be anticipated and managed systematically. If the organisation lacks the foresight and neglects this change preparation, the employees will eventually become incompetent in their jobs and underperform.

(d) Lack of Aptitude for the Job

In some instances, as job requirements evolve and the organisation provides the necessary training to help the affected employees upgrade their skills and knowledge, the employees may however be unable to keep up. This may not be due to the lack of trying on the part of the employees but rather due to a lack of aptitude or capacity to learn.

(e) *Poor Attitude or Commitment*

On the other hand, sometimes, an employee may resist change or show disinterest in learning new skills/knowledge. This poor attitude will lead to the employee becoming a weak performer. In other cases, an employee may be competent in his job but shows a pure lack of commitment or diligence to perform. The poor attitude may even be deliberate and borders on defiance. At times, it may also be that the employee is facing personal/family or health problems, and these underlying factors affect his focus and commitment at work. In some instances, an employee may also slide backwards due to resentment over a matter (say, he may not be happy with the organisation's policy or decision in rejecting a request from him).

Dealing with Weak Performance in New Employees

D6.22   Most organisations impose a probation period for new employees joining service, typically 3–6 months depending on the seniority level of the job. The purpose of the probation period is to allow the organisation to have the opportunity to assess whether the new employee is competent for the job and a suitable fit for the organisation. It also allows the new employee to assess his liking for the organisation.

D6.23   Very often, the tendency is for an organisation to cut the new employee some slack during his probation period, on the consideration that he is new to his job. Some line managers are soft-hearted. If the new employee selected/recruited by the line manager is not shaping up, the manager may be inclined to be soft and not prepared to admit that it has been a mistake hiring the person. Work targets may be set lower than the actual standard expected of a full-functioning employee. While it may be the organisation's kind way of showing empathy to a new employee, this may not be an entirely wise move. As the probation period is a precious window of opportunity for the organisation to assess the employee, it should make effective use of the probation period. The organisation should critically assess the new employee as comprehensively as possible, by subjecting him to various challenges on the job. Considering that the employee is unfamiliar with the new job, the focus of the assessment can be on the employee's learning ability, core competencies (which are independent of the job or operational nuances), as well as his organisational fit.

D6.24   Throughout the probation period, it is important for the reporting officer to closely monitor the new employee's performance. The probation period must not be treated in a cursory manner like a mere administrative routine. The assessment of the employee must be thorough and honest.

Deficiency in Performance

D6.25   At any time during the probation period, should a new employee show any deficiency in his learning ability or core competencies or display a poor work attitude that affects his performance, the reporting officer must manage the employee proactively and systematically as follows:

(a) Communicate personally to the employee, highlight the specific areas of his underperformance and/or poor work attitude and specify the remedial actions that the employee must take to close the performance gap(s). Document the conversation.

(b) Continue to monitor the employee's performance closely. If there is no evidence of progressive improvement shown, inform the employee personally and highlight those specific areas where performance gap still exists. Give a deadline. Inform the employee that if he does not show any progressive improvement by the deadline, the organisation has the discretion to terminate his employment without waiting for the probation period to expire. Document the conversation.

D6.26   Organisations must be cognisant that not all new employees will receive unfavourable feedback well. Some may choose to leave, especially if the labour market is tight. Notwithstanding this dilemma, organisations must do the necessary to assess and provide honest feedback to their new employees. It is better to lose the new employee if the fit is not there, rather than add on a weak performer to the organisation.

Poor Fit with Organisational Culture

D6.27   Many organisations put their new employees through a structured induction/orientation programme to help them navigate the organisational system (for example, the organisation's history and culture, its hierarchical structure and the approval levels to get work done). Additionally, many organisations also have a buddy system where a suitable peer colleague would be assigned as a buddy to the new employee to help him integrate into the team and peer social circle. However, in spite of these support systems, not all new employees will assimilate and settle in well into their organisations.

Organisational fit depends very much on individual personalities and personal preferences. A misfit in culture can be so pronounced that it impedes the employee's work performance severely enough to make him an underperformer. Or the employee may become difficult to manage over the long term, thus making it a sub-optimal outcome for both the organisation and the employee.

Extended Probation

D6.28   An organisation should have a provision in its employment contract to allow the extension of the probation of a new employee if it needs more time to assess the employee. The organisation has the discretion to decide on the length of the extended probation. Typically, the extended probation is equal to the length of the first probation or may be half of it.

D6.29   Extension of probation should be considered if, and only if, the organisation feels that given more time, there is a fair chance for the employee to fully prove himself in performance and pass probation eventually. On the other hand, if the organisation assesses that the employee is clearly unsuitable and has a low chance of passing probation even if given more time, extending his probation will not serve a useful purpose.

D6.30   The extension of probation should be communicated personally to the employee as well as in writing. The specific areas of underperformance and remedial actions required from the employee to close the performance gaps must be stated clearly. The employee should also be informed that if he fails his extended probation, he will be terminated in employment.

Exit via Termination or Resignation

D6.31   Contractually, an organisation may terminate the employment of a new employee at any time during the probation period (including the extended probation period). There is no obligation for the organisation to wait till the expiry of the probation period to do so. But the organisation may also choose to let the entire probation period or extended probation period run its full course, so as to give the new employee the maximum time possible to prove himself and turn things around. However, at times, the organisation may already assess the new employee to be clearly unsuitable and even if he is given more time, there is a low chance for him to succeed. In such circumstances, it would be practical to signal to or advise the employee to leave without waiting for the probation period to end. By being resolute, both parties will not waste more time and can move on earlier.

D6.32   The termination of employment should be communicated personally to the employee and in writing. As a good practice, the organisation (the management or Human Resource) should document the employee's underperformance or other factors that render him unsuitable. The discipline to document the basis of the termination action is to check that the organisation has acted objectively and responsibly and that the termination decision was not arbitrary or at the whim of the line manager.

D6.33   In many instances, when a new employee is made aware that he is not likely to pass probation, he may opt to resign instead of being terminated in employment by the organisation. The organisation should allow this (and even nudge the employee to do so) as resignation is a less contentious (and face-saving) manner for the organisation and the employee to part ways over a failed hiring.

D6.34   It is pertinent to point out that once an employee is confirmed in employment, handling weak performance will become more onerous (see elaboration in the next section). Therefore, it is important for the organisation to make effective use of the probation period to critically assess a new employee's suitability to remain in employment. If a new employee is unsuitable, it is vital to manage him out promptly, either via termination (by the organisation) or resignation (by the employee).

Dealing with Weak Performance in Existing Employees

D6.35   When an existing employee (that is, those who are already confirmed in employment) falls into weak performance, the organisation will need to find a solution to rectify the problem, as weak performance will exact a long-term heavy cost to the organisation if left unaddressed. The solution must however be targeted and matched to the cause of the weak performance. Actions that do not address the cause(s) will be unproductive and ineffective.

Job Transfer

D6.36   If an incumbent employee who is formerly well-performing suddenly falls into weak performance after being posted to a new job position, it usually signifies a mismatch of the person to the job. However, the organisation must first ascertain whether it is due to lack of effort or commitment on the part of the employee. At times, an employee may resist new challenges, preferring to remain in the same job for many years, at the risk of becoming silo (or narrow) in skills and knowledge, which is not good for his long-term employability. If this is the case, the organisation must render career counselling to the employee to let him understand the critical need for him to broaden his job exposure to enhance his employability. This is especially so if his current job position is at risk of facing obsolescence. Additionally, job transfers within the organisation are the management's prerogative (if the transfer does not entail a change to the detriment of an employee with regard to his terms of employment) and are done either to cater to operational requirements or as part of its talent management strategy to develop and enhance employees' capability. Over-accommodating employees' preferences will impede the organisation's resource utilisation as well as its long-term capability development.

D6.37   If the organisation is satisfied that a lack of effort/commitment and/or resistance to new job challenges on the part of the employee is ruled out as the probable causes, then the organisation must consider whether it is a mismatch of the person to the job. A fact-finding interview with the employee and line manager would be necessary. It may be that the new job posting requires a different personality from what the employee is, and/or a different set of competencies from what the employee possesses or is capable of. If it is a case of job mismatch, then the solution would be to re-fit the employee to another job. A good job posting should be a balance between leveraging sufficiently on the employee's natural strengths and yet give enough room to stretch the employee out of his comfort zone to provide new learning.

Skills and Knowledge Upgrading

D6.38   If an employee's weak performance arises out of skills and knowledge obsolescence, the organisation should bear some responsibility for it. After all, an organisation has a moral duty to help its employees keep their skills and knowledge current and relevant to their jobs, and systematically and proactively train and re-train its employees to move in tandem with the evolvement of their jobs. If this is not already done with foresight, then at least at the signs of weak performance shown by employees, the organisation must quickly take remedial action and expedite the skills and knowledge upgrading for its employees.

Performance Management Protocol

D6.39   If an employee's weak performance is not due to a job mismatch or skills/ knowledge obsolescence, then the most probable cause would be poor work attitude, as in the lack of commitment or diligence to perform. In such instances, the organisation must systematically manage the employee's performance to rehabilitate him back to a level of satisfactory performance. This calls for a structured performance management protocol for managing weak performers. More is elaborated in the next section.

Weak Performers in Super Competitive Organisations

D6.40   In a super competitive organisation where high performance is a norm, it is common for an employee (typically professional and executive) to voluntarily leave the organisation once he is informed that his performance is below expectation. Where the performance goals and work targets are clear and specific, the employee may, on his own initiative, approach his line manager or Human Resource to work out an amicable parting of ways, usually by resignation. These professionals and executives are typically paid competitively and they take it as their side of the bargain to deliver what is expected of them. Since these employees will work out their own exits, there is usually no need to wait for the year-end appraisal to give them a negative appraisal. Neither is there a need to trigger a structured performance management protocol to manage their weak performance. The exits of these employees are usually quiet and hassle-free, much as non-events for the organisation.

Weak Performers in Small Enterprises

D6.41   Most small and medium enterprises (SMEs) are lean in manpower due to their tight budget. When work teams are small, every member counts and each must pull his own weight, as often there are few or hardly any other employees to fill the gap for the weak performer and the SME will not have the budget to hire an extra headcount to keep the work moving. For this reason, most SMEs can ill afford to accommodate weak performers and must manage their weak performers expediently.

D6.42   In reality however, most SMEs do not have in place any structured performance management protocol in the form of a Performance Improvement Plan (PIP) as practised in large organisations (the PIP is covered in detail under the section "Performance Management Protocol for Weak Performers"). With small work teams, it is common for the boss (owner) to work closely with most of his employees. That being the case, weak performance will often quickly surface to the attention of the management/boss (which is unlike the case in large organisations where a weak performer may lie low and "hide" under the radar). The general practice in SMEs is that once alerted to a weak performer, the reporting officer (or boss himself) will counsel the said employee to level up within a specified (usually short) deadline, failing which he will be terminated in employment.

D6.43   The expedient way of managing weak performers by SMEs is possible because most SMEs are non-unionised. In the case of unionised organisations, the unions are likely to insist that the employee undergoes a structured PIP so as to give him a full and final opportunity to level up his performance before he faces termination in employment.

D6.44   While many SMEs want to shed their weak performers expediently and in a fuss-free manner, this is not always possible if hiring is difficult in a tight labour market. Quite often, if the sub-performance of an employee is not "crippling", the SME may have to show restraint and tolerate the sub-performance for longer or until such time a replacement can be hired.

Performance Management Protocol for Weak Performers

D6.45   Large and established organisations typically have in place a systematic and structured performance management protocol to manage their weak performers. The performance management protocol typically consists of these steps that are undertaken in sequential order:

Performance Management Protocol for Weak Performers

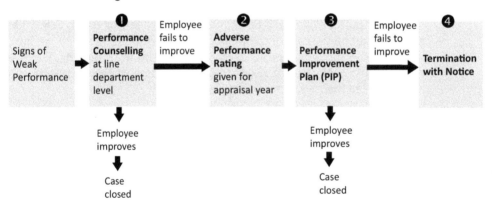

Performance Counselling

D6.46   In a best-case scenario, a reporting officer should always be closely in touch with how his direct report is performing on the job at all times.

Through regular performance feedback and coaching (if it is done), any slack in performance will be picked up by the reporting officer. The reporting officer should do a first round of performance counselling to the employee.

D6.47 The primary purpose of performance counselling is to address performance issues at the earliest opportunity possible so that remedial action can be taken by the employee promptly to close his performance gaps. This will reduce the possible negative consequences for both the employee and the organisation should the performance issue go unaddressed and drag on. The cost to the organisation will be a loss of productivity and effectiveness, while for the employee, it may well lead to a blemish in his career record.

D6.48 Performance counselling should not be seen as something "ominous" or take on any tone of "censure". It should be viewed as a normal (albeit a bit more intense and assertive) way of performance feedback and coaching from the reporting officer, with a sharper focus on the areas that the employee needs to quickly improve on. It is in fact part and parcel of an employee's learning process as he navigates and adjusts to the organisation's expectations while managing his own work tempo.

D6.49 Performance counselling is a process taken at the reporting officer or line manager level. That being the case, the format of performance counselling is usually less structured and often depends on the personal management style of the individual reporting officer or line manager. Human Resource may be alerted but should not be involved in the performance counselling session. Notwithstanding, to be effective, performance counselling should incorporate the following components and steps:

(a) *Performance Requirements*
Explain the job requirements and organisation's expectations clearly again to the employee, in terms of (i) work targets and (ii) competency-based behavioural standards. Ensure that there is no room for ambiguity. Cite work examples or illustrations specific to his job context.

(b) *Performance Gaps*
Review the employee's performance and point out the shortfalls against the requirements. Be specific. Cite actual work examples, incidents or any feedback from other sources (such as other line managers whom the employee has work interactions with).

(c) *Improvements Needed*

List the remedial actions and improvements needed from the employee to close his performance gaps. Be descriptive. Give illustrations specific to his job context.

(d) *Help and Support*

Ask the employee what help he needs to close his performance gaps, for example, on-the-job coaching and training. Arrange to offer the help/support as reasonable. The employee must take some ownership and cannot hold the organisation at ransom over the help/support to be offered to him to close his performance gaps. The employee should fundamentally be qualified for the job that he is hired for or is holding. For example, if the employee is an engineer, one expects him to possess engineering expertise befitting an engineer, and not expect the organisation to offer him training in basic engineering. Likewise, a human resource manager is expected to possess basic to advanced knowledge on human resource management concepts and not expect the organisation to train him in human resource management from scratch.

(e) *Monitoring and Review*

Inform the employee that his performance will be monitored, in order to track his progress and ensure that he is on the right track. Set a schedule to hold one-to-one sessions to review his progress.

D6.50 Performance counselling must be distinguished from the Performance Improvement Plan (PIP) which is administered to weak performers who have officially been assessed as having failed to achieve the threshold/minimum performance level and have been given an adverse performance rating (after due moderation) at the end of the annual appraisal period. While performance counselling is initiated and done at the line manager level, the PIP process is often initiated by the organisation's management (or Human Resource, on behalf of management) that serves to put an employee on official notice that he is given a last chance to improve his performance, failing which he will face the possibility of termination in employment.

D6.51 Because performance counselling is taken at the line manager level, it may go undocumented and therefore is usually not entered into the employee's personal file record. Indeed, there is often no real necessity for a strict documentation regime for performance counselling, since it is viewed as part and parcel of performance coaching by a line manager. That said, some circumstances warrant proper documentation. Where the line manager has reason to believe that an employee may persist to be a weak performer and may eventually be placed under an official PIP process, then it is best for the documentation to start from the performance counselling stage. This is so that the organisation can trace the entire length of time, the resources put in, and the opportunities given to the employee to improve his performance before the organisation takes punitive action on the employee. If the organisation is unionised, there is a stronger need to do documentation, as the employee may seek representation by the union which will invariably query the management. Where there is such necessity for documentation, the line manager should record the content of the performance counselling (with dates specified) and forward it to Human Resource to be entered into the employee's personal file record for future reference.

Adverse Performance Rating

D6.52 Performance counselling is meant to guide an employee to close his performance gaps. The ideal outcome is that with more intensive guidance and nudging, the employee will be able to attain the required performance level. However, not all cases have positive outcomes. Sometimes, in spite of repeated and prolonged performance counselling, an employee may not improve sufficiently and may persist to be a weak performer.

D6.53 An employee who persists in his weak performance will fail to meet the overall threshold/minimum performance level for the appraisal year. At the end of the appraisal year, he will be officially assigned an adverse performance rating (after the due moderation process).

D6.54 The key point to note about assigning an adverse performance rating to an employee is that it must not come as a "surprise" to the employee. In other words, during the course of the appraisal year, the reporting officer or line manager should already have flagged out the employee's performance gaps and carried out performance counselling with him. The performance counselling should have been documented. If the employee has never been prior informed of his performance gaps and has not been given any performance counselling, he will more likely challenge the adverse performance rating. If the employee is represented by the union, it would probably argue that the employee must first be made aware of his performance gaps and given a fair opportunity to improve before an adverse rating is warranted. The employee's contention would be weaker if the work targets and performance expectations as well as the actual achievements are clear and evidence-based.

D6.55   The performance moderation panel that reviews the line manager's recommendation for an adverse rating must be satisfied that there is adequate data/evidence on the employee's weak performance before endorsing such a rating. This is where documentation of the performance counselling comes in. Such documentation should be presented to the moderation panel. The adverse rating must not be a case of personal bias or victimisation by the line manager. In case of any challenge by the employee/union, the management must be able to defend the basis for the adverse rating.

Performance Improvement Plan

D6.56   When an employee has been assessed (and endorsed by the moderation panel) that his performance falls below the threshold/minimum performance level, he will be assigned officially with an adverse performance rating for the said appraisal period.

D6.57   The next step taken by most organisations is to place the employee on a Performance Improvement Plan (PIP). The PIP is viewed as a structured intervention process initiated by the management against the employee. It serves to put an employee on official notice that he is given a last chance to improve his performance, failing which he will face the possibility of termination in employment.

Trigger of PIP

D6.58   *Which adverse rating will trigger a PIP?*
It is important that the organisation has a clear policy on the trigger of PIP in adverse performance cases. Typically, all adverse ratings that fall below the threshold/minimum will trigger the PIP. However, some organisations choose to adopt a more lenient approach and will only trigger the PIP for the last (or worst) rating and not the second-last rating. An example is shown below. This conservative approach is probably an arrangement that the organisation has committed to the union. Fundamentally, the union recognises the gravity of the PIP; that once the PIP is triggered, the employee's employment is in jeopardy should he fail his PIP. Therefore, the union will tend to urge the management to go slow on triggering the PIP.

Overall Rating (with corresponding Performance Intervention)	
A	Outstanding contribution. Exceeds job requirements in many areas.
B	Major contribution. Fully met job requirements and exceeds in some areas.
C	Good contribution. Met job requirements.
D	Marginal contribution. Improvement needed in some areas of job requirements. → *Continue with Performance Counselling at line department level.*
E	Unacceptable outcomes. Major shortcomings in many areas of job requirements. Significant improvement needed for continued employment in current position. → *Trigger Performance Improvement Plan (PIP) by Human Resource on behalf of management.*

D6.59   Whatever policy the organisation decides to adopt on the trigger of PIP (that is, at which specific adverse rating the PIP will be triggered), what is important is the transparency of the policy and the consistency of application. The PIP policy should be stated in the Employee Handbook and/or the performance management framework and it warrants publicising it at the start of every new appraisal period. It would not do for the organisation to act at its whim and fancy to trigger the PIP selectively (or randomly) on some adverse performance cases and not others. An inconsistent practice will be challenged by the union and employee and will be seen as biased and not in good faith.

Timing to Initiate PIP

D6.60   The PIP is usually initiated immediately following the closing of the annual performance appraisal cycle, that is, after the performance moderation panel has endorsed the adverse rating for the employee. For example, if the moderation exercise and all the performance ratings of employees (of the preceding appraisal year from January to December) are finalised in March, the PIP can be initiated from 1 April. Typically, the responsibility rests upon

Human Resource (HR) to initiate the PIP process. In some large organisations, the respective line managers or department heads may be tasked to initiate and conduct the PIP for their employees and keep HR updated.

Length of PIP

D6.61   The organisation has the discretion to decide on the length of the PIP. Typically, the PIP is 3–6 months, depending on the seniority level of the job. The length may also depend on the nature of the job, because for certain jobs, it may not need that much time to see the employee's improvement in performance.

Communicating the PIP

D6.62   Typically, HR and the line manager/head will hold a joint session with the employee to inform him that he has been placed under the PIP. At the session, the following should be communicated clearly to the employee:

(a) the performance requirements that the employee must fulfil;
(b) the specific performance gaps of the employee (cite actual examples);
(c) the improvements needed from the employee (give illustrations);
(d) the length of the PIP period, that is, the deadline for the employee to meet his performance requirements;
(e) the interim reviews by the line manager during the course of the PIP; and
(f) the consequences of his failing the PIP, which is most likely termination of employment with notice. This should be stated with absolute clarity and assertiveness without any room for ambiguity whatsoever.

D6.63   At the joint session, the employee should be given an opportunity to seek clarifications and give feedback. On the improvements needed, the line manager/head may allow the employee to suggest the action plan for himself (which will be subject to the agreement of the line manager); this will help strengthen ownership and commitment from the employee.

D6.64   The joint session should be followed by issuing a PIP letter to the employee, stating all of the above communication points. It is a common practice for organisations to require the employee to sign an acknowledgement on the PIP letter. If the employee declines or refuses to sign the PIP letter, HR or the line manager should make a note on the copy retained by the organisation. In unionised organisations where the employee is represented by the union, HR will inform the union that the PIP letter has been issued to the employee.

Interim Reviews during PIP

D6.65   HR should institute interim reviews by the reporting officer (or line manager) during the course of the PIP. For example, if the PIP period is 3 months, the interim reviews may be held at the end of every month (end of Month 1 and Month 2); whereas if the PIP period is 6 months, the interim reviews may be held bimonthly (end of Month 2 and Month 4). The scheduled interim reviews should not preclude the reporting officer from engaging and guiding the employee at any time in the normal course of work interaction.

Outcomes of PIP

D6.66   There are two possible outcomes of the PIP, which are as follows:

(a) *Employee passes the PIP*
The employee makes sufficient improvement to close his performance gaps by or before the expiry date of the PIP. HR should issue a letter to the employee to inform him that he has met his performance requirements and has been taken off the PIP.

(b) *Employee fails the PIP*
The employee fails to make sufficient improvement to close his performance gaps by the expiry date of the PIP. HR and the line manager/head should hold a joint session with the employee to inform him of the negative outcome. HR should follow up with managing the employee out of the job, through termination, resignation or demotion. See more elaboration in the next subsections.

Extended PIP

D6.67   If the employee is represented by the union, should he fail his PIP, the union may appeal on his behalf to the organisation to allow an Extended PIP as the final chance to the employee. The management is at discretion to accede to or reject the appeal. That said, some organisations have by practice acceded to such appeals from the union on a "regular" basis, so much so that an Extended PIP becomes an expectation, or even an "entitlement".

D6.68   Generally, it is not advisable for an organisation to allow Extended PIP. After all, assuming that the organisation's performance management framework has been diligently followed through, the employee would already have undergone performance counselling at the line department level and have had ample opportunities to make improvements even before the PIP is triggered. Therefore, the PIP should be the final chance given to the employee. There should not be yet another final after the final. If an organisation makes an exception to allow an Extended PIP, say, to accede to strong appeal from the employee or union, or on account of extenuating circumstances, it is best that the organisation makes its position clear that it is a one-off special concession and not to be cited as a precedent for future cases.

Instituting Early PIP

D6.69   *Can a PIP be triggered <u>before</u> an employee is given an adverse performance rating?*
Some organisations may put an employee under PIP if he fails to improve after performance counselling, and not wait until the year-end appraisal; that is, the PIP is triggered even before the employee is officially given an adverse performance rating. The reason for doing so is to deal with the weak performer expediently. Understandably, going through the entire PIP route is a very long-drawn process, usually taking more than a year.

D6.70   Organisations that do not have the patience to carry weak performers for such protracted periods may choose to trigger a PIP if, at the performance counselling stage during the course of the appraisal year, there are already clear signs that the employee is not likely to meet performance requirements. However, taking such early action to trigger a PIP is usually only possible in non-unionised organisations. If an organisation is unionised, the union is likely to insist on "proof" of weak performance before an employee is officially put under PIP. To the union, a final performance rating that has gone through moderation by a moderation panel gives added assurance that the case is a bona fide one of weak performance. This is the union's way of protecting employees against any unfair bias or victimisation (say, a reporting officer may be overly strict in his assessment or may be wanting to manage the employee out for reasons other than weak performance).

D6.71   For non-unionised organisations, the onus to ensure that an early PIP is justified should rest on Human Resource. A reporting officer requesting to put an employee on early PIP should be required to surface the case to HR and the line head. HR should do the due diligence of reviewing the evidence of weak performance (for example, documentation of the employee's poor-quality work or mistakes) before instituting an early PIP.

Termination

D6.72   When the employee fails the PIP (or the Extended PIP), the next step is for the organisation to terminate his employment on account of poor performance. The organisation should be resolute in this decision, as otherwise, the performance management protocol would lose its purpose.

D6.73   Poor performance is not misconduct per se. Therefore, the termination must necessarily come with due notice or salary in lieu of notice. After informing the employee that he has failed to make sufficient improvement to pass the PIP, the organisation should issue a termination letter to serve notice of termination to the employee. The length of notice would be the contractual notice as provided in the employee's term of employment. Some organisations, on compassionate grounds, may provide a slightly longer notice to the employee. For instance, if the employee fails his PIP sometime in the last quarter of the year, and if his contractual notice ends just before Christmas, the organisation may allow the employee to stay till the end of the calendar year, so as to avoid the awkwardness for the employee leaving service just before Christmas. Likewise, if the employee's contractual notice ends just before, say, Chinese New Year (CNY), the organisation may allow the employee to stay till the end of the month after the CNY. The delay in executing the termination of employment is also sometimes done to enable the employee to qualify for his fixed bonus if it is due soon.

D6.74   In some instances, instead of letting the employee serve out the notice period, the organisation may instead pay salary in lieu of notice so that the employee may leave service immediately and avoid the awkwardness of serving out the notice. This practice is more common for middle to senior positions. Most employees will appreciate this approach, as it makes it easier for them to attend job interviews and/or start their new jobs elsewhere as quickly as possible.

Resignation

D6.75   It is fairly common to see some employees opting to resign once they are informed of being put on PIP, as they may feel embarrassed, although the PIP is confidential in nature. Some may also consider the PIP to be a blemish in their career record, and so prefer to start afresh elsewhere. Whereas some will attempt to go through and pass the PIP in a bid to remain in employment, but when informed of the failure to pass PIP, they would tender resignation to avoid bearing a record of being terminated in employment. Organisations are typically glad to accept the employee's resignation as an amicable parting of ways.

Demotion

D6.76 In some instances, an employee may negotiate to be reassigned to a lower job in order to save himself from being terminated in employment. The employee is more likely to be someone at a more mature age and finds it more difficult to find alternative employment elsewhere.

D6.77 A job that comes with a lower job grade than the employee's current job position will require a salary reduction and a demotion of the employee's job grade. The organisation should be at liberty to decide on the new salary, new salary range and new job grade for the employee, pegging to other employees in the same or equivalent job role.

D6.78 The organisation should consider the request for demotion favourably only when these conditions are met by the employee:

(a) The weak performance of the employee in the first place was not due to poor work attitude or low commitment. In other words, only employees with good/satisfactory work attitude deserve a second chance to remain in employment.

(b) The employee must possess the necessary competencies and attributes for the lower job. For example, if an Operations Manager fails his PIP, say, on account of poor skills in managing resources and supervising staff and requests to be reassigned as an Operations Executive, he may be considered favourably if he possesses adequate competencies to be effective as an Operations Executive. However, if he has failed his PIP on account of questionable competencies in the operation domain, then a demotion to a lower job role will not eliminate the problem.

D6.79 If the organisation decides to allow a demotion in lieu of terminating the employment of the employee, the organisation should document the reasons for doing so, including the organisation's assessment of the employee's suitability and competencies for the lower job role. A new appointment letter should also be issued to the employee, stating the new salary, new salary range and new job grade. The employee should be required to sign his acceptance on the appointment letter.

Union Representation and Appeal on Performance Issues

D6.80   In a unionised organisation, an employee who is a union member may seek representation by the union when he runs into performance problems. However, it is pertinent to note that it is a union member's personal choice whether to seek union representation or otherwise. One cannot presume that it is always the case. There may be union members who prefer to keep a low profile to preserve the confidentiality of their performance records instead of involving the union to represent them. Therefore, before the organisation engages with the union on an employee's performance matter, the organisation must first ascertain with the affected employee whether he plans to seek or has indeed sought union representation on the matter. The line manager and HR must however not influence or be perceived to influence or pressure the employee not to seek union representation. The message to the employee must be that it is entirely up to his choice.

D6.81   In some unionised organisations, the collective agreement may stipulate a requirement for the organisation to inform the union of any union member who is put on PIP. The collective agreement may even specify that a union representative must be present when the PIP is communicated to the employee.

D6.82   A union member may seek union representation at any of these stages:

(a) when he receives an adverse rating at the end of the appraisal year; or
(b) when he is put on PIP; or
(c) when he fails his PIP; or
(d) when he gets terminated in employment on account of poor performance.

D6.83   It is in the interest of the organisation to address any feedback or employee grievance as soon as it is raised by the union. This is because the later it is, the more onerous it will be for the organisation to handle. If the union/ employee raises the issue at any time before the employee is terminated in employment (on account of poor performance), the matter will be dealt with as an internal staff matter. However, if the employee is already terminated, the union/employee may resort to raising the matter to the external authorities. In the case of an employee who is a union member working in a unionised organisation, the union/employee has the option to appeal to the Minister for Manpower. Whereas for an employee who is a non-union member or working in a non-unionised organisation, the employee can appeal to the Employment Claims Tribunals (ECT).

D6.84 Once the appeal goes to the Minister or ECT, the organisation will be called upon to substantiate its performance assessment and termination action. If the organisation cannot substantiate the employee's poor performance, the termination may be viewed as baseless or without just cause, and the organisation will risk being ordered by the Minister or ECT (as applicable) to reinstate the employee or make compensation to the employee. Such an outcome may also cause some damage to the organisation's reputation.

D6.85 For the organisation to substantiate its performance assessment and termination decision, documentation of the evidence of the employee's poor performance is key. In the absence of documentation/evidence, the organisation will risk losing the case/defence. Therefore, whenever the line manager/head and Human Resource are alerted to a case of weak performance which has the potential to escalate into a PIP and termination case, diligence must be applied to the documentation of the case from start to end.

D6.86 Most small and medium enterprises (SMEs) do not have the resources to undertake a structured performance management protocol (including a PIP) carried out over a protracted time to deal with weak performers. In practice, it is common for SMEs to just verbally inform their weak performers that if they fail to improve within a specified deadline, they will be terminated in employment. However, as employees are increasingly aware of the appeal avenue to ECT, it is advisable for SMEs to put in place a proper PIP policy and practice, or at least document the evidence of the employees' weak performance and manage the cases carefully and responsibly, especially if a termination decision is made.

Confidentiality in Dealing with Performance Cases

D6.87 In dealing with performance cases, organisations must remember to observe confidentiality. An employee's performance is a confidential staff record.

D6.88 In observing confidentiality, the dos and don'ts for the organisation are summarised below:

(a) The organisation must not disclose an employee's performance record to any irrelevant parties. In holding discussions on an employee's performance matters, the organisation should confine it to only persons directly involved in managing the performance matter (for example, the line manager/head and Human Resource officers).

(b) It would be erroneous for the organisation to disclose information on an employee's performance record to the union without first obtaining explicit consent from the affected employee. For example, if the union requests the organisation to furnish a name list of employees who have been given adverse ratings, it is not proper for the organisation to furnish such a list without the expressed consent of the affected employees. If an employee (who is a union member) wishes to seek union representation for his performance issue, the organisation should first obtain the said employee's confirmation on this before engaging with the union or furnishing any confidential information on the case.

D6.89 An organisation cannot name and shame its poor performers publicly even if it is just to send a message to all its employees on upholding a strong performance culture in the organisation. Revealing the identity of poor performers publicly is a breach of staff confidentiality. Below is an iconic actual case:

Naming the Poor Performers Publicly at Surbana Jurong

On 14 January 2017, The Straits Times reported that Surbana Jurong terminated the employment of a number of employees as part of its performance management review. It was said that the terminations were not a retrenchment exercise, but "rather a small number of poor performers were communicated with and released".

In his email to all the staff, the Group Chief Executive Officer said that "the group cannot allow a small proportion of poor performers to weigh down the rest of the organisation". The Group Chief Executive Officer added that "there were no retrenchments".

Of the 54 employees who had been axed, 18 were members of either the Singapore Industrial and Services Employees' Union (SISEU) or Building Construction and Timber Industries Employees' Union (BATU). The company was criticised for the way they handled the cases. The two unions hit back through Facebook and challenged the company's assertion that these employees were poor performers. The terminations were done about two weeks before the Chinese New Year.

Following the public outcry, the company started talking to the two unions. Several days later, the company issued a joint statement with the two unions, highlighting that they were working closely to provide an "equitable and mutually agreeable arrangement" for the affected employees, and to help them find new employment. Eventually, the two unions reached a settlement with the management of Surbana Jurong to pay an ex gratia payment to the affected employees.

On 7 February 2017, then Manpower Minister Lim Swee Say, speaking in the Parliament, rapped Surbana Jurong for publicly labelling its employees as "poor performers". Minister Lim said the manner in which the company had laid off the 54 employees, followed by criticising them publicly in a strongly worded letter to all staff and a statement to the media was totally unacceptable. He added that all companies, especially major employers, are expected to conduct their HR practices in a responsible and progressive manner.

Conclusion

D6.90   It is best to minimise the incidences of weak performance. Stringent selection in the recruitment process and diligent performance assessment during the probation period are a must. Giving timely performance feedback and coaching and accurate and honest performance ratings will help give early signals for interventions and minimise the deterioration of performance within the organisation.

D6.91   Not proactively surfacing and managing weak performers and using retrenchment to part ways with them is not a good option and organisations should refrain from working on that premise. For further discussion on letting go of weak performers under the guise of retrenchment, please refer to Volume A, Chapter A10 "Retrenchment".

D6.92   Dealing with weak performers requires a structured protocol and a systematic follow-through. However, protocol and process aside, as with all people management functions, it takes an art to handle weak performers – to guide, motivate, counsel and push, in order to rehabilitate an employee back to satisfactory performance. It requires the line managers to have the willingness and patience to help the weak performers, and at the same time without compromising the need to uphold the organisation's performance standard.

D6.93   The accountability to manage weak performers rests with all layers of the organisation's management – from the reporting officers in being alert in spotting weak performance and being proactive in doing performance feedback and coaching and performance counselling, to the line heads and the performance moderation panel in being firm in assigning an adverse performance rating to the affected employees, to Human Resource in being diligent in following through with the Performance Improvement Plan for the affected employees, and to top management in being resolute in managing out the recalcitrant weak performers. In short, be proactive, timely, systematic and resolute.

D6.94   Managing weak performers "up" and if that fails, "out" is a serious people function. An organisation must never be laissez-faire about it, as otherwise the population of weak performers will gradually grow in size and will take over defining the organisation's performance culture. Indifference or nonchalance in managing weak performers certainly impedes an organisation's continual progress and success. In today's highly competitive operating environment, an organisation that trends downwards in performance instead of upwards is set for an ominous end. Organisations must surely avoid this outcome.

References

1. "Unionists Speak Out Against Sacking of Surbana Jurong Employees". The Straits Times, 21 January 2017
2. "Surbana Jurong Says It Could Have Better Managed the Dismissal of 54 Workers". The Straits Times, 24 January 2017
3. "Parliament: Surbana Jurong Labelling Workers It Fired as Poor Performers Not Acceptable, says Lim Swee Say". The Straits Times, 8 February 2017

Performance Management and Industrial Relations

Focus of this Chapter

In the last six chapters, we have covered different aspects of performance management in detail. As performance management is very much a sensitive people issue, employees may have an emotional reaction when their performance report cards are revealed to them. In unionised organisations, a performance management issue may be taken up as an industrial relations matter and escalate into an industrial dispute.

This chapter is dedicated to the industrial relations dimension of performance management. It discusses the typical industrial relations issues and the concerns of the aggrieved employees and also highlights the common approaches taken by unions and employees in seeking resolution on performance management issues.

The Law and Contract on Performance Management

Absence of Employment Act and Contractual Provisions

D7.1   In Singapore, the Employment Act (EA) is silent on performance management. Implicitly, it is treated as a matter to be dealt with by the employers or between the employees and their employers. There is also no legal requirement to include performance management as a key employment term to be specified in the employment contract. It is rare to find employers incorporating any elements of their performance management frameworks in their employment contracts. The performance management framework and processes are normally mentioned in the organisation's employee handbook or shared as a standalone staff circular or document.

D7.2   In view of the above, an employee has no recourse to fall back on the law to pursue a case regarding a performance issue except through an appeal to the Employment Claims Tribunals arising from wrongful termination. He also cannot rely on his contractual right unless a performance matter has impacted or breached a term in his contract (such as his contractual salary being cut on account of his performance). An employee working in a unionised organisation who is represented by a trade union however enjoys some protection under the Industrial Relations Act (as elaborated in the next subsection).

Negotiation as an Industrial Matter

D7.3   The Industrial Relations Act (IRA) permits a trade union to negotiate with a unionised organisation on "industrial matters" which have been defined as "*matters pertaining to the relations of employers and employees which are connected with the employment or non-employment or the terms of employment, transfer of employment or the conditions of work of any person*". However, 6 items have been classified as non-negotiable: (a) hiring, (b) assignment of duties, (c) job transfers, (d) promotion, (e) dismissal and reinstatement and (f) retrenchment. Performance management per se is not one of the 6 non-negotiable items. Arguably, performance management issues may be subject to collective bargaining (that is, negotiation by the union) as they pertain to the relations between the employee and employer and are connected with employment and hence would be classified as "industrial matters" which are negotiable.

D7.4   While the IRA may allow a union to negotiate on performance management issues, the actual practice does not bear this out. Unions generally do not proactively and vigorously bargain on such matters. Organisations seldom involve or consult their unions when they implement or change their performance appraisal frameworks. Even in organisations that embrace good labour–management relations, while the management may engage the union to seek its feedback when it is considering a revamp of its performance management framework, this engagement is not viewed as a negotiation per se, as it is usually the management that will eventually decide on the construct of the performance management framework.

D7.5   While unions are seldom involved in the construct of an organisation's performance management framework, they are however keenly concerned with the applications of performance appraisal results, such as how an employee's rating will affect his salary increment and bonus, or in the case of an employee nearing statutory retirement age, how it will affect his qualifying for re-employment. If the union perceives that the organisation applies the performance ratings of employees unfairly or unreasonably in a manner that affects the employees in monetary or employment terms, the union will represent the employees to negotiate with the organisation. The negotiation may be either on a collective or individual employee basis, depending on the issues and the number of employees involved, as provided under the IRA.

Does Unionisation Impact Performance Appraisal?

D7.6   *Will the mere presence of a union in the organisation influence how performance appraisal is conducted?*
Unionised organisations and their Human Resource (HR) departments are not likely to say that there is any effect. The official line is likely to be one that the organisation believes in driving a performance culture and performance appraisals will be done in a fair, progressive and responsible manner. However, the real picture at the line department level may be more nebulous. Some line managers may be abrasive, unreasonable or high-handed in doing performance appraisals. Favouritism and personal bias (whether consciously or otherwise) can be quite common. The presence of a union will to some extent provide a check on such behaviours as line managers are likely to exercise more restraint to avoid employees complaining to the union. Some unions and organisations may have jointly established some procedures or protocols for reporting officers or line managers to observe which aim to give more transparency and fairness to managing employees including their performance. These are good for the organisations and employees.

D7.7   There may however also be less than positive (and unintended) effects arising from the presence of a union. In unionised organisations where the union presence is strong and the industrial relations climate is vigorous, line managers may "learn" to avoid getting into a tussle with the union on people issues, including performance appraisal. The line manager is aware that giving an employee an adverse performance rating may require him to face a barrage of questioning, first from HR and next from the union if the employee raises his grievance to the union. At times, depending on the prevailing priorities or concerns of HR, the line manager may even be quietly advised on the side to "soften" his stance in the interest of labour–management harmony or other bigger industrial relations issues. After some time, line managers may just relegate. Rightly or otherwise, the line managers gradually become conditioned to being more prudent (and even wary) in giving adverse performance ratings. Some may turn to being "nice guys" and give "safe" performance ratings to employees even if the cases warrant harsher ratings. Such prudence is in fact just mere avoidance.

D7.8   While such a prudent or politically expedient approach in performance appraisal will avoid industrial relations issues and reduce the incidence of employee grievances, unfortunately, it will over time lower the performance bar and stifle the building of a vibrant performance culture in the organisation. Employees are not better off as they will be deprived of knowing their actual performance levels and the opportunities to learn and improve themselves.

Hot Button Issues on Performance Management

D7.9   Employees, particularly rank-and-file employees and junior executives, are generally not enthusiastic about performance goals setting, performance feedback and coaching. Their primary concern is the year-end performance rating, as it will affect their performance-linked rewards (such as salary increment, bonus and promotion). Those who are nearing retirement age and whose performance has been hovering on the borderline will also be concerned about whether they will qualify for re-employment.

Common Employee Grievances on Performance Appraisal

D7.10   Invariably, at the conclusion of a year-end performance appraisal exercise, not all employees will walk away happy or satisfied with their performance ratings. The common reasons for their dissatisfaction usually stem from their perception (which may be true or otherwise) that unfairness has occurred in the performance appraisal. These perceptions of unfairness may involve one or more of the following:

(a) favouritism shown by a line manager towards his favourite employee;

(b) prejudice shown by a line manager towards an employee whom he dislikes;

(c) prejudice shown by a line manager towards an employee who has a close relationship with the predecessor manager whom the said line manager is not on good terms with;

(d) favouritism shown by a line manager towards those employees who were his ex-staff from his previous organisation and who have followed him over to the current organisation;

(e) preferential treatment for new graduate entrants vis-a-vis non-graduate long-serving staff;

(f) preferential treatment given to sales and revenue-generating staff and neglecting backroom support staff; and

(g) a good rating given by the direct reporting officer (as claimed by the reporting officer) but is subsequently slashed by the counter-signing officer or performance moderation panel.

D7.11   In unionised organisations, an employee who is a union member and who is aggrieved over his performance results will usually seek help from the union to represent him to raise his grievance through the organisation's grievance handling procedure or performance appraisal appeal avenue.

Low Performance Rating on account of High Sick Leave

D7.12   One of the hot button industrial relations issues regarding performance appraisal is when the organisation is seen to mark down an employee's performance rating on account of high Sick Leave (SL) record. Some organisations frown on employees with high SL consumption and view them as unreliable and disruptive to teamwork and operations, and therefore assign a default rating or put a cap on the rating for such employees. This approach is controversial. One should not confuse performance with SL consumption. Performance appraisal should strictly be based on an employee's performance and not on SL consumption per se. This has been discussed in Chapter D4 "Performance Appraisal". The crux of the matter lies in whether the employee's high SL has adversely impacted his performance and if so, his performance should be assessed and rated accordingly. On the other hand, if an employee puts in decent (or good) performance despite incurring high SL (say, he puts in extra hours to make up for his SL absence or he works smart to achieve results), his performance should be rated accordingly.

D7.13   In recent years, the tripartite partners (the Ministry of Manpower, Singapore National Employers' Federation and National Trades Union Congress) have made repeated exhortations to employers to give consideration to employees' health and well-being and therefore no employee should be penalised on account of high SL. With this sanction, employees and unions have become more vigilant on this matter. Organisations need to tread carefully on this issue. If an organisation marks down an employee's performance rating on account of high SL but is unable to substantiate that the high SL has adversely impacted the employee's performance or caused disruptions to work, then it is most certainly inviting censure and creating an industrial relations problem for itself.

Low Performance Rating on account of Disciplinary Record

D7.14   Another hot button industrial relations issue is the organisation assigning a default adverse performance rating or scaling down the rating (usually by one notch) if the employee has committed misconduct. It is debatable whether this is entirely fair as one may argue that the employee has already been punished for the misconduct and hence should not be penalised for another time unless his performance has been adversely affected arising from the misconduct.

D7.15   Fundamentally, employees should be appraised based on their fulfilment of performance requirements. The relevant question is this: *Taking all performance requirements as a whole, what weightage does the misconduct bear to the whole?* Viewing the misconduct vis-à-vis the sum total of the employee's performance requirements would be a fairer way to decide on the performance rating for the employee. Please refer to Chapter D4 "Performance Appraisal" for a more detailed discussion.

D7.16   Whatever policy or practice the organisation adopts in coupling an employee's performance rating with a misconduct record, it calls for prudence and reasonableness. If the organisation is unionised, it pays for the organisation to secure the union's acceptance of its policy. What is important too is the consistency in applying the policy. It will not do if the organisation scales down the performance rating selectively for some affected employees and not others.

Low Performance Rating on account of Absence due to Union Activities

D7.17   Not all unionised organisations enjoy harmonious labour–management relations. In some organisations where the relationship is tense, performance appraisal can be the wick that starts a fire.

> Case Example
> A union official was given an adverse performance rating. The line manager cited the reason that the said employee (union official) had spent too much time attending to union matters and had neglected his primary work as a salaried employee in the organisation.

D7.18   Such incidents can be explosive and potentially detrimental to labour–management relations. The "hardline" stance may be taken by the organisation's management or may be isolated cases of some line managers who focus clinically on assessing their employees on work deliverables and do not care about the relationship matters between the union and the organisation. Fundamentally, it boils down to how the organisation's management and its line managers view the union officials'/leaders' contribution to the organisation. If the organisation views that the union is value-adding by helping to align, unify and galvanise employees towards achieving organisational goals, it will see the union officials' absence from work (due to union activities) in that light. Whereas if labour–management relations are less than cordial, the organisation may view the union as disruptive or not value-adding.

D7.19   In the instance where it is an isolated case of a line manager being hardline in his approach and it does not represent the organisation's stance, usually, the management (or Human Resource) will intervene to salvage the situation and avoid an explosive fallout with the union. To prevent this type of incident, often, the headcount for the active union official may be put under the Human Resource department so that the salary cost of the active union official does not affect the cost of any line department. Alternatively, he may be posted to a department which is headed by a line head who better appreciates industrial relations or takes a more amiable stance with the union.

Negotiation Outcomes on Performance Issues

D7.20   In a unionised organisation, an employee who is not satisfied with his performance rating may seek union representation to raise his grievance to the management (assuming he has already attempted in vain to resolve his grievance through the internal appeal avenue or grievance handling procedure). How a union responds tends to be somewhat individualised for each union; it mostly depends on the thinking of its key union officials. Some unions (union officials) may take a strong and very protective position for their members, whereas others go for a more measured (cautious) approach, considering the significance of such grievances relative to the larger industrial relations issues, to avoid an affront with the management.

D7.21   There are several underlying reasons why a union may prefer to take a measured approach with regard to dealing with performance-related issues:

(a) First, performance management is a subjective matter that is often difficult to pin down on what's right and what's wrong. If the union has a good relationship with the management, it will be mindful that being over-reactive carries a risk of jeopardising the harmonious labour–management relationship which may have taken many years to build.

(b) Second, each performance-related grievance case is unique and individualised. Pursuing one case may require a lot of information gathering and sieving through what are facts and what are mere perceptions or opinions. It requires hearing from both the employee and the management, and since the matter is subjective, it requires the union to be discerning about who or what is "right" or "wrong". More often than not, the issues are usually nebulous or convoluted. The process is invariably time-consuming and the union may not have sufficient bandwidth to delve deep into each case.

(c) Third, there are instances where the union is aware that the employee (the complainant) does not have a "pretty" track record of performance and work attitude (say, through feedback from other co-workers or union members). If the union indiscriminately fights the case for the said employee, it may turn out to be embarrassing for the union if ample evidence is produced by the management to show that the employee is a problematic worker. It will make the union look undiscerning and even gullible to believe untruths from its member (the said employee).

D7.22   Given the foregoing reasons, it is not surprising that most unions take a measured, dispassionate and cautious approach to handling performance-related issues. There are also times when the union does not resonate with the employee's complaint, but because it feels obligated to represent and serve its members, it will take up the employee's case; in which case, the union will usually engage the management to try to secure a face-saving outcome for the said employee (say, lower salary increment or bonus instead of nothing) rather than to pressure the management to tweak or upgrade the rating.

D7.23   Generally, when a union represents employees on performance-related issues, the outcome will depend considerably on (a) the strength of the labour–management relations in the organisation and (b) the personal chemistry between the key union officials and the management representative handling the case. Sometimes, there are also "politics" played out – say, the management may relent in a particular case to let the union official win some credit in the eyes of union members and such goodwill will be "brownie points" to be traded when the occasion calls for it in future.

D7.24   Assuming that a case has some justifications for the union to engage with the management, the outcome (or settlement) may be any one of the following:

(a) raise the employee's performance rating to one notch higher or to a satisfactory rating;

(b) give a chance (say, 3 months) to the employee to perform and thereafter the management will re-evaluate his performance;

(c) retain the performance rating but negotiate to enhance the increment and/or bonus (higher than the quantum that would be accorded based on the original performance rating);

(d) let the employee resign with an ex gratia payment package (the package may comprise salary in lieu of notice, pro-rated Annual Wage Supplement and bonus, and in more generous cases, an additional top-up payment); and

(e) let an employee nearing the retirement age leave service on early retirement with the Employment Assistance Payment.

D7.25   Realistically, in the domain of performance management, there is not much room for a union to exert influence on the organisation or to dictate what the construct of its performance management framework should be. Performance management is multi-faceted and involves complex dynamics. Judgment and subjectivity are inevitable. The most important safeguard that a union can secure is to ensure that the organisation has a fair and transparent process and there is some check and balance within the performance management framework. The framework should allow an aggrieved employee to make an appeal under the organisation's grievance handling procedure and for the management (or Human Resource) to look into the matter. Beyond that, a union will just have to deal with each grievance as it comes in a measured approach and with an open mind.

Potential Conflict of Interest
in Union Representation on Performance Issues

D7.26   In the earlier decades, a rank-and-file union was prohibited by the Industrial Relations Act (IRA) to represent executives who managed or supervised rank-and-file employees who were represented by the said union. The IRA was amended twice over the last two decades to allow rank-and-file unions to represent executives: (a) first in September 2002 to allow individual and limited representation of executives by rank-and-file unions and (b) again in April 2015 to allow collective and full representation of executives by rank-and-file unions.

D7.27   With the amendments in the IRA paving the way for rank-and-file unions to represent executives, it has become a plausible scenario for both a rank-and-file employee and his reporting officer (who is an executive) to be members of the same union. This situation can potentially give rise to a conflict of interest if a dispute or grievance arises on performance appraisal. If a rank-and-file employee is not satisfied with his performance rating and seeks union representation to raise his grievance to the management, the union will be caught in an awkward position. The union will have to challenge the reporting officer (who is also its member) on his basis for the assessment of the rank-and-file employee. It may be that the adverse rating for the rank-and-file employee was given by the reporting officer, or it may also be that the rating came from the counter-signing officer or the moderation panel. Whatever the case, Human Resource or the management should step in to handle the case as the matter is considered an industrial matter. The reporting officer (who is a union member) must be excused or prevented from being put in a conflict of interest to face off his own union. This is workable if the incidents are infrequent. If they are rampant, the management may be tempted to reorganise the work and roles and convert some of the executives to become individual contributors in order to avoid having them supervise and appraise direct reports.

Industrial Disputes on Performance Issues

D7.28   If a complaint or grievance on performance rating remains unresolved after negotiation between the union and the management, an industrial dispute arises. The dispute may be escalated to the Ministry of Manpower (MOM) for conciliation. From experience, MOM has rarely received such disputes.

D7.29   Under the IRA, if a dispute is not settled after conciliation, the union and the organisation may jointly refer the case to the Industrial Arbitration Court (IAC) for arbitration. From records, it does not appear that the IAC has ever received a dispute on performance-related issues. One can postulate the following to be plausible reasons:

(a) While an employee may be comfortable to enlist the union's help to negotiate with the management on his performance issue up to the conciliation stage, he may shy away from having his case disclosed and arbitrated in an open court. IAC cases may be reported in the media, and if this happens, the employee's performance issue will be made public. Even if he "wins" the case at the IAC, his future job search may become jeopardised as some prospective employers may have lingering questions and doubt about him.

(b) The organisation may also likely avoid bringing a performance-related dispute to the IAC because of the time and effort required, not to mention the potential reputational damage if the IAC rules in favour of the employee. Even if the IAC rules in favour of the organisation, what it gains is only in intangible form – that it has been steadfast and successful in defending a performance issue, thereby sending the right message to the rest of its employees.

D7.30   If an employee is terminated on the grounds of poor performance, his union may represent him to appeal to the Minister for Manpower. If the termination is found to be without just cause, the Minister may order the organisation to reinstate the employee to his former position or compensate him. If the Minister is satisfied that the termination is with just cause, the employee's case will end there as the Minister's decision is final and binding on the parties. For a more detailed elaboration, please refer to Volume A, Chapter A9 "Termination and Dismissal".

D7.31   It is necessary for organisations to deal with performance issues (specifically, weak performance) with a firm hand in order to drive and build a performance culture. However, it must be handled sensibly and tactfully. The case of Surbana Jurong (shared in Chapter D7 "Dealing with Weak Performers") where 54 employees were let go on account of their performance attracted a lot of negative publicity for the company. It serves as a reminder to organisations that they must conduct their human resource practices (specifically involving termination of employees) in a responsible and tactful manner.

Performance Management Issues in Non-unionised Organisations

D7.32   Non-unionised organisations comprise predominantly small and medium enterprises (SMEs) which tend to have less structured performance management frameworks. For example, it is less common to find SMEs using a bell curve to regulate their distribution of performance ratings. SMEs are more concerned with seizing business opportunities and survival; how many or what proportion of employees get "A" or "B" rating is, relatively, a small matter to them. Their focus is on how to increase revenue and create a bigger increment budget and bonus pool to reward their employees; how to apportion the sharing, although a consideration, is less important.

D7.33   Many of the smaller SMEs may not do performance appraisal regularly and hence their employees may not even have performance ratings (and most employees are not bothered by that and life goes on – they get their increments and bonuses). Hence, for many SMEs, it is academic or insignificant to talk about grievances and issues surrounding performance ratings.

D7.34   In a situation where an employee is dissatisfied with his performance appraisal, he may appeal to the management/boss directly. The appeal may also go to the Human Resource department (if it exists). The follow-through will depend on whether the organisation has a clear and transparent grievance handling procedure. If the organisation does not have a clear resolution procedure or if the management/boss is not persuaded to diligently address the grievance, the aggrieved employee may just suppress his dissatisfaction and become demotivated. Next, he may likely resign from the company. Given the difficulty in attracting and retaining employees, often, SME bosses would bend backwards or give the benefit of the doubt to the aggrieved employees for the sake of maintaining their morale and retaining them.

D7.35   If an employee is terminated on account of poor performance and wants to challenge the termination, he may appeal to the Employment Claims Tribunals (ECT). This has been discussed in Volume A, Chapter A9 "Termination and Dismissal".

Civil Suits on Performance Issues

D7.36   It is not common to find an employee pursuing a civil case on performance issues. A civil suit between an employer and an employee must be premised on a breach of contractual terms that are contained in the employment contract. Performance rating or fairness in performance appraisal is not a contractual term. However, if the case involves termination of employment or a cut in the contractual remuneration arising from (unfair) performance appraisal, it may constitute a breach of contract and form the basis for an employee to file a civil suit against his employer.

D7.37   Notwithstanding that an employee may feel that he has a valid basis to file a civil suit, he may be circumspect in doing so. Proceedings at the civil courts are open to the public. Taking this route of action will expose the employee's performance record publicly. It is understandable that an employee will shy away from this publicity, unless the case involves great injustice, and the employee is resolute about seeking redress.

D7.38   The magnitude of the stake at hand is also a deciding factor. Civil suits invariably involve high legal fees. If a senior management executive is terminated and it involves huge monetary loss (such as notice pay, bonus and share option incentives), then a civil action may make sense.

Potential Triggers for Rise in Performance-related Disputes

Workplace Fairness Legislation

D7.39   A new legislation – the Workplace Fairness Legislation (WFL) as it is called in the interim – is expected to be enacted in 2026 to better enhance, support and enforce workplace fairness in Singapore. The new WFL will create awareness amongst employees about workplace discrimination. With this, we can expect that more employees will challenge their performance appraisals on the basis of discrimination. The fact that subjectivity cannot be totally avoided in performance appraisal, it would be convenient for a disgruntled employee to file a complaint that he has been discriminated against on account of his personal attributes.

D7.40   To avoid running afoul of the new WFL, organisations will be forced to be more transparent and objective in dealing with performance management and appraisal. Reporting officers must proactively make observations, counsel their staff and document the observations and conversations, as evidence is key when an organisation needs to defend its decisions on performance management and appraisal against allegations of discrimination. Suffice to say, organisations must step up their rigour of managing weak performers (particularly in documenting poor performance) so that they can be better prepared to handle any potential challenges that may arise from the WFL.

Growing Population of PME Workforce

D7.41   As the number and proportion of PMEs (professionals, managers and executives) grow in the workforce, we can expect that performance management will receive more attention since PMEs are more mindful of their performance report cards and understandably so, since they are materially impacted in their career growth and advancement by their performance appraisal results.

D7.42   Additionally, with the growing representation of PMEs by the unions, the number of industrial disputes on performance-related issues is poised to rise. It is expected that the focus will be on the applications of performance results, such as how an employee's rating will affect his salary increment and bonus and his chances of promotion.

Hybrid Working

D7.43   The rise of hybrid working may potentially give rise to more issues related to performance appraisal, in particular, how to appraise an employee fairly for work done outside the workplace. Organisations must move away from appraising employees based on "face time" to appraising based on work results.

D7.44   For fair appraisal to be possible, performance goals and work targets must first be spelt out clearly so that there is a clear basis for appraising an employee. Organisations that have been less than rigorous in this aspect must therefore step up their discipline to do this important part of performance management.

Performance Management: The Challenges, Realities and Alternatives

Focus of this Chapter

The preceding chapters (D1–D7) have covered quite extensively the features, processes and practices of performance management. While there are common features and processes across all organisations, their practices and successes vary considerably. This is because performance management is contextual; no two circumstances are the same.

This concluding chapter consolidates the key issues that have been covered in the preceding 7 chapters on performance management and distils some critical observations — the realities, problems and challenges. The use of performance ratings to determine rewards and other significant employment matters is what makes performance management complex, contentious and difficult.

We touch on the proposition for organisations to do away with performance management entirely, which we cannot, because there are yet no better alternatives. Finally, we consider various measures that can make performance management work better.

Performance Management: The Intent and Applications

D8.1   At the core, a performance management framework is meant to help an organisation drive, improve and sustain the performance of its employees through the following processes:

(a) *Performance Planning and Goals Setting*
Set out expectations on what results employees should focus on and deliver and the competencies that they should demonstrate.

(b) *Performance Feedback and Coaching*
Provide feedback to employees on job performance as well as coaching and guidance to help them learn, improve and sustain performance.

(c) *Performance Appraisal*
Assess employees' performance, achievements, challenges, strengths and developmental needs and provide a fair basis for follow-up actions such as rewards determination and career management for employees.

(d) *Dealing with Weak Performers*
Manage weak performers and help them level up, and if that fails, manage them out.

Using Performance Ratings to Determine Rewards

D8.2   Linking performance management with reward design is an important mechanism to drive performance behaviours. Organisations must pay competitively to attract and retain employees. To justify the remuneration paid, they need employees to perform and deliver and one needs performance management as the mechanism. Rewarding employees for their performance in the form of increments, bonuses and other monetary forms is one practical and common way to give reciprocation for results delivered by employees. To have a systematic way to differentiate the amount of increment and bonus that an employee should be rewarded with, one must necessarily use performance ratings.

Using Performance Ratings for Other Significant Employment Matters

D8.3   Besides being used to determine variable increments, bonuses and other monetary rewards, performance ratings are also extensively used as one of the important considerations to decide on other employment matters, including the following:

(a) consider whether to promote an employee;
(b) determine whether to select an employee for an overseas or expensive training program;
(c) decide whether to extend the contract of a term-contract employee;
(d) consider whether to offer re-employment to an employee approaching the statutory retirement age; and
(e) determine whether an employee should be selected for retrenchment if there is redundancy.

Performance Management: The Challenges

D8.4   Organisations face numerous challenges in performance management. We have examined these challenges in the earlier chapters under each of the performance management processes. As these challenges can significantly impact the success of performance management, it bears to highlight the key ones, understand them better and explore possible ways to deal with them.

Common Overarching Challenges

D8.5   There are challenges that affect multiple performance management processes. The key ones include the following:

(a) *Obsession with Performance Ratings*
It is understandable that employees can become obsessed with their performance ratings since ratings impact their rewards (increment and bonus) and careers (promotion, contract renewal, re-employment and retrenchment). In organisations that use performance ratings extensively and make big differentiations in rewards based on individual ratings, it fuels employees' obsession with ratings to the extent that the organisation culture can turn very competitive and toxic.

(b) *Disinterest in the Purpose of Performance Management*
When obsession with performance ratings sets in, ratings become the end in itself. Employees show less interest in the other purposes of performance management such as (i) benefitting from the feedback of their reporting officers to gain awareness of their own strengths and developmental areas and (ii) leveraging on their

guidance and coaching to make improvements and enhance their competencies. It is not uncommon to find employees and their reporting officers short-circuiting the performance management process flow – they jump straight to performance ratings. The other processes like performance goals setting, feedback and coaching and performance critical conversation are skipped or at best cursorily done. They do not appreciate the significance and benefits underlying these processes.

(c) *Involvement of Judgment and Subjectivity*
Much that we try to put some science into performance management, there is no question that judgment is involved. Setting performance goals and targets/standards, appraising performance (especially for qualitative standards and competency-based behaviours) and arriving at performance ratings are not science. Judgment is required and hence subjectivity will inevitably creep in (it is a matter of the degree).

(d) *Sensitivities of Human Egos and Emotions*
In performance management, the reporting officer needs to evaluate the performance and behaviours of his employees and be honest in giving feedback, including laying out their weaknesses (or blind spots). These touch on human egos and emotions. Most employees will find negative feedback hurting, even if it is backed by evidence and given in good faith. In a competitive work environment, employees strive to do well relative to others, since everyone is sharing the rewards pie which is finite. Competition inevitably arouses human egos and emotions, which are all sensitive to manage.

(e) *Lack of Understanding and Commitment*
Employees and line managers generally do not expend effort to understand the performance management framework (which spans performance goals setting, performance feedback and coaching and performance critical conversation). Organisations may put in considerable attention and resources into educating their people managers (reporting officers) on performance management. However, it is the enforcement that is necessary to ensure that the performance management processes are diligently complied with and this is where the shortfall usually lies.

(f) *Lack of Information and Data*
Performance management requires information and data. In many situations, securing sufficient, accurate and reliable information/data

is an impediment to setting performance goals and targets/standards. Market conditions are volatile and usable data is hard to come by. Internally, most organisations do not have robust information systems to generate the requisite data readily for planning and decision-making. As a result, assumptions have to be made and judgment used, thus bringing about subjectivity.

D8.6   There are also challenges that are specific to a certain performance management process and are related to the execution of the said process. We discuss these in the sequence of the performance management process flow.

Challenges in Performance Goals Setting

D8.7   Wrong Goals or Wrong Level of Targets/Standards
For performance goals and targets/standards to be correctly set, one has to rely on information/data. One must interpret the available information/ data, contextualise them and make realistic assumptions to extrapolate or project, and then go about calibrating the level of performance targets/ standards. All these require judgment grounded on experience, insights and good faith. If one makes an inadvertent error in any of these steps, performance goals may become off the mark in the following ways:

(a) wrong performance goals are selected which are not in sync with the organisational strategy or priorities; and/or
(b) performance targets/standards are set at too low or too high levels.

D8.8   Not all Goals can be SMART
Another challenge in setting performance goals is that not all goals can satisfy the SMART (specific, measurable, attainable, relevant and time-bound) criteria. It is generally not difficult to find goals that are SART, but it is a common challenge to find relevant and meaningful goals that are quantifiable and measurable. Since reporting officers and employees generally prefer or (more likely) are cajoled to select measurable goals to make assessment more objective, they may resort to selecting narrowly defined and easy-to-measure goals, even if they are not as relevant or material to the organisation.

Challenges in Performance Feedback and Coaching

D8.9   Performance feedback and coaching, though useful, are not put into practice as often as they should. While many organisations have mandated performance feedback and coaching, it is difficult to enforce at the ground level and therefore compliance is usually low. We summarise the underlying causes or challenges below:

(a) employees may feel discomfort in receiving feedback (especially if it is negative) as their egos may be hurt;

(b) during coaching, employees may feel apprehensive about being too honest in revealing their weaknesses to their reporting officers for fear that it may impact their performance appraisal;

(c) reporting officers may not be adept at crafting their feedback effectively and delivering them sensitively;

(d) reporting officers may not be adequately trained in coaching and lack the knowledge and experience in selecting and applying appropriate interventions for staff development; and

(e) reporting officers and employees may not appreciate the purpose and benefits of performance feedback and coaching as they are focused only on performance ratings.

Challenges in Performance Appraisal

D8.10   Appraising performance and contributions is not straightforward. It must be done with reference to the targets/standards set at the start of the performance appraisal cycle. The targets/standards set are premised on assumptions made. The actual performance and results delivered by employees are the culmination of the employee's effort as well as the impact of environmental events and organisational factors. How much of the results are attributed to the employee's effort is judgmentally based on available evidence supplemented by subjective assessment by the reporting officer.

D8.11   Challenges in appraising performance are aplenty. We list the key ones below:

(a) accuracy of rating (including being over-stringent or over-lenient);
(b) personal bias;
(c) recency effect;
(d) halo and horn effects; and
(e) central tendency effect.

These challenges have been discussed in detail in Chapter D4 "Performance Appraisal".

D8.12   Translating performance outcomes to a performance rating is somewhat judgmental and subjective in most situations. If the reporting officer or line manager is keen to please his direct reports, he will err in being generous with performance ratings. Honesty in assessment is compromised.

Challenges in Performance Moderation

D8.13   Performance moderation helps reduce rating errors and enhances consistency and fairness in performance ratings. The mere presence of this step would have nudged some appraisers to treat performance appraisal more seriously and objectively, lest they are viewed as sloppy people managers by their own seniors.

D8.14   In performance moderation, forced ranking and bell curve are invariably used as tools to moderate the performance ratings of employees and regulate the proportion of employees in various performance bands. Employees and their reporting officers are often (rightly or wrongly) unhappy about the results and curse the tools when they do not get the performance ratings that they want. How the bell curve is used is critical; for example, whether deviations (exceptions) are allowed when there are valid circumstances justifying such. Inter-department competition and politics also add on to the dynamics (tension) played out during performance moderation sessions. All these require Human Resource and the moderation panel chairperson to act in a measured, circumspect and above all, firm manner, to be able to manage the dynamics, emotions and sensitivities at performance moderation sessions.

Challenges in Performance Critical Conversation

D8.15   Notwithstanding that performance critical conversations are useful and serve as an important platform for reporting officers to understand the development needs of their direct reports, the conversations are seldom seriously done and appreciated. The lack of interest and commitment often stem from the mutual discomfort of both the reporting officers and employees. Not everyone is comfortable with holding a conversation on something as serious as wrapping up a year's worth of performance. It has much to do with managing expectations. Even a good performer who is scored with a "B" rating may express disappointment if he is expecting an 'A' rating. Reporting officers dread employees becoming defensive, disappointed and bitter. Employees, on the other hand, dread the reporting officers being critical and insensitive.

Performance Management: The Realities

D8.16   Can the many challenges associated with performance management be overcome or mitigated? To answer the question, let us first examine the realities that encircle performance management.

Dichotomy of Interests

D8.17   Performance management is not the end in itself. Organisations manage performance as a means to drive performance to meet and support their business, operational and corporate objectives and priorities. The end goal of the organisation is to thrive successfully – to be profitable (in the case of commercial organisations) or to provide public services efficiently and cost-effectively (in the case of public organisations).

D8.18   Performance management touches on interest issues of the two parties, the employees and the organisation – rewards, employment security and career progression (for employees) and financial performance and organisational effectiveness (for the organisation). While there is a nexus and sharing of fate between the employees and the organisation (in that if the organisation fails, the interests of employees will be jeopardised), the interests of the two can never be fully aligned. On the side of the organisation, it has to contend with the expectations and priorities of its shareholders and other stakeholders besides employees. On the side of the employees, they have their own financial, emotional and social well-being and needs to meet.

D8.19   The incomplete congruence of interests (or simply, dichotomy) between the employees and the organisation is the root of the tension underlying the use of performance management to govern the interests of employees (as in rewards, employment security and career progression). The nature of the dichotomy is summarised below:

> - The organisation wants to achieve a higher profit, so it will require more effort from its employees, hence it uses performance goals setting to set higher expectations. Performance appraisal and moderation (with bell curve and forced ranking methods) will in turn regulate the total cost of rewards.
> - On the other hand, most employees are primed to resist excessive pushing by the organisation to meet higher performance expectations.
>
> As a result, there is often a tango and negotiation between the employees and their reporting officers in setting performance goals and targets/standards and the resulting performance ratings.

Performance Management Deals with People Emotions

D8.20   In performance management, one cannot avoid having to deal with the emotions of people. This being the case, performance management issues cannot always be managed clinically. Many employees see performance ratings as more than a report card on how well they have performed. They are disturbed if the ratings do not meet their expectations. An employee is also mindful if his co-workers obtain better ratings than him. Understandably so, the use of bell curve and forced rankings in performance management rouses competition. Performance ratings not only impact rewards but also affect the pride and emotions of employees.

Execution of Performance Management Depends on People

D8.21   To operationalise performance management, we need policies, processes, forms and tools. These alone, however, do not guarantee a good outcome from performance management. It requires the commitment and willingness of the people in the organisation to execute performance management activities in a meaningful way. How employees are called to participate, talked to and treated contributes critically to the success of performance management.

D8.22   The people side of performance management includes how the management, reporting officers, employees and Human Resource view and execute performance management. Reporting officers, especially, play a pivotal role as they are the conduit between the management and employees; they can make or break performance management.

> • Even if the general culture in an organisation is toxic, an employee can still be motivated and perform well if the relationship between the employee and his reporting officer is functioning and respectful.
> • On the other hand, notwithstanding that the general culture in an organisation is positive and the organisation has done everything right in the design of its performance management framework, an employee may be badly managed and become demotivated if his reporting officer does a poor job of setting performance goals, providing performance feedback and coaching and appraising performance.

D8.23   The quality of the relationship between the reporting officer and his direct report has a direct and significant impact on how performance is managed. How a reporting officer interacts with the employee on daily and routine work activities will shape the performance management process.

- Does the reporting officer engage the employee in dealing with work issues and solving problems?
- Is there rapport and trust between the reporting officer and the employee?
- Do they talk openly in two-way communication?
- Does the employee feel safe and comfortable approaching and talking to the reporting officer when he has an issue?
- Does the reporting officer listen? Does he show care and concern?
- Does the reporting officer show interest and commitment in developing the employee?

Organisational Culture and People Management Philosophy Impact Performance Management

D8.24 Performance management practices are also dependent on organisational forces at play, predominantly so with (a) the organisation's culture and (b) its people management philosophy.

D8.25 Every organisation has its own unique culture – how people communicate and relate to each other, leadership and management styles, attitude towards work and performance and how employees collaborate or compete.

> *How culture can impede holistic performance management...*
>
> - If the work culture is laissez-faire, we cannot expect employees and reporting officers to be serious in performance goals setting and accountability.
> - If people are always guarded as communication is not open and transparent, we cannot expect employees and their reporting officers to have any meaningful and deep conversations on performance feedback and coaching.
> - If the culture is competitive and people are self-centred, one can expect strong contention on performance ratings and rewards distribution.

D8.26 Likewise, the people management philosophy of an organisation provides an important context for the execution of the performance management processes. If human capital is highly valued and the essential people management policies and frameworks (such as training and development, promotion and career management) are sound, congruent and properly installed, performance management will likely be treated with diligence and respect. Organisations that have successful performance management practices believe that investing in the development of their employees goes hand-in-hand with the pursuit of profit and organisational success because simply, better employees will make a better organisation.

> *How people management philosophy can impede holistic performance management...*
>
> If the organisation views its employees as cogs to be maximised solely for its financial gain, the management will have a very transactional mentality in the way it views and treats human capital. Performance management will just be about extracting the maximum effort from employees. Nurturing and long-term development of employees will be out of the equation. This attitude will cascade from the management down to the reporting officers. Performance feedback and coaching will be neglected. The performance-critical conversation will only focus on highlighting an employee's performance gaps.

Dynamic Operating Environment Complicates Performance Appraisal

D8.27   All organisations operate in a dynamic environment that never stands still. It is hence inevitable that performance management is subjected to the same vagaries of change. Performance planning and goals setting are premised on the organisation's strategic plan and objectives as well as based on assumptions made on the operating environment (such as competitors' activities, consumer behaviours and local and global economic conditions). All these are subjected to change and impact performance planning and goals setting materially.

D8.28   As conditions change, the assumptions that were used for setting performance goals may not hold true throughout the entire performance management cycle. This affects the validity of the performance goals and targets/standards set and poses a challenge in appraising the performance of employees at the end of the appraisal year. Interpreting performance results in a dynamic context and translating them to performance ratings is an art, requiring judgment and decision-making in good faith.

Tension and Mistrust over Performance Coaching and Appraisal

D8.29   There is an inherent tension between performance coaching and performance appraisal. For performance coaching to be effective and beneficial to the employee, he should be honest in revealing his weaknesses and anxieties to his reporting officer so that the reporting officer can be specific in coaching and guiding him to do better. However, since the reporting officer is also the one to do the appraisal, the employee is understandably worried that such honesty about his weaknesses/anxieties may jeopardise his performance appraisal. It requires trust and good faith between the employee and his reporting officer to mitigate this concern.

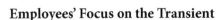

Employees' Focus on the Transient

D8.30   Increasingly, more employees embrace a transient mentality towards the organisations that they work in. They are more loyal to themselves and their own careers than to their organisations. When one accords less permanency to a job and an organisation, his interest and focus will be more short-term. He has less motivation and tenacity to stay on course and address issues that he believes are not right or sub-optimal. Encouraged by tight labour market conditions, many employees would prefer flight to fight; they simply look elsewhere for better conditions.

D8.31   Given the above, an employee who is displeased with any aspect of performance management may easily go into a resigned state and start seeking other opportunities to move on to. This explains the general apathy displayed by many employees. Their transient mentality leads to disinterest in the performance feedback and coaching by their reporting officers. When employees are not enthusiastic, their reporting officers will also not be inspired to invest in their development.

Technology Displacing the Human Touch

D8.32   As performance management is an annual affair and given the large number of employees covered and many stakeholders involved, organisations need to have their performance management processes systematically and efficiently administered. Organisations go for standardisation and use technology to execute their performance management processes. While this provides efficiency and orderliness, the personal touch that is required in performance management is undermined somewhat. The use of electronic workflow encourages and facilitates the employee and the reporting officer to avoid seeing each other for the entire performance management cycle. Some systems used by organisations even allow the performance critical conversation to be done digitally, with the employee and reporting officer signing off on a digital conversation that is typed into the appraisal form.

The Alternative:
Is it Feasible to Discard Performance Appraisal?

D8.33   Given the numerous challenges and stack of realities surrounding performance goals setting, performance appraisal and performance moderation, it is not surprising that some organisations have come to ponder whether to do away entirely with a structured performance management framework.

Are There any Real Alternatives?

D8.34   While the notion may be tempting (and even liberating), doing away with performance management begs the following questions:

- *How would the organisation coax results from its employees?*
- *How would it differentiate one employee's performance from another?*
- *How would it reward its employees, if not on the basis of performance? Service and loyalty? At the line manager's discretion?*
- *What would meritocracy mean to the organisation and its employees?*

Unless there are persuasive answers to the above questions, there are no good alternatives to having a performance management framework, onerous and imperfect though it may be.

D8.35   *Can we do away with performance appraisal (throw the contentious bell curve out of the window) and keep only performance goals setting and performance feedback and coaching?*
While this seemingly looks convenient to do, some amount of assessment (aka appraisal) is unavoidable. Without that, how would an employee's results or contribution be weighed, and consequently, how would his rewards be determined and defended? If an employee's continued employment depends on his performance, without any appraisal/assessment, what would such decisions be based on? We are back to square one.

D8.36   There are organisations that choose to dispense with using appraisal/moderation tools such as the bell curve and forced ranking, but this is not to say that performance appraisal (or some form of assessment in one way or another) can be dispensed with. One must not come away with the mistaken notion that appraisal/assessment is unnecessary or optional. We use Netflix as an example to illustrate this point.

> Netflix articulates a very clear people culture. Two important tenets of its culture are: *"Netflix expects High Performance. Netflix pays at the Top of the Market."*
>
> **High Performance**
> Like every company, Netflix tries to hire well. Netflix has stars in every position. Unlike many companies, adequate performance at Netflix gets a (generous) severance package so that we can open a slot to find a star for that role. Within Netflix, we do not do "top 30%" or "bottom 10%" rankings. Employees should focus on staying as the top 10% relative to the pool of global candidates.

> **Pay at Top of Market**
> One outstanding employee gets more done and costs less than two average employees. We endeavour to have only outstanding employees (stars). There are no fixed salary increments. Every year, every employee is re-aligned to the top of market pay.

> Comments
>
> - That Netflix uses neither the bell curve nor forced ranking does not mean that it does not appraise/assess its employees. Quite the opposite. Performance assessment is rigorous and ongoing. When an employee's performance is less than outstanding, he is offloaded promptly. Only star performers get to keep their jobs.
>
> - Since every employee who stays in Netflix are star performers, there is no such notion of tiering their pay/rewards based on individual performance ratings (on a rating scale of ABCDE). All (retained) employees are by default "A+" performers and accordingly, every employee's pay is pegged to the top of the market.

D8.37   *Taking a wider and longer lens, will performance appraisal still be relevant as the workforce and jobs continue to evolve?*
Today, jobs no longer thrive on speed and precision as in the factory jobs of yesteryears. The world continues to evolve unabated. From coping with a VUCA (volatile, uncertain, complex and ambiguous) world, since the hit of the Covid pandemic, we now have to adapt to a new world that is BANI (brittle, anxious, nonlinear and incomprehensible). Employees must use cognitive discretion, creativity and enterprise to deliver results for the organisation to help it survive and thrive. And different times call for different deliverables. Performance expectations will change. Organisations must have a mechanism to steer and drive the new behaviours in employees. If not through performance management, then what would that be? In short, we cannot do without performance appraisal/assessment in one form or another (period!), although the format and tools of appraisal/assessment may vary or change.

How Can Performance Management Work Better?

D8.38   If we decide that we cannot do away with performance management, how can we improve it to make it work better? Which features or processes can be tweaked? Before we go into that, we have to be cognisant that there is neither a universal nor best performance management framework. Everything is contextual. What works for one organisation may not work for another. In most cases, the challenges and frustration experienced with performance management have less to do with its design and features per se; rather, the pain points are usually related to how performance management is being executed. As it is a people process, it is not something that can be done in a standard cookie-cutter way; invariably, there will be some messiness. Moreover, as performance appraisal touches on human emotions, we have to also accept that it is impossible to have every employee coming away happy at the end of a performance appraisal cycle.

Generic Improvements

D8.39   Some improvements can be made that are not specific to a particular feature or process of performance management. These are fundamental aspects that underpin the entire or most parts of performance management. Making improvements in these aspects has a wider impact.

Build Trust

D8.40   Performance management requires trust. Employees must trust that their reporting officers and management will act fairly and in good faith in the following aspects:

(a) Goals setting must be premised on a fair middle ground and not leverage on ambiguity (due to incomplete or imperfect data/information) and make assumptions that will "take advantage" of the employee and put him in an unfavourable position.

(b) An employee who opens up to his reporting officer about his weak spots during the performance feedback process should not have it backfire on him; the reporting officer should reciprocate the employee's openness by giving him more targeted guidance and coaching and not cut him down to size for his weaknesses.

(c) Performance moderation done by the management must be fair and objective and not be clouded with political undercurrents. An employee should get the performance rating that he truly deserves and not be more or less favourably treated because his line head has clout or no clout.

D8.41   To make the change, the management (senior leadership) must start with good intentions and an open mind. They must be genuine and circumspect in dealing with performance goals setting, appraisal and moderation as well as linking rewards to performance. They should communicate their intentions to employees and back up with judicious decision-making and actions. This is a journey and not a one-off exercise. Trust earned must be continually tendered. Human Resource should keep a watch out to alert and prompt the management to stay on course.

Get Employees on Board

D8.42   The organisation must invest time and effort to educate its employees on the purpose and principles underlying performance management. Most importantly, employees need to appreciate how performance management (if executed properly) impacts and benefits them. The task of educating employees on performance management usually lies with Human Resource (HR), since HR is the overall process owner.

D8.43   Reporting officers and line managers must be familiarised with the features and processes involved in performance management — goals setting, feedback and coaching, appraisal and moderation (including the use of bell curve and forced ranking as tools of moderation) and performance critical conversation. They need to understand how these pieces fit together and interplay. Most importantly, they must be convinced of the importance of performance management and appreciate how it helps them manage, motivate and develop their employees. They must understand the critical role that they play in executing performance management and ensuring its success.

Equip Reporting Officers with Performance Management Skills

D8.44   For performance management to be executed well, reporting officers and line managers/heads must be skilled and effective in handling the various performance management processes — goals setting, feedback and coaching, appraisal and critical conversation. They must be trained and equipped with the following skills:

> Performance Goals Setting
> Understand how to align and translate the organisation's strategies/objectives to the employees' performance goals. Adept at setting SMART (specific, measurable, attainable, relevant and time-bound) goals. Able to exercise good judgment in setting targets/standards fairly and at the appropriate levels to provide enough challenge to employees.

Performance Feedback and Coaching
Be observant in picking up work incidents that constitute learning points for employees. Adept at crafting specific and appropriate performance feedback messages, focusing on work behaviours/actions of employees. Able to deliver feedback clearly and tactfully with the right use of words, body language and tonality (without being personal and condescending). Show confidence and empathy in handling employees' emotions and sensitivities. Understand various intervention methods (such as counselling, coaching and on-the-job training) and apply the right methods suited to the context and needs of employees.

Performance Appraisal
Able to exercise sound judgment in appraising employees' achievements and competency-based behaviours and scoring employees fairly in performance rating. Be cognisant of possible rating errors (including over-stringency or over-leniency, personal bias, recency effect, halo and horn effects and central tendency effect) and strive to avoid them.

Performance Critical Conversation
Able to conduct meaningful conversations on performance review and encourage employees to be open with sharing their strengths, development needs and career aspirations. Able to listen empathetically and speak clearly to be understood. Able to give honest feedback to employees and encourage them to sustain and improve their performance. Able to handle employees' emotions and sensitivities and bring the conversation to close on a positive note.

Leadership by Example

D8.45   Doing performance management is not an easy task. Organisations must demonstrate visible commitment and support their line managers in their efforts. Support should not be just lip service. The management should lead by example. If the senior leaders do not do performance management properly for their next-in-line (who are likely to be line heads), the laissez-faire mentality and approach will cascade down to line managers and other reporting officers.

D8.46   If an organisation genuinely believes in the importance of performance management and people development, it should mandate this as an expectation of its people managers. People development should be stipulated as a competency requirement for its people managers. Those who do a good job in developing their direct reports should be duly recognised and taken into account for their overall performance.

Process-specific Improvements

D8.47   As each performance management process comes with its own set of challenges, organisations can look into measures that are specific to each process and targeted for addressing the specific challenges associated with each process.

Improving Performance Goals Setting

D8.48   The following measures will go some way to improve performance goals setting:

(a) *Information Sharing*
Share information on the organisation's strategy, objectives and priorities as clearly and openly as possible with line heads (within the reasonable bounds of business confidentiality). Line heads can translate and cascade down to the reporting officers. While organisations must be mindful about guarding business-sensitive and confidential information, the information (selectively) shared should be sufficient to enable reporting officers to craft meaningful performance goals.

(b) *Quality Check on Performance Goals*
Not all reporting officers are impeccable in crafting performance goals. Line heads should do a quality check to ensure that the performance goals for the entire department are relevant and aligned (with the organisation's priorities), coherent and comprehensive (mapped to the department's annual plan with no gaps in coverage) and fair (in relative standards expected of employees).

Improving Performance Feedback and Coaching

D8.49   The main bugbear surrounding performance feedback and coaching is employees' discomfort over discussing their weaknesses (or developmental areas) with their reporting officers. This is understandable since the reporting officer is also the one to appraise the employee. Employees worry that such sensitive information may put them at a disadvantage when appraisal time comes. Yet, for employees to benefit meaningfully from feedback and coaching, honest sharing is vital so that reporting officers can understand their employees better and go about helping them improve in a more targeted way. To overcome this obstacle, trust is the way to go. Only with trust, then can employees feel safe and assured that their reporting officers have good intentions and are not out to "trap" them.

D8.50   *How to build and sustain trust?*
Merely verbally espousing it just won't do. Trust in a reporting officer can only be earned and not mandated. It cannot be built overnight. The reporting officer must manifest by his behaviours or actions that he is a fair person and genuinely cares for the employee's well-being and development. The following aspects of a reporting officer's behaviours/actions will form the basis of trust:

(a) be professional, objective and consistent in dealing with work and people matters;
(b) be fair and firm in treating all employees without showing prejudice and bias;
(c) practise open communication and let employees feel safe to raise work issues;
(d) give a listening ear to engage with employees and show care and concern for their well-being and professional development; and
(e) when an employee shares honestly on his weaknesses (or developmental needs), reciprocate by putting in interventions (such as extra coaching or specific training) to address the employee's developmental needs in a more targeted manner.

Only with positive experiences accumulated over time, employees will put their trust in their reporting officers. This then sets a favourable stage for meaningful performance feedback and coaching.

Improving Performance Appraisal

D8.51   It is idealistic to expect a perfect performance appraisal considering the various challenges and realities that envelope it. However, we can put in effort to make it as fair as possible.

D8.52   The following measures will go some way to improve the accuracy and fairness of performance appraisal:

(a) *Apply Evidence-based Judgment*
To improve accuracy and objectivity in performance appraisal, good information and evidence are required. Reporting officers should collect and document information/evidence in the course of interacting with their employees over work, noting down the employees' achievements and performance lapses, as well as the competency-based behaviours they have demonstrated while carrying out work. This may appear tedious, but it is necessary so that performance appraisal is evidence-based and defensible.

(b) Re-evaluate Assumptions Made

When performance goals and targets/standards are set at the start of the appraisal period, invariably, assumptions on the operating conditions and parameters (such as economic climate, consumer demand and competitors' activities) must have been made. By the end of the appraisal period, many events could have happened and made some of the assumptions materially wrong. Adverse circumstances may have arisen that are beyond the control of the employee. This means that if the performance of the employee is measured against the original goals and targets/standards, the assessment will be off the mark or even invalid. It is necessary to do a critical review of the assumptions made, evaluate the shifts and take these into consideration when appraising the employee. For consistency in principle, the converse should also apply. If circumstances turn favourable not by the employee's effort, it should also be taken into consideration when appraising the employee's results. How much to adjust or discount is a matter of judgment, which should be made judiciously in good faith.

    (c) Avoid Rating Errors

Reporting officers must remain vigilant not to fall prey to making common rating errors, such as over-stringency, over-leniency, personal bias, recency effect, halo and horn effects and central tendency effect. Reporting officers should always take a step back to re-examine the initial ratings they have assigned to employees and check for consistency and relativity before finalising the ratings. If the reporting officer has several direct reports, it may also be helpful to force-rank them before determining their performance ratings.

Improving Performance Moderation

D8.53   The purpose of performance moderation is to do a cross-calibration across the organisation to arrive at a common "ruler" to achieve consistency in appraisal standards so that the final performance ratings assigned to employees are accurate and fair as much as possible. It prevents cases of over-leniency (which is a common problem) and over-stringency (albeit much less common).

D8.54   Doing performance moderation is often a tedious (even painful) exercise; it usually requires a lot of management time and resources. However, it cannot be skipped or glossed over. The mere provision of performance moderation in itself will condition reporting officers and line heads to be more circumspect in assigning performance ratings to their employees.

D8.55   Given that performance moderation is an important check-and-balance process that is here to stay, it bears to make it work well. Some pointers are shared below:

(a) *Sensible Use of Bell Curve*
While the bell curve is a practical tool for calibrating and normalising the distribution of performance ratings, one should not use it rigidly regardless of the circumstances. The moderation panel should exercise judgment when there are valid circumstances warranting a tweak of the bell curve. One must appreciate that the bell curve is only a means; the end is an accurate and credible spread of performance ratings that truly reflect the different performance levels of employees. Satisfying technically the normal bell curve should not be the end in itself.

> - If a particular department has brought in overall stellar results, it is fair and realistic to allow more employees from the said department to earn good ratings. The bell curve quota for the said department can be tweaked accordingly to accommodate it.
> - Likewise, the reverse should also be practised. If a particular department has brought in overall disappointing results, the bell curve can be tightened to reduce the number of employees from the said department to earn good ratings.

(b) *Not to Tamper the Bell Curve for Inappropriate Reasons*
If, say, the labour market has shifted to paying higher increments and bonuses, it is better for the organisation to correspondingly raise its budget for increment/bonus to keep competitive with the market. It would be inappropriate to relax the bell curve just to allow more employees to earn better ratings to justify being paid higher increments/bonuses. Since performance ratings are meant to reflect the employees' performance, the messaging to employees would be confusing (and wrong).

(c) *Special Provision for Curated Employee Groups*
Bell curves are suited for a random population. For specially (and stringently) curated groups, it may be a challenge to force a bell curve. Specially curated groups may include C-suite officers or a select group of mission-critical employees (say, the product research team for an organisation for which success is highly dependent on product innovation, or pilots in an airline company). In any given year, a few C-suite officers or mission-critical employees may not fare as well as their peers, but it is highly unlikely that they will fit into the "Met Few Expectations" or "Met Some Expectations" performance bands. Since

their contribution (or non-contribution) has an extremely high impact on the organisation, the normal scenario is that a weak performer would be managed out swiftly. Only those who make the cut and are faring well are allowed to remain in employment. Therefore, one should not insist that performance ratings for these specially curated groups fit into a normal bell curve. In Annex D8-1, we delve deeper into how performance management can be modified for specially curated employee groups and for illustration, we highlight the specific performance management practices for commercial pilots.

(d) Sufficient Time for Moderation Process
Performance moderation is usually a tedious and tiring process and is compounded by the need to meet a deadline. In the rush for time (and given the voluminous number of appraisal results), the moderation panel may at times skim through cases and not do enough due diligence before endorsing the preliminary performance ratings given by the reporting officers or line heads. Worse, in a bid to resolve "conflicts" in assessment in an expedient manner, the panel may sometimes resort to using voting to determine the outcome. Voting allows political manoeuvres to creep in (for example, line heads may form a pact with one another to game the voting). This should be avoided. The right thing to do is for the moderation panel to allocate sufficient time and number of sessions for performance moderation to be conducted with rigour and thoroughness. The chairperson must be effective in steering the flow of the deliberations and encourage candid discussions (for one, he should refrain from making comments and revealing his preferences too early). Human Resource should provide clear and concise data and analysis of the performance ratings (broken down by job grades/levels and departments) so that the panel can direct their attention to the pain points. Line heads should have on hand the information and evidence to justify the performance ratings they have given to their employees.

Improving Performance Critical Conversation

D8.56   The annual performance management cycle should end with each reporting officer holding a performance critical conversation with every one of his direct reports individually. The performance critical conversation gives closure to the employee on putting in one year's efforts. It should also offer key takeaways for the employee to move on to the next year.

D8.57   The performance critical conversation should be holistic and cover the following areas: (a) the final performance rating assigned to the employee, (b) his strengths, (c) his weaknesses (or developmental areas) and (d) learning and developmental plans for him.

D8.58   To make performance critical conversations more effective, reporting officers should pay attention to the following aspects:

(a) *Do Not let the Conversation be Derailed*
A complete performance critical conversation must cover the four areas (a) to (d) as mentioned above. Unfortunately, quite often, the conversation stops at (a). Once the final performance rating is revealed to the employee, the conversation is derailed as the employee becomes engrossed (or obsessed) with the "why" of his performance rating. To handle this uncomfortable situation, the reporting officer should redirect the employee's attention to the specifics of his performance – in what aspects he has fared well and where he has room to improve and discuss with him on how improvement can be achieved. Essentially, it is to bring the employee to focus on the longer-term objective of developing himself and eventually achieving his career aspiration, rather than to obsess over his performance rating for the past year. Depending on the situation and mood, the reporting officer may reverse the conversation order by revealing the performance rating last.

(b) *Do Not Play the Blame Game*
Reporting officers must be given to understand that it is unprofessional to play the blame game and paint themselves as the good guys. To avoid confusion and blame attribution, the organisation should strongly forbid the reporting officer to inform the employee of the preliminary performance rating (given by the reporting officer).

Improving Management of Weak Performers

D8.59   It is not difficult to design and install a performance improvement framework that comes with policies and processes to deal with weak performers. Most organisations mandate that a weak performer who is given an adverse performance rating be put under a Performance Improvement Plan (PIP) where he will be closely monitored in his performance and must level up within a deadline, failing which, his employment will be terminated.

D8.60   The challenging part is to get reporting officers to appraise their weak performers honestly and assign an adverse performance rating. Most line managers shy away from giving adverse performance ratings to weak performers. Their reluctance is usually attributed to their concern for breaking the rice bowls of the weak performers should they fail the PIP and become managed out.

D8.61   The reality is that to genuinely help a weak performer, one should not wait till the end of the appraisal period to put him under the PIP (after assigning him an adverse performance rating). Performance problems should be nibbed in the bud, that is, addressed as early as they are identified. When a reporting officer observes that an employee is struggling to keep up his performance, he should intervene straightaway by (a) counselling if it is a case of attitudinal problem or (b) giving extra guidance and targeted training if it is a case of knowledge or skills gap, and follow up with close monitoring to address the performance gap. Performance issues should be discussed candidly during the performance feedback and coaching sessions throughout the appraisal period. Addressing performance problems only when the PIP is instituted after the end of the appraisal period may at times already be too late. The organisation would have lost precious time in rehabilitating a weak performer. Early intervention increases the chance of rehabilitating a weak performer successfully.

Roles of Stakeholders in Performance Management

D8.62   The success of performance management cannot just rely on good design of framework, policies and processes. It is people who drive performance management. It takes concerted will, diligence and commitment from the organisation's senior leaders and people managers (reporting officers) to tackle the challenges and push on with performance management. Human Resource as the custodian, owner and facilitator of performance management plays a critical role. So too for the employees themselves, as their interest and participation in the performance management processes make or break its success.

D8.63   The roles that each stakeholder group must play are summarised below:

Roles of Senior Management

1. Direct and ensure that the performance management framework is appropriately designed and aligned with other human capital functions and initiatives.
2. Inspire and forge a culture where employees and line managers take performance management seriously.
3. Inspire and instill confidence in employees and line managers that the management is trustworthy, judicious and fair in performance goals setting, performance appraisal and determination of rewards.
4. Drive discipline and diligence in executing the policies and processes under the performance management framework.

---

5. Cascade and articulate corporate goals and focus to facilitate line managers to set performance goals and targets/standards.
6. Judiciously decide to refine and adapt performance management practices and tools (such as bell curve) to make performance management work well.
7. Direct and steer performance appraisal and moderation to produce sensible outcomes.

Roles of Human Resource

1. Design, upkeep and own the performance management framework, ensuring that it is functional and aligned with other human capital functions and initiatives.
2. Support the management in initiatives to forge a culture where employees and line managers take performance management seriously.
3. Support the management in instilling confidence in employees and line managers that the management is trustworthy, judicious and fair in performance goals setting, performance appraisal and determination of rewards.
4. Lead the execution of the performance management framework and educate and guide the stakeholders in doing so.
5. Monitor and help ensure that the organisation's corporate goals and strategic initiatives are suitably cascaded to enable line managers to set performance goals and targets/standards.
6. Do eyeball check on the (directional) correctness and quality of performance goals and targets/standards set by line managers.
7. Administer the entire performance management cycle and all the processes and provide advice and assistance to management, line managers and employees. Make the processes and tasks less tedious and burdensome.
8. Review the performance appraisal results submitted by line managers to spot inconsistencies and advise review.
9. Facilitate and support performance moderation to enhance accuracy, consistency and fairness in appraisal.
10. Advise and administer the determination of rewards (bonus and increments) using inputs from the performance results.
11. Oversee and ensure relevant recommendations in performance appraisal reports are collated for follow up (for example, promotion, transfer, re-employment, training and development).
12. Direct and ensure that weak performers are picked up for Performance Improvement Plan.
13. Deal with appeals and performance-related grievances jointly with line heads.

The actual roles of Human Resource vary from one organisation to another. In large organisations where the framework and policies are clearly documented and processes are well established, the line heads and managers are more independent and involved in executing the annual performance management exercise. In this situation, Human Resource will focus on overall performance planning and management.

Roles of Line Managers (or Reporting Officers)
1. Understand and appreciate the purpose, benefits and features of performance management and its significance in managing and developing employees.
2. Understand the organisation's corporate/business objectives and strategic initiatives and help explain them to direct reports.
3. Identify suitable performance goals and craft the goal statements. Set targets/standards at appropriate levels for direct reports.
4. Actively observe the work behaviours of direct reports and pay attention to their work output/outcomes and identify relevant incidents and information that can constitute performance feedback and learning points.
5. Construct performance feedback messages descriptively and accurately focusing on the behaviours and actions of the direct reports (and not directed at the persons or their character/personalities).
6. Deliver performance feedback with the right choice of words, body language and tonality.
7. Embrace a developmental orientation in giving performance feedback and coaching as well as addressing feedback from direct reports.
8. Consolidate and review the work and contributions of the direct reports for the year and appraise them accurately and objectively using evidence as well as judicious judgment in good faith.
9. Engage the direct reports purposefully during the performance critical conversations (held individually), explaining their final performance ratings and discussing their developmental needs.
10. Follow up on action matters related to the direct reports' development such as training and other developmental activities (for example, stretch assignments and transfers).

Roles of Employees
1. Understand and appreciate the purpose, benefits and features of performance management.
2. Understand the organisation's corporate/business objectives and strategic initiatives.
3. Identify suitable performance goals and craft the goal statements as best as possible.
4. Embrace and engage actively in performance feedback and coaching given by the reporting officer with an open mind, making the best use of it.
5. Reflect, consolidate and document the work done for the year as well as factors that have materially affected one's performance favourably or unfavourably. Do self-appraise if it is required.
6. Engage the reporting officer actively and purposefully with an open mind during the performance critical conversation. Share one's views. Clarify doubts and reflect on feedback raised by the reporting officer.
7. Follow up on action points that have arisen from the performance appraisal and agreed upon with the reporting officer.

Closing

D8.64   Performance management is the core mechanism to drive alignment and performance within the organisation. If carried out properly, it gives the organisation a definite competitive edge.

D8.65   Unfortunately, not many organisations have been able to make performance management work effectively. Challenges assail performance management. We have suggested various measures that can possibly mitigate the challenges and improve performance management. The measures should be undertaken in concert to have a better impact.

D8.66   Getting performance management right is never-ending. As organisations continue to evolve, so too must their people strategies evolve, including how to manage and motivate employees. While performance management is complex and difficult to tackle, it is not an option for organisations to dismiss, neglect or make light of it. There is no other way for organisations to succeed and sustain success except by continually managing and motivating its employees to perform and deliver results.

Annex D8-1

Example of Modified Performance Management for Special Employee Groups

Performance management features and practices can be designed or modified to suit special employee groups. The nuanced performance management for special employee groups cannot be done in isolation; they must be integrated with and supported by appropriate recruitment and reward policies and practices so that the overall management of such special employee groups is congruent and holistic.

Special Employee Groups

Special employee groups are likely to be in specialised professional fields such as *commercial pilots, medical doctors, researchers, scientists* and *management consultants*. To enter these professions, one has to meet stringent criteria and the road to attaining professional accreditation requires extensive investment in time and effort. Their stay in the chosen professions is likely to be lifelong. To remain in their professions, they may be required to periodically undergo professional assessment for re-certification or clock enough continual professional development hours to keep current in their knowledge and skills.

Organisations that employ these special employee groups usually treat them separately from the rest of the workforce. The reason is because the quality, competence and contribution of these employee groups are vital to the organisation. Invariably, they are the backbone of the organisation's core business or function.

- For airlines, pilots perform the core function of flying aeroplanes.
- Medical doctors are the lifeline in healthcare institutions.
- For organisations that are highly dependent on product or service innovation to compete in the market, their research teams and scientists are vital.
- Management consultants are the revenue generators as well as subject matter experts in professional services firms.

The remuneration structure and pay progression for these special employee groups must necessarily be different from those of other employees. In terms of the job hierarchical structure housing these employees, it tends to be quite flat with only a small number of senior positions taking on management or leadership roles. In other words, most of these employees remain as individual contributors in their careers. Notwithstanding, the impact of their contributions to their organisations is high and critical.

Recruitment and Employment Practices

Organisations are very strict in hiring these employees in terms of academic/ professional/technical qualifications, competencies and aptitude. Due to the stringent selection criteria, employees who enter into employment are touted as competent.

As the performance of these special employee groups impacts the organisation materially, most organisations take proactive steps to monitor and review their performance so as to ensure that only effective performers remain in the system. To begin with, these employees have high and stringent performance standards to meet. Professional discipline is often non-negotiable. Because of their professional ethics, they are diligent in maintaining their work standards and observing strict discipline. These professionals rarely produce sub-standard work or are sloppy about discipline. Peer reviews are strict and commonly applied. Invariably, the fraternities of the respective professions are fiercely protective of their professional standards and will frown on a black sheep or bad apple. If an employee flounders, the organisation is fast to take corrective measures to help him get back on track, or if the situation is untenable, he will be managed out swiftly. In view of the stringency in recruitment and performance and discipline management, those who remain in employment are regarded as competent and are well-respected.

- For commercial pilots, their work and competence are periodically and systematically checked by licensed reviewers. If a pilot breaches a fundamental rule (say, consuming alcohol within X hours before operating a flight or violating an important safety rule), the punishment is hefty; the pilot may be sacked or lose his flying license.

- For medical doctors, their work is often reviewed by senior peers of a medical board within the healthcare institution. Patient safety is paramount; a breach will be reported to the Singapore Medical Board for review and possibly incur a censure or worse, a suspension of license or struck off the medical register.

- For management consultants, the quality of their solutions and deliverables are constantly subject to scrutiny by the project leads and/or managing partners of the firm, together with critical feedback from the client companies that they serve.

Reward Practices

Organisations tend to pay competitively for these employees, and they regularly benchmark the market trends to ensure that their pay levels do not trail behind. Generally, these employees in the same role or job grade/level are paid about the same increment and bonus; the differential that is accorded to individual performance, if any, is usually relatively small. The size of their increment/bonus will depend on the performance of their organisations and the prevailing market norms. Most of these employees expect fair and good pay but are not too "obsessed" with differentiated increment/bonus vis-à-vis their peers based on individual performance. In the case of commercial pilots, the preference for egalitarianism is strong.

Performance Management Practices (using Commercial Pilots as illustration)

We now highlight the performance management practices for commercial pilots. For the other special employee groups, the practices may differ in some ways due to the uniqueness of each profession.

Job Ranks for Pilots

First, it is necessary to give a little background on the job ranks of commercial pilots to give context to the performance management of pilots.

There are essentially only two ranks: First Officer and Captain. The number of First Officers and Captains depends on the number of aircraft and types and number of flights operated by the airline.

To qualify as a First Officer, one must have completed the lengthy and vigorous cadet pilot training program and cleared all the certification requirements. Some years later, to be considered for training and selection to be a Captain, the First Officer must have attained the required number of flying hours and sectors (one sector means one take-off/landing). The aspiring Captain must go through the "command" training and be certified for the rank of Captain. One is generally considered to have "arrived" when one attains the command rank of Captain.

Some Captains may subsequently be appointed as Line Instructor Pilots or Instructor Pilots, whose key accountabilities are to train and check on other pilots (after being licensed as checkers). Notwithstanding their additional roles, they continue to operate flights (like the other Captains).

Some are also appointed to the management ranks in roles such as Assistant Chief Pilot, Deputy Chief Pilot and Chief Pilot. These appointees "double hat" and continue to operate some flights periodically (like the other Captains) because fundamentally, they are still Captains and they need to clock flying hours to maintain their flying licenses and recency.

For appointment of Captains to instructor or management roles, the airline would consider their non-technical competencies on top of their technical competencies. Captains who are offered such roles may decline the offer, as some prefer to focus on flying and not get involved in other responsibilities. Indeed, after some years in a management role, a Captain may opt to return to operate flights on a full-time basis.

Generally, pilots do not battle to outdo each other for better performance. They just need to ensure that they operate their flights safely and smoothly and pass all the required tests and checks to maintain their flying license and recency. In operating a flight, there are strict technical procedures and operation protocols that they must comply with. The room for them to deviate and operate differently is limited.

In terms of the remuneration package, pilots are paid a basic salary based on whether they are First Officers or Captains. In addition, they are given a flying allowance and other allowances as well as corporate bonuses. If a Captain is appointed as an Instructor, he will be paid an instructor allowance. Likewise, if he serves in a management role, he will be granted an allowance for it. These allowances are removed once they relinquish their roles. These roles are not linked to the performance ratings of pilots. In fact, as we soon share, pilots do not have performance ratings!

Performance Goals and Targets for Pilots

Commercial pilots know specifically what they are supposed to deliver in terms of performance and professional standards. Their job description is clear. Performance goals setting is not needed as flights to be operated are assigned to them by the system under very strict rules and protocols (such as a pilot must have enough rest between two flights). Their deliverables are to complete the flights safely and make the flights comfortable for the passengers.

The nature of the work of pilots is not subject to market vagaries. Pilots just operate the flights that are assigned to them, regardless of the number of passengers on board and the fares paid to the airline. It is not for pilots to choose the (more challenging or easier) flights. The overwhelming majority of the flights are non-events. Occasionally, pilots have to deal with unexpected events such as technical and medical incidents, air turbulence, adverse weather conditions and diversions – all of which are part of their duties.

Pilots usually take an interest in knowing the directions and developments of their airlines, particularly initiatives and events that may impact their profession. They find satisfaction in the work itself and see less need to compare and compete with co-workers.

Performance Feedback and Coaching for Pilots

For the general employee population, the same reporting officer who provides performance feedback and coaching is also the one who will appraise the performance of the employee. This is however not the arrangement for pilots. The typical modus operandi is that for administrative, flight scheduling and welfare matters, they report to the Chief Pilot (Fleet Management or Operations) who acts as their reporting officer. On training, development and safety matters, the pilots take guidance from the Chief Pilot (Technical/Development) supported by a team of instructor/trainer/specialist pilots. This arrangement has enabled the pilots to engage the Chief Pilot (Technical/Development) and his team openly and deeply without fear of repercussions.

Performance Appraisal for Pilots

As with most other professionals, pilots tend to dislike having their performance evaluated. They see themselves as competent professionals who are self-driven to maintain professional competence and performance.

Pilots must have a valid license to operate aircraft. They are subject to checks, audits and tests periodically by licensed checkers who are appointed by the regulatory authorities. The evaluation result is either "Competent" or "Not Competent" (that is, Pass or Fail). The standard to get a Pass is upheld consistently and stringently. If a pilot fails, he will be grounded (not allowed to fly) and sent for retraining and thereafter evaluated again until he has regained a Pass.

Technical scores for pilots are generated for the flights that they have operated. The focus is on the technical competencies which are highly specific and procedural. If they operate the flights "normally", there will be little variations in the technical scores. The pilots are not chasing ratings that are better than "Pass". In fact, the airlines do not have "better-than-Pass" or "marginally Pass" ratings. Giving a pilot a performance rating other than "Pass" or "Competent" will certainly not resonate well with passengers. To passengers, they are entrusting their lives to a pilot when they take a flight. The pilot cannot be less than "Competent". Imagine if passengers find out that their flight is operated by a pilot who has been rated C- (C minus), D or E!

Performance Moderation for Pilots

As pilots are periodically checked, audited and tested by licensed checkers who independently evaluate and decide whether a pilot is "Competent" or "Not Competent", there is no such thing as performance moderation or intervention by their airline's management.

Performance Critical Conversation for Pilots

Performance critical conversation takes the form of a debrief immediately after a pilot has been checked, audited or tested upon. The checker will share his findings and observations. The pilot may seek clarifications (if any). Sometimes, the checkers may make comments and surface scenario questions for discussion and learning.

Managing Weak Performance for Pilots

With the periodical checks and reviews of the technical scores of the pilots, those who are trailing will be surfaced for prompt counselling and re-training. The airline will not allow a pilot's performance to deteriorate, otherwise the credibility of the entire pilot population in the said airline will be at stake. Being professional and mindful of the disrepute that he may bring to the pilot community, the pilot who is off track will take his situation very seriously and shape up. Suffice to say, a formal (and protracted) Performance Improvement Plan (PIP) is not required.

Competency Frameworks

Focus of this Chapter

Organisations compete for committed and competent people. Collectively, the competencies of the individual employees and quality of the leadership constitute an organisation's human capital capabilities. Every organisation needs strong human capital capabilities to survive and thrive. It cannot be overstated that the quality (or competence) of employees is a prerequisite for any organisation to deliver performance and succeed.

Competence of employees is measured through competencies. This chapter takes the readers through the concept of competencies and how to develop a competency framework. We examine the ways to identify, select and define competencies and use the competency framework to assess employees and apply the competency results to integrate with and enhance the organisation's overall human capital management. We also discuss the challenges involved in developing and using a competency framework.

To have a more targeted discussion, we focus on the competencies of professionals, managers and executives (PMEs). Towards the end of this chapter, we touch on competencies for non-executive employees briefly.

Competencies Explained

The Discovery and Study of Competencies

D9.1   During the early to mid-20th century, organisations mostly used job-based functional/technical knowledge and skills to assess, select and hire employees. In the 1960s and 1970s, there was a shift towards behavioural competencies, emphasising observable behaviours that lead to success on a job. Competency models started to emerge, incorporating interpersonal skills and other behavioural traits over and above job requirements that specify functional/technical knowledge and skills. Studies found that behavioural factors were more telling of an employee's performance.

D9.2   Notably, the study of competencies began in earnest in the early 1970s when Dr David McClelland (an American psychologist) published an article demonstrating that behavioural traits and characteristics are much more effective than aptitude tests in predicting who will and will not be successful in job performance. In every job, some people perform more effectively than others. Superior performers tend to do their jobs differently and possess different characteristics compared to their peers (who may be equally knowledgeable and skilled) with average performance. Superior performers did things such as exercising good judgment, noticing problems, taking actions to address them and setting challenging goals. They demonstrate these behaviours relatively independent of their skill proficiency and experience level. McClelland's postulation is that competencies matter more than functional/technical knowledge and skills in predicting superior performance.

The Theory behind Competencies

D9.3   Different researchers studying the linkages between performance in jobs and personal characteristics, behavioural traits, knowledge and skills have defined the term "competencies" somewhat differently, depending on the organisational and job context and particularly, how they frame superior performance. Let's look at a few.

> Hay McBer (the research and consultancy company founded by American psychologist Dr David McClelland) had defined competencies as *"personal characteristics that can be shown to cause or predict effective or outstanding performance in a particular job within a particular organisation. These personal characteristics include deep-seated traits as well as readily observable skills and behaviours"*.

In a paper written by Dr Lyle M Spencer Jr (co-founder of Competency International and President and CEO, Hay McBer Centre for Research and Technology) in 1991, he defined competency in layman terms as *"an underlying characteristic of an individual that can be shown to predict superior or effective performance in a job"*. He elaborated that competencies can be personal characteristics such as motives, self-concept and knowledge and skills.

Professor Richard E Boyatzis (an American professor and expert in the field of emotional intelligence, behaviours and competency) simply called competency as *"an underlying characteristic of a person which results in effective or superior performance in a job"*.

Another definition of competency is *"a cluster of related knowledge, skills and attitudes that affects a major part of one's job that correlates with performance on the job, that can be measured against well-accepted standards, and that can be improved via training and development"*. This definition has been synthesised from the suggestions of several hundred specialists in human resource development who attended a conference about competencies in Johannesburg, South Africa in October 1995.

What are Competencies Made of? The Iceberg Model

D9.4   The various definitions of competencies cited above reveal the common notion that competencies comprise the following components:

(a) personal characteristics such as motives, traits and self-concept;
(b) knowledge; and
(c) skills.

D9.5   Hay McBer used a "Competency Iceberg" to capture and explain the various components. The iceberg shows the visible and non-visible components of competencies:

- *Knowledge and Skills (Visible)*
  These are above the water level and are readily observable and more easily assessed and developed through training.

- *Motives, Traits and Self-Concept (Hidden)*
  These are below the water level which are hidden and more difficult to observe but are more impactful. These are central to a person's personality and are enduring, that is, much more difficult to change or develop.

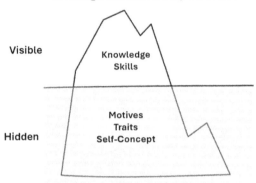

Iceberg Model of Competencies

Visible — Knowledge / Skills

Hidden — Motives / Traits / Self-Concept

D9.6   Using the Iceberg Model, Spencer and Spencer went on to articulate 5 types of competency characteristics as follows:

1. **Knowledge**
   Knowledge and information that a person has in specific content areas. An accountant's knowledge of balance sheets is an example. (Knowledge refers to the theoretical and practical understanding of a subject and involves facts, information and concepts acquired through education, training or experience.)

2. **Skills**
   The ability to perform certain physical and mental tasks. A sales executive's ability to make a sales presentation is a skill (how effective the presentation depends on other competency characteristics such as his motivation and self-confidence).

3. **Motives**
   The things a person consistently thinks about and wants that cause actions. Motives drive, direct and select behaviours and action paths. Examples are the need for achievement, power and affiliation.

4. **Traits**
   Physical characteristics and consistent responses to situations or information. Examples are stamina, tenacity, resilience and emotional composure.

5. **Self-Concept**
   A person's attitudes, values or self-image. Examples are self-confidence and team spirit versus personal achievement.

D9.7 *What is the connection between Competencies, Work Behaviours and Job Performance?*

A person's competencies comprise the knowledge and skills that he possesses, as well as his motives, traits and self-concept. Knowledge is about understanding a subject matter, while skills are about putting that knowledge into practice to perform specific tasks/activities. Skills can be honed through practice and experience. Motives, traits and self-concept are the driving forces that generate the intent and propensity/inclination for a person to acquire knowledge and apply it to skills. Once set into motion, the result is manifested as work behaviours which then lead to job performance. The following diagram summarises the interrelation between all these components.

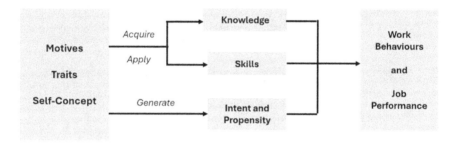

Importance of Competencies

D9.8 The concept of "competencies" entails that one looks beyond just knowledge and skills to predict an employee's performance. A competency model puts the focus on a person's motives, traits and self-concept as important determinants for superior performance. Put simply, knowledge and skills are only the basic (or threshold) requirements for a job; these do not sufficiently predict superior job performance. A very qualified, knowledgeable and skilful person may not necessarily produce superior performance. He may lack the aspiration and drive. Or his manner of dealing with issues and working with people may hamper him from getting the best outcomes. These factors (aspiration, drive and attitudes) are embedded in his motives, traits and self-concept. They generate the intent, inclination and attitudes that shape one's behaviours and actions and therefore determine the quality of work outcomes. This is especially so for complex jobs.

> Zwell International which had conducted many searches for Chief Financial Officers (CFOs) found that superior CFOs do not necessarily understand balance sheets or other aspects of finance better than the average CFOs. More importantly, what they possess is the ability to partner with Chief Executive Officers (CEOs) to understand business issues and impact and influence the organisations using their financial acumen. They are able to help business heads improve revenues and reduce cost through better ways of managing assets and resources. In short, it is competencies (not just knowledge and skills) that differentiate superior performers.

D9.9   In today's environment where knowledge and skills can become obsolete rapidly and with the abundance of information available through the internet and artificial intelligence (AI) products such as ChatGPT, the advantage enjoyed by an individual who possesses information, knowledge and skills is eroded.

D9.10   At the organisation-wide level, the competencies of employees and leaders collectively constitute the organisation's workforce capabilities. Competencies are the leading indicator of performance and organisational success. The relationship is a straightforward one:

> *Employees have high competencies → employees will perform their jobs well and deliver good work outcomes → organisation will show effectiveness in what it does → high probability for organisation to be successful.*

Classifications, Types and Groupings of Competencies

D9.11   In most competency frameworks, competencies are classified according to the area of focus and emphasis. A common way to classify competencies is as follows:

(a) *Core competencies*
(b) *Leadership competencies*
(c) *Functional/Technical competencies*

Core competencies and Leadership competencies almost always have the elements of intent and propensity/inclination which are derived from a person's motives, traits and self-concept. Whereas for Functional/Technical competencies, the emphasis is on knowledge and skills.

Core Competencies

D9.12   Core competencies are critical to an organisation. Most organisations term them as "core" because the competencies are applicable to all job families and all job levels.

D9.13   Core competencies may be clustered according to their purpose or emphasis. An example of clustering of core competencies is shown in the table below:

Core Competency Clusters	Examples of Core Competencies
Achievement and Excellence	Taking Ownership. Initiative. Execution and Results. Bias for Action. Concern for Governance/Order. Concern for Quality.
Cognitive Capacity	Analytical Ability. Analysis and Judgment. Critical Thinking. Conceptual Thinking. Sense of Perspective.
Help and Service	Service Orientation. Empathy. Concern for Others.
Influence and Collaboration	Communication and Influence. Collaboration. Relationship Building. Cultural Sensitivity.
Personal Effectiveness	Tenacity. Resilience. Information Seeking. Self-confidence. Decisiveness. Organisation Commitment.
Relevance and Growth	Change Orientation. Growth Mindset. Sustainability Mindset.

More examples of how core competencies may be clustered are shown in Annex D9-1 (based on the core competency models by Hay McBer and Dr Michael Zwell).

D9.14   When one dissects a core competency, it becomes obvious that it comprises a varying mix of knowledge and skills and a person's motives, traits and self-concept:

- Some core competencies emphasise more on intent, drive and attitudes. For example, core competencies such as "taking ownership", "bias for action", "tenacity", "resilience" and "growth mindset" have little to do with knowledge and skills. Rather, these shout out about a person's motives, traits and self-concept which drive his intent and propensity/inclination to behave in a certain way.

- There are also core competencies that require a fair amount of knowledge and skills besides just having the motive and inclination. For example, a core competency like "customer focus" will require a person to have good knowledge of customer service and the skills to serve and delight customers. Core competencies such as "communication and influence" and "relationship building" are also similar examples that entail a good amount of acquirable knowledge and teachable skills other than just the need for motive.

- On the other hand, a core competency like "decisiveness" involves a heavy dose of motive, traits and self-concept in that the person must be willing and bold enough to make judgement and take calculated risks in decision-making. Yet at the same time, decisiveness can be improved by having the knowledge of the issues on hand and the pertinent skills to make effective decisions confidently.

D9.15   SkillsFuture Singapore (SSG) has developed and published a set of 16 Critical Core Skills under 3 clusters (SSG uses the two terms, skills and competencies, interchangeably). These critical core skills (or competencies) are applicable to all sectors and job families, and Singaporeans are encouraged to acquire and possess them to remain future-ready. In that sense, it can be said that these are put forth by SSG as the desired "core competencies" for Singaporean workers. Organisations looking to develop their own competency frameworks may take reference from these and use these as a basis to hire and train their employees.

Competency Clusters	Competencies
Thinking Critically Cognitive skills that are needed to think broadly and creatively in order to see connections and opportunities in the midst of change.	1. Creative Thinking 2. Decision Making 3. Problem Solving 4. Sense Making 5. Transdisciplinary Thinking

Interacting with Others Learning from other people is one of the most effective ways to acquire new skills and ideas. Being effective at interacting with others means thinking about the needs of other people, as well as being able to exchange ideas and build a shared understanding of a problem or situation. Increasingly people need to be able to combine their technical skills with those of others to succeed.	6. Building Inclusivity 7. Collaboration 8. Communication 9. Customer Orientation 10. Developing People 11. Influence
Staying Relevant Managing oneself effectively and paying close attention to trends impacting work and living provide the strategies, direction and motivation for technical skill development.	12. Adaptability 13. Digital Fluency 14. Global Perspective 15. Learning Agility 16. Self-Management

Critical and Supplementary Competencies

D9.16   In developing a competency model, some organisations tend to select a fairly long list of core competencies, particularly if the organisation has many job roles and many people are involved in the selection process for the core competencies. A long list of core competencies has its disadvantages:

(a) the core competencies may vary in degrees of criticality and applicability across different job families;

(b) having too many core competencies may dilute the attention of the few that are truly critical; and

(c) employees may feel daunted by a long list of core competencies expected of them.

D9.17   For the above reasons, organisations may consider dividing their shortlisted/ selected core competencies into two subsets: (a) critical competencies and (b) supplementary competencies.

D9.18   Whether a core competency is termed as "critical" or "supplementary" will depend on the nature of the job role for a particular job family. If relevancy is emphasised, different job families may be assigned with different sets of critical and supplementary competencies. In other words, the critical and supplementary competencies are "customised" for each job family. An example of this customised approach is given in the following table:

Job Roles/ Families	Core Competencies	
	Critical	Supplementary
Marketing and Sales	Taking Ownership. Execution and Result Focus. Communication and Influence. Relationship Building. Growth Mindset.	Analytical Ability. Tenacity. Resilience.
Human Resource	Taking Ownership. Analytical Ability. Communication and Influence. Service Orientation.	Change Orientation. Empathy. Effective Negotiation. Collaboration.
Finance	Taking Ownership. Analytical Ability. Information Seeking. Concern for Governance.	Change Orientation. Collaboration.
Engineering	Taking Ownership. Analytical Ability. Information Seeking. Concern for Governance. Solution Focus.	Change Orientation. Collaboration.

D9.19   Some organisations may prefer a more simplified approach. A few critical competencies may be selected as a common set and applied to all job families, while each job family may have different supplementary competencies.

Leadership Competencies

D9.20   As the name implies, "leadership competencies" relate to managing, developing, motivating, aligning and inspiring people, as well as leading the organisation (at least in a functional area). Leadership competencies are usually applied to senior-level executives (aka management personnel). However, some organisations choose to use a broader application and apply leadership competencies to all employees who are people managers. Usually, the organisation will use a job level as a proxy "cut-off" line to apply leadership competencies (for example, leadership competencies may apply to employees who are in job grade [X] and above).

D9.21   Common leadership competencies include: (a) strategic vision, (b) critical thinking and judgment, (c) leading and developing people and (d) influencing and inspiring. The leadership competency framework developed by the Glasgow City Council as shown below provides some examples of leadership competencies:

Leadership Competency Framework by Glasgow City Council

Leadership Competency Clusters	Examples of Competencies
Personal Qualities	Self-belief. Self-awareness. Drive for improvement in public service. Personal integrity.
Setting Direction	Seizing the future. Intellectual flexibility. Broad scanning. Contextual astuteness. Drive for results.
Delivering Service	Leading change through people. Holding to account. Empowering others. Effective and strategic influencing. Working effectively with others.

Functional and Technical Competencies

D9.22   Functional and technical competencies encompass all knowledge and skills that pertain to specific functional domains that are required for running an organisation (such as business and marketing, sales, customer service, finance, human resource, legal, information technology, procurement, engineering, production, quality control, operations, logistics, risk management and audit).

D9.23   Functional/technical competencies incorporate the requisite academic, professional, trade and accredited qualifications/certifications that validate one's knowledge, skills and experience to perform competently in a specific domain area.

D9.24   Small organisations have a preference to set out functional/technical competencies to add on to their core competencies, so as to make their competency frameworks more "complete". These organisations use functional/technical competencies as a basis for hiring and appraising their employees. They find comfort in knowing that their employees possess the requisite functional/technical know-how (or expertise) to perform the jobs that they are hired for. As small organisations usually do not have many job families, their lists of functional/technical competencies would be quite manageable.

D9.25   In the case of large organisations, they typically opt not to specially create a list of functional/technical competencies for their competency frameworks. The rationale is that they view functional/technical competencies as role-based skills requirements. If the organisation has many job families, it will end up with a long list of functional/technical competencies which will make its competency framework very unwieldy. More importantly, these organisations tend to believe that functional/technical competencies are just basic requirements and not the differentiating factor in performance. Moreover, functional/technical competencies stand a higher chance of obsolescence.

D9.26   If an organisation chooses to set out functional/technical competencies, it should have the competencies elaborated in different proficiency levels with the accompanying behavioural markers (these are covered in the later sections of this chapter). Samples of proficiency levels and behavioural markers have been provided for human resource management and financial management in Annex D9-2. Those who prefer more granular details will find the behavioural markers in these two samples too generic (since the financial management competency has been defined as a composite of the key financial management knowledge and skills, and likewise for the human resource management competency which has been constructed as a composite of the relevant knowledge and skills related to human resource management). If more granularity is preferred, the financial management competency and human resource management competency may be further broken down into sub-domain areas as follows:

Financial Management	Human Resource Management
• Financial Transaction Management	• Manpower Planning and Recruitment
• Transaction Due Diligence	• Salary and Rewards Design
• Financial Closing	• Benefits Design and Management
• Group Accounting and Consolidation	• Performance Management
• Financial Analysis and Reporting	• Learning and Development
• Financial Planning and Budgeting	• Employee Relations and Industrial Relations
• Cash Flow Management	• Career Management and Staff Deployment
• Cost Management	• Talent Management and Succession Planning
• Treasury Management	• Organisation Development
• Taxation	• HR Information System and Analytics
• etc.	• etc.

D9.27   Organisations which are keen to have detailed functional/technical competencies for various job families may refer to the skills frameworks published by the SkillsFuture Singapore (SSG). Specifically for human resource (HR), HR practitioners can refer to the Body of Competencies (BOC) for HR management and development published by the Institute of Human Resource Practitioners (IHRP) which shows a comprehensive and granular list of HR functional competencies.

D9.28   While more granularity for functional/technical competencies is useful in guiding employees in their professional knowledge/skills upgrading, too much attention channelled into this direction may inadvertently subtract the focus on core competencies. The most effective functional leader (say, a chief financial officer or chief human resource officer) is often not a professional who excels in the subject domain alone; more importantly, he needs to be outstanding in the core competencies.

Workplace Skills

D9.29   All employees whose work involves administrative tasks (for example, professionals, managers and executives (PMEs) and backroom employees) are expected to have some common workplace skills at the basic (or threshold) level to be able to "move around" and operate effectively at the workplace. These include the following:

(a) basic communication skills,
(b) basic writing skills,
(c) basic interpersonal skills,
(d) basic comprehension skills and
(e) office technology skills.

D9.30   The purpose of mentioning workplace skills in this chapter is to raise awareness of these basic skills being prerequisites (that is, bare essentials) for employment for PMEs and backroom employees. While these skills are essential, they are not useful as a predictor or differentiator of superior performance. For this reason, these skills are not considered as competencies.

D9.31   That said, certain job roles require particular workplace skills at a higher proficiency level. For example, jobs in sales, business development and human resource require jobholders to have a higher level of interpersonal skills to communicate, persuade and influence, in which case these requirements may be encapsulated under "communication and influence" and considered a core competency.

Summary of Competencies and Skills

D9.32   For ease of reference, a recap of the various types of competencies is provided in the summary table below:

Types of Competencies	Examples
Core Competencies (which may be sub-divided into Critical competencies and Supplementary competencies)	Taking Ownership. Analytical Ability. Problem Solving. Execution and Results. Bias for Action. Sense of Perspective. Tenacity. Agility and Resilience. Communication and Influence. Collaboration. Relationship Building. Information Seeking. Solution Focus. Innovation and Creativity. Change and Growth Orientation. Cultural Sensitivity.
Leadership Competencies	Strategic Vision. Leading and Developing People. Influencing and Inspiring. Critical Thinking. Harnessing Diversity. Global Orientation.
Functional/Technical Competencies	Business and Marketing. Sales. Customer Service. Finance. Human Resource. Legal. Information Technology. Procurement. Engineering. Production. Quality Control. Operations. Logistics. Risk Management and Audit.
Workplace Skills (not part of Competency Framework)	Basic Communication. Basic Writing Skills. Basic Inter-personal Skills. Basic Comprehension Skills. Office Technology Skills.

Identifying and Selecting Competencies

D9.33   Once an organisation has decided to establish a competency framework, the next step is to identify and select the appropriate competencies that will suit its context and needs. To give more focus, we navigate and explain the process of identifying and selecting competencies for a competency framework for a professional/manager/executive (PME) workforce. For non-executive (that is, rank-and-file) employees, we suggest a simplified competency framework and discuss this towards the end of this chapter.

D9.34   The more common ways that organisations can use to identify and select competencies for a competency framework are the following:

(a) Behavioural Event Interviews (BEI) method
(b) Expert Panel method
(c) Organisational Forward Review method

Behavioural Event Interviews

D9.35   The Behavioural Event Interviews (BEI) method involves interviewing two groups of employees for every job position: (a) the superior-performer group and (b) the average-performer group.

D9.36   The employees selected for interview will be individually asked about the typical things that they do daily or regularly and the thoughts that they have when they engage in what they do – that is, the employees are probed about the *What, How* and *Why* about doing their work. Care must be taken to use open questions so that the interviewees will be free to give their own answers. Closed and leading questions that invite only Yes/No answers must not be used, as otherwise, they will skew the interview responses. To validate the interview responses, the employees should be asked to cite critical incidents, so as to better uncover how the employees react to situations and deal with them. The focus of the interview is not on the employee's knowledge and skills but rather on his mindset about doing his job, which essentially hinges on his motives, traits and self-concept (see definitions of these in paragraph D9.6).

D9.37   The interviews will generate a large amount of action statements, action verbs and thoughts from the interviewees. The BEI interviewer (usually a senior human resource officer or an external consultant engaged for the project) must plough and sieve through the information to identify behaviours and personality traits that are: (a) common to both groups of performers and (b) unique to only the superior performers. The behaviours/traits that are typically exhibited by only the superior performers (and not the average performers) point to the differentiating competencies that drive superior performance, while those behaviours/traits that are demonstrated by both groups of employees are considered the threshold level job requirements.

D9.38   The data gathered on the behaviours/traits that distinguish the superior performers from the average performers form a rich library of information to enable the organisation to deliberate, distil and eventually shortlist the desired competencies for the said job position. The organisation's management should do a critical review and sanity check on the shortlisted competencies to ensure that the competencies correlate with performance and have minimal overlap. The final list of selected competencies will form the competency requirements for the specific job position.

D9.39   The above process (paragraphs D9.36–D9.38) is then repeated for all the job positions to be studied. By comparing the shortlisted competencies for all job positions, the organisation will be able to identify those that are common across all or several job families. These competencies can then be selected as the core competencies.

D9.40   The BEI method is a tedious and time-consuming process, especially if an organisation has many job families/positions. To do a "shortcut", the organisation may consider applying the BEI method only for selective job positions that are considered as anchor or benchmark jobs – these are mission-critical job positions and are typically occupied by a large number of jobholders. The core competencies identified for these anchor/benchmark jobs can then be extended to cover all job families, including non-anchor/benchmark jobs.

D9.41   It is pertinent to point out that the BEI method has a major disadvantage. It uses "lag" data – that is, the information gathered from the superior performers is based on current (or past) events. Therefore, the core competencies identified and selected using the BEI method cater to the current/prevailing organisational context and circumstances. What if the organisation undergoes change and transformation and jobs evolve? The organisation will need additional or new future-oriented core competencies. The BEI method which relies on interview data from current/past events may not serve to identify the new future-oriented competency requirements. The organisation will have to use another way, the Organisational Forward Review (OFR) method to apply foresight and identify the new future-oriented competencies. We discuss the OFR method in the later part of this section.

Expert Panel

D9.42   The Expert Panel (EP) method involves in-depth deliberations by a panel of experts (comprising senior executives) who are familiar with the jobs to be studied. Different panels may be convened for different job positions since it is not realistic to expect a single panel to be familiar with all job positions.

D9.43   Panel members will be asked to reflect and recount (a) the typical behaviours, actions, thought processes and characteristics observed of superior performers whom they have worked with and (b) the same for average performers.

D9.44   To facilitate discussion, the panel members may be asked to submit the lists (a) and (b) prior to the actual panel session. The project manager (usually a senior human resource officer or an external consultant engaged for the project) will consolidate the lists, clarify as necessary, and cluster similar observations/statements accordingly. The consolidated behaviours/actions which appear in list (a) but which are not found in list (b) can be considered as competency requirements that characterise superior performers. These should be shortlisted for arriving at the core competencies for the organisation.

D9.45   Next, the panel session will be convened to review, analyse, supplement and validate the proposed competency requirements. There may be several rounds of deliberation before confirming the final list of competencies to be selected for the organisation's competency framework. Before confirming the choices, the definitions of these competencies should be prepared and validated by the panel to ensure that there is a common understanding of the competencies (and their constituent elements). The process of defining the competencies will also help ensure that there is no or minimal overlap among the competencies.

> The Expert Panel method was used in an actual project when an airline wanted to identify the core or differentiating competencies (not technical skills) for the pilots. Eventually, 11 differentiating competencies were selected for the entire pilot community (of different ranks). To give more focus, only 7 differentiating competencies (that are chosen from the total 11) are set for each pilot group. Henceforth, pilots are assessed on 7 differentiating competencies apart from the requisite technical piloting skills.

D9.46   The EP method is a tedious and time-consuming process, as it may involve many panels if the organisation has many different job families. Same as for the BEI method, the organisation may consider a "shortcut" by focusing only on anchor/benchmark jobs. The core competencies identified for the anchor/benchmark jobs can then be extended to cover all job families, including non-anchor/benchmark jobs.

Organisational Forward Review

D9.47   Both the Behavioural Event Interviews (BEI) and Expert Panel (EP) methods are time-consuming and resource-intensive involving many stakeholders (many interviewees in the case of BEI and many panel members in the case of EP). In most situations, given limited time and resources, organisations would use the Organisational Forward Review (OFR) method to select the core competencies, perhaps with the guidance of an external competency consultant.

D9.48   Under the OFR method, an organisation embarks or leverages on a strategic or corporate planning exercise, where it takes stock of its strategic direction, performance, challenges and opportunities. The planning and review exercise will invariably generate new strategic action plans for the organisation that will help it navigate the evolving business environment and ensure continued success. These new insights form timely and critical inputs for the organisation in establishing its competency framework to equip its employees with the right competencies going forward.

D9.49   In arriving at a set of relevant and future-oriented core competencies, it is important for the organisation to take into account the following factors:

Vision and Mission	The vision and mission of the organisation serve as goal posts to provide context to the organisation's strategic plans and actions. These vision, mission, goals and strategies will suggest the need for certain core competencies for employees, especially those in mission-critical job roles.
Core Values	Most core values point towards the importance of certain core competencies. For example, the core value "excellence" points to core competencies such as "professionalism" and "quality focus". "Trust" as a core value, depending on how it is defined, may point to "taking ownership" as a core competency.
Strategic Changes	The aspirations and changes that an organisation wants to pursue must be considered in selecting the relevant and future-oriented core competencies. Some of the current competencies that have hitherto enabled employees to produce superior performance may not remain as relevant or effective as the organisation's focus undergoes change.

	For example, "concern for order" which has been valued by many organisations in the past is now less emphasised, except for certain job roles that focus on ensuring order and governance. "Growth mindset" and "change orientation" are seen as more relevant given the rapid changes in the operating landscape. "Cultural sensitivity" is emerging as an important competency as organisations become more globalised and diverse. "Sustainability focus" is also gaining attention as a future-oriented competency.
Competency Profile of Employees	The selection of relevant and future-oriented core competencies will send the message to employees about the change in job and performance requirements. It will also position the organisation to select the right internal candidates for promotion and suitably competent job candidates as new hires. The aim is to find ways to move the competency profile of the organisation's workforce to what it desires to have for the future.

D9.50   Organisations embarking on developing a new competency framework that is future-oriented must also take steps to pivot their workforce from the existing state (say, one that is anchored on an existing competency framework) to the desired future-ready state. The entire journey of change would involve the following steps:

Step 1 *Organisational Forward Review*	Consider the organisation's vision, mission and core values as well as its aspirations, strategic initiatives and challenges. Consider how these impact the organisation's expectations of its employees in terms of work behaviours and deliverables. Consider the strategic changes that the organisation intends to pursue – including those affecting organisation culture, business and operational models, decision-making protocol, work flows and processes.
Step 2 *Identify and select the Future-oriented Core Competencies*	Evaluate how the changes in Step 1 affect the existing job positions and work deliverables required from employees. Deliberate and generate a list of relevant and future-oriented core competencies that employees must possess to deliver superior performance in

	the new scenario. If the organisation has a large workforce and many job families, focus on the mission-critical or anchor/benchmark job positions that involve many jobholders. Where necessary, convene an Expert Panel for selective jobs to do the deliberation and review. Finalise the list of core competencies and their definitions.
Step 3 *Stocktake on Current Human Capital Capability*	Examine the current key (mission-critical) job positions in the organisation and the profiles of the existing employees including their performance, capabilities and limitations. The collective average is an indication of the organisation's current human capital capability.
Step 4 *Identify Competency Gaps*	Compare the organisation's current human capital capability (in terms of the current core competencies of its workforce) with the list of future-oriented core competencies desired by the organisation going forward. Map out the gaps.
Step 5 *Action Plan for Closing Competency Gaps*	Devise plans and initiatives to close the competency gaps identified under Step 4, that is, to shift the organisation's human capital capability from its current state (determined under Step 3) to the desired state (determined under Step 2). The plans/initiatives may include training and development for incumbent employees and/or hiring of new talent.

Summing up …

D9.51   From experience, during the initial deliberation, many core competencies will look appealing and relevant and will be picked up for the check-out cart. The result will be an overloaded cart with many competencies. Having too many core competencies is neither desirable nor practical; it will dilute the focus and overwhelm employees. Therefore, the organisation must be judicious in selecting only those competencies that can truly shape and generate the work behaviours that lead to superior performance. Pick only the essentials and leave out those that are "good to have".

D9.52   Another consideration is that competencies must be those that can be described with observable behaviours; otherwise, the competencies will be too abstract for employees to grasp, let alone acquire and practise. The competencies selected must also be clearly defined. One example is communication; it is important to specify whether the communication competency should be written or oral. It is not advisable to combine both written and oral communication skills as one competency because many employees are strong in one but not the other. Moreover, most jobs do not require the jobholder to be proficient in both. For example, it does not serve any purpose to insist that sales personnel must write well when their jobs do not require them to do so.

D9.53   Selection of core competencies cannot be a cut-and-paste exercise, say, merely copying what another organisation has. What works for organisation A may not work for organisation B. Competencies must be contextualised based on the aspirations, needs and circumstances specific to the organisation.

D9.54   Some further pointers on selection and housekeeping for core competencies are given below:

(a) A core competency must not be too "multi-dimensional". For example, a core competency articulated as "emotional intelligence" has many dimensions of behaviour embedded. Likewise, for something articulated as "personal effectiveness". Having multiple dimensions in one single competency will pose a challenge in defining the competency and the behavioural markers. It will also be very difficult to assess and rate an employee on the said competency as he may be strong in some dimensions and weak in others.

(b) Core competencies that are selected must have no or minimal overlap. For example, "pursuit of excellence" has some overlap with "quality focus". Same for "relationship building" and "collaboration". If the organisation has selected one as a core competency, the other that has overlap should not be selected.

(c) Some core competencies are related (such as, one leads to the other) and therefore can be combined. For example, "communication" and "influence" may be combined. Same for "change orientation" and "growth mindset".

(d) Some attributes and skills should be taken as a given (or a threshold job requirement). An example is "professionalism" for executive employees. An organisation may however still select "professionalism" as a core competency if its employees are lacking in this area and it wants to reinforce the requirement. Likewise, "customer focus" can be taken as a given, but if an organisation's employees are lacking in this aspect, it may list it as a core competency to affirm its importance and transform its customer service culture.

(e) Some competencies such as "agility and resilience" and "change orientation" are widely adopted. Be it as it may, an organisation must define the said competencies and describe the behavioural markers in its own context (taking into account the unique challenges it is facing) instead of copying from other organisations.

Developing a Competency Model

D9.55 Once an organisation has identified and selected its competencies (which may include Core, Leadership and Functional/Technical competencies), the next step is to define the competencies, set out the proficiency levels and describe the behavioural markers for each proficiency level. We elaborate on these steps.

Defining the Competencies

D9.56 To define a competency, one must first understand the dimensions (as below) that characterise a competency:

(a) intent, propensity, commitment, effort and persistence involved (in demonstrating certain behaviours);
(b) intensity and frequency (of showing the said behaviours);
(c) complexity of the issues or situations (to be dealt with); and
(d) impact of the behaviours on other stakeholders and the organisation.

D9.57 Crafting definitions of competencies is an art and requires a good command of the language as well as astute discernment. A good definition should be precise (accurate), concise (succinct), incisive (clear and sharp) and elegant (neat). We share some examples below for illustration.

Core Competency	*Taking Ownership*
Definition	*The willingness and commitment to own the issue, take charge, follow through and produce results.*

The words "willingness and commitment" denote a person's intent and propensity; these are the underlying characteristics of a person. The phrase "to own the issue, take charge, follow through and produce results" describes how taking ownership is done (which are largely observable and may also be measurable). The words "produce results" convey the desired impact of taking ownership; it does not mean just being busy with activities.

Core Competency	*Pursuit of Excellence*
Definition	*The inclination, intent and effort to excel and be the best in whatever one is doing.*

This competency "pursuit of excellence" first requires the desire and intent to want to excel, hence these aspects have been included in the definition statement. Intent alone will not produce the desired output, there must be effort and persistence and even innovation; these can be incorporated into the behavioural statements. As this is a generic competency which can be used for all job roles/levels, the phrase "be the best in whatever one is doing" is all encompassing.

Leadership Competency	*Strategic Vision*
Definition	*The propensity and ability to look at issues from a strategic or higher vantage point and place facts and issues in a broader context and longer time horizon.*

The word "propensity" denotes a natural inclination. However, propensity alone is not enough; one must have the "ability". The rest of the statement highlights how "strategic vision" should be demonstrated in terms of breadth and time dimension.

Setting and Naming the Proficiency Levels

D9.58   *What is a proficiency level?*
The level of competency that is demonstrated by an employee (through his observable work behaviours) is called the proficiency level. As all competencies have a range of depth and intensity, they can have various proficiency levels that are discernible. The higher the proficiency level, the more depth and intensity of the said competency will be demonstrated through the employee's work behaviours. Each proficiency level will have a set of behavioural markers to describe what is meant by that said proficiency level.

D9.59   There is no fixed rule on the number of proficiency levels to set. Organisations that prefer more granularity go for 6 levels, while others may go for 4 or 5. Generally, organisations apply a standard number of proficiency levels to all their selected competencies. In other words, if an organisation has decided to go for 5, then every competency will have 5 levels of proficiency for the sake of uniformity and ease of administration, especially if competency assessment is used as part of performance appraisal.

D9.60   There is no fixed rule on how to serially number the proficiency levels. Most organisations number the proficiency levels from "1" (being the lowest) to "5" (being the highest). Some organisations, however, in wanting to emphasise that behaviours at the lowest level are unacceptable, choose to number it as "0" or even "–1".

D9.61   Some organisations give a "name" to the proficiency levels other than just using numeric labels. The intent is to help employees better appreciate what level of proficiency they have attained (say, basic or intermediate or advanced level). Two examples of naming proficiency levels are given below:

Proficiency Level	Example 1	Example 2
	Proficiency Name	Proficiency Name
0	Foundation Minus	Awareness
1–2	Foundation	Basic
3–4	Foundation Plus	Intermediate
5	Advanced	Advanced
6	Advanced Plus	Expert

D9.62   Some organisations apply a uniform expectation (that is, requirement) of proficiency attainment on their employees based on job seniority. For example, all managers in the organisation may be required to attain proficiency level 4 in all the competencies that they are assessed on, while all directors may be required to attain proficiency level 5. Such standardisation makes it easier to apply the competency framework for performance appraisal. The caveat is that the organisation must ensure that the behavioural markers for proficiency levels 4 and 5 for all competencies are correctly pinned down and appropriately set for managers and directors respectively.

Describing the Behavioural Markers

D9.63   Each proficiency level of a competency must have a set of behavioural markers to describe what is meant by having or exhibiting that said proficiency level. The necessity to do so is simple. Competencies must be manifested through observable behaviours, otherwise there is no evidence of the competency and assessment will not be possible. Simply put, an employee is assessed on his competencies based on the behaviours that he demonstrates – how he thinks, talks, deals with people and situations, takes actions, solves problems and what results he produces. Behavioural markers articulate these. An employee's behaviour is compared against the behavioural markers of the proficiency levels of a competency; if his behaviour matches the behavioural markers for a particular proficiency level, he is considered to have attained the said proficiency level for that competency.

D9.64   In crafting behavioural markers for each proficiency level, one must look at the following dimensions of a competency:

(a) intent, propensity, commitment, effort and persistence involved (in demonstrating certain behaviours);
(b) intensity and frequency (of showing the said behaviours);
(c) complexity of the issues or situations (to be dealt with); and
(d) impact of the behaviours on other stakeholders and the organisation.

Behavioural markers must be sufficiently differentiating, changing in gradation from one proficiency level to the next. The differentiation must be discernible and meaningful.

D9.65   Crafting behavioural markers requires analysis and skill. Some pointers are given below:

(a) behavioural markers must be written using precise words that are carefully chosen to flash out the gradation between the proficiency levels;

(b) behavioural markers must be contextualised using terms/lingo that are relevant to the organisation so that employees can understand them and relate to them as "goal posts";

(c) the behaviours described must be observable; and

(d) while it is good to be comprehensive and detailed, it is not practical to have too many and long behavioural marker statements, as it will make it cumbersome and tedious to use. As a rule of thumb, 2–3 short behavioural maker statements for each proficiency level should be sufficient. The higher proficiency levels usually require more marker statements. Keeping it simple, concise and clear is key to minimising errors in competency assessment.

D9.66   When a first draft of behavioural markers is done, it is advisable to validate the draft by applying it to "known" employees (that is, employees who are regarded as superior performers, average performers or weak performers). The validation and checking will enable the behavioural markers to be refined and recalibrated.

D9.67   We share two examples of competencies with proficiency levels and their corresponding behavioural markers for illustration.

Competency	*Pursuit of Excellence*
Definition	*The inclination, intent and effort to excel and be the best in whatever one is doing.*
Proficiency Levels and Behavioural Markers	
1	• Focus on completing the job within the timelines. • Do just enough to meet the basic requirements.
2	• While getting the job done, try to do it better. • Try to do better but cannot sustain; quite easily distracted.
3	• Show interest and effort to do a good job. • Explore ways and execute to produce better output and quality.
4	• Show passion and consistent effort to produce good work. • Diligently push the boundaries to improve the status quo.

5	• Show passion and great effort to consistently produce excellent work. • Relentlessly and single-mindedly pursue excellence and set new standards.

Competency	*Collaboration*
Definition	*The desire, effort and ability to work effectively, cohesively and synergistically with others towards common goals, by leveraging different perspectives and strengths.*
Proficiency Levels and Behavioural Markers	
1	• Focus on own needs and job; cooperate with others only when asked. • Typically stick to own ways of working, unless asked to change to align with others. • Indifferent to teamwork. Not at all helpful.
2	• Generally, help others and consider the interests of others. • By and large, cooperate without prompting. • Try to deal with differences with others (not avoiding).
3	• Consider the interests of others, support others and generally work well with them. • Approach persons within own work contacts/areas and collaborate. • Can deal with some differences and tension.
4	• Seek and support opportunities for collaboration at organisational level. • Blend own efforts and views with those of others to achieve synergistic results. • Able to work with tension and resolve differences effectively.

5	• Actively create and facilitate opportunities for collaboration, enlist the right persons (usually multiple stakeholders) and integrate divergent interests, perspectives and strengths. • Always build on and sharpen others to enhance collective achievements. • Take the lead in ably resolving major differences.

Competency Framework (Sample)

D9.68   A sample competency framework (of Company ABC) is provided in Annex D9-2. It covers the following: (a) definitions and categories of competencies, (b) importance of competencies, (c) overview of the Critical, Leadership, Supplementary and Functional/Technical competencies selected and their definitions, (d) competency requirements matrix for different job levels and job families/roles, (e) proficiency levels and the associated behavioural markers for the selected competencies and (f) competency assessment.

D9.69   The sample framework has been specifically designed to cater to the needs of Company ABC. Organisations should design their own frameworks to suit their own unique context and needs. To better appreciate the competency framework shown for Company ABC, the following points should be noted:

(a) Company ABC has decided to sub-categorise its Core competencies into Critical and Supplementary. Other organisations may opt to keep it simple by just having one type of Core competencies.

(b) Company ABC has chosen to include Functional/Technical competencies in its competency framework, although the definitions and behavioural markers are rather generic since each functional area (for example, Human Resource) is represented by a single competency and not divided further into sub-functions (for example, manpower planning and recruitment, learning and development) for more granularity. Other organisations may opt not to include Functional/Technical competencies in their competency frameworks and have them parked under job requirements instead (which can be spelt out in job descriptions).

(c) On the number of competencies, Company ABC has decided that each employee will have a total of 10 competencies, where the permutations of competencies (Critical, Leadership, Supplementary and Functional/Technical) depend on the employee's job level and job family/role. The permutations are spelt out in a competency requirements matrix. Organisations may consider any other options and permutations to suit their needs and employee profile. For example, using the sample of competency framework for Company ABC shown in Annex D9-2, one may instead allow Leaders/Managers to have 5 Critical and 5 Supplementary and Functional/Technical competencies in addition to the 3 Leadership competencies, thus making a total of 13 competencies. The permutations are limitless; each organisation should decide what it needs, balancing being ideal and practical. On the other hand, a competency requirements matrix is not even necessary if an organisation so decides to have a standard list of core competencies that applies to all its employees.

Competency Assessment

Assessing the Individual Employee

D9.70   To assess the competencies of an employee, one must observe his work behaviours – how he thinks, talks, deals with people and situations, takes actions, solves problems and what results he produces.

D9.71   In assessing a particular competency, the assessor will compare the employee's behaviours against the behavioural markers of the various proficiency levels of the said competency. The assessor will select that particular proficiency level showing behavioural markers that best match with the observed behaviours of the employee. The selected proficiency level is taken as the employee's assessed proficiency for that competency. Competency assessment is done one competency at a time. The process is repeated for each competency that is relevant or has been selected for the employee.

D9.72   In assessing an employee on competencies, it is important to focus on the typical (or representative) behaviours demonstrated by the employee consistently (or at least, often enough) and not the one-off or occasional behaviours. The typical (or representative) behaviours are akin to the employee's work habit, and they reflect the motives, traits and self-concept of the employee, which are all components of competency, other than knowledge and skills (please refer to the Iceberg Model of Competencies elaborated in paragraphs D9.4–D9.7).

D9.73   *Where would an assessor gather the information and evidence on an employee's behaviours to assess his competency?*
To be able to capture the information and evidence, an assessor must be alert and observant in his interactions with the employee. His "radar surveillance" must be turned on, so to speak. The sources of information and evidence include the following:

(a) observations of his participation and contribution during meetings or discussions – the questions he raises, views expressed and suggestions given;

(b) reports and proposals prepared, noting the quality of the thought process, the degree of accuracy of facts presented and the organisation of ideas;

(c) minutes of meetings written, noting the grasp of the points of discussion;

(d) conversations with colleagues and customers – the manner, style and clarity of the communication;

(e) decisions made or actions taken – how problems are resolved, the quality of the outcomes and timeliness;

(f) daily work interactions, noting the employee's state of mind, whether calm and composed and in control or distraught and losing his cool; and

(g) performance feedback and coaching sessions, noting his motivation, confidence and priorities.

D9.74   Other than daily and regular work interactions, where necessary, the organisation may deliberately create special opportunities to enable a closer assessment of an employee on his competencies. For example, an employee may be assigned to work on special projects (such as stretch assignments) where his competencies will be put to a stringent test (aka under a microscope). The employee may be made to report to a different assessor (other than his regular supervisor) for such special projects, as having multiple assessors will enable a more holistic assessment of the employee. Such in-depth and intense assessment of an employee's competencies is a common talent management initiative when organisations want to identify their high-performing and high-potential employees to groom them for key leadership positions.

D9.75   Assessing an employee on competencies involves human judgment; subjectivity cannot be totally avoided. This is the case even if behavioural markers of proficiency levels of competencies have been carefully described. Matching an employee's observed behaviour to a proficiency level requires interpretation and discernment and also depends on the assessor's leaning towards being strict or lenient. The challenges of assessment (such as subjectivity, personal bias, leniency bias and recency effect) have been covered in Chapter D4 "Performance Appraisal".

Assessing and Tracking an Employee's Progression in Competency

D9.76   For every job position, the proficiency requirements will be set for each competency that has been selected for the said job. The proficiency requirements may differ from competency to competency, to take into account the nature of the job role as well as the job level. An employee's actual (assessed) proficiency levels for his competencies are then compared against the proficiency requirements for his job position. We illustrate with two examples (Human Resource Executive and Finance Executive) as shown below. Assume that both job positions are of the same job level/rank.

Core Competencies	Proficiency Level					
	HR Executive			Finance Executive		
	Required	Actual	Variance	Required	Actual	Variance
Taking Ownership	3	3	0	3	4	+1
Analytical Skills	3	3	0	3	3	0
Communication and Influence	4	3	−1	3	3	0
Concern for Governance	3	3	0	4	3	−1

Notice that the proficiency requirements for the two jobs are not the same. The HR Executive is required to have a higher proficiency for "Communication and Influence", whereas the Finance Executive is required to have a higher proficiency for "Concern for Governance". This is logical, given the different nature of the job roles. However, some organisations may opt to simplify by standardising all the proficiency requirements for an entire job level/rank, regardless of job family/role (for example, all executives of job band [X] must have proficiency level 3 for all their competencies, and for job band [Y], the requirement for all is proficiency level 4). While this approach may not be entirely "correct" (since it ignores the different job natures), it is done for the sake of practicality, especially if the organisation has many job families/roles.

D9.77　If an employee is being assessed over a period, his progression in competency proficiencies can be tracked easily. If the organisation has put in interventions (such as training and development, coaching and mentoring, job rotations and assigning stretch assignments) for the employee, the tracking of his proficiencies over time provides a validation of whether these interventions have borne fruit.

Changes in Competency Proficiency Levels for Employee Mr X

Core Competencies	Proficiency Level			
	2021	2022	2023	2024
Taking Ownership	3	3	3+	4
Pursuit of Excellence	3	3	3+	3+
Communication and Influence	3	3+	4	4
Execution and Result Focus	3	3	3+	3+
Change and Growth Orientation	2	3	3	3

The jump from one proficiency level to the next is a big step forward, given that there are not many proficiency levels. The use of "+" gives indication that the employee is making progress.

Results of Competency Assessments

D9.78　All said and done, when the competency assessment is completed for an employee, the line supervisor and/or line head should review the results. The following scenarios will emerge:

Employee's Actual Competency Results versus Competency Requirements	
Closely Matched	Employee in the right job role and job level. Also check his performance level; logically, his performance should hover around "Fully Meet Expectations".
Small Positive Variance	Check if his performance is also at the higher end of the rating scale. If so, there is alignment between his competencies and performance.

Big Positive Variance	Review the competency results to ensure accuracy (no over-leniency). Check against his performance level. What are his strong competencies? Consider how he can be tested for a higher job role (say, given stretch assignments).
Small Negative Gap	Check his performance level, whether it is also borderline. Is the employee new to the job role? What are his weak competencies? What could be the reasons? Will more time to familiarise with the job help? Consider how training or other interventions can help him improve.
Big Negative Gap	Review the competency results to ensure accuracy (no over-stringency). Check against his performance level. Was he wrongly hired or wrongly promoted? Find out the background and draw lessons from it. What are his weak competencies? Are these related to knowledge and skills or motives, traits and self-concept? Consider the type of interventions to be given (training or counselling).

Assessing the Organisational Capabilities

D9.79   At the organisational level, the competencies of employees can be aggregated to arrive at the average. The analysis can be done for different job levels and job families. This gives a useful and holistic view of the organisation's overall strengths and weaknesses of its workforce, which taken as a whole, represents the organisation's capabilities. At the same time, it will provide good insights for the organisation to consider how best to leverage on its obvious strengths and what interventions (such as recruiting new hires with different profiles, training and development such as mentoring, coaching, counselling and job rotations) can be made to shore up its weaker competencies.

D9.80   The organisation's competency proficiency profile can also be tracked over time to show the progress. If the organisation has made specific interventions for its weaker competencies, tracking the progress of the said competencies will offer insights into whether the interventions are bearing fruit.

Changes in Competency Proficiency Levels for the Organisation

| Core Competencies | Average Proficiency Level | | | | | |
| | Executives | | | Managers | | |
	2021	2022	2023	2021	2022	2023
Taking Ownership	3.2	3.3	3.5	3.9	4.1	4.2
Pursuit of Excellence	3.3	3.3	3.4	3.9	3.9	4.0
Communication and Influence	3.1	3.2	3.2	3.8	3.9	4.0
Execution and Result Focus	3.4	3.4	3.6	4.0	4.2	4.2
Change and Growth Orientation	2.1	2.3	2.4	3.4	3.6	3.5

"Change and Growth Orientation" is the weakest competency for this organisation, while "Execution and Result Focus" is relatively stronger than other competencies. If the organisation is operating in a fast-changing industry, the weakness in "Change and Growth Orientation" will be a concern. The organisation should explore what interventions it can make to uplift this competency in its employees.

Competency Framework for Rank-and-File Employees

D9.81   The concepts and features of the competency framework for professional, managerial and executive (PME) employees can logically be applied to rank-and-file (non-executive) employees. However, for practical reasons, most organisations do not do that. Generally, organisations prefer a simpler framework to deal with the competencies and performance assessment of rank-and-file employees. The main reasons for taking a simplified approach include the following:

(a) Rank-and-file employees generally work under clear instructions and follow prescribed work processes and are not given much room to make discretionary decisions. That being the case, their competency requirements are less complex and more homogeneous.

(b) The impact of superior performance from a rank-and-file employee is much lower compared to that of a professional/managerial/executive employee. While a rank-and-file employee's motives, traits and self-concept are also differentiating factors for performance, because the impact on performance is less significant, organisations tend not to invest too much time and resources to develop an elaborate competency framework for them.

D9.82   The common competency factors applied to rank-and-file employees include: (a) job knowledge and skills, (b) effort and diligence, (c) initiative, (d) customer and service focus, (e) communication, (f) teamwork, (g) discipline and reliability and (h) adaptability. A sample of a competency framework (with behavioural markers) for rank-and-file employees is shown in Annex D9-3.

Applying Competencies in Human Capital Management

D9.83   Core competencies are integral to various aspects of human capital management and development. Competencies underpin many human capital functions and initiatives, including the following:

(a) recruitment and selection,
(b) performance management,
(c) competency and skill-based salary structure,
(d) learning and development,
(e) promotion and succession planning and
(f) organisation development.

Recruitment and Selection

D9.84   Hiring right is critical. Assessment of job candidates should primarily be based on their competencies (and organisational fit). Interviewers should size up the candidates' past performance and experiences to assess their competencies by looking for evidence of how they have thought, behaved and acted in past situations.

D9.85   Some large and established organisations use assessment centres to assess the core competencies of candidates. The use of assessment centres is time-intensive and expensive, so it is usually reserved for candidates whom organisations intend to make heavy investment in (for example, scholarship candidates who if selected will be on sponsored education and bonded to serve the organisation upon completion of their study). The exercises and tests used in an assessment centre are usually based on "generic" core competencies, such as breadth and depth of view (commonly termed as helicopter view), analytical ability, critical thinking, communication and influence, resilience, adaptability and self-confidence.

D9.86   Hiring based on competencies is important. While knowledge and skills can be acquired through training and development, core competencies that are primarily anchored on a person's motives, traits and self-concept (see the definitions in paragraph D9.6) are innate characteristics and less trainable. An organisation that hires the right people with the right motives, traits and self-concept will have the right enduring competencies in its workforce capabilities.

Performance Management

D9.87   Most organisations appraise their employees on two aspects: (a) work targets and (b) competencies. For some job roles, it is straightforward to set clear and quantitative work targets – for example, a salesperson may be given a sales target of [$X] per month, or a production operator may be given a target of [X] units produced per month. However, not all jobs can have clear and quantitative work targets, especially so for backroom administrative job roles – for example, it is not as straightforward or meaningful to set [X] number of reports prepared or [X] number of letters issued as a work target for an administrative executive. For job roles where work targets are somewhat nebulous, the performance appraisal of the employee will lean more heavily on competency assessment. For more elaboration on how competency assessment is used in performance appraisal, please refer to Chapter D1 "Overview of Performance Management Framework" and Chapter D4 "Performance Appraisal".

Competency and Skill-based Salary Structure

D9.88   Competencies and skills can be used to calibrate salary level and increment. As competencies are predictive of performance, it is logical to use competencies as one of the factors to steer salary progression. In Volume B, Chapter B5 "Salary Ranges" and Chapter B6 "Salary Increments", we have mentioned that a learner should start at the bottom of the salary range for his job level. When he becomes more competent, his salary will progress, to eventually reach the maximum point of the salary range, which is appropriate for an incumbent at the expert level. Although this approach is logical and fair (and the ideal approach), in the Singapore context, seniority in service (and not competency progression) tends to take a disproportionate weightage in the determination of increments, particularly for increment policies for rank-and-file employees in unionised organisations.

D9.89 The consideration of competencies/skills in calibrating salaries is also evidenced in the Progressive Wage Model (PWM), where one of its four pillars relates to salary progression based on skills acquisition. For more elaboration on PWM, please refer to Volume B, Chapter B14 "Managing and Raising Wages of Lower-Wage Workers".

Learning and Development

D9.90 Performance appraisal will surface performance gaps and competency shortfall of individual employees. To plug the gaps and shortfall, a competency framework with detailed descriptions of competencies and proficiency behavioural markers provides a basis to plan and design interventions and training programs.

D9.91 *Can competency shortfall be addressed through training and development?* First, we need to know what the cause of the competency shortfall is. Competencies comprise the following: (a) knowledge, (b) skills, (c) motives (such as the need for achievement, power or affiliation), (d) traits (such as tenacity, agility and emotional composure) and (e) self-concept (such as values, attitudes and self-confidence). While shortfall in knowledge and skills can be addressed through training and development, it is not as easy for the rest. Self-confidence can be improved through developmental initiatives (say, coaching, mentoring and counselling), but requires more time and effort. Traits, values and attitudes on the other hand are much more difficult to change. More is discussed in Chapter D11 "Employee Training" and Chapter D12 "Employee Development".

Promotion and Succession Planning

D9.92 When an employee is considered for promotion, the consideration is not only on performance. The employee must also be assessed to be of good potential to take on a higher job position. How is potential assessed? The employee's competencies provide the basis for his assessed potential – weak competencies indicate weak potential and strong competencies indicate strong potential.

D9.93 Succession planning is about selecting and preparing employees with potential to take up bigger and critical roles. Knowing the competencies and the proficiency levels required for the bigger jobs will provide a basis to select the right candidates and develop them to fill the positions. Aspiration is important, as an employee with no hunger to climb the corporate ladder will not be motivated. Competencies relating to achievement motivation, bias for results and growth mindset are good proxies in sizing up the aspiration of an employee.

Organisation Development

D9.94   Organisation development (OD) is a planned and systematic process aimed at enhancing an organisation's effectiveness and adaptability and the overall well-being of its employees. It entails appropriate strategies and interventions to improve the organisation's structure, processes, culture and people. Change management, which is a fundamental aspect of OD, aims to facilitate the transition from an organisation's current state to a desired future state while ensuring that its employees are equipped and ready to navigate and embrace the change.

D9.95   For OD to be effective, the organisation must align and strengthen its core competencies to support its overall strategic direction. Many OD interventions involve developing or refreshing a competency framework, so as to identify the core/critical competencies required for the organisation's future success. Training and development interventions should follow to strengthen the new (desired) core competencies.

Challenges and Limitations of Competency Frameworks

Challenges in Development and Assessment

D9.96   The two biggest challenges faced by organisations in building and using competency frameworks are as follows:

(a) *Time and Resource-intensive*
It is tedious and resource-intensive to develop a good competency framework. Selecting and defining competencies and analysing and describing the behavioural markers for various proficiency levels are no easy tasks, but they are important.

(b) Judgment and Subjectivity in Competency Assessment
Some subjectivity in assessing competencies is inevitable as it involves observing and applying judgment to make sense of the behaviours. Behaviours are observable but most are not exactly measurable and quantifiable. While the proficiency behavioural markers (aka the ruler) may give clear narratives of the behaviours, it requires the assessor to make his own interpretation of the observed behaviours to match them against the ruler.

Relevance in Industry 4.0

D9.97   In today's rapidly changing operating landscape, knowledge and skills can become obsolete quickly. New knowledge and skills are required, such as digital literacy, data analytics and sustainability (green) skills.

D9.98   It is easier to acquire new functional/technical competencies if one has the motivation, initiative and tenacity to learn them. One may also use competencies such as collaboration and persuasion to enlist others to help provide the required technical/functional competencies.

D9.99   With changes in the operating environment, technology and business model, some core competencies may become relatively less important, while some may emerge to be more relevant. Competencies such as growth mindset, resilience, learning agility, adaptability and critical thinking are now becoming more important. Competencies such as taking ownership and achievement motivation will not go out of fashion.

References

1.   D.C. McClelland. "Testing for Competence Rather Than Intelligence". American Psychologist, 28, 1–14, 1973
2.   L.M. Spencer Jr. "Job Competency Assessment". In H.E. Glass (ed.), Handbook of Business Strategy, 2nd edn. Warren, Gorham & Lamonte, 1991
3.   R.E. Boyatzis. The Competent Manager. Wiley: New York, 1982
4.   S.B. Parry. "The Quest for Competence". Training, July 1996
5.   M. Zwell. Creating a Culture of Competence. John Willey & Sons Inc.: New York, Chichester, Weinheim, Brisbane, Singapore and Toronto, 2000, pp. 23, 25–52
6.   Glasgow City Council. "Leadership Competency Framework". https://www.glasgow.gov.uk/CHttpHandler.ashx?id=4082&p=0. 11 February 2024

Annex D9-1

Generic Competency Models (showcasing Core Competencies)

Competency Model by Hay McBer

Hay McBer is the research and consultancy company founded by American psychologist Dr David McClelland.

Core Competency Clusters	Examples of Core Competencies
Achievement and Action	Achievement Orientation. Concern for Order. Concern for Quality. Initiative. Information Seeking.
Helping and Human Service	Interpersonal Understanding. Customer Service Orientation.
Impact and Influence	Impact and Influence. Organisational Awareness. Relationship Building.
Managerial	Developing Others. Directiveness. Teamwork and Cooperation. Team Leadership.
Cognitive	Analytical Thinking. Conceptual Thinking.
Personal Effectiveness	Self-control. Self-confidence. Flexibility. Organisational Commitment.

Competency Model by Michael Zwell

Dr Michael Zwell is a globally recognised competency and talent management expert.

Core Competency Groups	Examples of Core Competencies
Task Achievement Competencies associated with performing a job well.	Results Orientation. Managing Performance. Initiative. Influence. Efficiency. Innovation. Concern for Quality.
Relationship Competencies that relate to communicating with and working well with others and satisfying their needs.	Teamwork. Service Orientation. Interpersonal Awareness. Relationship Building. Conflict Management.
Personal Attributes Competencies intrinsic to an individual and that relate to how people think, feel, learn and develop.	Analytical Thinking. Conceptual Thinking. Decisiveness. Decision Quality. Stress Management
Managerial Competencies that specifically relate to managing, supervising and developing people.	Motivating Others. Empowering Others. Developing Others.
Leadership Competencies that relate to leading an organisation and people to achieve an organisation's purpose, vision and objectives.	Visionary Leadership. Change Management. Building Organisational Commitment. Establishing Focus.

Annex D9-2

Competency Framework of Company ABC (Sample)

Definition of Competencies

The Company defines "Competencies" as *"those skills, knowledge, motives, traits and self-concept, that in the right combination, differentiate top performers from the average."*

Categories of Competencies

The Company adopts the following 4 categories of competencies:

1. Critical competencies
2. Leadership competencies
3. Supplementary competencies
4. Functional/Technical competencies

These competencies are applicable to all professionals, managers and executives and above.

Importance of Competencies

The Company will use Competencies for its organisational development and human capital management and development, including the following:

- to select the right hires;
- to determine promotion (both performance and competencies will be considered);
- to appraise employees in the annual performance appraisal;
- to assess skills and capabilities gaps to identify learning and development needs for employees;
- to select candidates for succession planning; and
- to foster a vibrant and performance-driven culture.

Overview of Competency Framework

The Competency Framework comprises the following components:

- Critical, Leadership and Supplementary competencies (with definitions)
- Functional/Technical competencies (with definitions)
- Competency Requirements matrix
- Proficiency Levels and Behavioural Markers of competencies
- Competency Assessment

The Competency Framework is the official source of all information and materials relating to competencies. It is to be owned and managed by the Human Resource department which shall be responsible for its maintenance, periodic review, refinement and update.

Critical, Leadership and Supplementary Competencies

Taking into account the number of job roles and job levels in the organisation, the Company has decided on Critical, Leadership and Supplementary competencies as listed below, together with the definitions. For more clarity and details, please also refer to the behavioural markers for each of the competencies.

CRITICAL Competencies

1. **Taking Ownership**
   The commitment to own the issue, take charge, follow through and produce results.
2. **Customer Focus**
   The desire and effort to consider the customers' needs and serve and delight customers (including internal customers).
3. **Pursuit of Excellence**
   The inclination, intent and effort to excel and be the best in whatever one is doing.
4. **Change and Growth Orientation**
   The inclination and drive to embrace and thrive on change, pursue personal and professional growth, and grow the Company, riding on opportunities.
5. **Execution and Result Focus**
   The inclination, ability and discipline to execute with tenacity, timeliness and effectiveness to deliver positive results, riding on opportunities and overcoming challenges.

LEADERSHIP Competencies

1. **Strategic Vision**
   The propensity and ability to look at issues from a strategic or higher vantage point and place facts and issues in a broader context and longer time horizon.
2. **Leading and Developing People**
   The desire and ability to lead, manage, motivate and develop people to perform at their best.
3. **Critical Thinking and Judgment**
   The ability to analyse, think critically and make sound and logical decisions under various situations.

SUPPLEMENTARY Competencies

1. **Collaboration**
   The desire, effort and ability to work effectively, cohesively and synergistically with others, leveraging different perspectives and strengths, towards common goals.
2. **Communication and Influence**
   The inclination and ability to listen actively, as well as communicate clearly and persuasively.
3. **Agility and Resilience**
   The willingness and ability to stay adaptable and versatile and bounce back despite challenges and setbacks.
4. **Information Seeking**
   The desire and effort to find out more, get to the root of the issue as well as gather and use adequate and relevant information to perform a job well or solve a problem.
5. **Solution Focus**
   The inclination and effort to focus on finding solutions to problems instead of focusing on the problems.
6. **Concern for Governance**
   The concern for order and accuracy and initiative to identify and manage risks and comply with regulatory and corporate requirements and policies.

Functional/Technical Competencies

To make the Competency Framework more wholesome, some Functional/Technical competencies have been included, as listed below, together with the definitions:

Business Orientation and Management
The ability to navigate the business environment and leverage on opportunities to achieve the best commercial advantage and results for the Company.

Prospecting and Selling
The ability to plan and execute prospecting and selling to maximise the conversion of sales leads to actual sales.

Financial Management
The ability to perform accounting and financial functions to ensure that accounts are complete, accurate and timely, and to manage the Company's financial resources effectively and structure its financial assets optimally.

Human Resource Management
The ability to plan, execute and deal with people initiatives and issues to support the Company in recruiting, managing, rewarding, developing, motivating, aligning and retaining the right people.

Operations Management
The ability to plan meticulously, organise systematically and execute efficiently the entire flow-through process from the confirmation of job orders to the final delivery of solutions to customers and other stakeholders.

Resource Management
The ability to plan, organise and manage the deployment of resources (including staff, money, facilities and materials) in a cost-effective manner to achieve optimal outcomes for the Company.

Procurement Management
The ability to plan, manage and execute procurement in a cost-effective, timely and efficient manner.

Project Management
The ability to plan and organise project timelines and resources, coordinate, execute and resolve issues to complete projects in a timely manner within budget and according to specifications and standards.

Workplace Skills

Apart from the Critical, Leadership, Supplementary and Functional/Technical competencies, some basic workplace skills are required to enable an employee to "move around" and function. Such workplace skills include (a) communication skills, (b) interpersonal skills, (c) planning and organising skills and (d) office technology skills. These are not covered and not part of this Competency Framework.

Competency Requirements Matrix

Every employee will have 10 competencies based on the permutations shown in the following table:

Type of Competency	Number of Competencies	
	Professionals and Executives	Managers and Leaders
Critical	5	5
Leadership	Not Applicable	3
Supplementary	5	2
Functional/Technical		
Total	10	10

The 5 Critical competencies are compulsory for all employees, while the 3 Leadership competencies are a must-have for all managers and above. The Supplementary competencies and Functional/Technical competencies will be selected from the full lists in the preceding sections. For example, for Managers and Leaders, 2 competencies will be chosen from the Supplementary and Functional/Technical lists for each individual employee that are relevant to the said employee's job role. For simplicity, each of the 10 selected competencies will be given the same weightage.

For illustration, the Competency Requirements matrix for three job families (Business & Sales, Finance and Human Resource) and Leaders/Managers are shown below:

Competencies		Job Family and Role			
		Business & Sales	Finance	Human Resource	Leaders/ Managers
Critical	Taking Ownership	✓	✓	✓	✓
	Customer Focus	✓	✓	✓	✓
	Pursuit of Excellence	✓	✓	✓	✓
	Change and Growth Orientation	✓	✓	✓	✓
	Execution and Result Focus	✓	✓	✓	✓
Leadership	Strategic Vision				✓
	Leading and Developing People				✓
	Critical Thinking and Judgment				✓
Supplementary	Collaboration			✓	Select 2 from the Supplementary and Functional/Technical lists
	Communication and Influence	✓	✓	✓	
	Agility and Resilience	✓			
	Information Seeking	✓	✓	✓	
	Solution Focus		✓	✓	
	Concern for Governance		✓		
Functional/ Technical	Business Orientation and Management	✓			
	Prospecting and Selling	✓			
	Financial Management		✓		
	Human Resource Management			✓	
	Operations Management				
	Resource Management				
	Procurement Management				
	Project Management				
	Total	10	10	10	10

Proficiency Levels and Behavioural Markers of Competencies

Every competency has 5 proficiency levels. For each proficiency level, there are several behavioural markers to explain the proficiency level. Behavioural markers describe the type of behaviour expected from an employee when he is at the said proficiency level for a particular competency.

For illustration, the proficiency levels and associated behavioural markers for two Critical competencies, two Leadership competencies, two Supplementary competences and two Functional/Technical competencies are shown below:

CRITICAL Competency
Taking Ownership The commitment to own the issue, take charge, follow through and produce results.
Proficiency Levels and Behavioural Markers
1   • Do what is told only. Little drive. Need frequent prompting.   • Show little willingness and effort to take charge and follow up.
2   • Generally, do what is required on his own. Need some prompting.   • Show decent effort to take charge and follow up.
3   • Do what is required with some drive. Need minimal prompting.   • Take charge and follow through; generally self-motivated.
4   • Always show drive and exceed requirements.   • Self-motivated. Take charge and follow through without prompting.
5   • Always show drive and make tremendous effort.   • Always self-motivated. Take charge and follow through even in difficult situations or dealing with major challenges.

CRITICAL Competency

Pursuit of Excellence
The inclination, intent and effort to excel and be the best in whatever one is doing.

Proficiency Levels and Behavioural Markers

1	• Focus on completing the job within the timelines. • Do just enough to meet the basic requirements.
2	• While getting the job done, try to do it better. • Try to do better but cannot sustain; quite easily distracted.
3	• Show interest and effort to do a good job. • Explore ways and execute to produce better output and quality.
4	• Show passion and consistent effort to produce good work. • Diligently push the boundaries to improve the status quo.
5	• Show passion and great effort to consistently produce excellent work. • Relentlessly and single-mindedly pursue excellence and set new standards.

LEADERSHIP Competency

Strategic Vision
The propensity and ability to look at issues from a strategic or higher vantage point and place facts and issues in a broader context and longer time horizon.

Proficiency Levels and Behavioural Markers

1	• Look at problems and issues narrowly within a confined context. • Unable to see matters and possibilities outside the situation on hand (aka: See the trees but not the bush).

2	<ul><li>Look at problems and issues on a wider context.</li><li>Able to see matters and possibilities that are on the fringe of the situation on hand (aka: See the trees and part of the bush but not beyond).</li></ul>
3	<ul><li>Look at problems and issues on a wider context. Able to see matters and possibilities that are further away (in other dimensions/aspects) from the situation on hand.</li><li>Vaguely sense some salient trends and implications (aka: See the trees and many bushes in the near vicinity but not beyond).</li></ul>
4	<ul><li>Look at problems and issues on a wide context and perspective. See matters/possibilities in other dimensions/aspects and long-term time horizons that are related to the situation on hand.</li><li>Can discern trends and developments quite clearly and connect them, forming a fairly clear picture (aka: See many bushes and shade of the forest).</li></ul>
5	<ul><li>Look at problems and issues on a very wide context and perspective. See matters/possibilities/implications confidently in many dimensions (such as societal, community and environmental) and long-term time horizon that are related to the situation on hand.</li><li>Able to connect disparate events and issues meaningfully, giving a coherent and useful picture. Visionary and insightful (aka: See the forest).</li></ul>

LEADERSHIP Competency

Leading and Developing People
The desire and ability to lead, manage, motivate and develop people to perform at their best.

Proficiency Levels and Behavioural Markers

1	<ul><li>Show basic interest with some effort to manage and guide staff but focus on immediate tasks and roles.</li><li>Tend to manage for trouble-free rather than leading and developing staff for better performance.</li><li>Avoid dealing with difficult staff issues and poor performers.</li></ul>
2	<ul><li>Show interest and put in effort to manage and mentor staff; occasionally go beyond their current job roles.</li><li>Try to lead and encourage staff and help them develop their capabilities but usually not able to sustain.</li><li>Manage and guide poor performers as a matter of requirement.</li></ul>

3	• Show interest and considerable effort to manage and mentor staff, often go beyond their current job roles. • Quite diligently guide and encourage staff to develop their capabilities. • Manage and guide poor performers with some diligence.
4	• Readily mentor staff and take interest in developing and helping them to grow. • Readily engage and encourage staff to perform well, showing care and interest in their well-being and development. • Look out for high-performance and high-potential staff and offer help to actualise their full potential. • Actively and diligently manage weak performers.
5	• Readily and passionately mentor staff and take interest in developing and helping them grow, generously sharing knowledge and skills. • Readily lead, engage and encourage staff to perform well, showing care and interest in their well-being and development. • Constantly look out for high-performance and high-potential staff and actively nurture them to actualise their full potential. • Actively and diligently manage weak performers in a decisive and timely manner.

SUPPLEMENTARY Competency
Collaboration The desire, effort and ability to work effectively, cohesively and synergistically with others towards common goals, by leveraging different perspectives and strengths.
Proficiency Levels and Behavioural Markers

1	• Focus on own needs and job; cooperate with others only when asked. • Typically stick to own ways of working, unless asked to change to align with others. • Indifferent to teamwork. Not at all helpful.
2	• Generally, help others and consider the interests of others. • By and large, cooperate without prompting. • Try to deal with differences with others (not avoiding).
3	• Consider the interests of others, support others and generally work well with them. • Approach persons within own work contacts/areas and collaborate. • Can deal with some differences and tension.

4	<ul><li>Seek and support opportunities for collaboration at organisational level.</li><li>Blend own efforts and views with those of others to achieve synergistic results.</li><li>Able to work with tension and resolve differences effectively.</li></ul>
5	<ul><li>Actively create and facilitate opportunities for collaboration, enlist the right persons (usually multiple stakeholders) and integrate divergent interests, perspectives and strengths.</li><li>Always build on and sharpen others to enhance collective achievements.</li><li>Take the lead in ably resolving major differences.</li></ul>

SUPPLEMENTARY Competency
Communication and Influence The inclination and ability to listen actively, as well as communicate clearly and persuasively.
Proficiency Levels and Behavioural Markers
1 <ul><li>Listen but not actively. Easily distracted. Seldom clarify.</li><li>Communicate rather unclearly.</li><li>Limited interest and capability to persuade and influence others.</li></ul>
2 <ul><li>Listen rather actively. Often ask questions to clarify.</li><li>Generally able to communicate or present information clearly.</li><li>Modest willingness and capacity to persuade and influence others.</li></ul>
3 <ul><li>Listen actively. Able to frame appropriate questions and probe.</li><li>Communicate clearly and able to convince, gaining believability.</li><li>Generally willing and able to persuade and influence others.</li></ul>
4 <ul><li>Listen actively and accurately. Able to frame effective questions and probe.</li><li>Communicate clearly, convincingly and confidently, gaining trust and confidence.</li><li>Willing and able to negotiate, persuade and influence outcomes.</li></ul>
5 <ul><li>Listen actively and accurately. Ask powerful questions. Probe insightfully.</li><li>Communicate clearly, cogently and concisely in simple terms, enlightening the audience.</li><li>Readily willing and able to tactfully persuade and influence others even on difficult or sensitive matters.</li></ul>

FUNCTIONAL/TECHNICAL Competency

Human Resource Management
The ability to plan, execute and deal with people initiatives and issues to support the Company in recruiting, managing, rewarding, developing, motivating, aligning and retaining the right people.

Proficiency Levels and Behavioural Markers

1	• Know the basics of HR functions and regulatory requirements. • Able to execute HR functions with close supervision. • Play a support role (unable to deal with non-routine people matters independently).
2	• Know the operational frameworks and practices of HR functions and regulatory requirements to a reasonable level. Has awareness of some market practices. • Able to execute HR routine functions with minimal supervision and non-routine tasks with some supervision. • Under broad parameters and principles and some supervision, able to produce and execute the simpler people initiatives.
3	• Good knowledge of the operational frameworks and practices of HR functions and regulatory requirements. Know the common market practices well. • Able to execute HR routine functions independently and non-routine tasks with minimal supervision. • By and large, able to advise line managers and staff on people matters. • Under broad parameters and principles, able to produce and execute fairly challenging people initiatives.
4	• Familiar with HR frameworks and practices at both strategic and operational levels. • Able to execute HR functions independently. • Able to advise management, line managers and staff confidently on most people matters. • Under broad parameters and principles, able to produce and execute complicated or sensitive people initiatives.

5	<ul><li>Has deep knowledge and application of HR frameworks and practices at both strategic and operational levels. Very attuned to the market trends and practices. An HR expert.</li><li>Able to conceptualise and design HR frameworks and execute well at organisation-wide level.</li><li>Able to advise senior management, line managers and staff confidently and with good insights on people matters.</li><li>Able to formulate parameters and principles, and plan and operationalise HR initiatives for both short-term and long-term horizons to drive the people agenda sustainably for the organisation.</li></ul>

FUNCTIONAL/TECHNICAL Competency

Financial Management
The ability to perform accounting and financial functions to ensure that accounts are complete, accurate and timely, and to manage the Company's financial resources effectively and structure its financial assets optimally.

Proficiency Levels and Behavioural Markers

1	<ul><li>Able to handle routine accounting tasks independently and non-routine ones under guidance.</li><li>Able to troubleshoot and rectify basic accounting errors.</li><li>Basic working knowledge of profit and loss and cash flow.</li></ul>
2	<ul><li>Able to handle routine accounting tasks independently and non-routine ones with minimal guidance.</li><li>Generally able to troubleshoot and rectify accounting errors of some complexity.</li><li>Adequate working knowledge of profit and loss, balance sheet and cash flow.</li></ul>
3	<ul><li>Able to handle accounting tasks (both routine and non-routine) independently.</li><li>Able to troubleshoot and rectify most accounting errors.</li><li>Good working knowledge of profit and loss, balance sheet and cash flow.</li><li>Able to perform some financial analysis and prepare and present financial and management accounting reports.</li></ul>

4	• Able to supervise the accounting function. • Able to troubleshoot and resolve complex accounting errors and analyse and identify the causes of errors. • Good understanding of capital markets and instruments, funding options and shareholders' value. Able to deal with bankers, investors and auditors. • Able to interpret complex financial analysis and costing matters well.
5	• Able to set the direction and structure of the accounting function. • Able to troubleshoot and resolve complex accounting errors and put in place system controls to avoid similar errors. • Deep understanding of capital markets and instruments, funding options and shareholders' value. Able to deal with bankers, investors and auditors with confidence. • Able to perform complex financial and costing analysis and offer useful insights to senior management. • Able to design and devise an optimal structuring of financing to maximise value.

For all competencies, the proficiency level expected of an employee depends on his job band. The higher the job band, the higher will be the proficiency level expected, as shown below:

Job Band	Proficiency Level Expected
Executive/Professional	PL2
Senior Executive/Professional	PL3
Manager and Senior Manager	PL4
Director	PL5

Competency Assessment

On an annual or periodical basis, employees will be assessed on their competencies. In the assessment, the employee's typical work behaviours (that is, how the employee performs his work – think, write, act and deliver) will be the focus. These will be compared against the behavioural markers of the proficiency level expected of the employee. A score (similar to that used for performance rating) will be assigned to the employee for each of the 10 competencies that he will be assessed on.

Rating	Met Some	Mostly Met	Fully Met	Exceeded	Far Exceeded
Score Range	0.1–3.0	3.1–4.5	4.6–6.5	6.6–8.0	8.1–10

A score range is provided so as to give more room to differentiate the competency levels of the individual employees. For example, if an employee has barely satisfied the "Fully Met" rating, he may be given a score at the lower end of the [4.6–6.5] range, whereas if he is a strong "Fully Met", his score should be in the higher end of the [4.6–6.5] range.

As the 10 competencies have equal weightage, the average score for the competencies can be easily computed. The overall competency score will form part of the individual employee's performance appraisal. It is relevant to point out that one cannot "compensate" a weak competency by a strong competency. For example, if an employee is strong in "Customer Focus" but weak in "Execution and Result Focus", it does not mean that these "square off" and that he should be complacent and remain status quo in these two competencies. The approach for the employee should be to continue to leverage on his strong competency to shore up his performance while at the same time make serious effort to improve on his weak competency through training and other developmental interventions. The Company will also endeavour to deploy an employee to roles that can make good use of his strong competencies.

Annex D9-3

Competency Framework
for Rank-and-File Employees (Sample)

	EFFORT AND DILIGENCE The effort and diligence to do one's best in the job.
	Proficiency and Performance Level
1	• Lack effort and urgency. • Do just enough to get by or what is told only.
2	• Able to deliver work within timeline but enthusiasm is absent. • Normally meet requirements.
3	• Show some drive and enthusiasm in work. • Always meet requirements.
4	• Always show drive and enthusiasm. • Often exceed requirements.
5	• Consistent high drive and enthusiasm. • Make a lot of effort and sacrifices; always exceed requirements.

	INITIATIVE The willingness and effort to take action without being asked.
	Proficiency and Performance Level
1	• Always need to be directed. • Often require supervision and prompting.
2	• Seldom need supervision. • By and large, do the necessary without prompting.
3	• Work without supervision. • Has some initiative to do a bit more.
4	• Work independently with motivation. • Often take initiative to do more or better.
5	• Self-starter. • Constantly alert to operational needs and quickly take initiative to do more or better.

	JOB KNOWLEDGE AND SKILLS The level of subject knowledge or product knowledge and job skills.
	Proficiency and Performance Level
1	• Some knowledge and job skills but inadequate. • Little interest to learn.
2	• Sufficient knowledge and job skills. • Some interest and effort to learn.
3	• Good product and work knowledge and job skills. • Keen to learn.
4	• Very good and up-to-date product and work knowledge and job skills. • Always willing to learn on his own.
5	• Expert product and work knowledge and job skills. Know well beyond the job scope. • Always make effort to learn continuously and at every opportunity.

CUSTOMER AND SERVICE FOCUS

The desire and effort to consider the customers' needs and serve and delight customers (including internal customers).

Proficiency and Performance Level

1	• Show reluctance to serve customers and others. Give mechanical responses. • Show little enthusiasm and consideration for customers.
2	• Do it strictly according to standard procedures. Do not probe or show empathy. • Do what is needed to serve customers, but not any extra.
3	• Serve customers happily and make effort to understand customers' needs and solve their problems. • Place importance on meeting customers' needs and do some extras sometimes.
4	• Keenly offer good service and probe underlying needs of customers and follow through. • Always put customer's needs as core and adjust and do extra to delight customers and build good relations with them.
5	• Consistently give outstanding service and probe to understand and anticipate customers' needs and provide solutions to their needs. • Always put customers' needs as core and go the extra mile to support customers and build long-term relationship based on trust.

DISCIPLINE AND RELIABILITY

The desire and effort to exercise discipline, follow rules and discharge duties diligently and reliably.

Proficiency and Performance Level

1	• Reluctant to follow rules. Always give excuses. • Often do not follow through. Sloppy and unreliable.
2	• By and large disciplined. Generally, do not give any trouble. • Generally, follow through. Quite reliable.
3	• Well-disciplined. Always respect rules. • Follow through diligently.
4	• Consistently well-disciplined. • Take accountability and follow through.

| 5 | • Consistently well-disciplined. Always set high standards.
• Always take accountability and follow through. Completely reliable and unwavering. |

TEAMWORK

The desire and efforts to cooperate and work effectively with others towards common goals.

Proficiency and Performance Level

1	• Reluctant to work with others. Cooperate if ordered. • Unwilling to consider others' views.
2	• Support teamwork when prompted. • Cooperate readily with others when called upon.
3	• Able to relate and work with others. • Cooperate and offer to assist others without being asked.
4	• Always cooperate with and assist others to achieve better results. • Able to combine own efforts with team goals to get better results.
5	• Actively seek and make effort to improve team's performance. • Always willing to help others and put team interest above personal needs.

ADAPTABILITY

The willingness, agility and effort to accept changes and adapt and adjust one's ways of thinking and working.

Proficiency and Performance Level

1	• Unwilling to change one's thinking and ways of doing things. • Unable to adjust to changes to work processes or methods.
2	• Accept changes to some extent. • Able to adapt to changes with some guidance.
3	• Accept changes generally. • Able to adjust to new ideas and ways of working fairly quickly with little guidance.

4	<ul><li>Accept changes readily.</li><li>Adapt quickly. Agile. Learn willingly and fast.</li><li>Take initiative to adjust quickly and move forward.</li></ul>
5	<ul><li>Always welcome and accept changes.</li><li>Initiate and able to maximise opportunities created by change; adapt and move forward swiftly.</li></ul>

COMMUNICATION
The ability and effort to listen actively, as well as communicate clearly.

Proficiency and Performance Level

1	<ul><li>Listen passively. Easily distracted. Seldom ask questions to clarify and probe.</li><li>Communicate rather unclearly.</li></ul>
2	<ul><li>Listen rather actively. At times, able to ask questions to clarify and probe.</li><li>Communicate with sufficient clarity to provide information.</li></ul>
3	<ul><li>Listen actively. Usually able to ask appropriate questions and probe.</li><li>Communicate clearly to convey the right messages.</li></ul>
4	<ul><li>Listen actively and accurately. Able to ask good questions and probe.</li><li>Communicate clearly to help the listener gain good understanding.</li></ul>
5	<ul><li>Listen actively and accurately. Able to ask very good questions and probe effectively.</li><li>Communicate convincingly in simple, precise, clear and cogent terms.</li></ul>

Job Grade Structure and Career Roadmap

Focus of this Chapter

This chapter examines job grade structure and career roadmap.

A job grade structure is essentially a hierarchy of jobs organised in a systematic manner based on their significance in terms of the know-how required, the complexity of problems and situations that the jobholder normally deals with, his accountability and the impact of his actions. The actual grade that an employee holds (commonly referred to as the employee grade) may or may not match the job grade of the job that he is performing, and we elaborate on the scenarios and shed light on the circumstances, including deliberate intentions, behind them. We also discuss position titles and how they are related to job grades and employee grades.

A career roadmap is a plan that maps out how an employee can progress upwards along the job grade hierarchy to actualise his career potential within the organisation. A career roadmap uses the job grade structure as the backbone and adds on other essential elements, including the competency requirements, progression timelines and developmental interventions to guide and help the employee achieve his career goal. We provide examples of career roadmaps designed for job families and individual employees.

Job Grade, Employee Grade and Position Title

Definitions and Differences

D10.1   *What is "Job Grade"?*
"Job grade" (also referred to as job level) indicates the relative hierarchy of a job in an organisation. For example, if an organisation wants to convey that Job A is more complex and impactful (and therefore more important) than Job B, it can use a job grade structure (say, labelled numerically from 1 to 10, with 1 being the lowest level and 10 being the highest level) to convey this. Job A (the more important one) may be assigned a higher job grade (say, 6), while Job B (the less important one), a lower job grade (say, 5), to convey that Job A is of a higher job level than Job B.

D10.2   *What is "Employee Grade"?*
"Employee grade" is the <u>actual grade</u> of the employee (the jobholder) who is performing a job. The "employee grade" is also called by a myriad of other names – for example, the Singapore Civil Service calls it the "substantive grade", Maybank Singapore calls it the "benefit grade", while some other organisations call it the "salary grade". The employee grade determines the employee's relative hierarchy/rank compared to his colleagues in the organisation. The higher the employee grade, the more senior in rank the employee is.

D10.3   *Are "Job Grade" and "Employee Grade" the same things? Are they always equal?*
The "job grade" refers to the grade of a <u>job</u>; it does <u>not</u> refer to the employee/jobholder. When we do job evaluation to rank jobs in terms of complexity and impact, we look strictly at the jobs and not the jobholders. We look at the job description and evaluate how complex the job is. If a jobholder is weak and underdelivers on the job outcomes, that is beside the point. We look at the fully intended job and not subtract any importance from the job, just because the incumbent jobholder underdelivers on the job outcomes. The reverse is equally applicable. If an incumbent jobholder overdelivers on the job outcomes (say, he is very senior and experienced), it should not raise the job grade of the job.

The "employee grade", on the other hand, centres on the employee/jobholder. The general and most common scenario is that the grade of the employee/jobholder will match (be equal to) the job grade of the job that he is performing (that is, if the job is grade 6, the employee will also be grade 6). This is logical and the goal, since we presume that an employee should be assigned to a job that he is suitably qualified for, and he will deliver the intended job outcomes as per what the job is designed for. That being the case, the employee should earn an employee grade equal to the job grade of the job. However, this is <u>not</u> always the case; there are exceptions when an employee may be of a lower grade or higher grade than the grade of the job that he is assigned to. We elaborate on these scenarios in detail under the section "Mismatched Job Grade and Employee Grade" in the later part of this chapter. Suffice to say, "job grade" and "employee grade" are two separate matters; they should not be treated as one and the same thing.

D10.4   *What is "Position Title"?*
Every job carries a "position title" (also referred to as "job title" or "job designation"). A position/job title conveys the nature, function and mandate of the job role. An employee (jobholder) who is performing a job will carry the said position/job title of the said job (usually reflected on his name card). This is for practical reasons. People dealing with the employee want to know who they are dealing with. For example, if one wants to contact the accounts department to resolve some billing issues, it is essential to know that one is talking to the accounts executive (and not, say, the HR executive). And if one needs to reach someone who has the mandate to make substantial decisions on financial matters, it is essential to know that one is talking to the finance director and not just the accounts executive.

D10.5   Having defined "job grade", "employee grade" and "position title", we now delve further into the nuances in using these terms. We illustrate with examples.

> Example
> A supermarket chain has many outlets. Each outlet is helmed by an Outlet Manager. The job grade of each Outlet Manager position varies with the size of the outlet, based mainly on the revenue and the number of staff. A newly hired or promoted manager is usually assigned to head a small outlet. If he performs well and has the potential and capacity to do more, he may be promoted and transferred to head a bigger outlet. Regardless of the size of the outlet and the job grade, the job position carries the position title of "Outlet Manager".

	Outlet 1	Outlet 2	Outlet 3
Location	ABC	DEF	GHI
Revenue	$10 mil per annum	$15 mil per annum	$25 mil per annum
Number of Staff	12	17	25
Job Grade	Grade M6	Grade M7	Grade M8
Employee Grade	May be lower or higher than Job Grade of job position. Please refer to section "Mismatched Job Grade and Employee Grade" in the later part of this chapter.		
Position Title	Outlet Manager	Outlet Manager	Outlet Manager
Name Card	Outlet Manager, ABC	Outlet Manager, DEF	Outlet Manager, GHI

The Employee Grade is an internal matter between the company and the individual employee; it is also confidential and not disclosed to the employee's colleagues (except for the management and Human Resource). The employee is paid salary and accorded benefits based on his employee grade.

The Job Grade is also an internal matter that is known only to the company's management and Human Resource, and not to external parties. Outlet Managers may however be made aware that the job grade of Outlet Manager positions ranges from M6 to M8. The job grades of the positions are reviewed periodically as the size of the outlets may grow or shrink as years go by.

To external parties (customers and vendors), the only known information is that the employee, being the Outlet Manager, is overall in charge of the outlet.

Example
Organisation XYZ has a job grade structure where the job grade for a Manager position ranges from M7 to M9. The organisation has done job evaluation to size up the Manager positions in Operations, Human Resource and Marketing.

	Operations	Human Resource	Marketing
Position Title	Operations Manager	HR Manager	Marketing Manager
Job Grade	Grade M7-M8	Grade M7-M8	Grade M8-M9
Employee Grade	May be lower or higher than the Job Grade of job position. Please refer to section "Mismatched Job Grade and Employee Grade" in the later part of this chapter.		

Stakeholders (colleagues, customers, vendors, job candidates and business associates) relate to the employees by their position titles. Internally, the employees are recognised for their Manager rank, but their exact employee grades are confidential. They are paid salaries and accorded benefits based on their respective employee grades.

Practices in Small Organisations

D10.6   Many small and medium-sized organisations do not have a job grade structure. Most have only position titles. These organisations rely on using a nomenclature for their position titles that convey a progression in hierarchy. For example: executive → senior executive → assistant manager → manager → senior manager → director and so on. Quite often, these job positions and position titles are created on an ad hoc basis, say, as and when an employee is promoted, or when the organisation onboards a new hire.

Importance and Purposes

D10.7   *What is the importance of Job Grade? What is it used for?*
The job grade for a job indicates the hierarchy (or importance/impact) of the job relative to other jobs in the organisation. When all jobs are arranged systematically from the lowest job grade to the highest job grade, a job grade structure is formed. A job grade structure forms the backbone of many human capital initiatives, including the following:

(a) *Organisation Structure*

An organisation designs its organisation structure to drive its business and operations. The structure will show how various functions are organised in a manner so as to deliver the intended outcomes in the most effective and efficient manner. Next, job positions are slotted into the structure based on the manpower resources the organisation thinks are needed to drive various functions and handle various tasks. Job hierarchies and reporting lines are thereby formed in the organisation structure. The job grade structure (denoting job grades for various job positions) should be in harmony with the reporting lines so that there is overall coherence in the organisation structure.

(b) *Salary Management*

The job grade denotes the relative importance, and therefore, the relative worth of a job. The more important the job (which hinges on its complexity and impact), the higher will be the job's worth, and therefore the jobholder performing the said job should be paid a higher salary. In organisations that have put in salary ranges, each job grade will be assigned a salary range ($X—$Y). The salary range sets out the lower limit ($X) and upper limit ($Y) on the monthly basic salary that the job commands. Please refer to Volume B, Chapter B5 "Salary Ranges" on how to create salary ranges for job grades. The more important the job, the higher will be the job grade, and correspondingly, the higher the salary range. Job grades therefore are the anchors for salary management.

(c) *Recruitment*

For a job position that is being filled, the job grade will provide a reference for the organisation to decide what employee grade to emplace the new hire. For example, if the new hire is very experienced and competent and can hit the road running, he may be offered an employee grade the same as the job grade for the position, whereas if the new hire is less experienced but nonetheless hired for his good potential, he may be offered an employee grade slightly lower than the job grade for the position while he learns the ropes after onboarding. The salary range that corresponds to the new hire's employee grade will guide the lower and upper boundaries of the monthly salary that can be offered to the new hire.

(d) *Performance Management*

Every job position is created and designed to deliver results for the organisation. For this purpose, every job position will have a set of performance goals (or work targets). The higher the performance goals, the more complex and impactful (and therefore more important) the job is. In short, the higher the job grade for the job position, the higher the expectations on the performance goals. To deliver the said performance goals, the organisation will also go about specifying the competencies as well as the corresponding proficiency levels that are necessary for performing the job well, all of which must be tied to the job grade for the job position. Please refer to Chapter D2 "Performance Planning and Goals Setting" for more elaboration on how reporting officers and line heads should use job grade as the reference point for setting performance goals and competency requirements for jobs.

(e) *Career Management*
In career management, the organisation develops career roadmaps for different employee groups (usually by job families) and selected individuals. A career plan uses the job grade structure as the backbone to map out how an employee can progress upwards along the job grade hierarchy to actualise his career potential within the organisation.

D10.8   *What is the importance of Employee Grade? What is it used for?*
The employee grade is simply the actual grade of the employee and denotes his rank (that is, where he stands) relative to the other employees in the organisation. The higher the employee grade, it follows that the higher the employee should be remunerated. This fundamental notion is borne out by some organisations calling the employee grade by alternative names such as "substantive grade" (Singapore Civil Service), "benefit grade" (Maybank Singapore) and "salary grade", presumably to convey that the employee will be remunerated based on his employee grade. The employee grade is personal to the employee and impacts him in other material ways (apart from just remuneration), which are summarised below:

(a) *Renumerating the Employee*
An employee will be paid salary based on his employee grade (and not the job grade of the job position that he is occupying). For example, if an employee occupies a job position that is job grade 9 while his employee grade is only grade 8, he will be paid a monthly salary within the salary range of grade 8 (and not grade 9). If the organisation tiers its employee benefits/perks based on grade, the employee will be accorded benefits/perks based on grade 8 (and not grade 9). Remunerating employees based on employee grade makes salary and benefits management fair and defensible. This is particularly pertinent

for rank-and-file employees in unionised organisations; unions want a transparent and objective basis for the accord of salary and benefits to individual employees, and not based on subjectivity or whim and fancy of the management.

(b) *Career Progression*
The employee grade tells the employee where he stands in the hierarchy of his organisation. Most employees have aspirations; they want to advance upwards in their organisation so that they can earn higher remuneration, besides other considerations (including status and authority). When an employee performs well in his job and earns a promotion, he will move up in his employee grade. Therefore, the employee grade is the means whereby an employee can track his career growth and progression.

D10.9   *What is the importance of Position Title? What is it used for?*
A position title aims to convey (in a succinct manner) the nature, function and mandate of the job role. It is relevant to people whom the employee comes to deal with – both internal colleagues as well as external parties. In business dealings and work interactions, people want to know who they are dealing with, in terms of their job role and rank in their organisations. Job role can be denoted by a descriptor in the position title, such as "marketing", "procurement", "finance" and "human resource". Rank (which gives a proxy of the mandate) can be denoted by nomenclature, such as "executive", "manager", "director" and "chief". Simply put, a position title that describes an employee's job role and connotes his decision-making authority facilitates the conduct of work and business. If one wants to reach someone who has the mandate to make substantial decisions on financial matters, one would want to speak to the finance director and not the accounts assistant, or be wrongly routed to someone in the human resource department.

Nomenclature of Job Grades and Position Titles

D10.10   It is relevant to remind here that job grade and employee grade are an internal matter known only to the organisation's management (including Human Resource); the information is not disclosed to external parties. Position titles, on the other hand, are information that is openly publicised to all persons, including colleagues, customers, vendors, business associates and the public in order to facilitate business dealings and work interactions.

Job Grade Nomenclature

D10.11 There can be many ways to name job grades. The simplest way is to name the job grades using either numbers (1, 2, 3 and so on) or alphanumeric (for example, A1, A2, B1, B2, C1, C2). Please refer to Example 1 and Example 2 below. While numbers and alpha-numeric are simple, it does not give sufficient "clue" regarding the job level. For example, in the alpha-numeric method, assuming that the lowest rung is set at A1, while it is intuitive that A2 is higher in hierarchy than A1, and B1 is higher than A2, and so on, there is however no clue whether B1 and B2 are at an executive level or whether C1 and C2 are at a managerial level.

Example 1	Example 2
Job Grades	**Job Grades**
G1 G2 G3 G4 G5 G6 G7 G8 G9 G10 G11 G12	A1 A2 A3 B1 B2 B3 C1 C2 C3 D1 D2 D3
"G" simply denotes "Grade". That is, G1 is Grade 1.	"A", "B", "C" and "D" supposedly denote different job levels but are not clear about what exactly these levels are.

D10.12 For the above reason, some organisations will create groupings for their job grades and wrap a unique alpha-numeric nomenclature around the groupings so that it provides some indication of the job level – whether the job grade is of executive level or managerial level. Please refer to Example 3 below:

Example 3
Job Grade Groupings (with Broad Bands). **Job Grades are shown in brackets.**
Associate (A1, A2) Executive (E3, E4, E5, E6) Manager (M7, M8, M9, M10) Director (D11, D12, D13)
"A" denotes "Associate". "E" denotes "Executive" and so on. By using unique alphabets, it provides an indication which job grades are of associate, executive, manager or director level.

D10.13   Some organisations use very broad job grade groupings, while others prefer more granular job grade groupings, which can be done by creating sub-levels within each job grade grouping. Compare Example 3 (with broad bands) above and Example 4 (with sub-leveling) below:

Example 4

Job Grade Groupings (with Sub-Levels). Job Grades are shown in brackets.

Associate (A1, A2) ◆ Senior Associate (A3, A4)
Executive (E1, E2) ◆ Senior Executive (E3, E4) ◆ Assistant Manager (E5, E6)
Manager (M1, M2) ◆ Senior Manager (M3, M4) ◆ Assistant Director (M5, M6)
Deputy Director (D1, D2) ◆ Director (D3, D4. D5)

Position Title Nomenclature

D10.14   Likewise, there are many types of nomenclature used for position titles. Organisations will create their own nomenclature to cater specifically to their array of jobs and arrange the titles in a logical hierarchical sequence. Different nomenclature may be adopted for backroom and frontline jobs, or even for selected job families. Some organisations prefer fewer hierarchical levels of position titles, while others prefer more, which can be done by creating sub-levels of a hierarchy (for example, manager may be expanded to assistant manager, deputy manager, manager and senior manager). The permutations of position titles are endless. There is no right or wrong; it is entirely up to the organisation to customise position titles to suit its own context and preference. Please see Examples 5, 6 and 7 below:

Example 5
xxx assistant (e.g., HR assistant, finance assistant) → senior assistant → executive → senior executive → assistant manager → deputy manager → manager → senior manager → assistant director → deputy director → director → chief xxx officer (e.g., chief HR officer, chief finance officer) → assistant chief executive officer → deputy chief executive officer → chief executive officer

Example 6
xxx assistant (e.g., account assistant) → senior assistant → associate → senior associate → executive → senior executive → assistant vice president → vice president → senior vice president → executive vice president → senior executive vice president → deputy president → president

---

Example 7
production operator → team lead → production supervisor/assistant engineer → senior production supervisor/engineer → production superintendent/ senior engineer → production head/engineering head → assistant general manager → general manager → deputy managing director → managing director

D10.15   Some nomenclatures of position titles are fairly "complicated" and not easily understood. For example, it may not be as intuitive to a layman that "executive vice president" is more senior in rank than "senior vice president" (see Example 6 in the table above).

D10.16   In the last few decades, there has been an obvious trend in inflating position titles. Up till the 1980s, a position title of "manager" appearing on one's name card would indicate seniority. Today, fairly young graduates (even new entrants to the workforce) flash a name card showing the title of "manager". It is also common to find a HR manager in a small start-up enterprise bearing a title called "chief people officer". The obvious intention of organisations in giving inflated and fanciful titles is to appeal to the aspirations (and ego) of the younger workforce.

D10.17   One must be cognisant that organisations are at liberty to set their own stringency in using nomenclature for position titles. Some are strict and conservative, while others are lax and more ostentatious in style. That being the case, we cannot assume that two persons bearing the title "Vice President" from two different organisations are equivalent in seniority in terms of their responsibilities (and remuneration level). For example, in Singapore Airlines, a manager carries a lot of responsibilities, and a senior vice president may helm a division with a few thousand employees or be accountable for revenue or expenditure in the hundreds of millions. This is seldom the case for those with equivalent position titles in small (and perhaps even in some large) organisations. Therefore, a position title is only indicative of the employee's nature of job role and his relative hierarchy in *his own organisation* but is seldom an accurate proxy of his job size vis-à-vis the general market. This has a bearing when we do job evaluation comparing jobs across several organisations in the survey sample – assessing job sizes just relying on position titles alone can be very misleading (please refer to Volume B, Chapter B5 "Salary Ranges" on how to make meaningful and accurate comparison of job sizes for jobs across different organisations).

How Job Grades and Position Titles Interplay

D10.18 Now that we have given some examples of nomenclature used for job grades and position titles, we showcase how job grades and position titles interplay. Again, the permutations are endless. It is entirely up to organisations to customise how to stack their job grades and position titles, so long as there is some logical and meaningful structure achieved. The simpler the better so that employees can understand easily and at the same time sufficiently intuitive for external parties to appreciate. We remind that job grades are information internal to the organisation (known only to the management and Human Resource), while position titles are information open and publicised to external parties (say, on the organisation's website, telephone directory and employees' name cards).

D10.19 One example of interplaying job grades and position titles is shown below:

Example 8					
Job Grade Groupings	**Job Grades**	**Position Titles**			
		Production	**Engineering**	**Human Resource**	**Info Technology**
Non-Executives (NE)	NE-1	Operator			
	NE-2	Operator		HR Assistant	
	NE-3	Team Lead	Technician	Snr HR Assistant	Asst Programmer
Executives and Professionals (EP)	EP-4	Production Exe	Technical Officer	HR Executive	Programmer
	EP-5	Production Exe / Snr Production Exe	Snr Tech Officer / Asst Engineer	HR Executive / Snr HR Exe	Snr Programmer
	EP-6	Snr Production Exe / Asst Production Mgr	Engineer	Snr HR Exe / Asst HR Manager	Systems Analyst
Managers (M)	M-7	Production Manager	Snr Engineer	HR Manager	Snr Systems Analyst
	M-8	Asst Production Controller	Asst Engineering Superintendent	HR Manager / Asst Dir, HR	Asst Project Lead / Project Lead
	M-9	Dy Production Controller	Dy Engineering Superintendent	Deputy Dir, HR	Project Lead / Snr Project Lead

Directors (D)	D-10	Production Controller	Engineering Superintendent	HR Director	IT Systems Director
	D-11				
	D-12	Chief Production Officer	Chief Engineering Officer	Chief HR Officer	Chief Information Officer
	D-13				
Top Leadership (T)	T-14	Assistant Chief Executive Officer			
	T-15	Chief Executive Officer			
	T-16				

D10.20   The nomenclature used for position titles need not follow strictly or match the nomenclature used for job grades. Take the case of Example 8 above – each job family falling within a job grade grouping may carry position titles that best reflect its unique function role (for example, for job grade M-7, the titles may be "production manager", "senior engineer", "HR manager" or "senior systems analyst").

D10.21   Strictly speaking, job grades are meant to be internal information, while only the position title is publicised to external parties. However, in some instances, the organisation may permit the employee to reflect the job grade of his job position (or his actual employee grade) on his name card along with his position title, especially if the job/employee grade shows some degree of seniority and gives a boost to his identity (and ego) and facilitates his business dealings and work interactions with others. Example 9 and Example 10 illustrate different approaches on what information is revealed to external parties.

	Example 9	Example 10
Person	John Tan	Peter Sim
Job Grade	Senior Management SM18	Executive Vice President EVP13
Employee Grade	Senior Management SM16	Executive Vice President EVP12
Position Title	Acting Chief Executive Officer	Head, Consumer Banking
Name Card	John Tan Acting Chief Executive Officer	Peter Sim Executive Vice President Head, Consumer Banking
	The job grade (SM18) and employee grade (SM16) are not shown on the name card; in any case, these are not very intuitive.	The title of "Head, Consumer Banking" indicates that he is overall in charge of consumer banking. However, it sheds no light on his hierarchy. Since he is of EVP grade (very senior), revealing his grade puts him in good stead when he deals with external parties.

D10.22   For some organisations, they keep things simple by giving the same names to both the job grades and position titles; that is, the job grade is already a description of the position title. One such organisation is Singapore Airlines (SIA).

> SIA Cabin Crew and Pilots
> SIA adopts the same nomenclature for the job grades and position titles for its cabin crew and pilots; that is, the job grade is also the position title. The employee is also given an employee grade equal to the job grade.
>
> • Flight Steward/Stewardess → Leading Steward/Stewardess → Chief Steward/Stewardess → Inflight Supervisor
> • Cadet Officer → Second Officer → First Officer → Senior First Officer → Captain

> For a Captain, apart from holding a professional job grade and position title, he may also be assigned a corporate position title when he is given an additional role. For example, he may be appointed as Assistant Chief Pilot (ACP) to manage the training and technical functions while continuing to operate flights as a Captain, albeit less frequently. A Captain may also be appointed to a management role such as Deputy Chief Pilot (DCP) to look after pilot affairs. He is Captain when operating a flight, and ACP or DCP respectively whenever he performs his corporate roles. The corporate appointments (ACP and DCP) do not derail the employee grade for the pilot; his employee grade remains as Captain (with exceptions sometimes). He continues to be paid salary based on the Captain grade and is paid allowances for his ACP or DCP appointment and also accorded staff perks reserved for ACP or DCP. He will relinquish the ACP or DCP corporate title should he return to operate flights on a full-time basis.

D10.23   Another example of position title nomenclature is seen in the Progressive Wage Model (PWM) that is endorsed by the tripartite partners (please refer to Volume B, Chapter B14 "Managing and Raising Wages of Lower-Wage Workers" for more details on PWM). In a nutshell, the PWM enables workers to earn better wages and enjoy better career prospects as they become better skilled and more productive. The PWM encompasses 4 ladders: (a) skills ladder, (b) career ladder, (c) productivity ladder and (d) wage ladder. Each sector-specific PWM comprises a career ladder that specifies the various job/position titles as the worker progresses upwards on the ladder by taking on higher job roles that use higher skills. Examples of the position title nomenclature for the cleaning sector and security sector are shown below. Organisations employing cleaners and security personnel are at liberty to develop their own internal job grade structures and apply the endorsed PWM position titles to their job grades.

PWM for Cleaning sector
Office and Commercial Site General/indoor cleaner → outdoor/healthcare/restroom cleaner → multi-skill cleaner or cleaning machine operator → supervisor
PWM for Security sector
Security officer → senior security officer → security supervisor → senior security supervisor

"Mismatched" Job Grade and Employee Grade

D10.24   The difference between a job grade and an employee grade is simply that the job grade centres on the job, while the employee grade centres on the employee/jobholder. The job grade and employee grade are two separate matters and should not be treated as one and the same thing. There are 3 possible scenarios on the interplay between the job grade and employee grade, as described below:

Scenario 1:   The job grade and employee grade are equal
Scenario 2:   The job grade is higher than the employee grade
Scenario 3:   The employee grade is higher than the job grade

D10.25   Scenario 1 (the job grade and employee grade are equal) is the most common scenario. That is, if the job is grade 6, the employee will also be grade 6. The general premise is that an employee should be assigned to a job that he is suitably qualified for and competent in performing it, and that being the case, the employee should logically be assigned an employee grade equal to the job grade of the job.

D10.26   Scenario 2 (the job grade is higher than the employee grade) and Scenario 3 (the employee grade is higher than the job grade) can also happen under certain circumstances, sometimes even done so by deliberate design and intention. We elaborate on these scenarios and circumstances in the ensuing sections.

Circumstances when Job Grade is Higher than Employee Grade

D10.27   *Under what circumstances will the job grade be higher than the employee grade?*
Usually, this happens when an employee is new to the job or is being tested on the job. The common circumstances include the following:

(a)   An employee is newly hired for a job and the organisation is cautious in assigning him an employee grade same as the grade of the job. This is especially so if the new employee is stepping up to a job that is of a higher responsibility than his previous job (for example, the employee may have been an Assistant Manager in his previous organisation and reported to a Manager in charge of a unit, while his new job in the new organisation is at Manager level and head of a unit). Since the new employee is untested at the said higher level of responsibility, the organisation may prefer to assign him an employee grade of, say, one grade lower than the grade of the Manager position. When he has proven his competence and passes probation, the organisation may upgrade his employee grade to match the job grade of the Manager position.

(b)   Many organisations adopt a "test-first" approach for employee promotions. Before an employee is promoted, he will be assigned to a job of the next higher grade (say, he is grade 7 and will be assigned a grade 8 job). He will be monitored for some time (say, a few months or even one year) in the higher job, during which time, he will be assessed on performance goals and competency requirements based on the higher job. If he performs decently, he will become promoted at the next promotion exercise. If he does badly or struggles, he will be re-posted back to a lower job (that matches his employee grade) and life goes on. Such "test-first" approach for a promotion policy is fairly common and serves to make promotions fail-proof since only competent persons are promoted. However, organisations must be mindful that the test period must be reasonable, in order to be fair to the employee. There are anecdotes where some organisations make their test periods unreasonably long (sometimes even stretching to a few years); this may be seen as exploitative since the employee is still remunerated based on his current employee grade and not the grade of the higher job. If an organisation is exploitative and delays promoting an employee for no valid reason, it risks losing the employee.

(c) The "test-first" approach is also a common approach adopted by many organisations in their talent management program for high-potential employees. In grooming and developing high-potential employees, they will be assigned to various stretch postings that are of a higher job grade. Those who live up to expectations will enjoy accelerated career progression with successive promotions.

Circumstances when Employee Grade is Higher than Job Grade

D10.28   *Under what circumstances will the employee grade be higher than the job grade?*

The scenario of the employee grade being higher than the job grade is less common. The circumstances include the following:

(a) Sometimes, due to business changes, jobs in an organisation may be lost. Experienced employees may be displaced. The organisation has the option of retrenching the displaced employees or redeploying them to other job vacancies in the organisation. However, these vacancies may be of job grades lower than the employee grades of the displaced employees. Notwithstanding the mismatch, the organisation may choose to retain and redeploy these employees if it values them for, say, their institutional knowledge or if they are committed and good performers. Such mismatch of employees with job positions may be temporary as the jobs may eventually grow in size or the employees may be refitted to other higher/bigger jobs subsequently when the opportunities arise, thus reverting to a normalised situation where the employees' grades will match with the grades of the jobs they hold.

(b) There are also instances where an organisation may deliberately deploy a more experienced and qualified employee to a "start-up" role (for example, a country manager position for a new overseas branch). A start-up role in a new area of operations may start small because it has not yet attained the scale of operations or revenue. Invariably, the organisation would want to grow the operations and revenue, and consequently, the start-up role will grow in size. By deploying a more experienced employee to helm the start-up role, the probability and speed of achieving the intended growth in operations and revenue is enhanced. Such an approach is deliberate and purposeful. If a more junior employee (whose employee grade matches the job grade of the start-up role) is selected, all things being equal, it may take a longer time to scale up the operations and revenue. The more senior employee helming the start-up role is not shortchanged as he is remunerated based on his own employee grade (which is higher than the job grade of the start-up role).

(c) There may also be situations where an organisation wants to "contain" an employee in a lower-graded job for whatever reasons. For example, if a relatively senior employee is a marginal performer and the organisation is unable to terminate his employment (for whatever reasons), the organisation may "contain" or "cold storage" him in a lower-graded job until he voluntarily leaves employment or reaches retirement. By moving the senior employee to a lower-graded job, it frees up the higher-graded job that the employee has previously occupied, and this allows the organisation to execute its desired manpower plan, including leadership rejuvenation.

Developing and Implementing a Job Grade Structure

D10.29 As a recap, a job grade structure is essentially a hierarchy of jobs arranged in a systematic manner, stacking up from the lowest job grade to the highest job grade in the organisation. Job grades are derived using criteria such as know-how, skills and experience required, the complexity of issues and problems to be dealt with, responsibilities entrusted and impact of actions. A job grade structure enables one to see the relative importance of different jobs in the organisation even if they are spread across different functions, different entities and different geographical locations (cities/countries).

Methods to Develop a Job Grade Structure

D10.30 In Volume B, Chapter B5 "Salary Ranges", we have described the steps involved in designing salary ranges. Before salary ranges can be constructed, a job grade structure must first be put in place (see Step 1 below).

> How to Design Salary Ranges
> Step 1: Evaluate Jobs to slot into a Job Grade Structure
> Step 2: Decide on the Organisation's Pay Philosophy
> Step 3: Do Salary Benchmarking
> Step 4: Construct Salary Range for each Job Grade

D10.31 In this section, we revisit Step 1 (Evaluate Jobs to slot into a Job Grade Structure). There are two ways to go about developing a job grade structure, which are the following:

(a) by evaluating jobs for their job sizes or
(b) by management assessment to derive a hierarchy of jobs.

Develop Job Grade Structure by Job Evaluation

D10.32 To develop a job grade structure by job evaluation is akin to starting from ground zero. It requires much effort and deliberation. We need to prepare a job description for each of the jobs to be evaluated. Ideally, we should evaluate all the different or unique jobs in the organisation.

D10.33 *What is meant by "evaluating" a job?*
By evaluate, we mean assessing the complexity and accountability of the job.

> - *Job complexity* is assessed by looking at the job attributes, such as knowledge and skills required, the span of control that the jobholder has over resources, number of subordinates, proportion of routine work versus uncharted work, degree of difficulty in problem-solving, leadership essentials to manage ambiguity and diversity, and risk and job hazards.
>
> - *Job accountability* is assessed by the job's impact to the organisation and the specific role of the jobholder in making the impact.

D10.34 *What is the outcome of job evaluation?*
To evaluate a job, we need an evaluation methodology to measure job complexity and accountability. Most organisations will engage a specialist compensation consultant for this. Each consulting firm has its own proprietary job evaluation methodology. In evaluating a job, each of the

attributes of the job will be carefully and methodically examined and a sub-score will be generated for each attribute. The sub-scores for all attributes will be added up (with assigned weightages) to arrive at the total job evaluation score for the said job using the prescribed formula in the job evaluation methodology.

> In evaluating jobs, some line heads may hold the view that handling a bigger volume of the same tasks (typified by someone who willingly and routinely puts in more hours) or doing a wider range of tasks of the same complexity level will earn more job evaluation points. Based on job evaluation methodology, such situations do not lead to more points. One must appreciate that job evaluation focuses on the job and not the jobholder. A more diligent jobholder who puts in more hours to do more of the same will not raise the value of the job per se. However, the jobholder may be recognised for his extra effort through performance appraisal where he may earn a favourable rating if his diligence leads to a higher contribution to the organisation.

D10.35   Having all the total scores of the evaluated jobs, we can see the score range (that is, highest score to lowest score). We can "chop up" the score range to a number of portions. Each portion will represent a job grade.

> Example
> Assume that based on the evaluation methodology used, the full score range for all the evaluated jobs stretches from 200 points (lowest) to 1100 points (highest). One can create, say, 12 portions. Each portion has a 15% spread from the minimum to the maximum, as shown below:

Points	200 to 230	231 to 265	266 to 305	306 to 352	353 to 406	407 to 468	469 to 539	540 to 621	622 to 715	716 to 823	824 to 948	949 to 1091
Grade	G1	G2	G3	G4	G5	G6	G7	G8	G9	G10	G11	G12

<u>Spread</u>
- 15% spread: For example, $200 \times 1.15 = 230$. Again, $231 \times 1.15 = 265$, and so on.
- If an organisation prefers to have more but narrower job grades, it can set a smaller spread of, say, 10%.
- On the other hand, if an organisation prefers to have fewer but broader job grades, it can set a bigger spread of, say, 20%.

<u>Job Grades</u>
Using a spread of 15%, a preliminary job grade structure has been constructed, from Grade 1 to Grade 12, which will cover all jobs in the organisation, from the lowest to the highest.

D10.36　If an organisation has many different jobs, evaluating all the different jobs will be very time-consuming and resource-intensive. Most large organisations will take a shortcut by identifying "benchmark" jobs and doing job evaluation only for these jobs. Typically, a "benchmark" job is one that has many jobholders or is a job that is familiar to most line heads in the organisation. These benchmark jobs therefore serve as "anchors" for the job grade structure. To ensure a good representation and a credible evaluation outcome, there should be enough benchmark jobs selected at the respective junior, mid and senior levels of jobs in the organisation.

D10.37　For non-benchmark jobs, the job evaluation is dispensed with. After the benchmark jobs have been evaluated, the organisation's management team can slot the non-benchmark jobs in between benchmark jobs by doing comparisons and using judgment to decide whether a particular non-benchmark job is lower, equal or higher than the benchmark jobs closest to it.

D10.38　With all the jobs (both benchmark and non-benchmark) slotted in, the result is a job grade structure setting out the hierarchy of jobs, stacking jobs one above the other, from the lowest to the highest. For this exercise, HR needs to enlist the senior management team (or line heads) to collectively deliberate and endorse the resultant job grade structure. It is vital to get the job grade structure right because salary ranges, employee benefits and promotions are based on that.

D10.39　It is relevant to comment here on the engagement of specialist compensation consultants to do job evaluation and construct a job grade structure. For organisations that can afford it, even the preparation of job descriptions can be outsourced to the consultant. Other than having access to the consultant's proprietary job evaluation methodology, another critical advantage is that the consultant is better positioned to moderate any bias of the line heads (being not under any pressure to bend to the organisation's internal power dynamics) and therefore can help inject more objectivity to the evaluation process. However, engaging consultants is costly, and hence it is usually beyond the means of most small and medium enterprises. For organisations that cannot afford the time and money to engage job evaluation consultants, the alternative is to simplify the approach and dispense with doing job evaluation. We elaborate on this alternative in the following section.

Develop Job Grade Structure by Management Assessment of Job Hierarchy

D10.40   For organisations that cannot afford the time and money to do job evaluation, the alternative is for the management to review the different jobs and make their own assessment on the relative importance of the said jobs and so rank them in hierarchy from the lowest to the highest.

- First, decide on how many job grades the organisation will require, looking at the diversity of job types/levels in the organisation. Say, if there are 30 different types of jobs, from Receptionist (lowest) to Chief Executive Officer (highest), then 10–15 job grades may be sufficient to cover the entire span of jobs.

- Next, slot all the different jobs into the job grades according to the assessed complexity and accountability of each job. Jobs that are considered to be of equivalent complexity and accountability should be slotted into the same job grade. Jobs that are of a lower/higher complexity and accountability should be slotted into a lower/higher job grade accordingly, skipping grades as warranted, bearing in mind the relativity. It is useful to start with benchmark jobs (that is, jobs that are common or familiar to most line heads) and compare the rest of the jobs against these benchmark jobs. For example, the organisation may first fix the job grades for an entry-level diploma holder position and a fresh university graduate position respectively. Another anchor job may be the first rung of a managerial position. With the job grades of these benchmark jobs in place, it is easier to slot in the other jobs.

- After the preliminary job grade structure has been constructed, the management may do a final review. Where some job grades have very few jobs slotted in, the management may decide to remove the said job grade (by merging with an adjacent job grade). The converse may also apply. If a job grade has many jobs slotted in, the said job grade may be expanded into two and the various jobs may be re-slotted into either one of the two

> "expanded" job grades to provide more differentiation. The objective of the review is to arrive at a final job grade structure that is coherent and meaningful.

D10.41   To do this exercise, the organisation will need to involve its entire line management team to provide inputs and collectively deliberate on the relative complexity and accountability of jobs. Usually, Human Resource will be tasked to facilitate or mediate the deliberation process.

D10.42   Granted that a job grade structure derived in this manner (without doing any job evaluation) will not be perfect. However, pragmatism is important. We need a job grade structure that can work reasonably well, not necessarily a perfect one. The job grade structure can be reviewed and finetuned after using it for some time.

Sub-levelling of Job Grades

D10.43   Sometimes, organisations start with a modest number of job grades and subsequently for specific reasons, create some "sub-grades" to increase the total number of job grades. There is no universal rule on the ideal number of job grades. Most importantly, the job grade structure must serve the needs of the organisation.

D10.44   The common reasons for organisations to create more job grades (which will lead to narrower salary ranges) include the following:

(a) *To provide more promotion opportunities and use promotion increments to accelerate salary progression for good performers*

> Example 1
> The original job grade structure has 2 grades for technicians:
> Technician → Senior Technician
>
> These can be expanded to 4 grades by having sub-grades:
> Technician 1 → Technician 2 → Senior Technician 1 → Senior Technician 2
>
> Under the original job grade structure, an employee progressing from Technician to Senior Technician will experience only one promotion, whereas under the new structure, he can experience three promotions if he reaches Senior Technician 2. With more promotions, the organisation may use promotion increments to accelerate the salary progression for good performers. This is a useful lever especially if the organisation has an annual increment matrix that is modest and rigid.

(b) To ensure that only good performers can reach the salary maximum point

> Example 2
> We illustrate using the same Example 1 above.
> The original Technician grade has a salary range of $1,600–$3,200.
> By splitting into Technician 1 ($1,600–$2,400) and Technician 2 ($2,100–$3,200), only a good performer will become promoted to Technician 2 and can reach the maximum salary of $3,200. An average performer will stagnate at Technician 1 and hence can only reach a maximum salary of $2,400 (instead of the original $3,200).

D10.45 An organisation may intentionally create more job grades to solve some human resource issues. For example, if the organisation has a sizeable number of employees in the Manager grade and if only a few of them can potentially progress to the next higher grade of Senior Manager, it may pose a morale problem. This is especially so if many of the managers are still relatively young and far away from the statutory minimum retirement age. To solve the morale problem, the organisation may add on another new grade above the original Manager grade, but set a salary maximum point that is only modestly higher than the salary maximum point of the original Manager grade. The organisation may rename the original Manager grade as Manager 1, and name the new grade as Manager 2. Only the better managers may be promoted to or be re-graded as Manager 2, while the rest will remain at Manager 1 grade.

D10.46 When an organisation creates sub-levels of job grades to increase the number of job grades, it will have two implications:

(a) The job grades will come with narrower salary ranges. That is, the spread between the minimum and maximum points of the salary range will be smaller.

(b) When an employee is promoted from one sub-grade to the next (say, from Technician 1 to Technician 2), the incremental increase in job responsibility is much less substantial than a promotion from one job grade to the next (say, from Technician to Senior Technician). In fact, the promotion from Technician 1 to Technician 2 may not even come with any appreciable change in job responsibility if, say, the sub-grade Technician 2 was created primarily to block off average performers from reaching the salary maximum point for Technician 2. That being the case, logically, the promotion increment that accompanies a promotion from one sub-grade to another sub-grade should be modest.

Broad Banding of Job Grades

D10.47   There are organisations that prefer fewer job grades. If they have started with many narrow job grades, they may decide to bundle these job grades to create broad job bands which will be in fewer numbers. This approach is called "broad banding". It is essentially merging a few adjacent job grades into a single broad job band. For example, the grades of Assistant Manager, Manager and Senior Manager may simply be merged into one single broad band of "Manager".

D10.48   When broad banding is done, there are two implications:

(a) The broad job band that is formed by merging job grades will come with a long salary range. That is, the spread between the minimum and maximum points of the salary range for the broad job band will be large.

Example

Original Job Grades	New Job Band
Assistant Manager ($3,500–$5,200) Manager ($4,500–$6,700) Senior Manager ($5,500–$8,200)	Manager ($3,500–$8,200)

The new job band will have a salary range that takes on the minimum point of the lowest job grade and maximum point of the highest job grade that have been merged into it (that is, $3,500 of Assistant Manager grade and $8,200 of Senior Manager grade, respectively).

(b) The job band being a broad one, it implies that an employee in the said job band may be assigned a level of responsibility that can vary very largely. This gives the organisation the leeway to stretch an employee for developmental purposes without the need to re-grade or promote him.

D10.49   Organisations that opt for broad bands usually do so for one or more of the following reasons:

(a) It prefers a flatter organisation structure, instead of one comprising many hierarchical levels, to support or align with its intended organisational culture.

(b) It wants to leverage on broad job bands to facilitate the lateral movement of its employees.

D10.50 Broad banding has its downsides too. There are two main disadvantages, as elaborated below:

(a) There will be fewer opportunities for promotion. The organisation must find other ways to motivate its employees, such as giving good bonuses.

(b) As broad job bands have long salary ranges, employees will be allowed to progress to the maximum point of the salary range of their respective job bands. The organisation must therefore be prepared for higher salary costs. To manage this, the organisation must have robust performance assessment and a strict performance-oriented policy/culture that stops weak performers from enjoying salary progression (for example, an employee must achieve a threshold performance to qualify for annual increment).

D10.51 Many new or "contemporary" organisations now go for broad job bands as the preferred way to manage the deployment of their employees. In the present era where businesses, operations and jobs change rapidly, broad bands give organisations the critical advantage to deploy and emplace employees with less restrictions and without the hassle to re-grade or promote the employees.

Implementing a New Job Grade Structure

D10.52 When an organisation develops a new job grade structure or revamps its old job grade structure, it will need to launch the new job grade structure in a calibrated and systematic manner. The steps involved include the following:

(a) Share an overview of the new job grade structure with the employees. Explain the purpose and uses of a job grade structure.

(b) Next, assign an employee grade to each employee based on the new job grade structure. Do note that the employee grade for an employee may match or not match the grade of the job position that he is occupying (please refer to paragraphs D10.24–D10.28).

D10.53 Most organisations do not reveal to their employees the job grades of the positions that they are occupying. The organisations regard the job grades as confidential and only management is privy to the information and uses it to make decisions on staff deployment and development. From the perspective of the employee, what matters most is his own employee grade.

Assigning Employee Grade to Each Employee

D10.54 When an organisation switches from an old job grade structure to a new one, every employee must be assigned an employee grade based on the new job grade structure. If there was previously an old job grade structure, it will involve mapping the employee grades over from the old job grade structure to the new job grade structure. Though sensitive, it presents a good opportunity for the organisation to rectify anomalies (if any) that might have accumulated due to legacy issues or events. For example, some employees may have been under-graded (or under-recognised), while others may have been over-graded (or over-promoted). The new employee grade assigned to an employee should commensurate with his level of competency (that is, the level of job the employee can competently perform). The key is to ensure internal relativity and equity.

D10.55 The main constraint (or "golden rule") that the organisation must abide by is that no employee when assigned his new employee grade should suffer any reduction in his salary range; that is, his new salary range must be equal or better, and not lower. If an employee is matched to an employee grade (say, Grade X) based on his competency level (say, using the hierarchy/complexity of the current job that he is performing competently), but his old salary range is higher than the salary range of Grade X, then it is untenable for the organisation to forcibly impose Grade X's lower salary range on the employee. To overcome this "obstacle", the organisation may adopt any one of the following approaches:

(a) Assign the employee to Grade X but allow him to retain his old salary range on a personal-to-holder basis; that is, he will be allowed to progress (via annual increments) to the maximum of his old salary range (which is higher than the maximum salary of Grade X). Should he be promoted in future, he will be placed on Grade [X+1] and adopt the salary range of Grade [X+1] and thereby be re-aligned with the organisation's new salary structure.

(b) Assign the employee to the next higher employee grade, that is, Grade [X+1] so that the salary range of Grade [X+1] can accommodate the employee's old salary range. To justify giving the employee a higher employee grade of Grade [X+1], the organisation should consider expanding the job portfolio of the employee; that is, stretch him to do more or take on higher responsibilities. However, this approach is only feasible if the employee has the ability (or aptitude) to take on more or higher responsibilities; otherwise, it is a non-starter and the employee leapfrogs to a higher salary range at Grade [X+1] (even better than his old salary range) which further compounds the anomaly (or inequity). For such a case, it is better to take approach (a) and place the employee at Grade X but allow him to retain his old salary range on a personal-to-holder basis.

D10.56   Suffice to say, assigning employee grades to employees requires a lot of judgment. Human Resource is usually tasked to do a first-cut proposal and flag out all anomalous cases to the line heads and management for attention and deliberation. The exercise must be done in good faith. That said, one must guard against over-leniency in assigning employee grades to employees as higher salary ranges for employees mean higher salary cost for the organisation down the road.

Upkeeping Job Grades and Position Titles

D10.57   Job grades, employee grades and position titles are invariably decided for jobs and employees to suit the organisation's prevailing people management philosophy and circumstances. Over time, they should be reviewed and refined as necessary should these factors change.

D10.58   Of the 3 items, position titles are more likely to change (or change more frequently) to keep pace with changes in running the business and organising the operations.

D10.59   The job grade structure, if designed properly, should last for some years before any changes are required. While the overall job grade structure may remain quite stable, the job grades for specific job positions should be reviewed and refreshed if jobs have changed materially, such as when new responsibilities are added, or the purpose or nature of job tasks have changed. Adding and removing job positions can also be expected now and then as business operations evolve, expand or shrink.

D10.60   Whenever a new job position is created, a job grade must be decided for it. One way to go about it is to compare the new job with other existing jobs that have some similarities. Another way is to consider who among the existing employees possesses competencies suited for the job (without being under-qualified or over-qualified for it). The employee grade of this employee will serve as a good reference. If, say, none of the existing jobs are similar and none of the existing employees can fit into that role, the organisation will need to evaluate the new job position (please refer to paragraphs D10.33 and D10.34 for the evaluation process).

D10.61   Generally, Human Resource (HR) is tasked to own and upkeep the job grade structure. HR must also ensure governance and accuracy in assigning employee grades (which affect the remuneration and staff benefits of employees). Employee grades should be reviewed at promotion exercises in consideration of the employees' competencies and readiness to take on higher roles. As for position titles, HR should work with line heads to jointly specify position titles; for this purpose, it would be useful for HR to develop rules and pointers to guide the line heads in specifying position titles so that there will be consistency across the organisation. Though position titles do not cost the organisation any money, wrong choices of position titles may affect the image of the organisation and confuse customers, employees and other stakeholders.

Career Management and Career Roadmaps

D10.62   *What is Career Management?*
Career management refers to the process of planning, staging and optimising an individual employee's career path within an organisation. An organisation may undertake career management at 3 levels as follows:

(a) *Career management at organisation-wide level*
To put in place policies, frameworks and training and developmental programs to support employees in continual upskilling and reskilling and building meaningful and progressive careers within the organisation.

(b) *Career management at employee group level*
To provide career paths/roadmaps based on employee groupings. An employee group may go by job seniority level (for example, executives and above) or by job family or occupational group (for example, finance, marketing or engineering). A group may also be based on employee profile, such as high-potential employees, management trainees/associates or lower-wage workers.

(c) *Career management at individual employee level*
Typically, these individuals are those whom the organisation wants to chart their careers with specific timelines to meet its strategic needs. For example, the organisation may need to prepare a new chief executive officer (or any other C-suite executive) within the next, say, 5 years, and

has identified a specific internal candidate, and therefore charts out a rather precise career and developmental plan to prepare him for the eventual role.

D10.63 *What is a Career Roadmap?*
A career roadmap is a document mapping out an individual employee's full career pathway within the organisation that will see him eventually reach the highest job position that is matched to his full potential. A career roadmap should contain the essential components that will help both the employee and the organisation navigate and realise the career roadmap, including the following:

    (a) career milestones that the employee will progress through with estimated timelines (for example, the estimated timeline (year) the employee will reach Manager grade or Director grade);
    (b) competency requirements for each career milestone;
    (c) training and developmental support that the organisation will provide; and
    (d) the proactive steps that the employee must take for his own personal/ professional growth (this indicates the ownership that he must demonstrate for his own career roadmap).

Objectives and Benefits of Career Management

Benefits to Organisation

D10.64 Career management is an essential supporting component of an organisation's talent management and succession planning program. It enables the organisation to plan, manage and optimise its human capital to meet its operational needs. It is akin to planning the movement of chess pieces on a chessboard. Without proactive career management for employees, it is much like the organisation leaving to chance how the chess game will pan out.

D10.65 Doing career management and providing career roadmaps to employees also signify an organisation's long-term commitment to develop its employees and help them actualise their career potential. It is a powerful value proposition to employees and prospective job candidates and thus will help the organisation better attract, engage and retain talent.

D10.66 For some organisations (especially those in niche industries), it is critical for certain management and specialist positions to be filled by internal talent who have built up experience and institutional knowledge of the organisation's multiple functional/operational areas and are also aligned with the organisational culture. Such attributes and experience are not found in external candidates. That being the case, career management for the category of high-performing and high-potential employees becomes critical for these organisations to fulfil their strategic manpower needs.

Benefits to Employees

D10.67 Career management and career roadmaps communicate to employees the career progression possibilities that are available to them within their organisations, as well as help align their career aspirations with the organisations' objectives and needs. Employees will feel better engaged and enjoy higher personal and professional fulfilment in pursuing a long-term career with the organisation.

D10.68 A career roadmap provides direction and gives clarity, serving as a "compass" of sorts to help an employee navigate his career progression and motivate him to upskill and enhance his competencies systematically and purposefully to reach his full career potential. In more specific terms, a career roadmap helps the employee stay focused, make smart and informed decisions about skills development and job posting options and track his own progress against his career goal.

D10.69 Whether a career roadmap will materialise or how soon it will happen depends on a myriad of factors – the most critical being the performance and readiness of the employee and the performance and growth of the organisation. If an organisation does not perform well or if an employee's personal circumstances change, the career roadmap may become derailed. Notwithstanding, whatever the outcome, in the course of realising the career roadmap, an employee would have undergone lateral postings and gained diverse job experiences, and these will enhance his overall and long-term employability.

Integrating Career Management with Other Human Capital Initiatives

D10.70 Career management cannot be done for its own sake (as an end itself) or as a perk for employees. It must also not be done in a vacuum as a standalone initiative. First, it must be aligned with the overall strategic manpower needs of the organisation and second, it must be fully integrated with other human capital initiatives, such as recruitment, staff deployment, rewards and recognition, training and development and talent management and succession planning.

Recruitment
If new hires are of the wrong profile, no amount of career management can rectify and career roadmaps are meaningless.

Staff Deployment
If good talented people are hired but wrongly deployed, it is a waste of talent. Career management for talented employees entails well-planned job postings that are both meaningful for the employees' development and productive for the organisation.

Rewards and Recognition
Career roadmaps invariably involve stretch assignments/postings for high performers to challenge and develop them. If they perform well, the organisation must be decisive in rewarding and recognising them. It is useless to have elaborate career roadmaps if the organisation only pays lip service to motivate and retain its talented employees.

Training and Development
For an employee to realise his career roadmap, he must meet the competency requirements for each career milestone. The organisation should provide training and development that are aligned with the employee's career roadmap so that they are purposeful and effective in supporting the employee to attain the required competencies.

Talent Management and Succession Planning
Career roadmaps for high-potential employees must be closely woven with the organisation's talent management and succession planning program. The essence of a career roadmap for a high-potential employee is to help him eventually reach the highest job position that is matched to his full potential. The organisation needs to take this "promise" seriously and make timely changes in staffing its key and leadership positions. Where there is a suitable internal candidate to fill a key/leadership position, all things being equal, the internal candidate should be given priority over an external hire.

Organisation's and Employee's Roles in Career Management

Organisation's Role

D10.71   Foremost, the organisation must have a desire to nurture people. For career management and career roadmaps to work, they must be contextualised to the needs of the organisation.

D10.72   To communicate a career roadmap effectively to the employee, the organisation must be open to sharing information on its strategic direction, business outlook, opportunities and challenges. The organisation should offer resources such as career advisory, job descriptions and self-assessment tools. Postings of internal job openings should be made on the staff portal so that there is transparency and employees can make informed decisions on the career opportunities available. It will be useful to have a career advisory hotline (manned by Human Resource) so that employees can have access to career counselling. It is also desirable to have career mentors that employees can approach for advice.

D10.73   Before an organisation embarks on career management for its employees, it should first undertake these actions:

(a) do a check and ensure that career management is aligned and integrated with other human capital initiatives;

(b) communicate a clear statement that both the organisation and individual employees have a role to play in making career management work – that while the organisation will provide work experience and learning opportunities, employees must take ownership to continually learn, take on new or additional roles, get involved in projects and stretch themselves beyond their comfort zones;

(c) put in place a job grade structure;

(d) have an up-to-date inventory of career milestone positions, including the job descriptions;

(e) mandate a requirement for all line managers/heads to hold proper career conversations with their staff during the annual performance appraisal exercise;

(f) provide a clear process for employees to raise requests for job transfers or apply for internally advertised job positions; and

(g) provide training and development programs to help employees acquire and meet the competency requirements for their career milestones. To bring about improvement in the general competency level of employees, make certain training programs compulsory.

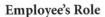

Employee's Role

D10.74 Employees must take ownership and be proactive in managing their own careers. While the organisation may provide opportunities and resources for learning and growth, the employee must make effort to seize the opportunities. They must be willing to take on an expanded job scope and stretch themselves to do more and stay committed to continuous learning.

D10.75 Given that a career roadmap is merely a plan and the fact that the realisation of the career targets depends considerably on the organisation's circumstances (for example, whether the organisation is performing well) and external factors, employees must manage their own expectations about career roadmaps. Ultimately, one must own and navigate one's own career.

D10.76 The employee should do an honest self-assessment of his own strengths, preferences and limitations so that he can choose and pursue a career path that is most aligned with his natural strengths, interests and passion. Having a conversation with a career coach will be useful.

Features of Career Roadmaps

Career Milestones, Job Grades, Competency Requirements and Progression Timelines

D10.77 A career roadmap will set out the various "career milestones" that an employee will progress through. A career milestone is a distinctive job level (or job band) that is distinguished from other levels/bands in terms of job size. For example, Executive, Manager, Director and Chief of Function are all typical career milestones. The job grades for each career milestone should be stated so that the employee can appreciate how he advances in the job grade structure as he realises his career roadmap.

D10.78 Each career milestone must also be accompanied by a set of prerequisites and competency requirements. This is to help the employee assess his own gaps so that he can go about fulfilling those requirements in a purposeful manner.

D10.79 Progression timelines for the employee to reach each career milestone should also be given, so as to manage the employee's expectations. The timelines are meant to be estimates only and need not be precise; a range (say, 3–5 years) should be sufficiently indicative. The progression timelines will give the employee an indication on the amount of time that he has to meet the prerequisites and competency requirements for his next career milestone so that his progression along the career roadmap will not be hampered or disrupted.

D10.80   To summarise, a good and complete career roadmap will contain the following information:

(a) the career milestones that the employee is expected to progress through and the respective job grades of the career milestones;

(b) the estimated progression timelines for the employee to reach the various career milestones; and

(c) the prerequisites for each career milestone, including the following:

- qualifications, trade/technical certifications, competencies and experience,
- acquisition of certain knowledge and skills and/or attendance of certain mandatory training programs and developmental activities before moving up to the respective career milestones and
- requirement of having undergone specific and critical work assignments before moving up to certain positions (for example, a few stints of overseas postings may be required before an employee assumes a key position at regional or global level).

Specialist Career Track versus Management Career Track

D10.81   If an organisation has an uncomplicated operation, it can make do with only one generic career path that all employees may progress upwards along its job grade structure.

D10.82   If an organisation has diverse businesses and operations, multiple job families and a sizeable employee population, it makes sense to create two (or even three) career tracks to cater to the different employee profiles and career aspirations of its employees. Traditionally, for an employee to rise to a higher job grade, he must manage people and do a general management job. However, in today's knowledge-driven economy, many industries require employees to be deep-skilled in their profession or technical craft (for example, a board-certified professional engineer, research scientist or product designer). Such high-performing professionals are experts in their respective fields and are able to contribute to their organisations in an impactful manner as strong individual contributors (without managing other employees). Many enjoy their professions and prefer to specialise and stick to their technical/professional career paths.

D10.83   It is common for large organisations to create at least two career tracks – a Management track and a Specialist track.

> **Management track** caters to employees who aspire to lead teams and manage people. These employees may be subject to deployment to various departments (functions) so that they can become familiar with the breadth of their organisations' operations.
>
> **Specialist track** caters to professionals (in professions such as finance, engineering, information technology and legal) who want to pursue advancement in their respective professions to reach expert level and continue as individual contributors in their organisations.

D10.84   The Specialist career track is aimed at lengthening the career path of high-performing and technically deep-skilled individual contributors who are a valuable asset to the organisation. By having a Specialist track to enable them to advance in their careers within the organisation, it will motivate and retain them in service. The organisation will be able to build a pool of technically proficient professionals with deep expertise and this will become its competitive advantage.

D10.85   For organisations that have two or more career tracks, these operate in parallel. The apex of the different career tracks may be equivalent in seniority (that is, the same or equivalent job grade).

> Example
> A hospital typically has a Management (administrative) career track and a Medical (professional) career track for its doctors.
>
> - The apex of the Management track is the Chief Executive Officer (CEO) who is accountable for the business and entire operations of the hospital but minus the medical aspects.

> - The apex of the Medical track is commonly referred to as the Chairman of Medical Board (CMB) who spearheads and oversees all medical professional matters. All doctors in the hospital will report to the CMB.
>
> The CMB position may be equivalent in job grade to the CEO position although administratively, the CMB may report to the CEO (so that the CEO can have overall oversight of the hospital when he deals with external stakeholders).

D10.86   If an organisation creates multiple career tracks, each career track must have salary ranges specified for their respective job grades. The salary ranges may be the same or different for the job grades under each of the career tracks. Having different (separate) salary ranges is logical because the demand and supply and market salary norms are different for the job positions under the different career tracks. For example, even assuming that an engineering manager position under the Management track is of equivalent job grade as an engineering lead consultant position under the Specialist track, these two positions may command different market salaries. Other than salary ranges and basic salary, other terms and conditions of employment should however be the same and consistent across the different career tracks where the job grades are the same.

D10.87   For illustration, samples of dual career tracks and triple career tracks are shown below:

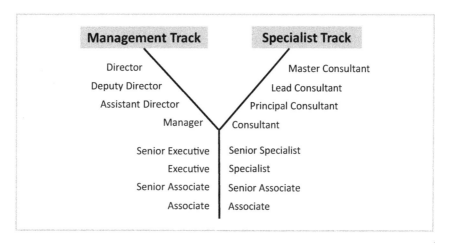

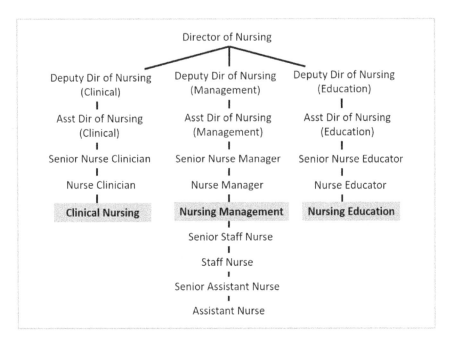

Career Roadmaps: For Individual Employees, Job Families and High-Potential Employees

Career Roadmap for Individual Employees

D10.88 A career roadmap for an individual must necessarily be very specific to the person. For the career roadmap to be meaningful, the management (or Human Resource or line management that is preparing the career roadmap) must first understand the employee's career aspirations and his motivational drivers. The employee's personal traits, strengths and limitations should be identified and taken into consideration to design the developmental plan under his career roadmap. Please refer to Annex D10-1 for a sample of an individual career roadmap.

D10.89 Given the heavy customisation needed for individual career roadmaps, they therefore require much time and effort to prepare. In view of this, organisations should be very selective on which employees should be given the "privilege" of having individual career roadmaps. Another consideration is that individual career roadmaps will invariably raise expectations for the employees, hence the organisation should assess carefully whether an employee is of good enough potential to advance in his career as well as whether he has the commitment to stay on long term with the organisation.

Career Roadmap for Job Families

D10.90   As it is not practical to develop career roadmaps for every employee, most organisations instead develop generic career roadmaps for job families. Even then, organisations tend to tier their efforts for different job families and focus more on mission-critical job families. For example, an engineering services company should have a career roadmap for its engineers. Likewise, a healthcare institution should have career roadmaps for its doctors, nurses and allied health professionals. Please refer to Annex D10-2 for a career roadmap sample for the finance job family.

Career Roadmap for High-Potential Employees

D10.91   Most large and established organisations have a talent management program specifically for employees with high potential. Some organisations recruit annually a batch of fresh degree graduates of high calibre and potential for their Management Associate scheme (or whatever equivalent name it may be called) which is de facto a talent pipeline for their key management positions. They will be deliberately assigned to different roles across the breadth of the organisation's operations to prepare them for leadership positions eventually. They will be nurtured, tested, closely monitored and tracked under a career roadmap. More details on career management for high-potential employees are shared in Chapter D14 "Talent Management and Succession Planning".

Challenges and Limitations of Career Management

D10.92   Career management and roadmaps are mostly prevalent in large and established organisations and are typically meant for executives and professionals. These organisations embrace a long-term view of their human capital and place a lot of emphasis on developing and retaining their employees. Career roadmaps in a systematic form are rarely seen in small and medium enterprises (SMEs). Many SMEs are concerned with survival and business viability and the small scope of operations poses a constraint in offering meaningful career paths to their employees. While some SMEs promote their capable and loyal rank-and-file employees to management positions over time, this usually does not arise from any deliberate career planning.

D10.93   There are several reasons why career management is not extensively embraced:

  (a) first, it is tedious and challenging to develop career roadmaps;

(b) second, given the rapid changes and disruptions arising from a continually evolving operating environment and technological advancement, organisations may be uncomfortable with a long-term commitment to advancing the careers of their employees;

(c) third, high staff turnover discourages organisations from proactively planning the careers of their employees; and

(d) fourth, at times, the career goals of employees may not materialise due to various individual factors. An employee's priorities may change. He may become more realistic and circumspect with more experience and self-reflection. Given the tight labour market, employees have a high tendency to seize opportunities and move on and navigate their own career plans that are not specific to any organisation.

D10.94   In closing, it bears to also highlight the limitations of a job grade structure. Job grade structure is the creation of Industry 2.0 (mass production) and 3.0 (computerisation and automation) Job grade structures provide a sense of orderliness, system and objectivity, which were all valued by organisations and employees. However, fast forward to Industry 4.0 (digitalisation and artificial intelligence), we see more volatilities in employment and less permanency of jobs. The nature and shape of jobs change faster and more radically. If a job is constantly evolving, its job grade will quickly become inaccurate or obsolete. It will be challenging to constantly re-grade jobs, and to compound the problem, it will get increasingly more difficult to understand and evaluate new jobs because of their "newness". Under Industry 4.0, employees will likely change employers more frequently. When an employee does not stay long enough with any organisation, the job grade structure of the said organisation will lose its significance to the employee.

D10.95   Given the challenges and limitations highlighted, organisations in steering forward must decide for themselves how much career management they want or should do for their employees and if so, how specific or granular the career roadmaps should be. It all depends on the organisation's context and circumstances. If a structured approach to career management is not practical (or meaningful), perhaps to adapt to a more general approach whereby the organisation continually nurtures and supports its employees in enhancing their knowledge, skills and competencies to help them stay steadfastly competent and versatile and with the ability to adapt with agility in the face of change. This way, as the organisation evolves and likewise its jobs, employees will be able to pivot and move in tandem with the organisation's needs.

Annex D10-1

Career Roadmap (Sample for Individual)

Career Roadmap for XXX [Name] as at XXX [Date]

Personal Particulars	
Qualifications	Degree in Business Administration
Experience	4 years in manpower recruitment and general human resource administration
Strengths	Communication. Service orientation. Taking ownership.
Challenges	Writing skills. Too obliging (don't know how to say "no").
Personality	People person. Quite compliant and not assertive.

Career Aspiration

To pursue a career in human resource management. Possibly to head the Human Resource department in the current company or an equivalent organisation within 10–12 years.

Career Planning

Milestone Positions	Senior HR Executive	Assistant HR Manager	HR Manager	Senior HR Manager	Head of HR
Timelines	Now	Add 2–3 years	Add 2–3 years	Add 3–4 years	10–12 years from Now
Competency Requirements	• Xxxxxxxxxx • Xxxxxxxxxx • Xxxxxxxxxx	• Xxxxxxxxxx • Xxxxxxxxxx • Xxxxxxxxxx	• Xxxxxxxxxx • Xxxxxxxxxx • Xxxxxxxxxx	• Xxxxxxxxxx • Xxxxxxxxxx • Xxxxxxxxxx	• Xxxxxxxxxx • Xxxxxxxxxx • Xxxxxxxxxx

Experience Enhancement

Move to other HR function areas including rewards design and management, employee relations and engagement, and talent management and development. Pace and timing will depend on opportunities and organisational needs.

To enhance appreciation of business and operational issues and to broaden perspectives, consider a stint in an operations department for 1–2 years, and/or to be assigned to projects/tasks outside of HR (for example, take minutes at senior management meetings, serve in inter-departmental committees/taskforces and participate in corporate planning sessions and other corporate-level initiatives).

Personal Learning

- Enroll for Graduate Diploma in Human Capital Management (1-year part-time course).
- Keep up with regulatory changes and evolving market practices.
- Attend courses on effective writing, thereafter to take minutes at senior management meetings and prepare reports for senior management.

Annex D10-2

Career Roadmap (Sample for Finance Job Family)

	Accounts Executive Senior Accounts Executive	Accountant	Finance Manager Senior Finance Manager	Finance Director
Qualifications and Experience	Accounting Diploma. Up to 6 years in Accounting.	Accounting Diploma or ACCA. 6–8 years in Accounting.	ACCA or equivalent. 8–15 years in Accounting/Finance.	ACCA or equivalent. At least 15 years in Financial Management.
Key Roles (not exhaustive)	Prepare P&L, balance sheet and cash flow statements. Perform reconciliation. Handle AP, AR and GST.	Prepare group consolidated accounts. Perform financial analysis. Oversee AP, AR and GST. Track usage of bank facilities.	Lead team to prepare financial reports/statements, management accounts, etc. Manage cash flow. Ensure integrity of financial data and accounting processes. Coordinate budgeting.	Strategise, develop and implement a financial plan to support business growth and operations. Advise on funding. Oversee cash flow and financial audit. Ensure high accounting standards and control measures. Devise plan for tax optimisation.
Core Competencies Required	Taking Ownership Quality Focus Concern for Governance	Taking Ownership Quality Focus Concern for Governance	Taking Ownership Quality Focus Concern for Governance Solution Focus Collaboration	Leading and Developing Others Strategic Vision Critical Thinking Concern for Governance Collaboration

Core Function Training	Accounting Standards Regulatory/Reporting Requirements Financial Closing Accounting Updates Payroll Processing GST	Consolidation of Group Accounts Fixed Assets Management Accounting Updates Financial Analysis Tax Computation	Financial Reporting Financial Operations Controls Cashflow Management Budgeting Tax Compliance/Planning	Financial Planning Strategic Financial Management Funding Strategies Financial Auditing Cash Management Solutions Strategic Tax Planning Investment Analysis and Advisory
Supplementary Training	MS Office Management Accounting Data Analysis	Data Analytics Cost Management Presentation Skills	Business Partnering Skills Recruitment Interview Skills Negotiation Skills	Managing Difficult Situations Design Thinking Financial Instruments
Training (Managing Self)	Time Management	Management Principles	Writing Effectively Emotional Intelligence	Influencing Skills Critical Thinking Skills
Training (Managing Others)	Communication Skills	Supervisory Essentials	Performance Management Stakeholders Management	People Management Skills Conflict Management
Training (Leading Others/Organisation)	Not Applicable	Not Applicable	Change Management	Strategic Planning Skills Industry 4.0

Employee Training

Focus of this Chapter

Training, learning and development are domains that aim at developing and enhancing human capabilities; they fall under human resource development (HRD). On the other hand, domains such as recruitment, rewards and benefits, performance management, employee conduct and relations, employee communication and engagement and industrial relations fall under human resource management (HRM).

Training, learning and development are big topics. We offer broad sketches and key salient features of these HRD domains in Chapter D11 "Employee Training" and Chapter D12 "Employee Development". The intention is to give readers a basic appreciation of these domains so that together with the other chapters spanning Volumes A to E, this book series enables human resource generalist practitioners to gain a complete picture of the entire spectrum of human resource – both HRD and HRM. Specialists in HRD must go beyond these two chapters to widen and deepen their expertise in HRD.

Employee Training, Learning and Development:
Similarities, Differences and Inter-relation

Employee Training

D11.1   Training is the process or action taken to enable an employee to acquire or improve specific job-related knowledge and skills that are required or relevant for his current or not-too-distant future job role. Training is often linked to performance improvement goals, normally precipitated from performance planning and review where performance gaps are identified. The organisation attributes the performance gaps to a knowledge/skills gap on the part of the employee and thereby uses training as the intervention to help the employee close the gap.

D11.2   Knowledge/skills gaps may arise in 4 possible scenarios:

(a) the employee is not meeting the knowledge/skills requirements of his current job role;

(b) the employee's current job role is affected by changes in the operating environment, and hence his current knowledge/skills are becoming obsolete and he has to reskill;

(c) the employee is assigned to a different job role and thus required to pick up new knowledge/skills; and

(d) the employee is earmarked for higher responsibilities and therefore has to upskill to prepare for the said role.

D11.3   Organisations may use training as an intervention to address any of the above four scenarios. The ultimate desired outcome is to improve the employee's performance and productivity, be it in his current job, evolved job, new job or higher job.

D11.4   Training is usually done in the form of structured and time-bound programs or interventions (such as short training courses and on-the-job training attachments) initiated by the organisation that focus on imparting specific knowledge/skills to the employee or to influence change in a specific aspect of his work behaviour.

Employee Learning

D11.5   While training is typically directed by the organisation (or the trainer on behalf of the organisation), learning is driven solely by the learner himself. Learning is the process by which individuals acquire or assimilate new knowledge, skills, behaviours and attitudes. Learning is motivated by passion and sense of achievement. Continual learning helps an employee remain employable and thrive.

D11.6   Learning can occur both formally and informally, through various channels, including formal training programs, self-directed learning, peer collaboration, networking and exposure, mentoring, coaching and experiential learning on the job.

D11.7 Increasingly organisations embrace the "learning organisation" concept by investing time and resources to put in place a rich and diverse offering of training resources (both formal and informal, physical and online) and make them widely available to their employees and encourage them to take ownership of their own training needs and learn continuously. The purpose is to foster a culture of continuous learning which in turn will fuel continuous improvement, adaptability and innovation within the organisation. This form of continuous learning goes beyond an employee's immediate job requirements. Rather, continuous learning is extolled as a life skill to help employees stay relevant and employable throughout their working life.

Employee Development

D11.8 Employee development goes beyond the employee acquiring specific job-related knowledge and skills for his current job role. Rather, it extends to preparing the employee for future roles and responsibilities within the organisation. In other words, developmental interventions focus on the employee as an asset to be enhanced, rather than be tied to any specific job role. The goal is to help the employee strengthen his core competencies (knowledge, skills, behaviour traits and self-concept) to help him actualise his full potential. From the perspective of the organisation, employee development serves to build and strengthen an internal talent pipeline that will become capable managers and leaders.

D11.9 Employee development can happen through many formats of interventions (such as job rotations, transfers, secondments, stretch assignments, mentoring and executive coaching and leadership programs) that provide the employee with exposure and challenges to help him sharpen his competencies, broaden his perspectives and so achieve personal and professional growth. Development is often considered a more long-term investment. We cover in more detail in Chapter D12 "Employee Development".

Similarities, Differences and Inter-relation

D11.10 Employee training, learning and development are all interrelated. They are all interventions that have a common purpose of enhancing an employee's capability (what he knows and how he thinks, behaves, acts and ultimately performs at work), yet there are nuanced differences that distinguish them. We summarise these briefly in the following comparative table:

Training	Learning	Development
Primary Focus		
To impart specific knowledge/skills to an employee or enhance his competencies or influence change in a specific aspect of his work behaviour.	The individual employee acquires and assimilates new knowledge, skills, behaviours and/or attitudes.	To provide an employee with exposure and challenges to help him sharpen his core competencies (knowledge, skills, behaviour traits and self-concept), broaden his perspectives and so achieve personal and professional growth.
Direction and Control		
Initiated and directed by the organisation.	Self-directed by the employee based on his desire and aptitude to learn.	Initiated, directed and facilitated by the organisation.
Format		
Usually in the form of structured and time-bound programs or interventions, such as short training courses and on-the-job training.	Learning occurs as the employee undergoes both formal and informal training and developmental programs/ interventions and through self-directed learning.	Various formats of interventions, such as job rotations, transfers, secondments, stretch assignments, mentoring and executive coaching and leadership programs.
Desired Outcome		
To enable the employee to become more competent and perform better in his job.	To enhance the employee's capability and employability throughout his working life.	To prepare the employee for future job roles and higher responsibilities to help him advance in his career.

Benefit to the Organisation		
Competent employees will improve organisational performance and productivity.	A culture of continuous learning will fuel continuous improvement, adaptability and innovation.	Nurturing an internal talent pipeline will strengthen the organisation's bench strength of capable managers and leaders.
Time Horizon		
Usually short-term	On-going	Long-term

D11.11   All three – training, learning and development – play an important and complementary role in building a skilled, resilient and capable workforce within an organisation. We delve into "Employee Training" in Chapter D11 and "Employee Development" in Chapter D12. We leave aside "Learning" as it is a wide topic going into adult learning which is beyond the scope of Volume D.

Value Proposition of Employee Training

Purpose of Training

D11.12   Organisations do not train their employees for altruistic reasons. They treat employee training as a means to an end, which is improved performance and productivity for the organisation. The simple link between these is summarised below:

> Well-trained employees → have better knowledge and skills → become competent in their jobs → work at a faster pace and produce better quality work → higher productivity and performance.

D11.13   While improved productivity and performance are the immediate and tangible goals of training, the benefit to the organisation often goes beyond just these. There are other positives that are generated from investing in employee training:

(a) when employees are trained and competent in their jobs, it will minimise performance gaps and reduce the management time spent on managing performance problems;

(b) better-trained employees are more confident and adaptable, which facilitates change management; and

(c) many employees and jobseekers understand the vagaries of the VUCA (volatile, uncertain, complex and ambiguous) world where knowledge and skills become obsolete quickly. They appreciate the organisation's investment in training them and this becomes a strong employee value proposition to them.

Training is Not the Panacea for All Performance Problems

D11.14 Notwithstanding the importance of employee training, it is not the panacea for all performance problems. It is common for line managers to try to dispose of performance problems of their staff by suggesting or mandating them to go for training. This is a common mistake that many organisations make and must be avoided. To use training as the solution when the problem is not due to a lack of knowledge and skills is tantamount to pouring time and money down the drain.

D11.15 When an employee is not performing up to expectations, there can be many reasons including the following:

(a) he has not been properly trained in the knowledge/skills required for the job;

(b) he has an attitude problem;

(c) he has not been given clear and correct instructions or he has misunderstood the instructions;

(d) he has not been given the necessary resources and support to do his work;

(e) he has not been given the cooperation required from his co-workers;

(f) he is distracted by a difficult personal or family problem;

(g) he has lost his motivation and is cruising at work as he intends to resign soon or retire early;

(h) he has become demotivated as he feels that his effort has not been recognised; and

(i) the organisation's policies, rules, processes and systems are not clear, or are not conducive for efficient work, or are obstructing the performance of work.

D11.16   As can be seen from the long list in the preceding paragraph, the possible reasons for a performance shortfall can be wide-ranging. It may be any one or a combination of the above reasons. Training is a relevant solution if and only if the reason(s) for the performance shortfall includes (a). Otherwise, it will be a wasted effort to prescribe training. In a nutshell, one should not immediately jump onto the training wagon when there is a performance issue. It is important to probe further into the matter to correctly diagnose the underlying reason(s).

Train or Buy Ready-Made?

D11.17   There are organisations which prefer to recruit "ready-made" employees from the labour market. That is, these employees come fully equipped with the requisite knowledge and skills for the jobs that they are hired for and therefore can hit the road running once they are onboard. Organisations are prepared to pay attractive salaries to secure these hires if they are urgently required and there is insufficient time to train internal staff.

D11.18   Indeed some organisations consciously adopt a strategy of dispensing entirely with internal training, preferring the convenience of just buying external ready-made talent. This strategy is feasible if the job positions are generic and ready-made candidates are readily available from the market. Examples are positions in human resource, finance, legal, information technology, public relations, office administration and facilities management. Most smaller organisations adopt this approach as they tend to operate in a just-in-time manner, with little or no lead time for a prolonged period of training.

D11.19   In the case of job positions that are mission-critical, or which are in niche functions that are unique to the organisation, it is much less feasible for the organisation to find ready-made candidates who can just plug in and perform from the word "go". The organisation will have no choice but to hire candidates at the entry level and then train internally.

The Dilemma to Train or Not to Train

D11.20   With a perennial tight labour market, many organisations experience high staff turnover as their employees are presented with abundant job opportunities elsewhere. Employers generally target experienced and well-trained employees to poach. For this reason, organisations may hesitate whether to train or not to train their employees. Through training, their employees become more marketable, and many will not hesitate to jump ship when they are given better offers. On the other hand, if the organisation holds back on training its employees, it will perform sub-optimally. Moreover, employees who are more aspirational are likely to quit if they see a lack of learning opportunities.

D11.21   The solution to the dilemma is therefore not a matter of "to train or not to train". There is no question about the need to train employees if it is the only way to improve performance and productivity. Rather than holding back training for fear that employees will leave after they are well trained, the organisation should find ways to engage and retain their employees through enhancing bonding and instilling loyalty. Organisations must have a holistic employee value proposition (EVP) that is compelling enough for their employees to want to stay on. The EVP should be a whole-of-organisation package comprising factors that appeal to employees, such as fair and competitive remuneration, job security, values alignment, conducive work environment and inclusive culture, career advancement, challenging and meaningful work, empowerment and autonomy and inspiring leadership.

D11.22   Organisations that are confident with their vision, strategic direction and employee value proposition are unfazed by the occasional ripples caused by staff turnover. For example, Singapore Airlines has been steadfast over the decades in training and developing its core employee groups, despite the peaks and troughs seen in the industry. The same goes for the Singapore Civil Service and many large and established corporations. These organisations are steadfastly committed to training and grooming their employees.

Areas of Training Focus

Knowledge, Skills, Competencies and Behaviours

D11.23   Organisations want better performance and productivity. This will come about when employees improve their knowledge, skills, competencies and behaviours. Training must therefore be focused on imparting specific knowledge and skills, and/or enhancing competencies and behavioural traits.

Knowledge

Knowledge forms the foundation for an employee to do his job. It enables the employee to understand the subject matter and the logic behind certain ways of doing things. Knowledge includes concepts, principles, theories, formulae, methods, regulations, system requirements and functionalities, precedents, statistics, industry practices and developments, etc. When an employee is equipped with knowledge and understands it well, he is more likely to do the right things and do the things right.

Examples of Training that enhances Knowledge

- A training program on Product ABC enables the sales executives to be familiar with the product features, target consumer market and industry competition.
- A practicum on Customer Relations Management (CRM) system enables all marketing/sales officers to be familiar with the functionalities of the new CRM system rolled out.
- A course on banking regulations for new banking officers instils their awareness of the regulatory requirements and how to manage risks of non-compliance.
- A seminar on "Workplace Fairness Legislation" for human resource officers informs them of the new legislation that will be enacted in due course.
- A conference on "The Artificial Intelligence Revolution" for executives raises their awareness on the impact of AI on businesses and jobs.

Skills

In many work situations, just knowing (having the knowledge) is not enough. An employee must be able to apply the knowledge through his skills and actions. Skills can be categorised as follows (with examples):

- *Technical skills*: Accounting skills, driving skills, selling skills, writing skills
- *Workplace skills*: Basic communication and interaction skills, office etiquette
- *IT and Digitalisation skills*: IT system operating skills, common software skills
- *Cognitive skills*: Analytical skills, comprehension skills, reasoning skills
- *Personal effectiveness*: Time management, stress management
- *Interaction skills*: Communication, presentation, public speaking, networking skills
- *Supervisory skills*: Delegation skills, supervision skills

Certain professional skills are highly technical and sophisticated. For example, a surgeon doing an operation on a patient, a litigation lawyer articulating a defense in court, a pilot operating an aircraft and a civil engineer designing the construction of a building.

Examples of Training that enhances Skills
- Trainees must attend and pass the course conducted by the Institute of Technical Education (ITE) on "Forklift Operations" to become certified as forklift operators.
- A course on Microsoft Excel Programming improves an employee's knowledge and skills in using the software.
- A course on "Handling Difficult Customers" for restaurant service staff equips them with skills to handle sensitive and difficult situations with customers.
- A course on "Effective Writing Skills" for new officers enhances their skills in writing minutes and producing reports for management.

Competencies and Behavioural Traits

Competencies comprise knowledge, skills, motives, traits and self-concept. Work behaviours are manifestations of how an employee showcases his competencies. Just going through some training to enhance knowledge and skills alone may not generate the desired work behaviours. The motive (or motivation), trait and self-concept of the employee play a big part. A knowledgeable and skillful employee may not produce superior performance if he is not motivated or if his trait and self-concept are not in congruence with what he wants to accomplish. Therefore, to influence an employee's work behaviour, the organisation must not only equip him with the necessary knowledge and skills, but it must also tackle his motivation and competencies.

Examples of Training that enhances Competencies
- A course on "Situational Leadership" for promising executives enhances their understanding of leadership styles and builds confidence in their leadership abilities, including influencing and decision-making. The training should be supplemented by developmental interventions such as mentoring and experiential learning.
- A practicum on "Coaching" equips new managers with skills in listening, giving feedback and asking questions. To be effective as a Coach, the manager must also sharpen his other competencies in people development, such as being familiar with the types and uses of developmental actions.

Training Needs Analysis

D11.24   Training costs money. Adding to that is the salary cost of the employees attending training (what is referred to as "absentee payroll") as training takes employees away from productive work. To be cost-effective, training must be purposeful and serve a business need. Logically, an organisation must do training needs analysis before making these decisions: (a) whether to provide training as the solution to a performance problem, (b) what types of training to be provided and (c) for whom the training should be provided to.

D11.25   Foremost in doing training needs analysis, the organisation must first ascertain whether training is relevant as a solution to address a particular performance gap or boost performance, as the underlying cause(s) for the said performance gap or challenges in boosting performance may have nothing to do with a deficiency in knowledge, skills or competencies. One must probe and analyse to accurately diagnose the underlying cause(s) and not be too quick to prescribe training as the "cure-all" solution.

Multi-dimensional Training Needs Analysis

D11.26   To do training needs analysis in a comprehensive and holistic way, one must not confine the analysis to looking at just knowledge/skills gaps in incumbent employees. That would be too simplistic. One must widen the scan to both macro-level issues that are confronting the organisation, as well as micro-level issues that are happening at the shopfloor and individual employees level. The time horizon should also not be confined to just the current; one must project to the future, so as to prepare the organisation to be future-ready.

D11.27   Training needs analysis should encompass as many relevant dimensions as possible, including the following: (1) strategic direction, (2) organisation structure, (3) business, (4) artificial intelligence, digitalisation and automation, (5) systems and processes, (6) regulatory requirements, (7) culture, (8) organisational development, (9) critical incidents, (10) manpower, (11) performance of the organisation, (12) performance of individual employees and (13) preparation to be future-ready.

D11.28　We delve into each of the above dimensions and elaborate how to analyse each dimension to ascertain whether there exists a training need that will help address any existing or emerging problems.

Dimensions	Analysis to ascertain whether there is a Training Need
❶ Strategic Direction	One should look at the organisation's strategic plan – what does it want to achieve now and in the near future? What must employees do differently or what new things must they do to help the organisation achieve these strategic goals? Are the employees already equipped with the necessary knowledge, skills, competencies and mindset orientation for what they must do?
❷ Organisation Structure	Is the organisation undergoing any merger and acquisition or any restructuring in the near term? If yes, how will it impact the employees' jobs? Will there be jobs that are made redundant and incumbent employees must be reskilled to be redeployed to other areas of need?
❸ Business	• Have customers' needs or expectations shifted? What must employees know or do to keep up with these changes? • Is there any rollout of new products and services? Are employees familiar with the features, target customers, pricing structure and selling strategy? If this is a key product/service, the scale and amount of training involved can be huge (this was the case when Singapore Airlines put the A380 aircraft into service in 2007). The management will need to deep dive into these areas to ascertain whether there are any gaps in the knowledge, skills, competencies and attitudes of employees, and if yes, how these can be addressed by training.

4 Artificial Intelligence, Digitalisation and Automation	Are there any operational areas and tasks affected by artificial intelligence, digitalisation or automation? How are work processes impacted? Which are the tasks that will be displaced or changed? Which jobs would have to be redesigned? What are the new jobs? What new knowledge, skills, competencies and attitudes must employees acquire to adapt to the changes? What are those critical competencies that will better endure these changes?
5 Systems and Processes	Are there any rollouts of new systems and business/operation processes? Employees must be trained on how to use the new systems and/or follow the new processes. If the above systems and processes are localised or the changes are minor, these can be managed at the line level; employees impacted by the changes may be briefed/guided at the working level by their supervisors. However, if the changes are organisation-wide and impact many employees, the training should be centrally planned, organised and executed.
6 Regulatory Requirements	Are there any new regulations introduced or soon to be introduced? How will it impact the organisation's compliance requirements? How will operational processes be impacted? Are the affected employees familiar with the changes? For example, when the Personal Data Protection Act (PDPA) was introduced in 2012 in Singapore, it had wide-ranging impact on how an organisation handles personal data of its customers, employees/jobseekers and the general public.
7 Culture	Do employees communicate openly and collaborate synergistically? Are there unhealthy competition and undercurrents? Do people feel safe talking and raising sensitive issues? Is the decision-making mechanism malfunctioning? Although training may influence some behavioural traits of employees (such as team mindset and collaboration), these "illnesses" cannot be rectified through training courses alone. It will require more extensive and in-depth organisation development initiatives (such as policies and practices, management resolve and leadership by example) to tackle these "illnesses".

❽ Organisational Development	Some organisations proactively undertake organisation development initiatives to instil in their employees certain mindsets that support their organisational agenda. For example, an organisation may want to nurture a service quality credo or extol employees to pursue excellence or develop an innovative mindset or raise employees' awareness of environmental issues to usher in a sustainability movement. Training can influence and help bring about the desired change in employees' attitudes and behaviours to some extent.
❾ Critical Incidents	Critical incidents are those that have a significant adverse impact on an organisation. Examples are fraud, corruption, a severe malfunction or disruption of business operations and a severe misstep committed that incurs censure by a regulatory authority. Whenever a critical incident happens, after the dust has settled, the organisation should review its policies and procedures to prevent the recurrence of similar incidents. This may require the relevant employees to be trained in the revised/new procedures, or refresher training should be conducted for all relevant employees.
❿ Manpower	Most organisations have some roles which are mission-critical or unique and thereby justify long-term and continual training and development to groom the employees. For example, in Singapore Airlines, pilots and cabin crew, as well as marketing and sales personnel and station managers are mission-critical roles. In banks, the Management Associate Program for the specially recruited management trainees is also one. Likewise in the Singapore Civil Service, there are specific talent schemes where the employees are groomed for critical positions. These mission-critical or unique manpower categories will entail very deliberate, structured and intense training and development interventions. Additionally, many large organisations have their talent management and career management plans for their high-potential and high-performing employees, all of which require systematic training and development interventions for these select groups of employees.

⑪ Performance (Organisation)	How is the organisation performing? Is it falling short of what it can potentially accomplish? There may be underlying reasons such as poor alignment of goals, lack of understanding of strategies and requirements, inefficient operational processes, sub-optimal resource deployment and lack of employee motivation due to poor design of rewards and recognition structure. Or it may be due to gaps in knowledge, skills, competencies and attitudes of employees, and if so, these would translate into training needs.
⑫ Performance (Individual Employees)	At every annual performance appraisal cycle, reporting officers are expected to hold a critical conversation with their direct reports regarding their training and development needs. After the conclusion of every annual cycle, Human Resource should comb through the appraisal forms and lift up the training needs of the employees, review them and consolidate into the annual training plan.
⑬ Preparation to be Future-Ready	The organisation must stay attuned to emerging trends with regard to operating a business, harnessing technology and managing people. What are the winds of change? • <u>Business</u> Is the business model showing signs of obsolescence? How can the organisation evolve to ride the wave? • <u>Technology</u> How have other organisations (the trailblazers and game changers) adopted cutting-edge technology? How can the organisation catch up before it is too late? • <u>People</u> What are the current demographics of the organisation's employees? Fast forward to 3–5 years, how will it look? What are the risks to the organisation's manpower pipeline? How is the organisation's succession planning for its critical/key positions? How does its leadership bench strength look like?

SkillsFuture Singapore (SSG) Skills Frameworks

D11.29　Under the ambit of the Industry Transformation Maps (ITMs), more than 20 industry-based as well as occupation-based skills frameworks have been developed by the tripartite partners. These skills frameworks are under the custody of SkillsFuture Singapore (SSG), the government agency tasked to drive the upskilling and reskilling of Singaporean workers. Each of these frameworks sets out the typical job roles in the specific industry, together with the critical functions and key tasks of each job role. Each skills framework also specifies the technical skills and competencies (TSCs) and the proficiency level required for the jobholder. Two examples of the TSCs are shown in Annex D11-1 and Annex D11-2. Organisations in those industries that are covered by the ITMs should find it useful to refer to the relevant skills frameworks to assess and identify any skills gaps and training needs for their employees.

4 Levels of Training Needs

D11.30　Training needs may be analysed and collated via 4 levels, namely:

(a) organisation level;
(b) job family level;
(c) job role level; and
(d) individual employee level.

The 4 levels of training needs will be amalgamated into the organisation's total training plan, which is usually done on an annual basis. A sample of an annual total training plan is shown in Annex D11-3.

Training Needs at Organisation Level

D11.31　The findings from the analysis of the various dimensions such as strategic direction, culture and organisation development may point to certain training needs at the organisation-wide level. For example, in rolling out a new performance management framework, all employees must be trained to appreciate and use it. Likewise, if the organisation wants its employees to embrace innovation at work, all employees should be trained in the concepts and techniques of innovation and how to apply them to problem-solving in their daily work.

Training Needs at Job Family Level

D11.32   Training needs analysis for a job family is quite common. For example, an organisation with a team of sales and marketing personnel will want everyone in the team to know their products well, including the product features and functionalities, key technical specifications and how to use the products optimally and maintenance for the products. Likewise, the organisation's IT team must keep abreast with the fast-paced advancements in information technology. Each mission-critical job family in the organisation must be assessed for its training needs.

D11.33   Given the changes in technology, business models and competitive landscape, some job families may become "sunset" roles, while new job families may emerge as "sunrise" roles. Organisations must examine whether their sunset roles can be redesigned and rejuvenated. As for sunrise roles, the organisations must examine whether their employees are well poised for them. All these will translate into training needs.

Training Needs at Job Role Level

D11.34   Career milestone positions are roles that see an employee experiencing an appreciable leap in job responsibilities. Manager, director and senior leadership positions are common career milestones. It is common to see organisations putting their newly appointed managers, directors and C-suite executives through specially curated and structured training programs to help equip them with the necessary competencies to handle the full rigour of their new roles. To illustrate, a sample of training needs for new managers and leaders is given below:

> Training for Managerial Competencies
> Managerial skills are essential for an individual to effectively guide, organise and manage the activities of his team. They include the following:
> (a) communication, (b) team leadership, (c) employee engagement, (d) grievance handling, (e) conflict resolution, (f) delegation, (g) performance appraisal and feedback, (h) managing weak performance, (i) motivating good performance, (j) developing people, (k) analysis, (l) problem-solving, (m) negotiation and persuasion, (n) decision making, (o) change management, (p) planning and budget preparation, (q) resource and financial management and (r) risk management.

Training for Leadership Competencies
Leadership and managerial functions are different. A leader focuses on creating and articulating a vision, driving changes, setting direction, putting competent people in the right places and inspiring employees. In practice, leaders are often also managers who manage people. Hence, effective leaders need managerial skills in addition to leadership competencies/skills.

Some essential leadership competencies include: (a) strategic thinking, (b) critical thinking, (c) design and system thinking, (d) perspecting (looking at different perspectives) (e) foresight ánd visioning, (f) influencing and persuasion, (g) advanced negotiation, (h) stakeholders' management and (i) executive presence and spokesmanship. Leadership competencies/skills can be honed through curated and structured training programs, but these are usually insufficient and must be supplemented by developmental interventions. These are covered in Chapter D12 "Employee Development".

Training Needs at Individual Employee Level

D11.35   In most large and established organisations, during the annual performance appraisal cycle, it is mandated that the reporting officer holds a critical conversation with his direct report regarding his training and development needs. The discussion usually looks at the actual performance of the direct report in comparison to the job requirements and performance expectations. It should also extend to career planning for the direct report.

D11.36   The critical conversation should probe the following points:

Shortfalls in Job Requirements and Performance Expectations
Are there any shortfalls in the employee meeting job requirements and performance expectations? If yes, what are the causes? What can be done to address the causes? Do any causes point to a deficiency in the employee's knowledge, skills, competencies and attitudes? Will training help close these gaps? What other developmental interventions will be useful?

Career Planning for the Employee
How long has the employee been in the current job role? Has he stagnated in his learning? Is he ready to take on higher or new responsibilities to stretch himself and/or broaden his perspectives and skillsets? What is the employee's natural passion and career interest? What new job role would suit him? What training and/or developmental interventions will help prepare him to achieve his career goals?

D11.37   Unless the critical conversation between the reporting officer and employee is open, sufficiently detailed and done purposefully, it is a common risk that the reporting officer may just dispose of his employee's performance issues by simply suggesting or mandating that he goes for training. For example, a reporting officer may simply decide that an employee who has repeatedly missed work deadlines is bad at time management and so suggests that he be sent for a "Time Management" course, without first uncovering the root cause of the problem. On the part of the employee, being sent for training is not a bad thing; at the very least, it means time off from work, hence he will not object to attending training. The organisation is the party that pays the price for dollars down the drain. The onus is on the line head as well as Human Resource to do a second-level check. Some organisations impose a cap on the training budget for each department – this is one practical way to "force" the line head to scrutinise the training requests surfaced by the reporting officers, and evaluate and prioritise the training needs. The "scrubbed" training needs are then collated by Human Resource and amalgamated into the organisation's annual total training plan.

How Do People Learn?

Theories of Learning

D11.38   People learn through a combination of cognitive, behavioural and social processes. The learning process is complex and varies from person to person based on factors such as individual aptitude and preferences and the nature of the subject (or content) to be learnt.

D11.39   There are diverse theories on how people learn, each emphasising a particular dimension of human behaviour. We briefly cite some of the theories here on how people learn:

> *Behavioural Learning Theory*
> This theory emphasises the association between stimuli and responses.
>
> *Cognitive Learning Theory*
> This theory views the mind as a processor of information, using processes like encoding, storage and retrieval of information.
>
> *Social Learning Theory*
> This theory highlights that people learn by observing others.

> *Experiential Learning Theory*
> This theory highlights that learning is a cyclical process involving concrete experiences, reflective observation, abstract conceptualisation and active experimentation.

> *Multiple Intelligences Theory*
> This theory highlights that individuals possess different types of intelligence, such as linguistic, logical-mathematical, spatial, musical, interpersonal, intrapersonal and more. In view of this, different individuals have different strengths and preferences in learning.

> *Motivation and Self-Determination Theory*
> This theory contends that learners are more engaged and motivated when they have a sense of control, feel competent and experience meaningful connections.

D11.40 Learning is a dynamic and multifaceted process, often encompassing a combination of the above theories and perspectives. Factors such as motivation, environmental influences and individual differences and preferences all play a role in shaping how people learn. What all this means is that when designing training content and delivery, one should consider the trainees' profiles, motivation and preferences so as to create engaging and impactful learning experiences and thereby make training as effective as can be.

70-20-10 Model of Learning

D11.41 The 70-20-10 model of learning suggests that individuals acquire new knowledge and skills in the following manner:

> • 70% of learning is acquired through *doing*
>   – what is termed as *experiential learning* when one learns on the job.
>
> • 20% through *observation*
>   – what is termed as *social learning* when one interacts with friends, colleagues, supervisors and bosses, peers and associates, and observes how they think, behave and act.
>
> • 10% through *listening and reading*
>   – what is termed as *formal learning* when one is put through training courses.

Experiential Learning: Learn by Doing

D11.42   Learning by doing means that the individual has the opportunity to practise what he is learning or what is being taught to him. Only when he practises by doing, then the learning "stays" with him, that is, the acquired learning gets internalised. This is especially so for technical skills that are manual or practical in nature (say, baking a cake or welding a pipe). Even for soft skills (say, leadership), an individual learns best when he is put to the test to apply his skills.

> Example
> If an individual wants to learn how to bake a cake, he may read a baking book for recipes or watch a video on baking. Such learning will be "fleeting" and will not register deeply enough. However, if he digs his hands into the baking process and attempts to bake a cake, the learning experience will stay with him.

> Example
> An individual who aspires to be a good leader may attend courses on "leadership" and read articles or watch videos on "leadership". While he can gather some principles of what constitutes good leadership, the test of his learning comes only when he is thrust into a situation to lead. He will try to recall what he has gleaned from courses/readings, but whether he can apply what he knows remains a question mark. Only by actually leading others, then he will learn through experience (including through self-reflection and feedback from others) and hone his leadership skills bit by bit and gain confidence.

D11.43   Experiential learning is the most effective way for an employee (being an adult) to learn. On-the-job experiences include special projects and assignments as well as day-to-day tasks that allow the employee to apply his learning. The "pain" of going through the process will help him assimilate and internalise his learning. Most of the time, one may not even be aware that one is learning while doing work and solving problems. Cumulatively over time through practice and perhaps some hard knocks, an employee will become a steady practitioner of the said knowledge and skills.

Social Learning: Learn by Observation

D11.44   Learning socially by observation means that the individual gets the opportunity to observe what others do (especially if the person he observes is an expert). By observing how others think, behave and act, the learner gets to pick up tips on what needs to be done, how things are done, and what pitfalls or mistakes to watch out for.

> Example
> Going back to the earlier example of learning to bake a cake. The individual may attend a baking class where the baking teacher holds a full-scale start-to-finish demonstration on how to bake a cake. Being onsite to observe up close and personal, the individual can pick up the essential steps to follow, feel the pace and witness what unforeseen obstacles may crop up in the kitchen and how to cope with them.

> Example
> Going back to the earlier example of learning to be a good leader. The individual may pick a person whom he feels is a good role model as a leader. He may seek mentorship from the person. By watching by the side of his mentor, seeing the actual scene (and drama) and feeling the tempo, he will be able to witness how his mentor deals with difficult situations, manages conflicts, holds steady during crises, upholds fairness and navigates moral dilemmas. Such real-life observations are much more powerful than say, attending a course on the principles of good leadership.

D11.45   Social learning includes learning through friends, peers and colleagues, where the interaction may be formal or informal. Learning can occur within a learning community, participation in collaborative projects, attendance at meetings or discussions and being mentored or coached by another party. Often, one may not realise that a lot of learning can be had from attending important meetings where high-level or challenging issues are discussed and debated upon. This is why some organisations deliberately expose their young and promising executives to such meetings and platforms. Many senior-level executives and professionals also participate in their own social or learning circles to exchange views and be exposed to new ideas and developments.

Formal Learning: Learn by Listening and Reading

D11.46   Formal learning happens in traditional and structured training programs, which include classroom training and seminars, conferences, workshops, online courses, training podcasts, etc.

D11.47　Contrary to the general perception of the significance of formal learning, this form of learning contributes the least to employees' learning. Yet many organisations invest most in formal training and take pride in tracking the number of training hours clocked by their employees in formal training programs. While it is useful for employees to pick up new ideas, theories, concepts, principles and frameworks from formal training programs, all these remain on the drawing board if they are not applied on the job. When the newly acquired learning is not translated into action, there is also no effective way to ascertain whether the employee has indeed imbibed the learning. Just by merely measuring the training hours clocked by the employee is no guarantee that any learning has in fact occurred.

Applying 70-20-10 into Employee Training and Development

D11.48　Appreciating the 70-20-10 model of learning is important for designing training and developmental interventions for employees. Formal training must be supplemented by both social learning and experiential learning to make learning holistic and effective for the employee. Having the employee attend a training course is only the first step; it should not end there. The employee should be given exposure to work with and learn from others to reinforce his learning. On the job, he must also be put to do challenging work to apply and internalise his learning.

Training Design and Delivery Formats

D11.49　Training programs may be designed and delivered in a myriad of ways. Training content may be generic or specially customised for the organisation. It may be designed and delivered by internal trainers or outsourced to external trainers. Training may also be done on the job or off the job. It may be delivered through physical means or cyber/virtual mode or a blended arrangement (that is, a hybrid of both physical and cyber). In designing training programs and delivery, it is also necessary to decide whether to take the teacher-centred approach or the learner-centred approach. Generally, adult learners like employees should find the learner-centred approach more effective for work-related training. There are however exceptions such as when we want to learn from subject matter experts (the teachers) who share their knowledge and insights.

Generic versus Customised Curriculum

D11.50   Ideally, a training curriculum should be customised for the organisation; the training content (say, the use of illustrations and examples) should be contextualised based on the actual work environment. Learning will be more effective if the employees can relate the simulated situations, issues and problems directly to their daily work.

D11.51   However, customisation and contextualisation entail a lot of effort and investment in designing the training. Hence, to make business sense, most organisations will customise their training only if the said training involves a large number of employees to be trained or the training is to be used repeatedly and frequently. Another factor for consideration is whether the training serves a strategic intent for the organisation. For example, if a public service agency wants to imbibe a new cultural mindset in its employees (say, to adopt a "servant leadership" mindset to serve its unique beneficiaries), a generic training program on "servant leadership" will not quite cut the ice.

D11.52   If the training topic is generic and only involves a small number of employees, the common practice is to enrol the employees in training programs that are available "off-the-shelf". For example, employees who are weak in communication can attend an external generic training course on "effective communication".

D11.53   There is a plethora of generic training courses available that are run by private training institutions and freelance training consultants. Some of these courses adopt the SkillsFuture Singapore (SSG) skills frameworks. Such generic SSG-based courses are popular with organisations for two reasons: (a) since the SSG skills frameworks are used, the training content is considered to be "curated" to some extent and (b) many of these courses qualify for substantial government subsidy.

On-the-Job versus Off-the-Job Training

D11.54   On-the-job training simply means that the training takes place when the employee is doing his work; that is, he works and learns simultaneously. Whereas off-the-job training means that the employee is released from work to attend training elsewhere; he may be attending classroom training or a seminar, workshop or conference, or doing online self-directed learning.

D11.55   On-the-job training is commonly referred to as "OJT". For OJT to be effective and meaningful, there must be a deliberate effort on the part of the supervisor to build learning element/content into the OJT. Merely assigning routine and repetitive work to an employee will not provide sufficient learning. The employee should be given challenging or incremental assignments that are paced to stretch his abilities little by little so that he learns as he performs the work. To help the employee assimilate his learning, the supervisor should point out where he has done well and where he can improve and how; a debrief after every major assignment should be done. We elaborate on OJT (including the merits and demerits) in the section "Types of Training: On-the-Job Training" in the later part of this chapter.

D11.56   Not all training can be done as OJT. This is especially so if the employee has to acquire cognitive knowledge (in terms of concepts and principles). Additionally, when the work environment is fast-paced, it is not always feasible to use the workplace as the "classroom" to impart cognitive knowledge. For example, if a forex trading officer in a bank has to acquire knowledge on banking regulations or the prevention of money laundering, it would not be feasible for the supervisor to impart the depth and breadth of the requisite knowledge to him while he is performing forex trades at break-neck speed in the bank's forex trading room. The officer should attend external training courses on the said topics instead.

Physical versus Cyber versus Blended Delivery

D11.57   The traditional model of training is one that involves the presence of the trainer and trainees in the same physical space and time. For example, trainees attend classroom training hosted by a trainer, or attend a seminar or conference to listen to a panel of speakers. Technology has since enabled a lot of training to be done virtually and online and these have fast become popular and mainstay options for employee training.

Virtual Training

D11.58   Virtual training refers to training that is hosted by a trainer, but delivered via cyber mode at a specific time during which trainees will log on to listen to and interact with the trainer. The advantage of virtual training is that it removes the constraints of physical space. It allows trainees to join a training session from anywhere in the world. It also allows large numbers of trainees without the logistic constraints of a physical training venue.

D11.59 Virtual training allows trainees to engage with the trainer and fellow participants since everyone logs on at the same time for the training session. However, most virtual training programs generally face the challenge of engaging their trainee audience. As the interaction is over cyberspace (say, over Zoom), there is generally a perceived "barrier", especially if trainees do not reveal their faces (they turn off the videocam on their devices). Trainees may feel bored and tune off after a while. Notwithstanding this drawback, virtual training remains useful for reaching out to a wide training audience from multiple geographical locations.

Online Training (or E-Learning)

D11.60 Online training is commonly referred to as electronic learning (e-learning) or mobile learning, which is remote and self-directed. The training program is accessible anytime and anywhere via a cyber link or a training app. Many self-directed learning programs come in bite-sized modules (say, in portions lasting 30 minutes each), thus enabling the trainee to fill his pockets of free time. The trainee may even multi-task productively while he learns (say, he may plug on to listen to a training audio while he works out in the gym). This gives the trainee the flexibility to manage his time and integrate his learning with the demands of work and other personal commitments.

D11.61 Another advantage of e-learning programs is that the content and delivery is consistent for the entire cohort of trainees across the whole organisation. It is not subject to the quality of trainers or their consistency in delivering the training.

D11.62 E-learning is generally passive in nature as the trainee does not get to interact with the trainer and fellow trainees. To mitigate this problem, e-learning programs are now increasingly designed to be highly animated and interactive. For example, the trainee may be required to respond to questions or complete an exercise (or win a game) before progressing to the next part of learning. If the e-learning program captures the responses (or scores) of the trainees, it will enable the organisation to track the pass rates, which in some way is an indicator of learning outcomes.

D11.63 E-learning programs generally require somewhat substantial investment in the design of course content. However, if the trainee population is large, the unit cost of upfront development should be acceptable.

Blended Training

D11.64   While virtual training and online training have their advantages, not all training programs can or should be done virtually or online. Ideally, training should be done in a social setting because social learning is a powerful way of learning. People are more motivated to learn when they can physically interact with others (the trainers and fellow trainees). Physical training also allows trainees to learn in a more focused manner, and at the same time, it gives room for the trainer to adapt in situ the training focus and delivery in pace with the trainees' learning progress and the mood in the room. Hence, training in the traditional physical format continues to be relevant.

D11.65   To marry the advantages of both physical and virtual/online training, this is where blended training comes in. Blended training simply means the combined use of both physical and virtual/online training; that is, it is a hybrid model. This approach allows different permutations of delivery methods. For example, the trainees may be required to do online learning to gain some background knowledge of the training topic. They may also be asked to do a pre-training self-assessment on how much they know about the topic. The trainees may then proceed to a physical training session. The knowledge gained from the online portion will give the trainees momentum to engage more actively during the physical class. The trainer can guide the trainees to deep dive into areas that need more elaboration. Following the physical session, the trainees may be asked to go online to complete a follow-up assignment which will assess their learning. The blended approach will shorten the time for physical sessions and therefore make it more feasible for busy trainees to integrate training with their work.

Gamification Training

D11.66   Gamification or gamified learning can be applied to corporate training and online courses. It is a learning approach that incorporates elements of game design and mechanics into training content and delivery to enhance the learning experience. The goal is to make learning more engaging, interactive and enjoyable by leveraging the motivational aspects commonly found in games. People want to win at games, and this motivates them to learn better so that they can win.

D11.67   A gamified training program that is well designed will incorporate the following features:

- *Narrative and Storytelling*
  Storytelling elements are used to provide context to the learning content to pique the learner's interest, making the learning more immersive and engaging.

- *Simulation and Scenario-Based Learning*
  Simulations or scenario-based learning are used to create realistic situations where learners can better relate to their work experiences.

- *Interactivity and Decision-Making*
  Learners are required to solve problems and make decisions as they navigate the game-learning, so as to promote interactivity and (simulated) accountability.

- *Challenges and Goals*
  Specific challenges and tasks are set for learners to complete, making it a goal-oriented learning to give motivation and some pressure to the learners.

- *Competition and Collaboration*
  Elements of competition are incorporated; the learner competes either against himself or against other learners. Learners are also given opportunities to collaborate with other fellow learners as a strategy to complete their learning tasks with better outcomes.

- *Achievement and Motivation*
  Game-like elements such as points, badges, levels and leaderboards are incorporated to create a sense of achievement and progression.

- *Feedback and Progress Tracking*
  Immediate feedback is provided to the learner on his performance and progress so that he understands what works and what doesn't.

- *Adaptive Learning Paths*
  Learning paths can be adjusted based on the learner's performance, thus ensuring a personalised learning experience (that is, not too fast and not too slow for the learner).

Types of Training

Orientation and Onboarding

D11.68 Orientation and onboarding constitute one form of training for new employees.

> Orientation
> New employees are usually put through an orientation program to familiarise themselves with the organisation's vision and mission, policies and people philosophies, work culture, products and services offered by the organisation and the industry landscape. The design of orientation program is usually entrusted to Human Resource so as to ensure consistency in content and delivery.

> Onboarding
> New employees undergo an onboarding process to help them settle into their jobs smoothly. The onboarding process comprises briefings on the employee's job responsibilities, the reporting structure, work processes, systems and methods and other resources within the department. Onboarding is usually carried out by the new employee's supervisor.

D11.69 In large and established organisations, the orientation program for new hires in executive and professional ranks may be rather elaborate and include team bonding activities and interactive sessions with the senior management. It may run intermittently spanning several months of the new employee's first year of service. To reduce the need for physical face-time so as to minimise disruption to work, many organisations have leveraged on online learning where the new hires are required to complete some self-directed orientation training before attending face-to-face briefings. Small and medium-sized companies on the other hand tend to have very simple and brief orientation for their new employees, focusing mainly on basic human resource matters such as terms and conditions of employment, company rules and office practices.

On-the-Job Training

D11.70 On-the-job training (OJT) refers to the process of acquiring knowledge, skills and competencies while performing the actual job at the workplace. The employees receive training directly within the context of their job responsibilities instead of learning in a formal classroom setting, OJT is a practical and hands-on approach to learning, as it allows employees to learn in real-world scenarios.

D11.71 The merits of OJT include the following:

> (a) *Real-world Application*
> Employees learn by doing tasks and activities that are part and parcel of their work. They see direct and immediate application of what they have learnt.
>
> (b) *Supervision and Guidance*
> Employees work under the guidance of their supervisors and/or experienced colleagues who can provide immediate, contextual and explicit feedback and support during the learning process.
>
> (c) *Customised Training*
> OJT is tailored for the specific job. The pace of OJT can also be adjusted to suit the learning agility of the employee.
>
> (d) *Building Relationships*
> OJT provides significant opportunities for the "trainees" to interact with the "trainers". Often, this positively imbues a sense of gratitude in the employees.
>
> (e) *Cost-effective*
> OJT takes place within the existing work environment, minimising the need for additional training facilities or resources. The employee is also producing some work output while learning.

D11.72 OJT is effective only if the trainees are properly briefed, guided and given clear instructions/information on how to go about doing their work. Many organisations have developed online learning videos on important operations showing how work is done, and the trainees are required to go through self-directed online learning before embarking on OJT at the workplace. Ideally, the OJT should include explaining the "why" behind work actions, apart from briefing on the "what" and "how". This helps ensure that the trainees learn intelligently and not mechanically.

D11.73   On-the-job training can have demerits, including the following:

> (a) *Competence of the OJT Trainer*
> Not every supervisor or experienced colleague (who is assigned to provide the OJT) is a good teacher. He may not have the motivation, aptitude, skills and/or patience to guide and support the trainee.
>
> (b) *Self-Interest of the OJT Trainer*
> In some instances, the experienced colleague may be unwilling to share his knowledge due to feelings of insecurity and fear of (potential) competition. For example, an experienced supervisor who has risen from the rank-and-file may not feel comfortable or happy to teach a new graduate executive who is perceived to be a threat.
>
> (c) *Time Constraints*
> Most employees are busy with their daily work routines and sometimes firefighting, hence they may have time constraints to provide thorough OJT to the trainee. Some may also see providing OJT as additional workload; more so, if they are not recognised for the effort.
>
> (d) *Sub-optimal Outcomes*
> The selection of the OJT trainer is critical. Otherwise, through OJT, bad habits and sub-optimal working methods of the "teachers" may be passed on to the trainees.

D11.74   OJT may not be suitable for some job positions, particularly if the position is a frontline role and customer traffic is high and the pace of work is fast. For busy frontline roles, from the perspective of protecting the organisation's reputation, it is not prudent to deploy a trainee to learn on the job, notwithstanding that he may be closely guided by another experienced colleague. If the trainee fumbles in front of a customer, it is likely to displease the customer and incur a complaint. In large organisations such as Singapore Airlines and the banks, the new cabin crew and bank tellers must first be properly trained in the mock-up cabin and bank counter, respectively.

Job Shadowing

D11.75   Job shadowing is one form of training where an employee (trainee) spends time following and observing an experienced person (like a shadow) on the job. The purpose is for the trainee to gain insights into a particular occupation or job role by directly observing the day-to-day activities and responsibilities of a person working in the said occupation or job role. The trainee gets a firsthand look at the knowledge, skills, tasks and challenges associated with the said job role. It is akin to taking a peep into another person's typical day on the job, aka "walking in his shoes".

D11.76 Compared to on-the-job training, job shadowing is more passive because the trainee is not involved hands-on. Notwithstanding that the trainee is only an observer, the trainee is encouraged to make thorough observation, interact with the senior as well as other co-workers (whom the senior works with) and ask questions on how work is done, the challenges and constraints and the gratification and letdowns. In short, the trainee should gain as much appreciation as possible of the highs and lows about the job role.

D11.77 Job shadowing generally caters to two types of trainee profiles, as elaborated below:

(a) *Job Shadowing for Junior Trainees or Career Entrants*
The trainee is typically someone who is interested in exploring a particular occupation/profession but does not yet know enough about the said occupation/profession. The trainee may request a job shadowing opportunity to better understand the requirements and challenges of the said occupation/profession and thereby assess his own suitability. This is a prudent approach, especially if there are somewhat high stakes involved in going into the said occupation/profession (say, one has to undergo extensive professional training to enter into the said occupation/profession).

> Example
> Healthcare institutions offer job shadowing attachments to students who are considering pursuing a medical career. Likewise, it is common to see students considering a veterinary career seek job shadowing internships with vet clinics. This is understandable, as a medical or veterinary degree is a heavy investment, and the specialised nature of the study makes it less fungible to switch to other careers.

> Example
> Under the government's Professional Conversion Program (PCP) for mid-career workers looking to switch careers, many organisations recruiting mid-career entrants through the PCP provide short job shadowing stints (say, a few days to a week) to potential candidates.

(b) Job Shadowing for Mature and Adaptable Candidates

Job shadowing is also suitable for mature and skilled "trainees" who are able to adapt quickly to take on a new role. They are usually highly independent executives/professionals who have a keen sense of observation to be able to pick up learning points and apply them. That is, the trainees will be able to perform the job role once they have sized up the nature, requirements and challenges of the role. Rather than providing oral briefing about the requirements of the role, job shadowing is a quick and practical way to familiarise the trainees with the role.

> Example
> A seasoned human resource practitioner who is assigned a new role as a conciliator with the Ministry of Manpower (MOM) for industrial disputes may job shadow an experienced MOM conciliator for a few weeks. He may also job shadow an experienced mediator at the Tripartite Alliance for Dispute Management (TADM) to learn the ropes for mediating employment claims. With his knowledge of the employment laws and background in human resource management, coupled with learning agility and the right aptitude, he should be able to pick up conciliation/mediation skills and the nuances in dealing with claimants and their employers.

Formal and Structured Training Programs

D11.78 Formal and structured training refers to organised training that follows a predetermined curriculum or program that is designed to impart specific knowledge, skills or competencies to employees in a systematic manner. Such training programs typically have a well-defined set of topics or modules of the subject matter and come with a defined set of learning objectives. The topics are arranged in a logical sequence, starting from basic concepts and progressing to more advanced levels.

D11.79 Structured training programs can take various forms, including formal education in higher learning institutions, corporate training programs, workshops, seminars and online training courses. The structured training approach is useful when the trainees' learning must be acquired in a systematic manner to achieve optimal learning outcomes, such as when concepts, theories, models and frameworks are involved.

D11.80   Structured training can be delivered in a variety of methods, such as lectures, tutorials, group discussions, role plays, case studies, assigned readings and individual/group projects.

D11.81   Case studies are particularly useful to facilitate learning. Trainees must read, analyse and pick out salient points from a case study. The learning gained is more enduring than if the trainee is left to just passively absorb the knowledge and information downloaded from the trainer. If a case study is based on real (actual) events, the real-world context lends authenticity, and this helps the trainee relate and retain his learning.

D11.82   Many large and established organisations rope in their senior executives (or leaders) as trainers (or facilitators) in their corporate training programs. While this may be a heavy investment in terms of senior management time, there are significant benefits, including the following:

    (a) it sends the message that the organisation believes in the importance of developing people and its leaders have a responsibility to ensure this;

    (b) it allows senior management personnel to interact directly with the employees (trainees) and assess their quality and motivational level to some extent; and

    (c) having to train (and take questions from the trainees) enables the leaders to reinforce their own expertise in the particular subject matter.

D11.83   If the structured training leads to certification, the trainee will need to pass an assessment test (or other forms of evaluation). Courses that are heavily subsidised by SkillsFuture Singapore (SSG) are likely to have a condition that the trainee must pass an assessment test as a validation of his learning. Post-course certification is also sometimes set as a prerequisite by organisations for a trainee to attain a career milestone, such as earning a promotion or appointment to a position or to be confirmed in service.

D11.84   When a large number of employees are to be trained, an organisation may, in a bid to save cost, resort to getting an external master trainer (who is a subject matter expert on the training topic) to conduct a train-the-trainers course for its team of internal trainers. The internal trainers will in turn train the other employees. While this approach may save some cost, the effectiveness of the training conducted by the newly minted internal trainers may be questionable. It is effective only if the internal trainers are already knowledgeable and credible in the said training topic. In addition, the external master trainer would invariably factor in the use of his proprietary training materials and methodologies and hence charge a higher fee for the train-the-trainers training. The resultant cost saving to the organisation may not be significant, taking into account the time cost of the internal trainers.

Team Huddle Sharing and Debrief

D11.85   Some line heads organise team huddles regularly (say, monthly, bimonthly or quarterly) to enable their department's staff to do peer learning. They typically share their experiences, new ideas and learning points that they have picked up. Team huddles are usually informal and unstructured; the format depends a lot on the leadership style of the line head as well as the team dynamics.

D11.86   In spite of its potential as a good learning platform, not all team huddles provide effective learning. The line head who initiates and facilitates the team huddles must proactively and creatively manage the sessions to ensure that there is good learning content. Otherwise, team huddles may gradually degenerate and become more of a social get-together (in which case, it may help enhance team bonding). In some instances, however, if the sessions are tense and negative, attending team huddles may even become an unwelcome chore.

Planning for Training

Annual Total Training Plan

D11.87   Many organisations prepare an annual total training plan (ATTP). Human Resource (HR) is usually tasked to prepare the ATTP. It starts with HR engaging the line heads to identify the training needs and activities for each department. The annual training plans for each department are then reviewed and consolidated into the ATTP for the organisation. A sample of an ATTP is shown in Annex D11-3.

D11.88   The advantages of preparing an ATTP include the following:

(a) It gives the organisation an overview of the training requests/needs submitted by the various departments and therefore facilitates the management to review and prioritise them before giving its approval. The management should review the ATTP in respect of whether it supports the organisation's strategic and operational needs as well as prioritise the training needs to keep the total training budget within the organisation's affordability.

(b) It provides the mandate for Human Resource to make arrangements for the training activities – either to plan, design and execute customised in-house training programs or register the employees for external generic training programs.

(c) The departmental training plans (which are part of the ATTP) also provide a basis for each department to plan its manpower deployment so that employees can be released for training.

(d) The organisation is able to monitor the extent of realisation of the ATTP. If the realisation rate is low, the management may look into the cause(s). For example, supervisors may be reluctant to release their staff to attend training, or the execution of in-house training programs is delayed, or certain training needs have become irrelevant due to changes in circumstances. The management can address the causes as necessary so that the ATTP does not degenerate into a mere paper exercise.

Training Roadmaps for Job Families

D11.89   Apart from preparing the ATTP, it is also useful for the organisation to prepare training roadmaps for the job families which are mission-critical for the organisation. A training roadmap for a job family essentially lists down the various training that employees should go through as they climb up the hierarchy in their respective job families. The training roadmap may comprise programs categorised as follows: (a) core functional programs, (b) supplementary functional programs, (c) managing self, (d) managing others and (e) leadership programs. A simplified sample of a training roadmap is shown in Annex D11-4.

Annual Training Budget

D11.90   With the ATTP pinned down, the organisation will be able to work out its annual training budget. The management should review whether the proposed annual training budget (comprising the approved training requests/needs from the departments as well as the organisation-wide training initiatives mandated by the management) is within its affordability. If budget affordability is tight, the management must prioritise its training needs and make hard decisions on which training programs are critical and essential, which are urgent and which are "good to have". The key consideration is that the approved ATTP and training budget must support the organisation's strategic and operational needs.

D11.91   The traditional index (or yardstick) used to estimate an annual training budget was 3–4% of payroll cost. Say, if an organisation spent $1 million on salary-related costs (comprising monthly salaries, bonuses, allowances and Employer CPF), it would be considered reasonable to spend about $40,000 on employee training and development. This index is less relevant today. The reason is that the index was formulated decades ago when employee training was mostly delivered as structured and physical programs. In present times when we have a huge proportion of training delivered in virtual/online and blended/hybrid modes, the unit cost of delivering training to an individual employee has changed drastically. Rather than rely on the index, organisations should assess their training budgets based on whether the proposed training needs are justified, and the training delivery modes are cost-efficient, so as to ensure that it is getting the biggest bang for its buck.

Measuring Employee Training

D11.92   Many organisations tend to use quantitative indicators to measure their employee training. The common ones are (a) training places per employee per year, (b) training hours per employee per year and (c) evaluation scores of training programs.

Training Places and Training Hours

D11.93   Many organisations track the number of training places taken up by their employees as well as the training hours clocked. The traditional norm averages are 4 training places per employee per year and 40 training hours per employee per year. While these are norm averages (across industries/ organisations), the actual number of training places and training hours vary substantially in individual organisations. Large and established organisations tend to provide more training, while small and medium enterprises (SMEs) mostly fall (far) below the norm averages. If OJT (structured) is included, it is not difficult to attain those figures.

D11.94   Some organisations take pride in meeting or exceeding the norm averages and believe that the more training places offered and the more training hours clocked by their employees, the more successful their training functions are. However, organisations should be cognisant that training places and training hours only measure the volume of training activities (that is, how busy their training functions have been); they have no bearing on the effectiveness of training and the transfer of learning to employees. We elaborate more below.

D11.95 The two indicators (training places and training hours per employee per year) measure the frequency and volume of training attended by an employee. For example, 4 training places per employee per year means that an employee attends training about once every quarter. Likewise, 40 training hours per employee per year means that an employee spends about 2% of his work hours in training. While these indicators show that employees have been provided with training opportunities, they do not guarantee the effectiveness of training. It all depends on whether the employee has been sent for appropriate (relevant) training, and even if he has, whether the training quality is good and he has learnt effectively.

D11.96 Another point to note is that the norm average of 4 training places per employee per year is an organisation-wide average. It does not mean that every employee should be given an equal number of training places. Logically, more attention should be given to training employees in mission-critical jobs as well as employees whom the organisation wants to groom. It serves no purpose if an organisation is resolute in providing the same number of training places to all employees just for the sake of equal treatment.

Evaluation Scores of Training Programs

D11.97 It is common practice that after an employee has attended training, he is asked to submit an evaluation form on the training. The evaluation will typically touch on the following aspects of the training program: (a) training content, (b) duration, (c) quality of the training materials, (d) competence of the trainer/facilitator and (e) relevance of the training to the employee's work. The evaluation will be summed up with an overall evaluation score (say, on a scale of 1–5) for the training program.

D11.98 Most organisations use the overall evaluation score as an assessment of the quality of a training program. To maintain the quality of training, the organisation may set a threshold overall evaluation score (say, 3.5/5 or 4/5) as a prerequisite to continue with a training program.

D11.99 Same as for training places and training hours, evaluation scores also do not measure or guarantee the effectiveness of training per se. While ensuring the quality of training programs is important and goes a long way to enhance the employee's learning, it does not guarantee that the employee has learnt well and/or would apply the learning into doing his job. A training program may be good, but if there are factors preventing a trainee from assimilating the learning (say, he is not motivated to learn or is distracted) or applying the learning (say, he is not given the opportunity to do so at work), then the objective of training is not achieved and the training cannot be considered effective.

Learning Outcomes

D11.100 *What is the correct (or meaningful) way to measure training effectiveness?* Training is never the objective itself. It is a means to an end. Organisations do not train employees for the sake of training per se. The purpose of training is to have employees improve their knowledge, skills, competencies and attitudes so that they can perform better at work. Simply put, higher work performance is the learning outcome that is sought after. Training is considered effective (and meaningful) only if there is an improvement seen in the employee's performance post-training compared to pre-training.

D11.101 Ideally, after an employee has attended training, he should be asked what he has learnt and how he would apply his learning to his work. The employee should be specific and elaborate on what kind of improvement he aims to see for himself. The employee's response should be documented (say, in a "Learning Outcome" form) and routed to his supervisor. With this information, the supervisor can provide opportunities that are targeted to allow the employee to apply his learning. The supervisor can thereby validate his improvement in work performance (or otherwise). To close the loop, the supervisor should be asked to provide his feedback to Human Resource on whether the employee has successfully assimilated and applied his learning at work. This should be done, say, 3–6 months after the employee has completed the said training. Human Resource should collate all the supervisors' feedback to get an overall indication of the success (or otherwise) of employee training. Such post-training follow-up is ideal (like a gold standard) but requires a lot of effort and discipline from line managers and Human Resource. Understandably, not every organisation will have the time and resources to do so.

Example

Employee A is a promising young executive who is being groomed for higher positions. He attends an in-house "Young Leaders Program" customised for high-potential staff. Upon completion of the program, he is asked to complete a Learning Outcome form. He states that he has learnt a lot about "leadership". In particular, he is aware that he has to improve his leadership decision-making skills – to be able to make objective and hard decisions and not be influenced by his emotions. As required in the Learning Outcome form, Employee A draws out the contrast between his "pre-training" self (the current state) and "post-training" self (what he aspires to be).

The Learning Outcome form is routed to Employee A's supervisor. The supervisor makes deliberate effort to put Employee A in challenging assignments and tasks him to lead his team-mates. The supervisor monitors Employee A closely and obtains feedback on his performance as a peer leader, particularly in his decision-making skills. If Employee A's improvement is validated, it indicates that the training has been effective.

Example

During the annual performance appraisal cycle, Employee B indicates his desire to attend a course on "Public Speaking". The supervisor supports his training request as Employee B is introverted and has low confidence. After Employee B completes the course, the supervisor arranges for him to do presentations at team level initially and followed by departmental level. The supervisor also provides feedback and coaching on the side. As Employee B's confidence grows, he is eventually assigned to do presentations at management meetings. Employee B's improvement is testimony to the effectiveness of his training, including the coaching by the supervisor.

D11.102 Very often, organisations neglect the essential and last step of checking on learning outcomes. Many just stop at doing evaluation of the quality of training programs. Even if an organisation diligently mandates that the trainee fills up a "Learning Outcome" form, whether it gets properly followed up depends a lot on the supervisor's diligence and interest in the matter. A supervisor who is keen on developing his staff will facilitate the employee to apply and internalise his learning. Simply put, an organisation can have a fantastic training plan, but it is what goes on at the shopfloor level that counts as effectiveness (and success) of employee training. With this in mind, it is important for organisations to instil a culture of developing people and make it a requirement for all supervisors/managers. Its leaders must show the way by walking the talk.

Training Administration

Planning, Execution, Evaluation, Monitoring and Reporting

D11.103 Employee training and development demands a lot of design and creative cognitive work, particularly if training is provided in-house. It also requires a lot of administrative coordination which can be voluminous.

D11.104 In very large and established organisations, the employee training and development function may take the form of a centre of excellence (COE) and is a unit or department (which may be separate from the Human Resource (HR) department) that is tasked with people development. The COE unit/department oversees the planning, execution and administration of employee training and development. It will likely have a team of full-time curriculum developers, trainers, coaches and facilitators and at times also complemented by a larger team of line trainers (these are line personnel who are identified as internal subject matter experts and assigned training responsibilities to impart their knowledge to other colleagues).

D11.105 In smaller organisations, however, the employee training and development function is typically part of the Human Resource (HR) department, where it may be handled by a HR executive/manager who is also handling other human resource functions. In this situation, the organisation is likely to do minimal planning for training and the HR executive/manager is performing mostly just training administration.

D11.106 How the employee training and development function is operated depends a lot on the organisation's policies and processes and availability of resources. Some have very elaborate processes, while others may simplify for expediency. For example, in small organisations, training may not involve any prior planning; rather, it may simply involve an employee making a training request, upon which the line manager considers and approves and is followed by the employee doing self-registration for the training course and getting the training vendor to bill the organisation directly. Notwithstanding the diverse ways the training and development function may operate, the common tasks are elaborated below:

Planning
1. Conduct training needs analysis.
2. Prepare the annual total training plan (ATTP) for the organisation.
3. Prepare training roadmaps for mission-critical job families.
4. Prepare the annual training budget.
5. Obtain management's approval for the ATTP and training budget.
6. For in-house training programs:
   Design the training content and delivery format.
7. For external training programs:
   Source for training programs and trainers, call for quotations/tenders, evaluate and negotiate service terms and appoint the training vendors/consultants, etc.

Execution
1. Publicise the training programs and course calendar and invite registrations from employees. Prompt or remind employees and their supervisors for cases where the employees are due to attend compulsory training programs.
2. Register external programs for employees and arrange payment to vendors.
3. Submit claims for training subsidies where applicable.
4. Remind supervisors to release employees for training.
5. Manage training logistics (including sourcing for external training venues).
6. Serve as the point of contact between the training providers and employees.

Evaluation
1. Request trainees to complete the Course Evaluation form upon completion of training. Compile the evaluation scores and follow up to make improvements to training courses and/or manage out the training programs with low evaluation scores.
2. Request trainees to complete the Learning Outcome form. Route the forms to the trainees' supervisors. After 3–6 months from the time a trainee has completed his training, request the supervisor to submit his feedback on whether the trainee has successfully assimilated and applied his learning at work. Collate all supervisors' feedback.

Monitoring and Reporting
1. Update the training records of employees.
2. Prepare monthly or quarterly and/or yearly training reports for management's review. The reports should provide analyses of the course evaluation scores and learning outcomes of the training programs. Make recommendations on how to make improvements.

Learning Management System

D11.107 As the training function involves high administrative load, most large and established organisations invest in a learning management system (LMS) to facilitate the management and execution of the training function. The LMS serves as a staff portal dedicated to employee training matters. If the organisation has an enterprise-wide human resource information system (HRIS), very often, the LMS is a module integrated into the HRIS. A good LMS should be able to handle the following tasks:

1. Allow employees to view their individual training roadmaps for the calendar year (that is approved by the line head and HR).
2. Allow the supervisors (reporting officers) to view the individual training roadmaps of their staff for the calendar year.
3. Allow the line heads to view the amalgamated training plan for their respective departments for the calendar year.
4. Show a training calendar (with the planned dates of training programs) so that employees can plan ahead for the year to select their training programs.
5. For each training program:
   Show the learning objectives, course syllabus, duration and planned dates, target audience and prerequisites for trainees.
6. For in-house training programs:
   Allow employees to register for training programs → route to supervisors to support → route to line head to approve → route to HR to follow up on execution.
7. For external training programs:
   Allow employees to raise training request (and attach e-brochure of the training program) → route to supervisor to support → route to line head to approve → route to HR to follow up (register the employee with the training vendor).

8. Upon completion of training:
   Allow the trainees to submit the Course Evaluation form and Learning Outcomes form → route to supervisors, line heads and HR → supervisors to submit feedback on learning outcomes.
9. Allow line heads and HR to track year-to-date utilisation of training places and training budget for the departments.
10. Allow HR to auto-generate training reports on (a) training utilisation (broken down by departments, job levels and job families), (b) training budget (broken down by departments, job levels and job families), (c) course evaluation for training programs and (d) feedback on learning outcomes from supervisors.

Training Bond

D11.108   A training bond is essentially a binding contract between an employee and the organisation (his employer) as a consideration for the employee to be sponsored for a training program.

D11.109   It is common for organisations to impose training bonds on their employees (or potential employees) when the cost of sponsored training is substantial (for example, scholarships or sponsorships for undergraduate or postgraduate courses or executive/management programs at prestigious business schools). This is particularly the case if the training is done overseas as apart from the course fees, an overseas training program will entail granting paid leave to a serving employee to attend the program, as well as providing travelling expenses and other living allowances and benefits.

D11.110   All training bonds will state a bond period, which is the length of service that an employee must commit to serving the organisation in consideration of being sponsored for the training program. The length of the bond period should vary based on the cost outlay of the training. In practice, there are huge variations in the lengths of bond periods as some organisations are more generous than others. The financial ability of the organisation also plays a part.

Examples in the Variations of Bond Period
- Organisation A imposes training bonds for training that costs above $5,000, while Organisation B and Organisation C use thresholds of $10,000 and $20,000 respectively. It depends on how strict or generous and how deep-pocketed the organisations are.
- For the same postgraduate course that, say, costs $50,000 to sponsor, Organisation D may impose a training bond of 1 year, while Organisation E may impose 2 years.

D11.111 A bond period invariably starts only <u>after</u> the employee has completed the training. This being the case, in essence, an employee is locked into service for a length of time longer than the actual bond period. For example, if an employee is sponsored for a part-time postgraduate course that lasts 1 year and if his bond period is 2 years, he is effectively locked into service for 3 years (1 year for study duration followed by 2 years of bond period).

D11.112 Under a training bond, all costs incurred by the organisation that are related to the employee's pursuit of the training program will be taken into account. These may include the following: (a) course fees and other administrative fees charged by the training institution, (b) salary (if the employee is granted paid study leave to attend the training on full-time basis), (c) airfare (if the training is overseas), (d) accommodation costs such as hostel fees, hotel charges or rented property (if the training is overseas) and (e) other allowances and benefits such as book allowance and per diem and warm clothing allowance (if the training is overseas).

D11.113 The training bond will state the liquidated damages (LD) that the employee must pay the organisation should he leave service without serving out the full bond period. There should be a provision for pro-rated LD should the employee serve a portion of the bond period before leaving the organisation. Some organisations may impose an interest cost on the LD.

D11.114 Human Resource is invariably tasked to monitor the employee's fulfilment of the bond obligation and take the necessary action to recover the LD should an employee break his bond. The employee's reason for leaving service will include resignation and termination/dismissal for reasons caused by the employee (for example, poor performance or misconduct). There are unique situations where fairly so, the organisation should waive the LD; for example, the organisation retrenches the employee due to redundancy or terminates the employment of the employee for whatever reason best known to itself (and is not attributable to the employee's fault).

D11.115 It is useful for organisations to bear in mind that merely relying on a training bond to retain an employee is not enough. If an organisation sponsors an employee for training and handcuffs him with a training bond and subsequently neglects developing him, the employee will lose motivation. Worse, if the organisation exploits its upper hand and deploys the employee to hardship postings to "maximise" its return. The employee will likely clock the time to serve out his bond but grudgingly and with low commitment. This is not an optimal outcome.

Training Subsidies

D11.116 In Singapore, many training programs and courses receive funding from various government agencies, the key one being SkillsFuture Singapore (SSG), which is a statutory board tasked to drive the upskilling and reskilling of Singaporean workers in order to build a Singapore workforce that is resilient, adaptable and future-ready. The SkillsFuture fund set up under the jurisdiction of SSG provides training subsidies to Singaporeans to encourage them to embrace lifelong learning and pursue fulfilling careers.

D11.117 Most of the courses approved under the Industry Transformation Maps (ITMs) receive generous SSG training subsidies of up to 70% of the course fees (or even 90% if the trainees are in a mature age band). In some instances, the organisation may also qualify for funding for absentee payroll, subject to a cap. The SSG training subsidies are applicable only for Singapore citizens.

D11.118 Due to the attractive training subsidies, many organisations are geared towards sending their employees only for funded programs. However, most of these programs are rather generic as they are designed to cater to employees from all organisations in a particular industry. For organisations which have sufficient resources, they should consider supplementing with customised training to make their employee training more holistic and effective.

Conclusion

D11.119 Training may be a solution to only some performance problems. Training must serve a business need. Whether employees should be trained and how the training should be designed and delivered depend on the business need.

D11.120 For training and learning to be more fruitful, employees must take ownership; they must not expect to be spoon-fed. They must want it and sometimes ask for it. The very spirit of taking ownership and wanting to learn and grow is a strong imperative.

D11.121 In-house organisation-wide training programs are more impactful when most of the employees including the senior management learn the same concepts and skills and acquire the same vocabulary. The employees will feel more encouraged and comfortable to start speaking the new lingo and applying what they have learnt at the workplace. The initial enthusiasm must however be continually supported and reinforced and this is best done through institutionalising management frameworks and systems that encompass the new learning.

D11.122 Organisations invariably see training as an investment to develop their employees to be more effective and productive. However, if we are not focused on the business need of training, we may easily go off track and mistake training output for training outcome. Training output which is usually expressed in the number of training places, training hours and employees trained, the amount of training dollars spent (as a percentage of payroll cost) and the evaluation scores of training courses are easily quantifiable. But these training output figures do not paint an accurate picture of training outcome. Training outcome is about improvement in performance and productivity, period.

D11.123 Improvement in performance and productivity is more likely to materialise if the orgainsational/operational environment encourages employees to learn continuously and supports them in applying what has been learnt to doing their jobs. Senior management's commitment is required to bring about the change.

D11.124 Training constitutes only part of human resource development. In Chapter D12, we dwell on employee development as well as highlight how training and development should be integrated with other human resource initiatives.

Reference

1. M. McCall, R. Eichinger and M. Lombardo, Center for Creative Leadership (a global non-profit provider of leadership development and pioneer in the field of global leadership research)

Annex D11-1

SkillsFuture Singapore (SSG) Skills Framework for Accountancy

Technical Skills and Competencies (TSC) Reference Document (Source: SSG. Effective Date: February 2020)

TSC Category	Financial and Transaction Management					
TSC	Financial Closing					
TSC Description	Carry out month-end closing and reconciliation to ensure financial records are maintained properly					
TSC Proficiency Description	L1	Level 2	Level 3	Level 4	L5	L6
		ACC-CRP-2002-1.1	ACC-CRP-3002-1.1	ACC-CRP-4002-1.1		
		Perform reconciliation on account balances	Perform month-end closing activities in a timely and accurate manner	Assess the technical aspects of financial accounting and reporting processes		

Knowledge			
	• Double-entry accounting • Accounting standards for tangible and intangible assets, inventory, financial assets, liabilities • Reporting needs of internal stakeholders	• Organisation's financial reporting framework in relation to the Financial Reporting Standards (FRS) • Accounting principles behind assets, financial instruments, leases, employee benefits, taxes, provisions and contingencies	• Organisation's financial reporting framework • Accounting standards and regulatory requirements • Best practices in managing organisation's financial information
Abilities			
	• Operate double-entry accounting systems using books of prime entry, journals and ledger accounts • Record transactions relating to sales, purchases, receivables, payables and cash • Calculate customer account balances and reconcile with totals	• Analyse financial data to understand the financial performance and position of the organisation • Prepare trial balances and forecasts • Calculate accruals and prepayments • Ensure that financial records are maintained properly	• Provide financial advice to the organisation's management on the financial position of the business • Implement best practices in preparing and managing the organisation's financial information

Annex D11-2

SkillsFuture Singapore (SSG) Skills Framework for Wholesale Trade

Technical Skills and Competencies (TSC) Reference Document (Source: SSG. Effective Date: November 2018)

TSC Category	Stakeholder and Customer Management				
TSC	Customer Relationship Management (CRM)				
TSC Description	Establish strategies, technologies and practices to manage and analyse data on customer interactions throughout the customer lifecycle, with the goal of improving business relationships with customers, assisting in customer retention and driving sales growth				
TSC Proficiency Description	L1	Level 2	Level 3	Level 4	Level 5	L6
		WST-DAT-2001-1.1-1	WST-DAT-3001-1.1-1	WST-DAT-4001-1.1-1	WST-DAT-5001-1.1-1	
		Maintain effective regular communication with customers, collect and check customer information with existing records and execute activities as part of the implementation plans for adoption of CRM capabilities	Engage with customers and execute implementation plans for adoption of CRM capabilities	Manage customer plans and develop implementation plans to drive adoption of new CRM capabilities	Initiate and drive customer relationships and formulate CRM strategies to improve business relationships with customers	

Knowledge			
• CRM strategies • Limitations of CRM • Opportunities of CRM • Types of CRM technology and tools • Processes involved in managing workflow • Methods for locating and entering leads in CRM tools • Methods to identify customers' preferences and needs for products • Methods used to communicate with customers to identify their preferences and needs • Processes to maintain record-keeping systems • Various methods of monitoring client satisfaction	• Methods to identify potential warm leads • CRM framework • Importance of understanding customers' preferences and needs on products • Techniques to build positive relationships with customers • Ways to solicit feedback on products	• Criteria for recommending investments in CRM tools and technologies deployment • Criteria for improving existing CRM practices and programmes • Processes involved in monitoring optimisation of CRM tools and technologies • Methods for drawing and communicate insights from CRM data • Conversion process for warm leads • Communication strategies to maintain positive relations with customers • Ways to evaluate the communication processes to improve relationships with customers • Procedures in developing and maintaining positive relations with customers	• Business benefits of CRM • Current and emerging trends and technologies in CRM • Competitive landscape in terms of CRM • Customer expectations in terms of CRM • Principles for evaluating investment in CRM technologies and tools • Principles for evaluating effectiveness of CRM technologies and tools • Customer acquisition, retention, loyalty and conversion

Abilities			
• Perform tasks related to implementation of new CRM capabilities deployment strategy • Input data into CRM tools to facilitate downstream tracking of prospective clients, manage accounts and opportunities • Use CRM tools to track calls, emails, to-dos or create email templates • Locate and enter leads in CRM tools • Add products to leads and opportunities • Use reports to track customer accounts that are at risk • Maintain records and documentation relating to customer relationships • Adapt to any special needs and diversity of customers • Monitor client satisfaction	• Execute plans for implementation of new CRM capabilities deployment strategy • Use CRM tools to track prospective clients, manage accounts and opportunities • Manage workflow, communicate with clients, and run reports on customers' buying history and behaviour • Manage CRM programmes • Engage customers to ensure products meet client needs	• Develop and manage plans for implementing new CRM capabilities • Manage and monitor optimisation of CRM tools and technologies • Draw and communicate insights from CRM data • Draw insights into team's performance and fine-tune sales processes • Develop and define customer journeys • Convert qualified leads to accounts, contacts and opportunities • Review existing CRM programmes • Develop CRM plans • Manage dissatisfied customers or deviant requests	• Define the applications of CRM technologies, tools and practices in the organisation • Lead identification of current and emerging trends, technologies, competitive landscape and customer expectations in terms of CRM • Assess and recommend investments in CRM capability areas • Drive optimisation of CRM tools and technologies to achieve customer acquisition, engagement, retention, loyalty and conversion across all channels and platforms • Formulate CRM objectives • Develop CRM strategies • Guide operational plan development to support achievement of CRM strategies • Set key performance indicators to evaluate CRM

Annex D11-3

Annual Total Training Plan (Sample)

Programs	Duration (Hours)	Format	Targets	Number	Training Hours	Fee Per Trainee	Subsidy	Remarks
Organisation Level								
On-boarding Orientation	6	In-house	All new staff	40	240	Nil	Nil	2 runs
Performance Appraisal	3	In-house	All new staff	40	120	Nil	Nil	2 runs
Innovation at Work	4	External	All staff	320	1280	$200		8 runs
Job Family Level								
Product XYZ Roll Out	3	In-house	Sales and Sales Support staff	30	90	Nil	Nil	
Presentation Skills	7	External	Sales Team Leads	2	14	$400	Nil	
IT Security	7	External	IT Executives	4	28	$600	SSG 70%	
Cashflow Management	7	External	Senior Finance Executives	2	14	$450	Nil	

Job Role Level

Telephone Etiquette	7	External	All Frontline staff	12	84	$350	SSG 70%
Performance Management	7	In-house	All new Managers	10	70	Nil	Nil
Change Management	7	External	Managers and above	40	280	$800	Nil	2 runs
Grievance Handling	4	External	Managers (nominated)	3	12	$600	SSG 70%
Dealing with the Media	7	External	C-suite Executives	3	21	$2,000	Nil

Individual Employee Level

Strategic Marketing	21	External	Head of Marketing (nominated)	1	21	$2,000	Nil
Graduate Diploma in Business	150	External	Executives with A/B Performance Rating (nominated)	2	300	$7,000	Nil	1-year bond

Add on: List of training needs for individual employees in each department (collated from annual performance appraisal forms and reviewed by line head and HR).

Total

Annex D11-4

Training Roadmap for Accounting and Finance Job Family (Sample)

Training Clusters/ Programs	Accounts Executive Senior Accounts Executive	Accountant	Finance Manager Senior Finance Manager	Finance Director
Qualifications and Experience	Accounting Diploma. Up to 6 years in Accounting Operations.	Accounting Diploma or ACCA. 6–8 years in Accounting Operations.	ACCA or equivalent. 8–15 years in Accounting/ Finance.	ACCA or equivalent. At least 15 years in Financial Management.
Core Functional	Accounting Standards Regulatory/Reporting Requirements Accounts/Financial Closing Accounting Updates Payroll Processing GST	Consolidation of Group Accounts Fixed Assets Management Accounting Updates Financial Analysis Tax Computation	Financial Reporting Financial Operations Controls Cashflow Management Budgeting Financial Auditing Cash Management Solutions Tax Compliance/Planning	Financial Planning Strategic Financial Management Funding Strategies Strategic Tax Planning Investment Analysis and Advisory

439

Supplementary Functional	MS Office Management Accounting Data Analysis	Data Analytics Cost Management Presentation Skills	Business Partnering Skills Recruitment Interview Skills	Financial Instruments Managing Difficult People/Situations
Managing Self	Time Management	Useful Management Principles	Writing Effectively Emotional Intelligence	Influencing Skills Critical Thinking Skills
Managing Others	Communication Skills	Supervisory Essentials	Performance Management Dealing with Grievances	People Management Skills Conflict Management
Leadership			Change Management	Strategic Planning Skills

Employee Development

Focus of this Chapter

In Chapter D11 "Employee Training", we highlighted the linkage among training, learning and development and dedicated the rest of the chapter to employee training.

This chapter focuses on employee development as a way to groom and develop employees. Training and development are complementary, with training focusing on the employee's short-term knowledge acquisition and skills enhancement, while development is about preparing the employee for future bigger roles, including changing work behaviours beyond knowledge and skills.

We examine the common types of developmental interventions, such as job rotations, postings, stretch assignments, special projects, mentoring and executive coaching. We look at the features and developmental value of these interventions.

Employee Development versus Training and Learning

D12.1   Employee training, learning and development have a common over-arching and fundamental objective, that is, they are essentially concerned with changing (and improving) employees' work behaviours and habits – how they think, react and deal with issues and people at work. All three play an indispensable and complementary role in building a skilled, resilient and capable workforce within an organisation.

D12.2   However, there are nuanced differences among the three in terms of (a) specific purpose and outcomes desired, (b) methods/formats involved and (c) time horizon. These differences are summarised in brief in the following table:

	Employee Training	Learning	Employee Development
Specific Outcomes Desired	Usually targeted at equipping the employee with essential and job-related knowledge and skills to handle the current job.	Entails an employee's self-motivation to acquire new knowledge, skills and experiences for self-improvement and personal and professional growth.	Prepares employees for future roles and responsibilities. Emphasises long-term career progression within the organisation. Often also aims at enabling the employee's personal growth, including moulding the employee's character and attitude.
Methods/ Formats	Usually involves a structured process to enable an employee to acquire specific knowledge/skills. Examples include classroom training, workshops, seminars, etc. Also include on-the-job training to learn new skills or address performance gaps.	A broad ongoing process that includes self-directed learning, informal learning and experiential learning. Examples include self-reading, research, talking to associates and subject matter experts, paying attention to the thoughts, words and actions of one's peers and supervisors.	Developmental interventions come in diverse formats. Examples include performance feedback, job rotations, postings, stretch assignments, special projects, mentoring and executive coaching.
Time Horizon	Immediate or short-term focus and effort by the organisation.	Continual and long-term focus and effort by the employee.	Long-term focus and effort by the organisation.

D12.3   From the perspective of the organisation, the primary purpose of employee development is to build and strengthen a pool of capable leaders, managers and professionals who will be ready to take on higher roles and lead and manage changes as the organisation evolves. Employee development must necessarily be future-oriented.

Target Groups for Employee Development

D12.4   Employee development requires investment dollars, resources, time and effort. Organisations must be targeted and purposeful in selecting the appropriate employee groups or specific individuals to be developed. Logically, more attention should be given to employees who will serve the organisation's needs and give better contributions in the long run.

D12.5   Generally, large and established organisations put more emphasis in developing the following groups of employees:

(a) high-potential employees;
(b) young and promising leaders;
(c) employees in mission-critical roles or core functions/services (such as international officers of global banks, pilots of airlines, industrial relations officers of the National Trades Union Congress, doctors of healthcare institutions and civil service officers in the elite Administrative Service);
(d) specialist talent; and
(e) new graduates hired under the organisation's special talent program (such as Management Associates Program or any other talent program of whatever equivalent name) as the organisation's talent pipeline.

D12.6   Organisations tend to pay lesser attention to developing their rank-and-file employees usually because of the large numbers involved, their narrower job scope and generally their lower bandwidth for career advancement. But there are exceptions; some organisations offer sponsored formal education to their rank-and-file employees to help them upskill and advance to higher (including management) roles. Maybank Singapore is one such example with several success stories over the years where junior staff and officers were sponsored for diploma/degree programmes, given career upgrading opportunities and progressed to management roles. Even in small and medium enterprises (SMEs), rank-and-file employees can advance their careers if they are diligent, aspirational and committed and, more importantly, have the support of their organisations.

Key Developmental Areas

D12.7   While an employee can leverage on his strengths to excel in his strong areas, to push his performance higher, he must identify the areas where he is weaker and work towards closing the gaps. In the case of an employee preparing for a higher role, he must likewise identify what it takes for him to meet the requirements of the higher role; the "gaps" are his developmental areas.

D12.8   An employee's developmental areas can span the following 5 areas: (a) knowledge and skills, (b) core competencies, (c) functional/technical competencies, (d) leadership competencies and (e) values. Collectively, enhancements in the above 5 development areas should lead to and culminate in changes to the employee's behaviours, actions and habits at work. These will be manifested in the employee's thinking, solutioning, planning, execution, decision-making, confidence and personal mastery and people relations. Ultimately, it should lead to better performance and outcomes for both the employee and organisation.

Knowledge and Skills

D12.9   Knowledge can be in the form of principles, concepts, models, frameworks, formulae, methods and information. Skills can be related to know-how regarding a method or process (for example, how to weld a pipe or how to bake a cake). Skills can also be related to something more cognitive – what is usually referred to as "soft skills" (for example, how to write good minutes of meeting or how to be good in public speaking).

D12.10   Knowledge and skills can be acquired through training, self-learning as well as various developmental interventions (such as performance feedback/coaching, mentoring and participation in special projects). After acquiring new knowledge and skills, the more the employee applies and practises what he has learnt in his daily work, the more they become deep-seated in the employee's ability.

Core Competencies

D12.11   Core competencies touch on an employee's motives, traits and self-concept, all of which influence his behaviour at work. Examples of core competencies are taking ownership, critical thinking, pursuit of excellence, collaboration, creativity, adaptability and resilience. Most organisations specify a set of core competencies as job requirements that apply across all job families.

D12.12   Core competencies are enduring. Advances in technologies may make functional/technical skills obsolete quickly, but they would not impact core competencies much. On the contrary, many core competencies become even more critical and relevant, such as creativity, adaptability and resilience. Please refer to Chapter D9 "Competency Frameworks" for more elaboration on core competencies.

Functional/Technical Competencies

D12.13   Functional and technical competencies encompass the knowledge and skills that pertain to specific functional domains (such as business and marketing, customer service, finance, human resource, legal, information technology, procurement, engineering, production, quality control and logistics). They incorporate the requisite academic, professional, trade and accredited qualifications/certifications to validate one's knowledge, skills and experience to perform competently in a specific domain area.

D12.14   While functional/technical competencies are acquired primarily through training and learning, they can be sharpened through developmental interventions such as mentoring by a subject matter expert and assignments that give the employee opportunities to apply and practise his newly acquired functional knowledge and skills.

Leadership Competencies

D12.15   Large and established organisations place heavy emphasis on developing the leadership competencies of their leaders and managers. They see the multiplier effect of having effective and inspiring leaders. Examples of leadership competencies are strategic vision, astute judgment and leading and developing people.

Values

D12.16   Organisations invariably have a set of core values that guide how they want their employees to behave and deal with issues and people. Common core values such as integrity, fairness, trust, respect and service have been adopted by many organisations.

D12.17 For organisations that groom their internal talent for key leadership positions, they tend to be particular that the internal candidates (that is, their future leaders) must have personal values that are aligned with the organisational values. Although not easy, values can be honed through reinforcement, broadening or changing a person's perspectives and helping him do self-reflection. This can be done through developmental interventions such as mentoring, experiential learning and critical incident debriefing.

Types and Formats of Developmental Interventions

D12.18 Employee development can happen through many types and formats of developmental interventions, with the following being the common ones:

(a) learning and development through the employee's daily work activities;
(b) stretch performance goals;
(c) performance feedback and coaching;
(d) participation in high-impact project teams, committees and taskforces;
(e) structured team activities;
(f) job rotations, transfers and secondments;
(g) special postings and appointments;
(h) acting appointments;
(i) exposure to senior-level events and platforms;
(j) mentoring and executive coaching; and
(k) training assignments and community of practice for the employee's subject expertise.

Learning and Development through Daily Work Activities

D12.19 Although not obvious to many people, developmental interventions can take place right within an employee's daily work activities. If a line manager is intent on developing his subordinate, he can consciously and possibly weave developmental interventions into almost every work interaction with the employee. For this reason, all line managers should have "developing people" as one of their leadership competencies. It should also be one of their key deliverables.

D12.20   The following are some examples of how an employee can be developed through his daily work activities:

(a) *Regular Staff Meetings and Discussions*
During such sessions, the line supervisor/manager can deliberately steer the discussion to stimulate learning. He may ask these questions to jostle his staff to think and reflect more deeply and broadly: *Why? Why not? What are the alternatives? What are the pros and cons of a proposed action?* He may deepen the discussion to touch on fundamental principles and concepts. He may also mention other dots (areas which may be related) and guide his staff to connect the dots to improve their systems thinking and visioning. He may also share the practices of other organisations to broaden their perspectives.

(b) *Important Meetings*
As a way to expose and develop an employee, a line supervisor/manager can deliberately include him in attending important meetings with a client, supplier or vendor, such as making a presentation to a prospective client, pitching for a project or resolving problems with a supplier or vendor. The line supervisor/manager can do a debrief after the said meeting to engage the employee, pose questions and have him summarise the key discussion points to test his understanding and deepen his learning.

(c) *Writing Minutes, Reports and Proposal Papers*
In many large established organisations (including the Singapore Civil Service), the ability to write effectively is an important skill expected of an executive. Such organisations require their young executives to write minutes of meetings, reports of incidents and visitations as well as papers for information and decision-making by the management. Many senior officers/executives in these organisations make the effort to vet and edit the minutes/reports/papers and return them to the young executives (who drafted the documents) to do the corrections. An executive who is conscientious will learn from studying the edits and over time, he will improve in his writing skills. Having to organise the content of the minutes/reports/papers will also help the executive improve his logical and systematic thinking and breadth and depth of analysis and perspectives. Over time, the executive will gain confidence in putting together documents for senior management. Such writing assignments are much more effective than having the executive attend

a writing course (although attending a writing course is still a good starting point).

(d) *Incidents Debrief*

Incidents happen periodically. Besides demonstrating how to resolve the incidents, the line supervisor/manager should highlight the learning points and coax the staff to learn to avoid or prevent as well as manage similar incidents in the future. The more painful the incident, the deeper the learning to be gleaned from it. To not do a debrief after a critical incident will be a missed opportunity for learning.

Stretch Performance Goals

D12.21   Setting challenging performance goals is one way to stretch and develop employees. Employees are "elastic". When employees are stretched (but not overly stretched), they will exert themselves more vigorously, work smarter and challenge themselves to get out of their comfort zones. If they are consistently and suitably stretched, over time, they will gain more confidence and find themselves progressing and bracing new heights and move closer towards their full potential. Employees who are innately aspirational and achievement-oriented tend to be game to take on stretch performance goals to challenge themselves, hence organisations can leverage on this to develop them.

Performance Feedback and Coaching

D12.22   Giving performance feedback and coaching has a lot of developmental value. As the feedback is contextualised and specific for the employee, it is easier for the employee to relate and appreciate. The changes or improvements that the employee makes after one feedback/coaching session may not be significant initially. However, cumulatively over time, the improvement can be substantial. The extent of improvement depends a lot on the depth and quality of the feedback/coaching conversation between the supervisor and the employee. For feedback/coaching to bring positive outcomes, the supervisor must be authentic in his intent to help the employee improve (and not done to criticise the employee), while the employee must reciprocate by keeping an open mind and having the humility to reflect and learn.

D12.23   Performance feedback and coaching is the only developmental intervention that can be done on a wide scale throughout the organisation and every employee can have access to it. However, to do performance feedback and coaching well requires commitment and discipline on the part of the supervisors. The reality is most supervisors (or line managers) do not have the habit of giving performance feedback and coaching diligently to their staff, either due to a lack of time and/or feeling not confident or comfortable to do so. Organisations should find it worthwhile to invest in training their supervisors/managers in performance feedback and coaching skills so as to realise the full developmental value (more have been shared in Chapter D3 "Performance Feedback and Coaching").

High Impact Project Teams, Committees and Taskforces

D12.24 One good way to develop employees is to give them an opportunity to do new things that are outside of their normal routine work. Doing new things is experiential learning. It allows an employee to discover new skills and strengths. This is where stretch assignments (or special projects) can offer great developmental value to employees.

D12.25 *What types of assignments are suitable for developmental purposes?* Periodically, organisations may be confronted with strategic and/or complex issues that are over and above their normal daily or routine operations. Some examples are provided below:

> - Review a major business process to remove bottlenecks and improve efficiency
> - Design and roll out an enterprise-wide IT system
> - Review the risk management framework following a severe fraud case
> - Identify ways to improve overall customer satisfaction
> - Address the trend of profit decline
> - Identify cost-cutting measures to reduce the organisation's expenditure
> - Develop a new business model to meet evolving customers' demands
> - Reorganise departments to remove duplication in functions and create synergies

Typically, such issues span across multiple functions (or departments) and therefore may involve conflicting interests of the affected departments. To tackle such issues will invariably require inter-departmental collaboration.

D12.26 For this reason, an organisation will usually form a project team or taskforce and appoint representatives from the relevant departments to serve on it. This way, the representatives will be able to contribute different perspectives to the issue and hack out a solution. Often, tension and conflict may arise because of the differing perspectives, interests and priorities of the parties (departments) as well as the personalities of the individual representatives; these will have to be addressed before a feasible solution can be hacked.

D12.27 To handle the assignment well, an employee assigned to the project team/ taskforce would need to demonstrate various competencies including the following: (a) taking ownership, (b) information seeking, (c) analytical ability and critical thinking, (d) imagination and creativity, (e) strategic vision, (f) communication and influencing, (g) negotiation skills, (h) conflict management and (i) collaboration. Employees therefore will have ample opportunities to hone in and sharpen these competencies.

D12.28 Regarding the selection and appointment of employees to serve on such special project teams/taskforces, the reality is that not all employees welcome the opportunity. The assignment is usually over and above an employee's normal job role and hence will bring added work stress. However, for employees who are high performers and aspirational (or ambitious), they tend to be more amenable to take on such assignments and see them as opportunities to learn as well as to demonstrate their capabilities. Organisations invariably look for candidates from amongst their talent pool of high-potential and high-performing employees to fill the key positions in the project teams/taskforces. They stand the highest chance of delivering good outcomes for the assignment. If they do well, they will become more "visible" to the management and organisations often leverage on this as a value proposition to encourage and motivate their select talent to give their best for the special assignment.

D12.29 Other than providing developmental value to the select talent who serve in key appointments in such project teams/taskforces, there are also developmental opportunities suitable for a wider group of employees. Many organisations rope in junior to mid-level executives on a rotation basis to attend meetings to take minutes or provide other secretariat support to the project teams/taskforces. Very often, taking minutes for meetings that involve multiple stakeholders can offer learning much more than just honing one's writing skills. Likewise, providing secretariat support for mega-scale events that involve multiple stakeholders also offers invaluable learning in many dimensions.

> In a meeting chaired by a senior person, one can observe how he starts the meeting, manages the flow, responds to questions, deals with a domineering character, prompts the quiet ones to speak up, manages tension and conflict, filters out distractions and brings the discussion to focus and eventually to a close. This form of learning is far more impactful than attending training on 'Effective Meetings" or watching a video on how to hold good meetings.

> For a mega-scale event, one can take note of the exacting requirements for executing the project including time planning, guest list management, logistics arrangements, formal protocol and etiquette, program content, contingency planning, resource management and delegation of duties. First-hand experience is far more impactful than attending training on "Project Management" or "Event Management".

D12.30 Many organisations have a sports and social welfare (SSW) committee that is tasked with organising sports and social activities for employees, with funding from the organisation. The committee is usually staffed by employee representatives who may be elected by employees or appointed by the management. Where it is by appointment, the organisation may make all its executives/managers take turns to serve a stint at the SSW committee. From the employee's stint at the committee, the management may observe whether he is adept and creative in organising events. In addition, it will also show whether the employee has a service attitude towards his fellow colleagues.

> Example
> Easmed Private Limited (a local company that distributes medical equipment and devices) has a culture where its SSW committee refreshes its members every year with new staff representatives. The SSW committee earnestly puts in effort and imagination to plan and organise very novel and interesting events/activities to reinforce the esprit de corps in the company. In serving on the committee, the staff representatives have the opportunity to demonstrate and hone their competencies such as taking ownership, planning, collaboration and creativity. The management also makes an observation of the service attitude and competencies of the staff representatives.

Structured Team Activities

Adventure Learning

D12.31 Team activities can be appropriate to inculcate and influence behaviours relating to communication, collaboration and trust. Team activities that involve adventure (such as outward-bound camp) can further help employees strengthen their self-confidence and "can-do" attitude.

> Example
> Easmed Private Limited organises annual adventure outings (such as canoeing, volcano trekking and white-water rafting) for its employees. Other than bringing management personnel and employees together for team bonding, the activities also challenge employees to try new things and build their confidence.

> Example
> In Singapore Airlines, cadet pilots go through adventure camp as part of their training, while new executives attend an outward-bound camp as part of their orientation program. Such programs help toughen the character of employees and build bonding.

> Example
> In a particular healthcare cluster, promising executives under its talent management program attend adventure camp where activities are deliberately designed to let the participants take the lead in execution. By the end of the program, the natural peer leaders amongst them clearly emerge.

Brainstorming Sessions

D12.32   Brainstorming sessions are another type of structured activity that can generate developmental value if they are properly conducted, and the participants are participative. Brainstorming can build up group energy and tempo and help ignite employees' creativity. Some organisations hold brainstorming sessions as part and parcel of their annual corporate planning exercise. The organisation may put forth a topic (which can be a pain point confronting the organisation) and organise brainstorming sessions for employees to contribute their ideas.

> Examples of Topics suitable for Brainstorming
> • How to improve overall customer experience?
> • What should be the next big thing (product offering) for the company to focus on?
> • How to reduce wastage throughout all areas of operations?
> • How to refresh the company's branding to better resonate with evolving customer expectations?

Competitions

D12.33   Competitions generate excitement and bring out the competitiveness in people. When people compete, they become more tenacious, resourceful and creative, and work harder and smarter. Some organisations use competitions as a developmental platform to spur their employees to scale new heights. However, the practice is not common, as it entails a lot of resources and expertise to plan, organise and execute. Additionally, if a competition is not well managed, it may generate unnecessary friction and adverse reactions from employees.

Job Rotations, Transfers and Secondments

D12.34   Job rotations, transfers and secondments serve dual purposes: (a) to meet the business and/or operational needs of the organisation and (b) to develop employees by broadening their exposure and enabling them to acquire new knowledge, skills, competencies and experience.

D12.35   Job rotations, transfers and secondments all involve a change in job role for the employee. He may be deployed to a new job role under any of the following contexts: (a) to another role in the same department, (b) to another department in the same organisation or (c) to another entity within the group or outside the group.

Intra-department Job Rotation

Employee is reassigned from one job role to another within the same department.

Example

A human resource officer is rotated from handling recruitment to benefits management.

Inter-department Transfer

Employee is transferred to another department within the same organisation/ entity.

Examples

- Executive A is transferred from Finance department to Corporate Planning department.
- Executive B from Singapore headquarters is sent for overseas posting to its Shanghai office.

> **Secondment**
> Employee is on temporary transfer (or "loan") to another organisation/entity, which may be within the group or outside the group.
> Examples
> - Executive C is seconded from the organisation to a subsidiary company within the group.
> - Executive D is seconded to a company of one of its business associates (say, to understand its operations in preparation for an eventual joint venture between the organisation and the said business associate).

D12.36   Many large and established organisations have a policy to systematically rotate/transfer their high-performing executives and managers as part and parcel of their talent management program to develop and groom them for bigger or higher roles. Job rotations/transfers are carefully planned in a purposeful manner in line with the individual employee's career roadmap.

> Example
> Under the Singapore Civil Service's elite Administrative Officers scheme of service, officers are cross-posted to various ministries spanning five sectors: central administration (for example, Public Service Division), economy building (for example, Ministry of Trade and Industry), infrastructure and environment (for example, Ministry of National Development), security (for example, Ministry of Home Affairs) and social (for example, Ministry of Social and Family Development) to develop them into leaders with whole-of-government perspectives and capabilities.

> Example
> In Singapore Airlines (SIA), executives (except those in the specialist tracks) are systematically posted to different departments every few years. Those from Sales and Business Development are posted to different countries and regions to expose and develop them. Executives who are earmarked for bigger roles may also be appointed to head subsidiaries or take up senior roles in joint venture airlines. The opportunity to run the entire business and operation of a separate entity is a development platform for the appointees, many of whom subsequently return to join the top management team. This manpower posting and development model has been steadfastly practised for decades and is arguably one of the main reasons why SIA has been able to fill the bulk of its C-suite positions with internal talent.

D12.37 Secondment is a special form of transfer. The organisation "lends" the employee to another entity (host organisation) within or outside the group, usually for a specific period. During the secondment, the employee has to abide by the host organisation's policies, work protocol and culture. This means a new work environment and requires the employee to show adaptability, resourcefulness and resilience. Secondments are usually reserved for high-performing employees whom the organisation wants to develop and help them broaden their networks. Additionally, if the secondment is to an entity outside the group, the employee is inevitably seen as a "flagbearer" of the organisation, hence a high-performing employee would be a more suitable candidate.

> Example
> The National Trades Union Congress (NTUC) sends its high-performing Industrial Relations Officers (IROs) to various government agencies (including the Ministry of Manpower) with the aim of enhancing their understanding of government policy-making and the regulatory landscape, as well as broadening their networks.

> Example
> The Singapore Civil Service has, in recent years, extended secondments of high-potential officers to private sector companies. The targeted host companies are trailblazers, such as Citibank, DBS, Grab, Google and Lazada. Such secondments enable civil service officers to understand the evolving business landscape, how technology disrupts business models, and how the regulatory environment can better support innovation and business transformation.

D12.38 Job rotations, transfers and secondments have very high developmental value because they prevent employees from becoming complacent and keep them on a continual learning curve. Given a new job role, the employee is put to handle new tasks, make new contacts, deal with different work issues and challenges and interact with different stakeholders. As the new job role is the employee's primary portfolio, it is a case of swim or drown. This is in contrast to other developmental interventions (such as having an employee serve on a project team/taskforce) which involve assigning the employee a secondary portfolio, in which case the employee may still preserve good performance in his primary job role even if he flounders in his secondary portfolio. In contrast, job rotations, transfers and secondments require the employee to learn quickly and acquire new knowledge, skills and competencies to survive and succeed in his new primary role. For more elaboration on the nuances, benefits and execution of job rotations, transfers and secondments, please refer to Volume A, Chapter A6 "Transfer and Secondment of Employees".

Special Postings and Appointments

D12.39   Some large organisations have a mechanism to appoint their high-potential and high-performing employees to take up special postings or appointments that have been uniquely crafted to stringently and comprehensively stretch the employees as well as assess and validate (or otherwise) their candidacy for future leadership positions. Quite often, it involves assigning the employee to work directly under a well-acclaimed and inspiring incumbent leader, guru or veteran. Invariably, the special posting/appointment will put the employee on a steep (even exponential) learning curve and is considered an invaluable developmental opportunity that is reserved only for very high calibre employees.

Example

In the Singapore Civil Service, a specially selected high-potential officer may be appointed as Principal Private Secretary (PPS) to the Prime Minister, Deputy Prime Minister or Senior Minister. Each appointment may last about 2 years. The track record shows that many of the PPSs later rose to become Permanent Secretaries of ministries or entered politics and became political office holders.

Example

In Singapore Airlines (SIA), a high calibre officer may be appointed as Staff Assistant (SA) in the Office of the Chairman and Chief Executive Officer. The SA also serves as the Secretary of the Management Committee, organising the meetings and writing minutes of meetings. A good number of SAs have eventually risen to become Senior Vice Presidents and beyond.

Acting Appointments

D12.40   Some organisations use acting appointments as a developmental intervention to try out and prepare an employee for a higher role (especially for positions involving leadership responsibility, such as head of unit, department or division). Essentially, the acting appointment is a "probation" for the employee's promotion to the higher role. Acting appointments typically last for 6 months to 1 year, and occasionally, longer. The employee will be given a job title of "Acting XXX" (such as Acting CEO or Acting Director of Marketing). The employee is tested on his suitability before being confirmed in the appointment, at which time, the "acting" prefix to his position will be dropped.

> Example
> The Singapore government has a practice of acting appointments. Occasionally, we see a political office holder being first appointed as Acting Minister for a period before he becomes a full Minister.

D12.41   While using an acting appointment is a prudent way to assess an employee for a higher (leadership) role, there is a downside to it. There is a possibility that the employee may not make the cut, in which case, the aftermath must be delicately and sensitively handled, to minimise the employee feeling a loss of "face". To mitigate the awkwardness, the "failed" candidate seldom reverts to his previous position; he is typically posted to another role (with the organisation's messaging that he is needed elsewhere to meet its business needs). With the potential downside, acting appointments should be used judiciously and only when a candidate has a reasonably high chance of succeeding. This way, the acting appointment serves more as a way to give the employee some "breather" time to scale up for the higher role before becoming confirmed in the appointment.

Exposure to Senior Level Events and Platforms

D12.42   Exposing employees to significant events, meetings, discussions and activities can "unnoticeably" develop them (that is, it does not require any posting or appointment or change of job role for the employee). The organisation can simply rotate its high-performing employees to do some "helper" or secretariat duties at significant events. This way, the employees get to attend and observe the events. Some examples of senior-level events and platforms that offer developmental value are given below:

> - Meetings with senior executives from the regional or global headquarters
> - Meetings with officials from the government agencies
> - Meetings with external auditors and consultants
> - Board meetings and corporate planning retreats
> - Business networking events (such as lunches/dinners/cocktail events)
> - Conferences and seminars

D12.43   When an employee attends a senior-level meeting that discusses strategic or significant issues, he can benefit tremendously by observing and listening intently to what is being said. He should be able to pick up concepts and ideas and better appreciate the principles and considerations behind the decisions and actions of the management personnel. He will become more adept in looking at issues from multi-dimensional angles, and better at connecting the dots. To benefit maximally, he must be curious and hungry to learn.

D12.44   Some junior to mid-level executives may feel uneasy or anxious when they are asked to attend meetings with senior management or very important persons (VIPs). This is part of the growth process. Regular exposure to such settings and personalities will help the employee acclimatise, build self-confidence and improve his executive presence. He will learn how these personalities frame their questions and responses, navigate through difficult and sensitive issues and present themselves. The acquired confidence and comfort level in interacting with people in high positions will stand the employee in good stead as he progresses up the career ladder.

Mentoring and Executive Coaching

Mentoring

D12.45   Mentoring is a way for a management person (the mentor) to share his experiences and insights with a more junior colleague (the mentee) and to offer guidance and advice.

D12.46   *Who are the mentees?*
         Mentoring program is usually offered only to high-performing and high-potential employees whom the organisation wants to groom for future leadership positions.

D12.47   *Who are the mentors?*
         Mentors are typically senior management personnel. Depending on how widely an organisation extends its mentoring program, the mentor-mentee pairings may be "tiered". For example, a mentee who is a manager may be assigned a mentor who is of departmental director level, while a mentee who is a deputy director may be assigned a mentor who is of divisional director level.

D12.48   For mentoring to be meaningful, three important features should be safeguarded in the mentoring program:

(a) *Confidentiality and Trust*

In a mentoring relationship, both the mentor and mentee may share private or personal information. For example, the mentee may share about his weaknesses and insecurities, while the mentor may share about his own personal journey and the struggles that he had overcome. Mentors and mentees should be reminded to treat all information obtained in the course of mentoring as private and confidential and not to be divulged to any third parties (including the supervisors of the mentee and Human Resource) without the expressed permission of the other. This trust must not be breached in any way.

(b) *No Reporting Relationship between Mentor and Mentee*

For a mentee to feel "safe" to open up to his mentor to seek help and guidance, he should not have to worry about exposing his weaknesses or vulnerabilities that may adversely affect his performance appraisal. For this reason, the mentor and mentee should not be in any reporting relationship; that is, the mentor should not be the reporting officer or counter-signing officer for the mentee's annual performance appraisal. Mentors should come from a division different from the mentee.

(c) *Mentor must be a Willing People Developer*

A mentoring relationship is a personal one; it requires the mentor to invest his time and energy to share and guide the mentee. If the mentoring assignment is "mandated" by the management (say, the mentor is assigned to mentor the mentee), but the mentor is an unwilling party, the mentoring will be carried out in a superficial manner. For a mentoring relationship to be meaningful, the mentor must be genuinely interested in helping the mentee grow professionally and personally.

D12.49   Mentoring programs rarely dictate any fixed frequency for meetings between the mentor and mentee. It is something for the mentor and mentee to work out. Most find it useful to meet, say, once a month or every bimonthly or quarterly to keep in touch. The key is for the mentee to feel comfortable in approaching the mentor should he need help and for the mentor to be accessible and available to help when needed.

D12.50   If a senior management person is well known for being an inspiring leader and/or passionate about developing people, he will be a popular choice as a mentor. However, as mentoring requires the mentor to invest his time, a mentor should not be overstretched by taking on too many mentees. Most organisations set a limit of 3 mentees.

D12.51   The tenure for mentoring is typically 1–2 years since it takes time for a mentoring relationship to warm up. A mentee may be assigned a new mentor after the tenure of the current one has expired. Most organisations "graduate" a mentee out of the mentoring program after he has reached a certain career milestone (say, director level). This will allow the mentor to accept new mentees.

D12.52   There are many variations of mentoring models in practice. Organisations adopt whatever model that suits the objective of their mentoring program. We share two commonly used models here:

> Mentoring Model A
> The matching of the mentor to mentee is mostly random. Sometimes, the organisation may let the mentee choose from a list of, say, 3 mentors (those who are available for mentoring or whose mentoring load is not maxed out yet). The organisation may also consider the personality profiles of the mentor and mentee (say, the mentee is somewhat an introvert; he may benefit from learning from a mentor who is an extrovert and has an affable personality).
>
> The format of the mentoring (including the frequency and intensity) is flexible and much left to the mentor and mentee to decide on, which largely depends on their mutual comfort level and commitment. When they meet, the social element is usually high, and the conversation is quite generic. The mentor may share some past significant events, the general direction and priorities of the organisation (perhaps just a little beyond the official messaging that is known to all employees). The conversation may occasionally go deeper into a subject matter, especially if it is the forte of the mentor. The mentor may also connect the mentee to other senior executives and help him navigate the power dynamics in the organisation.
>
> Mentoring Model B
> In this mentoring model, the matching of mentor to mentee is more deliberate and purposeful. The organisation will select a mentor who has deep subject matter expertise in the field that the mentee is being groomed for. As the mentor has walked the path before, he will be able to offer invaluable guidance and insights to the mentee. The mentoring relationship is much like a guru-disciple relationship. Many mentors and mentees form enduring bonds and continue with their mentoring relationships even after the official tenure has ended.

D12.53   In terms of monetary cost, a mentoring program has zero or negligible cost (some organisations provide their mentors with a token annual budget of, say, $100–$300 for meals and miscellaneous expenses).

D12.54   The real cost of mentoring is in the management time invested. By roping in its management personnel as mentors, the organisation is able to impress upon them that they have a collective responsibility to help the organisation groom its next batch of leaders. For mentors to be effective, they should be trained in mentoring skills and be guided on their roles and how best to deliver maximum developmental value to their mentees.

Executive Coaching

D12.55   Executive coaching is geared to help the employee do self-discovery and take ownership to initiate change and/or improvement to achieve personal growth. The focus is not on daily workplace challenges (which should be tackled through ongoing performance feedback and coaching with the reporting officer) but on the deeper and more fundamental matters relating to the employee's longer-term and holistic development. The executive coach helps the employee reflect and take stock of his current state and project to where he wants to be. Essentially, it is to help the employee align his professional and personal attainment with his life passion and purpose.

D12.56   The executive coach's role is not to spoon feed the employee with solutions. The employee must find the solutions and decide for himself. The executive coach guides the employee to reflect by asking him incisive questions about himself. The employee speaks mostly and the executive coach listens, probes and guides the employee to focus and filter his thoughts to achieve clarity.

D12.57   For executive coaching to be effective, the employee must be very honest and open to reveal and discuss his reservations, weaknesses, idiosyncrasies and aspirations with the executive coach. The conversations between the executive coach and the employee must be kept strictly confidential and not be shared with the employee's supervisors and Human Resource. The trust must not be breached.

D12.58   Due to the characteristic of executive coaching, the reporting officer will not be suitable to double up as an executive coach to his direct report. If the reporting officer assumes the role of an executive coach, the employee will be apprehensive in revealing his flaws and "true self" for fear that his performance rating will be jeopardised. Some reporting officers do however have excellent and trusting relationships with their direct reports (but this is not common); in which case, the reporting officer may incorporate executive coaching along with giving performance feedback to his direct report.

D12.59 Since having the reporting officer double up as the executive coach is rarely a viable option, executive coaching is almost always conducted by a certified external executive coach. This is however an expensive investment. In view of that, executive coaching is mostly adopted by large and established organisations for their senior management staff only. Executive coaching is rarely used in small and medium enterprises.

Training Assignments and Community of Practice

Conducting Training

D12.60 An employee may be asked to conduct training in his area of expertise. This may seem like the employee is "giving" learning and not receiving for himself. However, the reality is that in order to train others well, the trainer must delve deeper into the subject matter to distil and crystallise the concepts. As Albert Einstein once said, "*If you can't explain it simply, you don't understand it well enough*". Giving training will motivate the employee (the trainer) to scale new heights to become even better in the subject matter.

D12.61 In designing and conducting training, an employee must also hone his competencies in presentation skills, engaging the audience and thinking on his feet, as well as strengthen his executive presence. These are excellent opportunities to learn and grow.

Community of Practice

D12.62 Joining a community of practice (COP) is a good way to keep abreast with the developments in one's professional domain. In large global organisations where each function (say, human resource) has separate teams spread across different geographical locations (say, HR in the global office and regional office as well as in each city/country that the organisation operates in), it is quite common for the organisation to form a COP for the various functional domains. For example, there may be COPs for human resource, finance, information technology, legal and marketing. The executives will meet periodically (usually over a virtual platform) to share and learn. E-newsletters or other forms of information exchange platforms may also be set up to facilitate information sharing and mutual learning. The COP is usually driven by the global head of function or a passionate member of the particular function/profession.

D12.63 COPs may also be set up beyond the confines of an organisation. For example, a HR director of an organisation may invite his counterparts from other organisations to meet periodically (either physically or virtually) to discuss common and trending issues, compare notes and keep abreast with professional developments. The impetus to form a COP is greater if the organisations or the said function/profession face common challenges. For example, if the organisations deal with the same trade union, they may attempt to stand together as a group and share practices so that they can forge a common ground to negotiate with the union. Likewise, if the profession is undergoing significant shifts or disruption (say, due to digital technology), a COP will be useful to help one keep abreast with the winds of change.

Structured Milestone Developmental Programs

D12.64 Large and established organisations often put in place special training and development programs for certain employee groups whom they want to nurture as a talent pipeline for future leadership positions. We highlight a few common ones.

Management Associates Program

D12.65 Some large organisations hire a certain number of fresh degree holders every year into their Management Associates (MA) program (or whatever equivalent name it may be called). The MA program is positioned as an elite talent development program with the objective of enabling the organisation to secure its share of top graduates to bring into its fold. Candidates for the MA program are typically fresh graduates from renowned universities with excellent academic results as well as outstanding non-academic attributes. They undergo very stringent and comprehensive assessment to earn a place in the MA program.

D12.66 The MA program is constructed to induct the employees systematically and comprehensively by giving them broad-based exposure to all aspects of the organisation's business and operations, including its strategic direction and priorities, management systems and processes, and policies and practices. Other than these knowledge-based aspects, the MA program also emphasises developing the employees' character and aligning them to the organisation's culture and values to build resonance and long-term commitment.

D12.67 MA programs usually last 1–2 years. A typical MA program contains the following components:

   (a) on-boarding orientation on the organisation's vision and mission, products and services as well as industry ecosystem;

(b) structured training on a broad range of topics related to the organisation's core operations and functions;

(c) outward-bound team-based activities;

(d) short attachments to various departments (say, 3–6 months) where they will be assigned special and challenging assignments;

(e) job shadowing of several senior colleagues;

(f) mentoring by specially selected mentors; and

(g) interactive sessions with senior management personnel.

D12.68   Since the MA program is primarily focused on the employees' development and the employees are rotated through different departments on short attachments, their headcounts are usually parked under a separate central pool (as supernumerary headcounts) rather than subsumed under any department's approved headcount. For this reason, MA programs are costly and viewed more as a long-term investment. Only large and established organisations can afford to have MA programs as part of their talent strategy.

Executive/Management Development Programs

D12.69   Many large and established organisations put in place specially designed or curated training and development programs that will better prepare or equip their employees as they attain career milestones or become appointed to mission-critical job roles.

> Examples
> - Organisation A requires all its new managers to undergo a "New Managers Program" within their first year of appointment.
> - Organisation B identifies its high-potential employees amongst its pool of graduate officers who have completed 3 years of service and puts them through a "Young Leaders Program" to better equip them as they progress higher in their careers.
> - Organisation C requires those employees earmarked to take up overseas postings as Country Heads within the next 1–2 years to undergo a specially curated training program to prepare them for their roles.

D12.70   Often, the specially curated executive/management training and development programs are customised to suit the organisation's needs and context. A typical program may comprise the following components:

(a) structured training by internal trainers;

(b) special topics by external trainers;

(c) online self-learning modules;

(d) team-based activities;

(e) special sessions (for example, fireside chats) with senior management;

(f) buddy system with an experienced incumbent; and

(g) mentoring by a senior management person.

Leadership Development Program

D12.71   Leadership development is crucial for organisational success because competent and effective leaders contribute to employee engagement, workplace vitality and overall performance. Simply put, good leaders have a huge multiplier effect.

D12.72   Leadership development refers to the intentional and systematic process of enhancing the skills, abilities and qualities of individuals in leadership positions. The goal of leadership development is to nurture effective and capable leaders who can inspire and guide others to achieve organisational objectives and excellence as well as think and manage strategically in a fast-changing operating environment. To ensure that their leaders are equipped for their roles, many large and established organisations have specially curated leadership development programs for their new or potential leaders who are selected as part of succession planning.

D12.73   Leadership development programs are often tailored to the specific needs and goals of the organisation, taking into account its culture, values and strategic objectives. First and foremost, an organisation must define the key competencies and attributes of leaders. Leadership competencies typically include the following: (a) leading and developing people, (b) influencing and inspiring, (c) strategic vision and foresight, (d) critical thinking and judgment and (e) imagination grounded on realism.

D12.74   While every organisation will customise their leadership programs to suit their own needs and context, the following components tend to be common:

(a) leadership topics and emerging management concepts conducted by professors or senior consultants who are experts (or authorities) in their fields;

(b) senior executive development programs in business schools of Ivy League universities (such as Stanford, Harvard, Columbia and Wharton); and

(c) executive coaching.

D12.75   Before the commencement of the leadership development program, it is also common to require the employee to go through the following assessments: (a) personal profiling assessment, (b) 360-degree feedback and (c) learning style assessment. The assessment findings will help the employee gain better awareness of self and how others (his subordinates, supervisors and peers) perceive him. If executive coaching is provided (which is usually the case), the employee is expected to share the assessment findings with the executive coach so that the executive coaching conversations can go into a deeper and more meaningful level.

Integrating Employee Training and Development with Other Organisational Initiatives

D12.76   As employee training and development programs can be resource-intensive and costly, organisations must plan and execute them purposefully and systematically. It bears to emphasise the following 3 important considerations:

(a) *Align with organisational needs*
Employee training is purported to serve the business/operations needs of the organisation. Employee development programs must produce outcomes that are useful for the organisation. Employees must be developed in the right competencies and trained in the areas of needs to address performance gaps, boost performance or prepare them for changes in business, products and services, operations and processes. For alignment to happen, the organisation must first do its needs analysis to identify the gaps that exist between its current state and the desired future state. These and more questions must be asked at both organisational and individual employee levels: *Which are the competencies that are the most lacking in the organisation's employee population? What will be the new competencies that the organisation will need as it navigates the changes in its business environment? Where are the performance gaps? What are the anticipated changes? What are the new initiatives? At the individual employee level, what are the competencies and functional/operational areas that the employee is weak in and needs training and development interventions to help him grow stronger?*

(b) *Target the right employees for development*
Organisations must be targeted and purposeful in selecting the appropriate employee groups or specific individuals to be developed. Even if the organisation wants its employee development interventions

to be broad-based and available to as many employees as possible, logically, it must apply a tiered approach and give more attention to those employees who can contribute more impactfully to the organisation. The same criteria should be applied to the execution of employee training programs because they cost money and employees' time away from work.

(c) *Support employees to apply learning at work*
Training and development are means to an end, which is performance and results for the organisation. Training and development enable employees to learn and enhance their knowledge, skills, competencies and experience. Employees must apply these in their daily work in order to give improved performance and results. Organisations must therefore enable their employees to do so by providing them with opportunities to apply their acquired learning. The likelihood of this happening is higher if employee training and development are conceived arising from the organisation's business/operational needs.

D12.77 Employee training and development cannot be done in isolation. To produce impactful outcomes, they must be reinforced and complemented by other human resource management and development initiatives as elaborated below:

(a) *Recruitment*
If hiring is done right, the organisation will have better hires. It is more effective to train, develop and mould the right hires. If hiring is wrong, the employees will not stay long, and this means wastage in training and development.

(b) *Rewards and Recognition*
Training and development will enable the employees to perform better. Rewards and recognition must be market-competitive, as good performers are mobile and may leave, thereby nullifying the investment and effort in training and developing them.

(c) *Career Progression*
As employees improve in their knowledge, skills and competencies through training and development, they will become ready to do more and take on bigger or higher job roles. Opportunities should be made available for the employees to perform in bigger/higher roles. Career planning (in terms of career roadmaps) should be done for the employees to guide them to advance in their careers.

(d) *Workplace Culture and Support*

For well-trained and developed employees to contribute optimally, they must be given meaningful work and have a conducive work environment (such as positive work culture, minimal political undercurrents and less bureaucracy) and be given enough empowerment and resources to do their work and use their talent and creativity.

D12.78 In closing, it is apt to highlight that employee training and development are not the task or responsibility of Human Resource (HR) alone. While HR can drive the employee training and development agenda, it takes a whole-of-organisation effort to make employee training and development happen. Supervisors and line managers must train, coach and guide their staff through daily work interactions and must also support interventions that benefit their staff's long-term career growth (for example, new job postings, release to attend training and their staff taking on secondary assignments), even if these may cause inconvenience to the department. For senior management personnel, they must support employee training and development by stepping up as trainers, mentors and resource persons, and additionally, forging and safeguarding a positive organisational culture that is conducive for employees to learn and grow.

Promotion

Focus of this Chapter

Promotion comes in many forms and permutations. It involves an interplay of job grades, employee grades, position titles and salary ranges. A promotion may be accompanied by a change in any one or more of these components, depending on how an organisation has set up its job grade structure and salary ranges, whether it has a practice of assigning employee grades to its employees and how it has designed its position titles. Suffice to say, promotion has a technical context. This, however, is not the focus of this chapter.

In this chapter, our focus is to critically examine the practices and nuances of effecting promotion, as well as the challenges and the right and wrong reasons for promoting employees. In practice, promotion is not a simple administrative action. It is a people and emotive affair. Employees and line managers have vested interests. There will be some tension between how the organisation packages the benefits that come with a promotion, what line managers want and what employees expect.

Importantly, a wrong promotion has long-tail adverse consequences. Promoting a currently productive employee without considering whether his capability and capacity will enable him to be effective at the higher job level can lead to bad outcomes for both the organisation and the employee. Organisations must avoid this as far as possible. Organisations should also go the extra mile to help newly promoted employees adjust and be successful in their new roles, as it will benefit both parties.

The Law on Promotion

D13.1   The laws on promotion are scant, as elaborated below:

(a) Employment Act (EA)
The EA does not contain any provision on promotion matters.

(b) Industrial Relations Act (IRA)
Section 18(2) of the IRA explicitly states that appointments and promotions are regarded as non-negotiable items for trade unions.

(c) Tripartite Guidelines on Fair Employment Practices
The Guidelines make mention of promotion as follows: "*Employers should adopt appraisal systems which are fair and objective, with measurable standards for evaluating job performance. This would help ensure that employees are assessed and promoted on the basis of merit.*"

Given the above, it can be inferred that in terms of the <u>decision</u> to promote an employee, it is entirely the management's prerogative.

D13.2   For a unionised organisation, its collective agreement with the union may contain a clause on the Promotion Increment (PI), as PI is a salary item, and all salary items are negotiable between the organisation and the union. The collective agreement however cannot state any union involvement in how decisions on promotions of employees are made, in accordance with IRA Section 18(2).

What is a Promotion?

Promotion in Layman's Language

D13.3   Promotion is commonly understood at the workplace as an employee progressing upwards in his career in the organisation. The phrase "progressing upwards in his career" connotes an increase in responsibilities and remuneration, and perhaps status and position title are supposedly to go up. It is celebratory.

The "Technical" Dimensions of a Promotion Action

D13.4   To organisations, the term "promotion" may involve changes in 4 "technical" dimensions: (a) job grade, (b) employee grade, (c) position title and (d) salary and salary range for the employee. Organisations may define "promotion" (in technical dimensions) differently to suit their own context. For one, if an organisation does not have any job grades, employee grades or salary ranges in place, then these 3 technical dimensions are irrelevant to its context and do not feature in its promotion actions.

D13.5   The terms "job grade", "employee grade" and "position title" have been explained in Chapter D10 "Job Grade Structure and Career Roadmap", and "salary ranges" in Volume B, Chapter B5 "Salary Ranges". We do a quick recap here.

Job Grade
It refers to the grade/level of a job, which indicates the job's complexity and accountabilities and its importance to the organisation. The higher the job grade, the higher the job is in the organisation's hierarchy of jobs.

Employee Grade
It refers to the rank of the employee (not the job) in the organisation's hierarchy. The higher the employee grade, the more senior the employee is in the organisation's seniority rank order. An employee may be conferred an employee grade that is equal to or higher or lower than the job grade of the job position that he is occupying, based on various contextual factors such as his competency and contribution level. His salary and staff benefits are based on his employee grade (and not the job grade of the job position that he is occupying) if the organisation uses employee grades. For example, if an employee occupies a job position that is grade 9 while his employee grade is only grade 8, he will be paid a monthly salary within the salary range of grade 8 and his staff benefits will also be based on grade 8.

Position Title
Every job carries a "position title" (also referred to as "job title", "function title" or "job designation"). A position title conveys the nature, function and mandate of the job role. An employee performing a job will carry the position title of the said job.

> **Salary Range**
> Each job grade is assigned a salary range ($X–$Y). The salary range sets out the lower limit ($X) and upper limit ($Y) on the monthly basic salary that the job commands. The more important the job, the higher will be the job grade, and correspondingly, the higher the salary range. In reality, salary ranges are only found in large and established organisations, and mostly in unionised establishments.

D13.6   Not all organisations have put in place job grades, employee grades and salary ranges (for example, most small and medium enterprises do not have these). In the case of position titles, unless it is a one-man set up, all organisations have employees placed in different job roles and hence a position title is a must for every employee.

D13.7   There are various possible scenarios arising from the different permutations of how organisations use the said technical dimensions. Four scenarios (the common ones) are elaborated below:

> Scenario 1
>
> | Job Grades | Employee Grades | Position Titles | Salary Ranges |
> |:---:|:---:|:---:|:---:|
> | ✓ | ✓ | ✓ | ✓ |
>
> This is mostly found in large and established organisations where a holistic system comprising job grades, employee grades, position titles and salary ranges has been put in place to convey the hierarchical structure in the organisation. Each job/employee grade has a salary range. Every employee will be conferred an employee grade (personal to himself, based on an assessment of his competency/capability), which may be equal to or higher or lower than the job grade of the job that he is doing. For example, if an employee is doing a job that is grade 9, his employee grade may be grade 8 (lower), grade 9 (the same) or grade 10 (higher); in more extreme cases, the differential between employee grade and job grade may even be more than one grade.

Scenario 2

Job Grades	Employee Grades	Position Titles	Salary Ranges
✓	✗	✓	✓

In this scenario, there is no such notion of conferring an "employee grade" to the individual employee. A simpler approach is taken here. Every employee (jobholder) is deemed to hold the grade of the job that he is occupying. That is, if an employee is assigned to a job position of grade 9, he will be accorded grade 9 and his salary and staff benefits will be pegged to grade 9. The organisation assesses the employee at grade 9 (the grade of the job that he is doing) and if his competency falls short, it will be duly reflected in his performance appraisal.

Scenario 3

Job Grades	Employee Grades	Position Titles	Salary Ranges
✗	✗	✓	✓

In this scenario, the organisation essentially incorporates the intent of job grades and employee grades into its position titles (in other words, all three dimensions are rolled into one, the position title). Each position title has a salary range. An example of such a system is the cabin crew and pilots of Singapore Airlines.

Cabin Crew: Flight Steward → Leading Steward → Chief Steward → Inflight Supervisor
Pilots: Cadet Officer → Second Officer → First Officer → Senior First Officer → Captain

All flight stewards are of the same hierarchy and enjoy the same salary range and the same tier of staff benefits. The same applies to all captains, and so on. The concept is straightforward and simple. All employees holding the same position title (in other words, doing the same job) are accorded the same salary range and staff benefits.

Scenario 4			
Job Grades	Employee Grades	Position Titles	Salary Ranges
✘	✘	✓	✘

This scenario is common in small and medium enterprises (SMEs) which mostly do not have any job grades, employee grades and salary ranges. They denote hierarchy through position titles. Career progression is by advancing through a string of job positions. For example: Executive → Senior Executive → Assistant Manager → Manager → Senior Manager → Assistant Director → Deputy Director → Director

D13.8   A detailed discussion on all the possible scenarios is neither intuitive nor essential in this chapter. Suffice to say, promotions are nuanced and contextual and if one works in a large organisation, one may encounter a unique way that defines a promotion.

How Promotion Benefits the Organisation

D13.9   Organisations may have varied reasons to promote employees. Some reasons are right and will lead to positive outcomes, while some reasons can be nebulous (we discuss this in the section "Getting Promotion Right"). Used correctly, promoting an employee should achieve the following multi-fold objectives for the organisation:

(a) to do the right and fair thing to accord the individual employee the grade that is commensurate with his competencies and responsibilities shouldered by him so that he can enjoy the right level of salary, staff benefits and hierarchical status;

(b) to advance the individual employee to a job level that matches his current level of capabilities, so as to stretch him and optimise his contribution to the organisation;

(c) to provide career progression to capable employees so as to continually motivate them and increase their commitment and thereby enhance retention of capable staff;

(d) to develop employees to their fullest potential and thereby strengthen the organisation's talent pool; and

(e) to send a positive message to employees that the organisation believes in developing internal talent, thereby enhancing its employee value proposition.

How Promotion Benefits and Impacts an Employee

D13.10 Promotions are celebratory events for employees. Looking at it in a broad and long-term view, an employee benefits from a promotion in the following ways:

(a) he can derive higher job satisfaction in performing a job that better matches his current capabilities; and
(b) he can advance in career and move closer towards actualising his potential.

D13.11 In immediate and more tangible terms, an employee benefits from the following changes that accompany his promotion:

(a) a higher job grade or employee grade (if the organisation has job/employee grade structures);
(b) a higher position title (generally happens for most cases, but not for some);
(c) a higher salary range (if the organisation has salary ranges);
(d) a promotion increment to raise his salary; and
(e) staff benefits tied to his higher grade or rank.

Higher Position Title

D13.12 Upon promotion, the job grade and/or employee grade of the employee should normally change, but not always, depending on how the organisation has designed those structures. Here, we focus on the changes in position titles which are optical.

D13.13 Organisations may design their position titles in various ways; it is a matter of preference. Two examples are shown below – one with finely differentiated position titles and the other with more broadly banded position titles:

Example 1: Finely Differentiated Position Titles

JG1	JG2	JG3	JG4	JG5	JG6	JG7	JG8	JG9	JG10
Exe	Senior Exe	Asst Mgr	Mgr	Senior Mgr	Asst Dir	Deputy Dir	Director		

Example 2: Broadly Banded Position Titles

JG1	JG2	JG3	JG4	JG5	JG6	JG7	JG8	JG9	JG10
Executive			Manager		Senior Manager		Director		

D13.14 Depending on the organisation's design of position titles, a promotion may come with or without a change in position title. An employee promoted from job grade JG1 to JG2 will have a change in position title in Example 1 above, while in Example 2, the employee retains the same position title.

D13.15 A change in position title conveys a sense of career progression for the employee. In reality, most employees value (or relish) a higher position title to accompany a promotion. While it is inconvenient (and even poor taste) for one to brag about one's higher salary or higher job/employee grade (which is an internal matter in the organisation), a higher position title makes one's career progression more visible (to friends/peers and future employers) and therefore gives the employee a sense of achievement. Since position titles are essentially free (that is, of no cost to the organisation), there is inherent advantage for organisations to adopt more finely differentiated position titles.

Higher Salary Range

D13.16 When the employee moves up in job/employee grade, he will become entitled to the (higher) salary range of his new grade. This means that henceforth he can enjoy salary increments until he reaches the maximum point of his new salary range.

Promotion Increment

D13.17 Upon promotion, the employee should receive a Promotion Increment (PI). The PI will be built into the employee's monthly basic salary.

D13.18   If the organisation is non-unionised, the quantum of PI is at the discretion of the organisation. Organisations may set a fixed PI (say, x% of salary or guided by a PI matrix or formula). On the other hand, some organisations prefer to make PI entirely variable based on the merits of each case. If the organisation is unionised, the PI will be negotiated with the union.

D13.19   If an organisation has salary ranges and if the employee's salary after incorporating the PI is lower than the minimum point of the salary range of the higher job/employee grade, the employee will also receive a top-up in salary to bring his salary to the minimum point of the said salary range.

> Salary Adjustment = PI + [Any top-up needed to bring to Minimum point of Salary Range]

If an organisation has no salary ranges, there will be no "minimum threshold" so to speak, on moving an employee's salary up after a promotion.

D13.20   The PI should be over and above the Annual Increment (AI) that the employee is receiving. The timing of PI and AI may be the same if the organisation coincides its annual increment exercise with its promotion exercise and applies the same effective date. But the timings may also be different (say, AI is effective on 1 January and PI is effective on 1 April).

D13.21   In a unionised organisation, the quantum for AI and PI would be negotiated between the organisation and the union and spelt out as separate amounts. On the other hand, in a non-unionised organisation where the AI and PI are decided solely by the organisation, if these are implemented together with the same effective date, the employee will usually receive a salary increment that combines both the AI and PI, without the separate amounts explicitly spelt out.

D13.22   Most organisations would calibrate their PI quantum to make it a meaningful promotion. For example, in a tight labour market where employees would change employment to advance their careers for not less than a 10%–15% increase in salary, then the organisation should aim to meet this threshold with both the AI and PI (combined) so that the employee feels that he can enjoy an internal career advancement that comes with a commensurate salary progression without the need for him to look for alternative employment elsewhere. For example, if AI is 4%, paying a PI of 6%–10% would make the total salary increase close to what the employee expects if he changes employment for a higher job. Paying the appropriate PI quantum is important, as one of the key objectives of promoting an employee is to retain and develop the employee. Please refer to Volume B, Chapter B6 "Salary Increments", Section "Promotion Increment" for more elaboration on determining PI quantum.

D13.23 *Does a promotion always come with a promotion increment?*
In the majority of promotions, an employee would receive a PI. However, in some rare instances, it may happen that an organisation considers that the employee's pre-promotion salary is already fair and competitive enough vis-à-vis his new position after the promotion. For such a case, the employee may not be given any PI (or given a nominal amount). Nevertheless, the employee moves on to a higher grade and he will enjoy the higher salary range pegged to the higher grade (assuming that the organisation has salary ranges) and perhaps better employee benefits as well.

Staff Benefits Tied to Higher Grade or Hierarchy

D13.24 Some organisations offer staff benefits that are differentiated by job grades/bands. Typically, benefits are differentiated broadly along these bands: rank-and-file employees → executives → senior management.

D13.25 If an employee's promotion puts him into a new job grade/band that qualifies for a higher tier of staff benefits, he will be accorded the higher tier of staff benefits accordingly.

D13.26 The common staff benefits that are differentiated by job grades/bands are (a) annual leave, (b) medical benefits, (c) insurance coverage, (d) transport allowance and (e) flexi-dollars for flexible benefits scheme.

Impact on Other Employment Terms

D13.27 Other than staff benefits, promotion will also entail an alignment to terms of employment that are tied to job grades/bands. Some common terms that may be impacted by promotion are:

(a) Notice Period
Notice period for resignation and contractual termination (including retrenchment) is usually differentiated by job bands. For example, an employee being promoted from the Manager job band to the Director job band may have his notice period increased from 1 month to 3 months.

(b) Union Representation

Unionised organisations will have an agreement with their unions on the delineation of job grades/bands that can enjoy full or limited representation by the union. Please refer to Volume E, Chapter E10 "Union Representation" for more details on this topic. If an employee is promoted to a job grade/band that affects his eligibility to enjoy union representation, he has to surrender his right for union representation accordingly.

Essential Human Resource Frameworks to Support Promotion

D13.28 To support and guide the management to make sound promotion decisions, information on the competencies and performance levels of employees is required. Therefore, the organisation must necessarily have a competency framework and a performance appraisal system. We highlight the salient features of the competency framework and performance appraisal system that are helpful for the understanding of "promotion".

Competency Framework

D13.29 A competency framework lays down the critical or core competencies and the required proficiency levels for different job grades. Using the competency framework, the organisation will be able to assess whether the employee has attained the requisite competency level for his current job and whether his competencies have improved or expanded to do the higher job at the next level. In some instances, competency requirements for the next higher job level may be quite different from those at the employee's current job level.

> Example
>
> In assessing whether a high-performing Sales Specialist is suitable to be promoted to a Sales Manager, it would be necessary to assess him against the competencies required for a Sales Manager role (such as sales planning, market analysis, management of pricings and discounts, sales training and team leadership) rather than his abilities to personally secure sales.

D13.30 Many large and established organisations have put in place competency frameworks that are customised to suit their organisational context. Most of these organisations specify that employees being considered for promotion to senior/leadership positions must demonstrate adequate proficiency in competencies such as critical thinking, strategic visioning and leading and developing people.

D13.31 In summary, a competency framework provides a checklist or platform to check against an employee's competencies and attributes to assess whether the employee can reasonably succeed in the next higher job grade. It provides some "science" to guide promotion decisions, although assessing an employee's competencies/attributes will still involve human judgment for which some subjectivity is unavoidable.

Performance Appraisal System

D13.32 Every organisation has a performance appraisal system/process in one form or another. In large and established organisations, performance appraisal is but only one component in the entire performance management framework. The other components that complement development and promotion of employees are performance planning (aka goals setting), performance review and coaching and performance critical conversation (between the reporting officer and employee).

D13.33 Performance appraisal takes stock of the employee's performance, work outcomes and contributions, competencies and strengths and areas for development. These are important and relevant inputs for considering whether an employee is suited or ready for the next higher job.

D13.34 In many small and medium enterprises, it is not uncommon for line managers to judge the performance of their employees without diligently first going through the rigour of a proper performance appraisal which requires checking against the employee's work outcomes and contributions, and strengths and gaps. The line manager would have decided on which employee to promote and then convey his recommendation to Human Resource (HR) and if pressured by HR, will complete the performance appraisal as an afterthought and work backwards to justify a promotion recommendation. This is not desirable.

D13.35 It must be emphasised that promotion decisions should be premised on proper performance appraisal so that the organisation can duly assess an employee's suitability and readiness for promotion. Otherwise, employees may be wrongly promoted which will bring about adverse long-tail consequences (we discuss this in the later part of this chapter).

Human Resource Policies that Impact Promotion

D13.36   There may be unique policies that exist in organisations that will impact the promotion of employees. Among such policies and considerations are the following:

(a) *Has the organisation designed narrow job grades or broad job bands?*
(b) *Are there dual career tracks for management and specialist roles?*
(c) *Does the organisation adopt a diversity and inclusion policy for its talent management?*
(d) *Does the organisation practise Acting appointments as a probation for promotion?*
(e) *Are there structured promotion regimes for specific professions or job families?*
(f) *Does the organisation do potential assessment for its employees and use it as a criterion for promotion?*
(g) *Is there a promotion quota?*

Narrow Job Grades versus Broad Job Bands

D13.37   Organisations that have put in place a job grade structure may have designed narrow job grades or broad job bands.

Narrow Job Grades
Under this option, many narrow job grades have been created. The organisation will have a tall hierarchical structure. The requirements in terms of responsibilities and competencies between one job grade and the next higher job grade will not be substantially different. Since there are many job grades, there will be more promotion opportunities for the employees. However, every promotion would logically come with a not-so-substantial salary adjustment.

Broad Job Bands
Some organisations choose to do the opposite of narrow job grades. Job grades are banded up, that is, a few job grades are combined to make a job band. With broad job bands (replacing the original job grades), the hierarchical

structure will be flat, comprising only a few job bands. Between two broad job bands, the difference in requirements in terms of responsibilities and competencies will be more substantial. Since there are few job bands, there will be fewer promotion opportunities for the employees. But each promotion should come with a more substantial salary adjustment.

D13.38 Most organisations prefer narrow job grades to broad job bands for the following reasons:

(a) Narrow job grades allow for more frequent promotions so that employees can better feel a sense of career progression and remain motivated. For broad job bands, since there are fewer promotions, the organisation must find other ways to motivate its employees, such as granting good bonuses, special performance awards/accolades or other recognition mechanisms.

(b) With more (narrow) job grades, it allows the organisation to control the salary progression of its employees better, since employees must earn their promotion before they can move on to the next higher salary range. Whereas for a broad job band, the salary range will be long (with a high maximum-minimum ratio), and employees will have the opportunity to progress to the maximum of the salary range.

D13.39 Although narrow job grades offer distinct advantages to organisations in managing the promotion and salary progression for their employees, some organisations have their own unique reasons or circumstances to go for broad job bands. For instance, where organisations undergo frequent mergers and acquisitions, they will inherit legacy job grade structures that need to be harmonised as one. Such an exercise can be complex and onerous. Broadbanding the job grades offers a viable solution, whereby several legacy job grades of almost equivalent levels can be combined into a single job band. Please refer to Volume B, Chapter B5 "Salary Ranges" for more elaboration.

Management Track and Specialist Track

D13.40 Large organisations would create multiple career tracks to cater to the career aspirations and strengths of different employee groups. Typically, there would be two career tracks, one for the generalists and the other for the specialists. Some organisations have multiple specialist tracks.

> Example
> An engineering company has a generalist track and an engineering track. Engineers who are passionate about engineering and want to excel in the profession will be channelled to the engineering track, where the apex will be Chief Engineer. Other engineers who wish to pursue management roles will go on the generalist track, where the apex will be Head of Engineering Division or Chief Executive Officer.

> Example
> A healthcare cluster has three career tracks for its nurses, namely (a) Management, (b) Clinical and Research and (c) Education. Nurses who perform well in managing inpatient services at the wards will go on the Management track. Those who wish to specialise in clinical roles working in collaboration with doctors to advance treatment protocols will go on the Clinical and Research track. Those who have a passion to be nurse educators to train junior nurses will go on the Education track.

D13.41　The creation of a specialist track avails more promotion opportunities to professionals who want to specialise in their fields. Many of these employees remain as individual contributors rather than managers of teams, but their value is in the deep expertise that they possess and their ability to resolve complex technical problems. By providing a suitable career track for specialist employees to advance their careers, the organisation enhances the retention of this talent group.

Diversity and Inclusion Policy

D13.42　With growing awareness of the importance of having a diverse and inclusive workforce, some organisations factor in diversity of talent for their recruitment as well as talent management (including promotion of employees). The value proposition for having a diverse and inclusive workforce is to introduce richness in perspectives and to have a balanced representation of different employee stakeholders to build a more holistic nexus and harmonious climate.

D13.43　There may be some challenges in pursuing a diversity and inclusion policy since most organisations would profess that all promotions should strictly be based on merit. The rational approach would be all things being equal (that is, if two candidates are of equal merit), then the candidate that can help boost diversity in the talent bench would have that extra advantage. There must be judicious balance in pushing the diversity and inclusion policy in promotion decisions.

Acting Appointments as Probation for Promotion

D13.44   Some organisations have adopted the practice of first trying out an employee in a higher role (especially for positions involving leadership responsibility, such as head of a section/department) on an "acting appointment" basis. The acting appointment typically lasts for six months to one year, and occasionally, longer. The employee will be given a position title as "Acting XXX" (such as Acting CEO, Acting CFO and Acting Director of Marketing). The Singapore government is one organisation with a very visible practice of acting appointments; some political office holders are first appointed as Acting Ministers for a period before they become full Ministers.

D13.45   In essence, an acting appointment serves as a probation for promotion. The employee is tested on his suitability and capability before being confirmed in the appointment, at which time, the "acting" prefix to his position will be dropped. Using an acting appointment as a probation for promotion is a prudent way for an organisation to assess an employee for a higher role. This prudence is especially important for senior leadership positions, where a wrong choice of candidate will be very costly for the organisation. However, there is a downside to this practice. The appointee may feel some unease. If the appointee is eventually not "confirmed", he will revert to his previous position, and this may cause a loss of face unless such occurrences are the norm in the organisation.

D13.46   One may argue that it is superfluous to use acting appointments as a probation for promotion. Organisations should find other means to assess an employee's suitability and capability before deciding to appoint or promote him. The organisation can test and stretch an employee by assigning some elements of the higher role (for example, complex assignments), without having to publicly give the employee an acting appointment. However, the reality is that this unofficial testing is not always possible. Some appointees may be appointed to an entirely different role, or the higher position may not be in the same vertical as the employee's current position (for example, the higher position is in an entirely different division, or even in another entity). It would not be as convenient or even feasible to test the employee in the higher role.

D13.47 It is pertinent to note that not all acting appointments serve as a probation for promotion. In some instances, an acting appointment is purely transient, and the appointee is only intended as a temporary fill-in. This usually happens when the higher position is vacated, and there are no clear candidates in sight, hence making it urgent to appoint a temporary fill-in to hold the fort while the organisation searches for a permanent replacement. From the onset, it is already clear that the appointee is not the chosen candidate for the vacated position (for whatever reasons). The organisation would usually set a limited tenure for the acting appointment, say, 6 months, and would even be transparent about this fact in its announcement of the acting appointment, whether internally or publicly.

> Example
> The CEO of ABC company announces that its Chief Executive Officer, Mr XXX will be stepping down with effect from 1 April 2025. The board will be searching for a replacement. In the interim, Mr YYY, aged 59, who is Director of International Marketing, will be Acting CEO from 1 April to 30 September 2025.

D13.48 All said, if an organisation has done its succession planning very proactively and built up an adequate bench strength of potential successors for its key positions, there should be less need for acting appointments. Acting appointments are in fact "awkward" for both the organisation and the appointee, and should be used judiciously.

Structured Promotion Regime for Specific Professions

D13.49 Certain professions go through a special and structured promotion journey. The promotion journey will require the employee to go through a structured regime of training and assessments to systematically surmount several professional milestones before reaching the apex of the professional career path. Each professional milestone invariably involves some assessment of competency and accreditation process. Some examples of these professions are doctors, nurses, engineers, architects, academicians, pilots, etc.

> Example
> The typical career path of a commercial pilot starts with being a Cadet Pilot. A Cadet Pilot must go through structured training and pass the mandatory assessments in order to "graduate" as a Second Officer. After some actual flying under the close guidance of instructor pilots, a Second Officer will be assessed whether he qualifies as a First Officer. The First Officer does actual flying for at least several years, to gather enough flying hours and sectors (one sector means one take-off and one landing) to qualify to be selected for training as a Captain. After completing vigorous "command" training and passing the mandatory assessments, the First Officer will be promoted to a Captain. While flying, a Captain will continue to be "checked" periodically by licensed instructor pilots to ensure that they remain competent and current in their knowledge of flight operation.

Potential Assessment

D13.50   First and foremost, an employee's performance and potential are two different things, although closely related, and it is not always a direct correlation. A high-performing employee may be of average potential, while a high-potential employee may show just average performance.

D13.51   Simply put, an employee with a high potential means that he is assessed to have innate abilities or attributes, or he has acquired the abilities through experience and exposure (such as critical thinking, analytical ability, strategic visioning and networking savviness) that stand him in good stead to assume higher roles in the longer run. Whereas an employee who is assessed as a good performer in his current role may have done well due to a number of factors, such as his good knowledge of his current work, his diligence and dedication, clocking extra hours and doing the lion's share of work, but this excellence does not guarantee that he can perform well in a higher role that calls for a different set of competencies.

> Examples
> - An expert engineer may not make an effective engineering manager.
> - A star salesperson may not make a competent sales manager.
> - The best professionals who are individual contributors may not always be the best candidates for management positions that call for managerial abilities.
> - Managing a team of 10 staff in the same function or unit is different from leading a team of 100 staff who come from different functions.

D13.52   To consider an employee for promotion, an organisation must consider whether he has the potential (that is, the competencies/abilities) to perform effectively at the higher job that he is to be promoted to. To guide promotion decisions, the organisation should use a checklist of the competencies and proficiency levels needed for the higher job, and systematically tick it against the employee, to assess whether he is suitable and ready for promotion. This step should never be skipped or glossed over. This cannot be over-emphasised. Otherwise, it would be setting up the employee for failure after his promotion.

> **Peter's Principle:**
> This is a management concept developed by Laurence J. Peter, based on the observation that people in a hierarchy tend to rise from their level of competence to their "level of incompetence", if the organisation makes the mistake of promoting employees purely based on performance in their current roles and not based on the competencies/skills needed in their future roles.
>
> Case Example
> John, an engineering graduate joined a company and performed well. He was promoted successively from Engineer to Senior Engineer, then Specialist Engineer, then Principal Engineer. All these years, he excelled in engineering and had been a hands-on expert. He had minimal requirement to manage other engineers. He treated all his junior engineers as buddies.
>
> When the Engineering Manager resigned, the organisation decided to promote John. As the new Engineering Manager, John continued to spend most of his time personally doing troubleshooting and solving engineering problems. He did not manage the engineers. Instead of helping his engineers learn, he often took over their assignments and problems. John also disliked dealing with other department heads such as the Finance Manager and the Production Manager. He even avoided dealing with the Chief Executive Officer as far as possible. He continued to immerse himself in doing his engineering stuff.
>
> The case of John is a common scenario in many organisations. He had moved from being at a high level of competence to a level of incompetence. It is a sad outcome for both John and the organisation.

Current Estimated Potential

D13.53   It is appropriate here to make reference to the Current Estimated Potential (CEP) system used or had been used by some organisations.

D13.54　*What is the difference between "Potential" and "Current Estimated Potential"?*

When we talk about an employee's potential to assume the next higher job role, we mean to assess whether the employee possesses the competencies/ abilities needed to perform effectively at the *next higher job* that he is to be promoted to.

CEP, on the other hand, is a "long-term" version of assessing an employee's potential. CEP is used to denote the specific job level that an employee is potentially able to reach *at the peak of his career*. For example, if a person is assessed to have a CEP of CEO, it means that the assessment (or rather, prediction) is that the person has what it takes to reach CEO level of the said organisation as *the peak of his career*. Simply put, CEP is a crystal ball forecasting about a person's "last stop" in his career (where he remains competent) and not just about his suitability or readiness to take on the next higher job role.

D13.55　In organisations that have embraced the CEP system, it is generally applied to their graduate talent pool (not rank-and-file employees), starting with the top-tier graduate officers freshly hired from renowned universities. The careers of these graduate officers are systematically managed according to their CEP. For example, if officer A has a CEP of CEO while officer B has a CEP of Division Head, the pace of promotion for officer A will be faster than that of officer B since officer A will have more ranks to attain before he reaches the peak or retires.

D13.56　Typically, a graduate officer is first given his CEP score after about two years in service. Thereafter, his CEP is reviewed every year or two years, assessed by different reporting officers or division heads. Due to this periodic or continual review, the potential assessment is labelled as "Current Estimated Potential", that is, the potential assessment is what stands at current review.

D13.57　The CEP system has its opponents. The contention is whether, at such an early stage of an employee's age and career, there is really enough information (or data points) to make an accurate assessment of his CEP. And whether it is helpful or even fair to use CEP to predetermine an employee's career trajectory, as in setting the pace of promotion for the employee.

D13.58　It is pertinent to note that Shell company and the Singapore Civil Service which had been using the CEP system for their talent management (including guiding promotion decisions) for many years, have already discarded the use of CEP. We discuss more on this in Chapter D14 "Talent Management and Succession Planning".

Promotion Quota

D13.59 Some organisations impose a promotion quota of, say, x% of the organisation's total employee population annually. Some may even apply the promotion quota in a more granular way, say, drilled down to each department and job level/band.

D13.60 The main rationale for imposing a promotion quota is to manage the number of promotions granted. Logically, there should be an overall check on the number of promotions. Promotions should be viewed as "significant" by employees; they should not be so common and granted loosely.

D13.61 There is no "magic" figure for setting promotion quota; much depends on the organisation's context. Some common considerations include the following:

- If an organisation has narrow job grades, there are more promotional opportunities for employees and hence a higher promotion quota is in order. The reverse applies if the organisation has broad job bands; a smaller promotion quota is logical.

- If an organisation is doing well and in an expansion mode with new and higher job openings being created, correspondingly, it should raise its promotion quota. On the other hand, for an organisation that is not doing well, it will need to manage its staff costs, a lower promotion quota (to accommodate only the critical and urgent promotions) is in order.

- In a year when an organisation has a higher attrition rate, the number of employees to be promoted will likely increase (assuming that the organisation may fill the vacated positions with suitable internal candidates).

- If a vast majority of the employees in an organisation are already conferred employee grades equal to the job grades of their respective job positions and if it is operating in a steady state, there should be fewer promotions. Conversely, if an organisation is young and growing fast with many employees stretching themselves to take on bigger roles or double hatting, more promotions will follow once the organisation starts to stabilise.

D13.62 Some line heads wrongly interpret a promotion quota to mean that each department is entitled to [x%] of promotions based on the department's staff strength. Human Resource and management must educate line heads to eradicate such wrong notions. A promotion quota is to manage the "maximum" and not to guarantee the "minimum" number.

D13.63 Suffice to say, a promotion quota should be used flexibly only to guide management's decisions on promotions and should be set and adjusted to suit the organisation's prevailing circumstances.

Getting Promotion Right

Examples of Promotions with Negative Outcomes

D13.64 Promotion is a staff action with a long tail. If the decision to promote is not substantially based on the core competencies and potential of the employees, it will likely have a long-term adverse impact on the organisation. Therefore, it is important that promotion decisions are made correctly to benefit both the employees and the organisation. To help the employees who have risen to leadership positions sustain their effectiveness and competence, organisations must provide continual exposure and learning opportunities for them through various developmental interventions.

D13.65 Following are some real-life cases where promotions of employees brought negative outcomes for the organisation. Their situations were aggravated because there was failure to keep the employees in performing shape when circumstances change. We can draw lessons from these cases.

Case 1: ABC Logistics
ABC Logistics has been in the trading and warehousing operations for some 30 years. A good number of employees have been with the company for more than two decades. They are loyal and perform decently well. Over the years, a number of them rose from the ranks and were promoted to department heads and managerial positions. Their promotions were primarily based on their past performance and service (aka loyalty to the company).

As management staff now, they continue to do a decent job in what they have been doing, in a business-as-usual mode. They are trustworthy and dedicated. However, they lack the exposure and managerial skills such as strategic thinking, business planning and managing the business and operations based on good economics. As a result, the company is not attuned to the changes in the market; it is still on its traditional and tried-and-tested business model. Adoption of new business operation models and technology is slow, and the inertia of the management staff are hindering the progress of the company. Meanwhile, customers' expectations are rising, and competition is more intense. Profit margin is dropping. The future of the company is not promising, although there are emerging opportunities in the supply chain industry.

Case 2: XYZ Paint Manufacturing and Trading

XYZ Paint Manufacturing and Trading started operations in Singapore more than 30 years ago, manufacturing and trading paint products for heavy industries. Over the years, sales have been good and production and operations generally smooth. XYZ has been consistently profitable, although there have been volatilities due to market conditions. In recent years, they have faced more competition and margin pressure.

The company has always treasured stability and pursued growth on an organic and steady basis. Staff turnover has been low; employees like the stability and not-so-pressurising work environment. Most employees joined the company without any prior relevant experience in the paint industry and rose from the ranks. The company values loyalty and has been promoting employees for their decent performance and dedicated service. Whenever employees hit the maximum points of their salary ranges, the management feels the pressure to promote the employees.

Many who rose to become department heads have continued to work hard, but they think and deal with issues in their traditional ways. They have hardly attended any management training or upgrading programmes. Their exposure to the external business environment is limited. Some work processes have improved, but these are hardly transformational in nature. The company now faces two major challenges – several managers are not effective as leaders/managers and many employees are being paid well above their market rates for the work that they are doing.

Case 3: RB Financial Company

A well-established financial services company in Singapore which has many outlets has always prized itself on retaining and rewarding employees who are reliable and trustworthy. Rightly so, as integrity and trustworthiness are crucial attributes for financial institutions.

Over the decades, the company had adopted the promotion-from-within philosophy. Employees were promoted mainly based on performance at current level and reliability. External mid-level hires were exceptions. The company was performing decently for many years partly because the operating environment then was more benign and much less competitive. As the financial industry opens up, competition has intensified greatly. Customers have become more demanding in respect of products and services and have also become more discerning on pricing. Depositors would shop around for better deposit interest rates, while borrowers are not hesitant to ask for lower financing rates, otherwise they would move their businesses to other financial institutions.

As the increasingly competitive operating environment unfolded, a number of managers and executives have found the going tough. They have been accustomed to the stable environment of yesteryears. As the company has never been in favour of letting go of the loyalists, it restructured and centralised a number of functions and created positions to let these managers/executives continue to contribute in a meaningful and productive way, while bringing in external hires to fight the new battles. With that, the company has an opportunity to move forward, while the long-serving employees are still being looked after in a decent manner.

Concurrently, the company has also started to emphasise on core competencies and potential when they consider employees for promotion. Over time, the quality of the management cohort has improved.

Some Learning Points

D13.66   In all the three cases, the companies had demonstrated good intentions to look after their employees. They promoted people based primarily on performance in their current roles, loyalty and reliability. Promotion was also used to reward and give recognition to the employees to retain them, and perhaps also to motivate other employees to stay on and wait for their turns.

D13.67   What was not obvious and considered was the long tail of a promotion. The companies did not consider the company's future needs and the changing operating environment. Whether the employees put at the company's management/leadership ranks were equipped to manage and lead the company in the mid to long-term had not been adequately weighed in. Promoting people based on performance and loyalty are arguably decent criteria at face value, and would even hold ground for years to come, but *if and only if* the business and operating environment remains static. However, this of course is never the case in this day and age. Change is a constant in the business world, and change occurs in an unabated breath. Only people who stay relevant and have a high level of core competencies, energy and resilience can remain effective amidst the changes.

D13.68   Promotion thrusts employees into higher job roles. What must not be neglected is the need for the organisation to provide continual exposure and developmental opportunities to enable employees to hone higher-level competencies and critical management skills and to keep abreast with changes in the business and operating environment and technological advancements. On the employees' part, they must have the motivation, potential, capacities and learning agility to upskill, reskill and scale greater heights.

Right and Wrong Reasons to Promote an Employee

D13.69   As promotion is not regulated by law, promotion decisions are entirely the management's prerogative. Organisations can choose to promote their employees in whichever way they like, using whatever criteria so decided by them.

D13.70   Organisations usually articulate their own officially acceptable criteria/ reasons for the promotion of their employees. At times, promotions are planned and implemented at regular timelines, yet at other times, promotions may be done ad hoc under pressurised circumstances. The following are what organisations usually cite as their official criteria/reasons to promote employees:

(a) to recognise an employee for taking on more or higher responsibilities;
(b) to recognise an employee for acquiring deeper or higher competencies;
(c) to reward an employee for his good performance and dedication;
(d) to allow an employee to continue to enjoy salary increments after hitting the maximum of his salary range; and

(e) to retain an employee in service (who has the intention to resign or who has tendered resignation) by counter-offering a promotion.

We discuss these criteria/reasons in more detail below to examine whether these (especially when applied as the sole or stand-alone criterion/reason) form a sound enough basis for a promotion action.

D13.71 Other than the common "official" criteria/reasons above, there are also "unofficial" (or covert) reasons for pushing promotion. In reality, promotions of employees often take on a political dimension, especially if the organisational climate is competitive and political. Line heads often attempt to use promotion as a tool to reward their own loyalists. By pushing their own candidates up the rungs of the corporate ladder, a line head can surround himself with loyalists who owe dues to him and thereby create a wall of security for himself.

Promotion for Taking on More or Higher Responsibilities

D13.72 Generally, in any organisation, the scope of most jobs will change over time. Some jobs will shrink and become smaller, while others will expand and become bigger.

D13.73 Organisations have the natural inclination to reward and compensate the incumbents of those jobs that are expanding. But there must be a word of caution here for organisations to better distinguish whether the job is expanding in terms of workload only, or in terms of complexity and higher responsibility. This distinction is important because the different scenarios would call for a different method of reward/compensation for the employee, and promoting the employee may not necessarily be the appropriate (or wise) move, as explained further below:

(a) *Job expansion by way of heavier workload*
Where a job expands with a heavier workload, it calls for higher efficiency from the employee, or alternatively, more headcount is needed. If the employee absorbs the heavier workload, he should rightfully be paid extra, either with overtime pay (if he is entitled to overtime pay under the Employment Act), a higher bonus, or a salary adjustment (if the increase in workload is not transient). As the job worth for the position remains unchanged, the employee should not be given a promotion, otherwise, he will move on to a higher salary range (if the organisation has salary ranges) and in time to come, his salary will exceed the worth of the job that he is performing.

(b) Job expansion by way of more or higher responsibilities
Where a job expands with higher responsibilities added on, the job becomes more complex and the job worth will increase. If the increase is sufficient to propel the job into the next higher job grade, then the employee should rightfully be promoted for doing a higher job.

Promotion for Acquiring Deeper or Higher Technical Competencies

D13.74   In many organisations, there would invariably be some employees in specialist roles. These employees are usually individual contributors, rather than managers of teams. The value of their contribution lies in their deep technical competencies, specialised functional skills or domain knowledge. They are an essential group that other co-workers and supervisors turn to, to get technical problems resolved or subject matter advice. In many instances, these specialist employees are a pillar anchoring the organisation's core operations.

> Example
> A company specialising in marine paint manufacturing requires chemists and coating specialists who are familiar with the properties of marine paints and who understand the operational nuances of the marine paint industry. These employees acquire their industry knowledge on the job, and at the same time, hone in their technical competence through further research and professional upgrading.

D13.75   For these specialist employees, it is critical for them to continually broaden as well as deepen and improve their professional/technical knowledge and competencies. The organisation relies on these specialist employees for a competitive advantage. The organisation therefore needs to encourage them to continually stay abreast of technical developments in their specialised domains and reward/compensate them for doing so. Career progression by way of promotion is one way to do so.

D13.76   Promoting employees based on specialist knowledge/skills/expertise and broadening and deepening of technical competencies makes economic sense for the organisation. An employee with higher technical competencies can produce higher quality work and/or take less time to complete a task. An experienced hand can cut through the chase and dive right into the crux of the matter and have invaluable insights into whether a method will work or not work. The higher efficiency and effectiveness delivered by a technically superior employee justifies a higher job worth for him, and hence a promotion. The career track for specialists can and should be lengthened to create a few more promotion opportunities to reflect the impact specialist jobs have on the organisation.

Promotion for Good Performance and Dedication

D13.77   On face value, promotion based primarily on the employee's good performance in the current role, plus dedication and dependability appears sound and persuasive. A very obliging employee who has done a lot of overtime work and taken on miscellaneous tasks that his supervisor cannot find a person to do should certainly be recognised and rewarded. However, rewarding him with promotion may not be an appropriate or wise move.

D13.78   There is no guarantee that an employee who is a good performer in his current role will succeed in a higher role, as the higher role may call for different competencies which the employee may have or not have. One must be mindful that an employee doing a high volume of the same tasks or dealing with many issues at the same level of challenge or using the same competencies is no guarantee that he can handle more complicated assignments or solve more complex problems that accompany the higher position. The decision to promote must ultimately take into assessment whether the employee can be competent and effective at the higher job level.

> Example
> An Accounts Executive who is highly proficient in keeping a full set of accounts, coupled with a meticulous nature and showing high dedication in producing accurate accounting records in a timely manner may be a star performer in his current role.
>
> However, promoting him to the higher role of Finance Manager will require him to prepare management reports, perform budget analysis, manage budget variances with the line departments and make presentations to the management on the financial health of the organisation and governance issues, as well as

highlight any financial risks. As Finance Manager, he will also be required to lead a team of 5 Accounts Executives. To succeed in the Finance Manager role, the employee would need higher competencies, such as (a) critical thinking, (b) analytical ability, (c) written and verbal communication skills, (d) relationship management skills, (e) strategic thinking and (f) leadership skills.

Promotion for Continued Salary Progression

D13.79 Many large and established organisations have salary ranges; each job grade carries a salary range. It is common to find line managers lobbying for promotion of their employees who have hit the maximum point of their salary ranges. Their worry is that without further salary increases, their employees may become demotivated.

D13.80 Promoting an employee for the sole reason of allowing him to continue to enjoy salary increases makes a very poor reason. Yet, many line managers push for it and organisations allow it. Sometimes, it may be because the organisation has been somewhat tardy in reviewing its salary ranges. As salary ranges become outdated and uncompetitive against the market, allowing an employee to stagnate at an outdated maximum point would seem unfair and also risk the employee resigning from the organisation. Therefore, the organisation invariably allows the employee to be pushed up to the next higher job/employee grade. Unfortunately, two wrongs (having outdated salary ranges for one, and promoting the employee for a wrong reason for another) do not make one right. The right approach would be for the organisation to review its salary ranges regularly to keep its salary structure updated and competitive and then hold the line against promoting employees for the wrong reason. One must however be realistic that salary ranges cannot go up indefinitely; there is a limit to employees continuing to enjoy salary increases.

D13.81 Done often enough, promoting employees beyond their job worth and their appropriate job/employee grade would lead to over-paying the employees in the long run as they will continue to receive salary increments until they reach the maximum point of the higher salary range. This will be expensive for the organisation. Worse, it will also lead to a population of employees who may be incompetent in performing their jobs at the higher job grade. These employees will be more susceptible to being retrenched when the organisation faces tough times.

Promotion to Retain Employee in Service

D13.82   Promotion to retain an employee may sometimes be done ad hoc and under pressurised circumstances when an employee (especially a high performer) lets known his intention to resign. Whether the decision to offer promotion to the employee is right or wrong depends on whether the employee has enough merits to earn a promotion, such as (a) he has already been doing an expanded job with higher responsibilities or (b) he has acquired deeper/higher competencies to enable him to perform a higher job.

D13.83   Often, because the offer of promotion is done under pressurised circumstances, the focus is on retaining the employee rather than scrutinising the merits of promotion. If there is insufficient merit for promotion, then while promotion may succeed in retaining the employee, it will exact a cost to the organisation in the longer term. The action also sends a wrong message to other employees that the organisation can be pressured into offering promotions.

Promotion to Reward Loyalists

D13.84   Promotion to reward loyalists is politically motivated. In reality, loyalty to the boss may not always equate to loyalty to the organisation. Anecdotal evidence shows that many loyalists leave the organisation to move with their bosses when the said bosses change jobs or employers.

D13.85   To build their loyalist following, line managers often use promotion as a reward. Invariably, promotion to reward loyalists will never be cited as the official reason to promote. Once the loyalist is picked for promotion, the line head will engineer a palatable "official" reason to push the promotion and lobby for support from the critical decision-makers (including Human Resource). Effort will be made to inflate credit to the loyalist for work delivered and make him more visible to the management. Competencies and potential to take on a higher job role are usually not broached. The loyalists just need to avoid mistakes that may ruin their chances of promotion.

D13.86   If such covertly driven promotions become the norm, the organisation will come to a state where many of its senior employees are less than competent in their roles. Worse, the organisation will have a divisive culture where line departments work to guard their own turf and interests rather than the interests of the organisation.

Disqualifiers for Promotion

D13.87   Some organisations set certain criteria or disqualifiers in considering employees for promotion. The common disqualifiers are as follows:

(a) minimum length of service (or lack of);
(b) employee's disciplinary record;
(c) employee's state of health; and
(d) employee's aspiration (or lack of).

Minimum Length of Service

D13.88   Many organisations set a minimum length of service (usually referred to as "time norm") that the employee should spend in a specific grade before he can be considered for promotion to the next higher grade. The rationale behind this criteria/disqualifier is that an employee would need time to familiarise himself with his current role, develop and excel in his current level of competencies and build a foundation before he can move on to acquire the higher level of competencies for the next higher job.

D13.89   The length of time norm usually varies from job level to job level. Time norms generally become higher at the more senior job levels, as understandably, the employee would need more time to develop and excel at the higher job levels. An example is given below (the time norms are shown in brackets):

JG1	JG2	JG3	JG4	JG5	JG6	JG7	JG8	JG9	JG10
Exe	Senior Exe	Asst Mgr	Mgr	Senior Mgr	Asst Dir	Deputy Dir	Director		
(2)	(3)	(3)	(4)	(4)	(4)	(4)			

D13.90   Exceptions may be allowed to promote an employee despite the employee having served less than the requisite time norm in his current job grade, under these circumstances:

(a) *Where the employee is assessed to be a talent of high potential*
"High potential" in simple terms means "high calibre". A high-calibre employee should need less time to learn and acquire competencies at each job grade, so he should be able to "fly" across the job grades in less

time than the rest of the cohort of employees (hence the colloquial term "high flier" to describe such talent). In fact, many organisations with a structured talent management programme to manage the career development of their high-flier employees would specify a separate set of promotion time norms for these high-flier employees that are truncated compared to those for the rest of the employees.

(b) *When a mid-career external hire (not a fresh entrant) earns his first promotion*
Very often, when a mid-career candidate is hired, the organisation may adopt a prudent approach in its employment offer. For example, if a candidate's competency is assessed to be somewhere between grade [X] and [X+1], the organisation may prefer to be prudent and offer the candidate to join at grade [X], instead of [X+1]. In this case, if the candidate performs well and soon proves to be competent enough to perform at grade [X+1], he should not need to satisfy the time norm specified for moving from grade [X] to [X+1].

Disciplinary Record

D13.91   Most organisations institute a disqualifier policy to bar or defer any employee having a disciplinary record from promotion. The degree of strictness may vary. Some common examples of policies are given below:

Example 1
Any employee who has received a disciplinary penalty (in whatever form) will be barred from promotion for 2 years from the date the disciplinary penalty is meted out.

Example 2
- Any employee who has received a disciplinary penalty that is a Verbal Warning or less will be barred from promotion for 1 year.
- Any employee who has received a disciplinary penalty that is a Written Warning or more severe action will be barred from promotion for 2 years.

D13.92   Some may argue that an employee's disciplinary record should be treated separately from his eligibility for promotion. The contention is that if an employee has already been duly penalised through a disciplinary action (say, with a written warning), it would not be fair to penalise him again by disqualifying him for promotion (assuming that he satisfies the other criteria for promotion). However, most organisations lean towards having a policy of disqualifying an employee from promotion for [x] number of years, where the duration of debarment is commensurate with the severity of the misconduct. The reason is a practical one. When an employee has committed a misconduct (say, he is given a written warning for being drunk at work or exhibiting unruly or unbecoming behaviour), to give him a promotion soon after (assuming that he satisfies the other criteria for promotion) would send confusing signals to other employees. The optics won't go down well. Putting a debarment of [x] number of years for promotion after a misconduct gives some space between the two events. That said, there should be a balance. Perhaps, the debarment should only apply to cases involving a written warning or more severe action. The debarment period should also be reasonable (say, 1–2 years, depending on the severity of the misconduct). An overly stringent approach may demotivate the employee (assuming that he would otherwise qualify for promotion).

State of Health

D13.93   Health is another factor that organisations may take into consideration in deciding whether to promote an employee, especially if the new/higher job role is significantly more stressful (for example, the job may require working across different geographical time zones, or frequent travelling). As promotion decisions are management's prerogative, it is not unreasonable for the organisation to stipulate health as an added criterion, to ensure that the employee has the vigour and stamina to shoulder higher job responsibilities. To gauge the employee's state of health, organisations may look at the employee's Sick Leave record or any other information that is openly available or disclosed by the employee.

Aspiration (or Lack of)

D13.94   Individual employees have different priorities and life goals, and priorities may change over time, depending on the life stage that one is in.

D13.95   Some employees may convey to their supervisors that they are contented with their current job level and do not desire to be promoted to a higher job. Some may even openly declare that they will decline if offered a promotion. If the employee does not have the aspiration to move up any higher on the career ladder, it would be regarded as self-disqualifying. The management should respect the wishes of the individual employees.

Z-Factors Impacting Promotability

D13.96   In some promotion cases, having satisfied all the "official" criteria that have been stipulated may still not be enough to land the employee a promotion. This is particularly true for senior positions. Organisations and decision-makers often consider other factors, many of which cannot be reduced to a written criterion. The decision-makers often use their intuitive sense of the candidates' potential for success. We refer to these as Z-Factors.

D13.97   There may be many Z-Factors. Different organisations have their own favourite lists (which are typically not formalised or documented). The common ones are highlighted below:

(a) *Visible Performance*
Not only must an employee have performed well, he must also be *seen* to do so. Visibility enhances believability. Publicising one's achievement, if done in a matter-of-fact manner and without inflation and without stealing credit from others, is acceptable and in fact essential. The relevance of this factor is unfortunately not favourable to someone who is too humble and reticent.

(b) *Personal Reputation or Brand*
A personal reputation/brand may be a career-enhancing or limiting factor, especially for senior positions. An employee with a positive or favourable reputation/brand will be in the good books of the key decision-makers. Building rapport (not political or clique connection) with the management personnel will be helpful. Personal reputation/ brand includes but is not limited to the following:

> competence ◆ reliability ◆ trustworthiness, integrity and credibility ◆ initiative ◆ vision, beliefs and charisma

Another dimension of personal reputation/brand is "likeability". Though it may seem unfair, someone who is likeable, especially by the key decision makers, and helpful to others enjoys some advantage (however, being too nice and helpful may be seen negatively when one is being considered for leadership roles). Likeability may include several attributes, including the following:

> physical disposition and presence (including grooming) ◆ mannerism and decorum ◆ sociability and people skills ◆ personality and charm ◆ eloquence

D13.98   If an employee shows interest and effort to get out of one's comfort zone (that is, one's primary domain of competence) and learn other subject matters and get involved in other work areas, it will also help decision-makers conclude that the employee has the zest, ability, breadth of knowledge/ experience and wider perspectives to ascend to a higher position. As one moves up the hierarchy, the importance of depth of knowledge gives way to breadth of knowledge and versatility. At the higher level, the employee must be able to see a bigger picture and connect the dots.

D13.99   These Z-Factors are unwritten criteria adopted by many key decision-makers. Even for employees at the lower ranks, visible performance, personal reputation/brand and likeability are factors that decision-makers consider subconsciously in assessing whether an employee should be promoted, over and above all the formal criteria that have been explicitly laid down. Oftentimes, the Z-Factors may even overshadow the formal or explicit criteria. That is life.

Promotion for Different Employee Groups

Promotion for Employees on Fixed-term Contract

D13.100 Many organisations have taken to hiring employees on fixed-term contracts (instead of permanent contracts) so that they can have better flexibility to adjust their staffing levels if the business situation calls for it. The proportion of employees on fixed-term contracts is on the rise and may even become the new default employment arrangement.

D13.101 Just like employees on permanent employment, employees on fixed-term contracts also need to be motivated. They too desire career progression. There is no compelling reason not to promote an employee on a fixed-term contract if he proves to be suitable and capable of taking on higher responsibilities. They should not be discriminated against just because they are on fixed-term contracts. Their promotion should be based on the same criteria as for permanent employees.

D13.102 For ease of administration, an opportune time to promote an employee on a fixed-term contract would be at the renewal of his contract. The renewal contract should spell out the job scope of the new/higher position, as well as the new salary and the terms of employment in respect of the new/higher position.

Promotion for Employees near Retirement Age

D13.103 Organisations should not deny a deserving employee promotion on account of age. As long as an employee, regardless of his age, takes on a higher job, he should be duly considered for promotion, based on the same criteria as applied to other younger employees. Age should not be a disqualifying factor.

D13.104 In reality, some organisations demonstrate reluctance to promote older employees, especially to key or senior positions. The general notion is that the older employee would usually be less energetic or dynamic, and perhaps also more risk averse (not to rock the boat), since he has a shorter runway to complete before he retires. This notion is debatable, but the reality is that many organisations hold such notions (or concerns). Their succession planning framework invariably favours the younger candidates (say, in the mid-40s) as successors to the key/senior positions if these become vacated.

D13.105 The Tripartite Guidelines on the Re-employment of Older Employees only has one advisory statement on career management for older employees: *"Employers are encouraged to adopt a forward-looking approach in guiding employees on their career development at various age milestones. For example, conversations with mature employees (around age 45) can be centred on their future career plans and potential training and support from companies, while those with senior employees (around age 55) can focus on relevant skills and training needed for re-employment."* The advisory statement appears to be "neutral" (or silent) whether employees near retirement age should be given opportunities to be promoted.

Promotion for Employees on Re-employment

D13.106 The Tripartite Guidelines on the Re-employment of Older Employees is silent on promotion of employees under re-employment contracts. Generally, we do not expect re-employed employees to go for bigger/higher roles while they are on re-employment. There may however be exceptions, especially if a re-employed employee is highly valued for his deep and specialised expertise. If say, the organisation calls for a new role that requires deep and specialised expertise and there are no suitable candidates amongst the younger employees, the new role may land on the re-employed employee. If the new role is bigger/higher than the role held by the re-employed employee, then in all fairness, the re-employed employee should be re-graded or promoted accordingly.

D13.107 A re-employed employee should arguably not be promoted at the expense of other younger candidates who are equally capable and suitable. All things being equal, the opportunity should be given to the younger employees, so that the organisation can develop and refresh its talent pool continually, which is essential for its long-term success.

Promotion for Employees on Secondment

D13.108 Employees who are on secondment to other organisations should not fall out of the radar for promotion. If a secondee has performed well in the host organisation and he takes on a bigger/higher role, there is no reason to deny him the promotion. However, to consider a secondee for promotion, the organisation (the employer of the secondee) will have to rely on the assessment of the host organisation on how well the secondee has performed, and also the weight of the higher responsibilities that the secondee has taken on at the host organisation. This presents a challenge, as the host organisation may apply a different stringency in assessment. Generally, most organisations would prefer to defer the promotion decision until the secondee returns to the organisation, and the organisation has a chance to do one more assessment before deciding on the promotion. This is understandable since promotion is a staff action with a long tail.

D13.109 For the above reason, it is therefore not advisable for organisations to arrange long secondments for their employees. If a secondment stretches for several years, the secondee will be delayed in his career progression. It would be more ideal to keep secondments to only 1–2 years, after which the secondee should return to the organisation to apply his learning and resume his career progression within the organisation. Organisations should take care not to make secondments an unattractive proposition for their employees since secondments are an important feature in any talent development programme to help employees broaden their work exposure. For this reason, if an employee has performed well for his secondment, it should weigh in his favour. Human Resource must ensure that the secondees are not "neglected" or "forgotten", because the divisions where the secondees come from may conveniently bypass them and focus on their own in-situ employees.

Administration of Promotion

Frequency and Timing of Promotions

D13.110 Organisations have different practices for implementing promotions to suit their own organisational context.

Annual or Half-Yearly Promotion Exercises

D13.111 Large and established organisations usually conduct an annual promotion exercise. Those who operate in a fast-moving competitive environment may even conduct promotion exercises every half-yearly to reduce the window period where their good performers may leave.

D13.112 The main advantage of having annual or half-yearly promotion exercises (versus implementing promotions in an ad hoc manner) is that when promotion cases are reviewed in one single batch by the management, it allows the management to compare the relative merits of candidates, ensure consistent application of criteria and standards, thereby enhancing credibility and ultimately leads to better promotion decisions.

D13.113 Since promotions are held annually or half-yearly, there will be one or two common dates for promotions accordingly. The promotion date usually coincides with the annual increment date. The promotion exercise and the annual salary review exercise are usually conducted concurrently, following the conclusion of the annual performance appraisal. This arrangement makes sense as it streamlines and compresses the salary administration tasks within a common window period.

D13.114 While the annual/half-yearly promotion exercises are expected to catch all promotion cases, there may be one or two exception cases handled off-cycle. These exception cases may happen due to unforeseen circumstances (for example, a critical position may be vacated unexpectedly, leading to the urgency to promote the successor to the role; or a new unit needs to be formed to tackle an unforeseen challenge, thus the urgency to assemble the team, which may require some employees to be promoted).

D13.115 Some organisations prefer to put both the promotion and annual increment dates as the first day of a new financial year, to facilitate budgeting of manpower cost. On the other hand, there are other organisations that choose to conduct their annual promotion and salary review exercises (usually held concurrently) several months into the financial year, so as to spread out the workload of the line managers, finance and human resource in tackling the major corporate exercises, including annual budgeting, headcount review, performance goals setting, performance appraisal, promotion review, salary review, bonus payment, etc. Each organisation should set its own timings that best suit its organisational needs.

Ad Hoc Promotions

D13.116 Many private-sector companies promote employees on an ad hoc basis throughout the year. This may be more prevalent in organisations or strategic business units where the head of the unit has a lot of authority and autonomy in managing the business, operations, finances and manpower.

D13.117 Small and medium enterprises (SMEs) mostly do not adhere to a common date for promotions. Often, they take staff actions, including the grant of salary increments and promotions as a response to staff attrition and recruitment challenges, or as and when a new position is created. Few SMEs would want the rigidity of adhering to a fixed window to take staff actions. For SMEs, flexibility, rather than consistency, is more critical.

Procedural Steps for Promotion

D13.118 For organisations that hold structured promotion exercises, the common administrative steps are as follows:

- Step 1: Recommendations for Promotions
- Step 2: Collation and Initial Screening
- Step 3: Evaluation and Decision
- Step 4: Implementation

D13.119 Organisations may not regimentally follow the steps above. For example, Step 2 (usually done by Human Resource) may sometimes be skipped. The practices within each step may also vary considerably across organisations. Much depends on whether the human resource functions are centralised at the corporate level or decentralised to the various business divisions.

Step 1: Recommendations for Promotions

D13.120 In large and established organisations, promotions are typically managed centrally by Human Resource. At the conclusion of the annual performance appraisal exercise, the line heads will be asked to submit their recommendations of employees for promotion. Each recommendation should be accompanied with a citation on the employee, covering:

(a) the employee's performance in his current role;
(b) the employee's competencies and attributes;
(c) the job scope of the higher position that the employee will be promoted to; and
(d) how the employee has been tested on shouldering the higher responsibilities in respect of the higher position.

D13.121 For small and medium enterprises (SMEs) that do not hold structured promotion exercises, the process of recommendation may be informal, such as the line head relaying his recommendation to the boss directly.

Step 2: Collation and Initial Screening

D13.122 In large and established organisations, the task of collating and screening recommendations usually rests with Human Resource (HR). The recommendations are screened to ensure that the candidates meet the basic qualifying criteria (such as promotion time norms, minimum performance level and professional/functional competency requirements). HR may query the line head if a case is considered weak or unjustifiable. A department that has too many recommendations may also be questioned. This is a sensitive matter; it takes a HR head who has been given a clear mandate by the management and who commands the respect of the line heads to do this.

D13.123 HR should summarise and tabulate all the recommendations by departments and/or job grades. The summary should detail the candidates' profile, covering:

(a) years in service (YIS);
(b) years in current job/employee grade (YIG);
(c) years in current appointment (YIA);
(d) past promotion records;
(e) performance ratings in recent years, say, for the past 3 years;
(f) attainment of competencies and professional/accredited qualifications;
(g) significant achievements/contributions; and
(h) key personal data of the employee, such as age and disciplinary records (if any).

The summary should be accompanied by the citation by the line head in support of the promotion. HR should also categorically state whether the employee satisfies the criteria for promotion and whether the justification for promotion is supported or otherwise.

D13.124 HR should also provide a simple analysis of the promotion trend, such as the following:

(a) the number of recommendations versus the staff strength of each department or business unit;

(b) the number of recommended promotions as a percentage of the organisation's total employee population, broken down by job levels/bands;

(c) the promotion numbers and percentages in the recent years (say, past 3 years) for each department or business unit;

(d) the promotion numbers and percentages in the recent years (say, past 3 years) for the organisation, broken down by job levels/bands; and

(e) the increase in salary cost for the promotions, and whether the respective department or business unit has the manpower budget to accommodate the increase.

D13.125 If initial screening is done thoroughly and the relevant/critical information is provided, it would facilitate decision-making by the management. The value-add by HR in this respect is important. Needless to say, HR should play the screening role diligently and not serve merely as a "post-box" or "secretary" to collate recommendations mechanically.

D13.126 In the case of SMEs, recommendations for promotions usually go straight to the boss. HR may collate the recommendations but perhaps without any real value-added screening. Much is left for the boss to decide. Since the numbers are small in SMEs, this process is feasible, but in large organisations, this would be untenable.

Step 3: Evaluation and Decision

D13.127 In SMEs, the boss (the business owner) may just confer privately with his line heads and decide on the promotions. The boss does not need to adhere to any timeline or protocol, as well as any pre-set promotion criteria, since he has full authority over the company. The main consideration for the boss is to reward and retain his good employees.

D13.128 The scenario in large and established organisations is a world apart, although different organisations will have their own process of evaluating and deciding on promotions. The typical arrangement is for the recommendations to be channelled to a management committee for evaluation and decision. The committee may comprise senior management executives (say, division heads) and chaired by the Chief Executive Officer (CEO). For promotions to senior leadership positions (say, divisional heads or C-suite positions), the Board Nomination or Remuneration Committee may play the decision-maker role. The gravity of involving a management committee or a board committee signals that the organisation takes staff promotions seriously, recognising that a wrong promotion decision will impact the organisation adversely for a long time to come. This is especially so for senior leadership positions in public-listed companies, where a strong candidate appointed at the helm may nudge the stock price up, while a "doubtful" candidate will bring about a muted response.

D13.129 The management committee will usually convene deliberation session(s) to review the recommendations for promotions. HR will serve as the secretariat for such deliberation sessions to present the recommendations. Line heads may be called in to clarify information or answer queries from the committee.

D13.130 Often, line heads may lobby key decision-makers for support in advance of the deliberation sessions. How efficient and productive the deliberation sessions run would very often depend on how HR can facilitate and steer the discussion. Members of the committee (say, the division heads) would each have their vested interest in the recommendations and would question one another on the justifications. This process is to find a common "ruler" or standard that is acceptable to all. If there is an impasse during the deliberation, the chairman of the committee will have to break the impasse. HR should also value-add by prompting the necessary questions and reiterating the fundamentals (such as the criteria, the purpose and the impact) if the deliberation goes astray.

D13.131 In some large organisations, candidates who have been recommended for promotion may be required to go through a promotion interview as part of the evaluation process. The Singapore Civil Service is one such organisation. All Division I Officers (including Permanent Secretaries) who have been recommended for promotion must attend a promotion interview convened by the Public Service Commission.

D13.132 Typically, the promotion interview panel will comprise senior management executives (say, division heads) appointed by the CEO. The interview panel is usually the same evaluation committee that decides on the promotion. A senior HR representative should also attend to normalise the strictness and to guide the panel, for example, to refrain from posing questions that may be perceived as discriminatory (such as questions concerning a person's religious beliefs or conveying a disadvantage for those who have young children).

D13.133 Having a promotion interview as an added avenue for evaluation has its pros and cons. A promotion interview allows the panel to know the candidate better, including checking his personal motivation, career aspiration and leadership philosophy. However, a common grouse from candidates (and their line heads) is that interviews favour those who are eloquent and disadvantage those who are less expressive or overly modest. It takes discernment on the part of the panel to sieve through what is relevant or not relevant, and important or not important. For example, some technical jobs do not require the jobholder to be eloquent. The panel must bear in mind the person-to-job fit, and not use a common yardstick to evaluate all candidates without regard to the position (and job nature) that the candidate is being promoted to.

Step 4: Implementation

D13.134 Execution of promotion decisions is invariably carried out by HR. A promotion will come with all or some of these changes for the employee: (a) a higher job/employee grade, (b) a higher salary range, (c) a promotion increment, (d) a change in employment terms and benefits tied to the higher job/employee grade and (e) a higher position title. HR should follow up on the necessary actions. In some cases, if the promotion decision is delayed beyond the scheduled promotion date, the employee must be paid the salary arrears.

D13.135 It is good governance to issue individual promotion letters to the promoted employees; just a public announcement (say, by way of a staff circular) does not suffice. This is especially so if the promotion involves a change in employment terms and benefits tied to the higher job/employee grade. The promotion letter should spell out the change in terms explicitly; preferably, the employee should be asked to sign his acknowledgement. The promotion letter thereby becomes the de facto new contract letter between the organisation and the employee.

D13.136 For candidates who have been aware that they were recommended for promotion (for example, they had attended the promotion interview), it is a good gesture for the organisation to inform them of the outcome, prior to the public announcement of the successful promotion cases. This communication is usually entrusted to the respective line heads. The line head must take care not to cause the candidate to become demotivated for not getting his promotion. If the candidate has not been aware of his recommended promotion (that is, the recommendation was submitted by the line head without the knowledge of the candidate), then it is best not to dwell on the promotion matter.

D13.137 Organisations invariably announce successful promotions internally to all employees. This is for practical reasons since the promotions of employees will involve changes to the organisation chart and reporting lines for employees. Internal announcements are usually done via staff circulars or company newsletters and/or posted on the staff portal. Sometimes, promotions/appointments must also be reported to the respective regulatory agencies. For example, for public-listed companies, the promotion/ appointment of certain senior/key executives must be reported to the Singapore Stock Exchange, while for the banks, certain appointments must be reported to the Monetary Authority of Singapore.

Human Resource as the Critical Gatekeeper

D13.138 The role played by HR differs considerably across organisations. In one extreme, HR may function as a mere "post-box" or "secretary" handling the collation, documentation and administrative follow-up on promotion decisions.

D13.139 On the other hand, some HR departments are very proactive and give high value-add to the entire promotion process by playing the gatekeeper role to ensure that promotion decisions adhere to the organisation's promotion policy and are based on sound justifications. The gatekeeper role covers these aspects:

(a) Review and filter recommendations from line heads to check against promotion criteria (such as promotion time norms, minimum performance level and professional/functional competency requirements).

If a recommendation is out of line, to convince the line head to drop the recommendation, failing which, to flag the anomaly or deviation for management's attention, as well as provide HR's recommendation.

(b) Perform analysis of promotion trends (such as number of recommendations versus staff strength, past years' promotion numbers and salary cost of promotions versus budget) and to flag anomalies for management's attention, as well as provide HR's recommendation.

(c) Guide the quality and robustness of the dialogue in the deliberation sessions on the promotion recommendations.

(d) Guide the professional conduct of the promotion interviews (if any).

(e) Provide sound recommendations on promotion increments to ensure internal parity and market competitiveness.

D13.140 If HR performs the gatekeeper role effectively, it will go a long way to ensure good promotion outcomes for the organisation. To do this, HR must be given a clear mandate by the management. The HR head must also be someone who is respected by the line heads for his competency, objectivity and impartiality.

Challenges and Other Considerations on Promotion

Promotion is an Emotive and Political Exercise

D13.141 Promotion exercises quite often involve emotions and politics. Understandably, line heads have vested interest in seeing their own employees get promoted, as promotions are often used as a tool to reward and motivate employees. Some line heads may also feel a "loss of face" to have their recommendations rejected, hence emotions must be managed both sensitively and sensibly.

D13.142 The quest for promotion will invariably lead to competitiveness among employees in the same cohort or department. Such competition, if it turns extreme, can be negative. When one person gets promoted, it may cause his competitors to feel envious and disappointed for not being promoted as well. This may bring about a drop in morale and work performance (at least temporarily). While promoting deserving employees is the right thing to do in employee development, it can be challenging to manage.

Wrong Promotions are Very Costly

D13.143 Wrong promotions will lead to the organisation having employees perform at their level of incompetence. Line heads enjoy the goodwill of promoting their "unsuitable" employees but may not stay long enough to face the long tail of wrong promotion decisions. It is not tenable to demote an employee on realising that he has been wrongly promoted. These employees are unlikely to leave, as most may not be able to find equivalent positions at similar salary elsewhere. Meanwhile, they may block the career advancement of other more suitable employees. Capable employees working under incompetent managers/leaders will become restless and unhappy and will invariably and quickly leave for better learning and advancement opportunities elsewhere. The organisation will suffer from inability to retain good talent. Suffice to say, wrong promotions impact an organisation adversely in multiple ways.

Insufficient Promotion Opportunities

D13.144 If an organisation is expanding, there will be new positions created that offer promotional opportunities for its employees. However, if the organisation is already in its mature state, promotional opportunities will depend on whether there is staff attrition at the middle/senior positions. In an environment where employees stay for a long time (facilitated by a higher retirement age), promotional opportunities will be limited. Good employees who do not see sufficient career advancement opportunities will soon look elsewhere.

D13.145 Additionally, with many organisations flattening their organisation structure in order to cut bureaucracy and reduce the distance from "command" to "ground", there will be fewer middle-level managerial or supervisory positions. Opportunities for promotion will be reduced. One way to mitigate this challenge is to create sub-grades within a broad job band based on differentiated competency levels for the individual contributors.

D13.146 Succession Planning in organisations often calls for more than just one successor candidate for each key position, often as an "insurance", in case of any attrition of the candidates. This in itself is a "paradox" and presents a dilemma. When say, there are three candidates being groomed for one key position, the remaining two candidates will be left without a promotion should the key position become vacated. They may then leave, and this means a loss of good talent for the organisation. Hence, the organisation must have a plan to take care of the career aspirations of the "unsuccessful" candidates in order to motivate and retain them.

Promotions when the Organisation is Not Doing Well

D13.147 If an organisation is not doing well, it will be difficult to support a higher manpower cost. Promotions may be a cost the organisation can ill afford. The organisation may tighten promotions and judiciously allow only the most critical and urgent cases of promotions to proceed (and often the management must explain to other employees why these few promotions are allowed despite belt-tightening). Freezing all promotions may undermine the organisation's human capital development thrust, which is a long game. A total promotion freeze may also send a very negative and gloomy signal to employees and dampen employee morale.

D13.148 In reality, when times are tough, the organisation may stretch an employee to perform at a higher level, but without officially promoting the employee and giving him any salary increase (by way of promotion increment). This may be feasible for a transient period. The employee may be promised a due promotion and reward when good times return. But the wait should not be too long.

Support the Employee to Succeed

D13.149 Organisations should support their employees to succeed after their promotion by providing guidance as they assume the higher position. This is especially so when an employee is promoted from an individual contributor role to a managerial role.

D13.150 In large organisations, new graduate recruits join in a batch. At some point in time, one amongst the cohort may rise faster than the rest. If these graduate officers are peers within the same unit/department, the relationship can become awkward when one of them is promoted and becomes the "boss" of the rest. The organisation should prepare the new manager on how to lead and manage his team who are his former peers. Alternatively, the organisation may consider deploying the new manager to head another unit.

Motivating Those Not Promoted

D13.151 For committed and good performers who lack the potential and competencies to be promoted, it can be challenging to keep them continually motivated.

Line managers should recognise their good work appropriately and enable them to gain more intrinsic job satisfaction. They should also have honest and forward-oriented conversations with these employees on their career growth, render guidance and provide opportunities for them to learn and grow. Most employees are appreciative of such intent and effort of their managers, even though they may not get promoted.

Balance Internal Promotions with External Hires

D13.152 It is commendable for an organisation to try to nurture its own employees and groom them for senior positions, instead of importing ready-made external talent to fill senior positions as and when vacancies arise. Grooming internal talent allows employees to grow their careers within the organisation. However, the disadvantage is the risk of having too much in-breeding which may then lead to herd thinking, as the internal talent may become too accustomed to the thinking pattern of the current leadership. External hires, on the other hand, can inject fresh/new ideas and alternate perspectives, as well as bring along new contacts. They may also see things (and flaws) that the existing employees do not see. For this reason, a hybrid model of having both internal promotions and external hires (particularly in subject matter areas where the organisation is not strong in) would be a better strategy for the organisation.

Drastic Actions to Correct Wrong Promotions

D13.153 If an organisation is undemanding or if the work culture is "benign", employees who are promoted to their level of incompetence may cruise along and hang on for longer or until they retire or quit on their own.

D13.154 However, if the organisation is facing market and competitive pressure and when its shareholders demand performance and accountability, the management will be forced to take drastic measures which may include major organisation restructuring and manpower rejuvenation. The likely outcome is that employees who are not performing competently vis-à-vis their employee grades and remuneration packages will be nudged to leave or contractually terminated or retrenched. It bears out that wrong promotions adversely impact not only the organisation but also the (wrongly-promoted) employees themselves.

Talent Management and Succession Planning

Focus of this Chapter

In the preceding chapters of Volume D, we discussed human resource frameworks and constructs covering performance management, competency frameworks, job grade structure, career roadmaps, employee training, employee development and promotion.

We round up Volume D with a discussion on talent management and succession planning which touch on how an organisation can manage and develop an internal talent pipeline and select and develop potential successors to fill its critical and leadership positions. Talent management and succession planning are necessarily supported by the said human resource frameworks and constructs shared in the earlier chapters.

For talent management and succession planning to be meaningful, an organisation must have a certain workforce size and fairly sophisticated human capital management capability. The discussion in this chapter is in the context of large or decently sized organisations. Notwithstanding, the concepts that underpin talent management and succession planning are also useful for smaller enterprises.

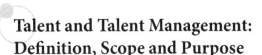

Talent and Talent Management: Definition, Scope and Purpose

D14.1   The term "talent" has often been loosely used to generically cover any employees or employee groups who are deemed to be of value to organisations. Terms like "local talent" and "foreign talent" have frequently been used. It appears that the term "talent", based on the context of its usage, actually refers to "manpower resource". Politically, it sounds better to call local manpower "local talent". It is also more persuasive to refer to foreign manpower as "foreign talent" so that the locals would perceive that the government is discerning in allowing only talent to be imported and not just any foreign worker (however, one must note that there has been no official definition for what is meant by "foreign talent" – does it refer to Employment Pass holders only? What about S Pass holders?)

D14.2   Similarly, the term "talent management" has been loosely used without a clear definition. Some organisations use "talent management" in the context of managing their general employee population, in which case it would mean the same as human resource management and development. Other organisations have in place talent management frameworks that are reserved for a specific segment of their employees – the high achievers, high potential executives, valued professionals and budding leaders – in which case "talent management" would be a component (or sub-function) under the ambit of human resource management and development.

D14.3   For clarity, we define the terms "talent" and "talent management" as what these refer to when used in this chapter. This is so that readers understand the focus and context of our discussion for this chapter.

Talent (as defined in this Chapter)

D14.4   In this chapter, "talent" refers to employees or employee groups whom the organisation has categorised as critical or important (or more important than the rest of its general employee population). That being the case, these select employees warrant special attention and additional measures to manage and develop them.

D14.5   Generally, for an organisation to select an employee as a "talent", the following 4 characteristics are used as filters: (a) performance, (b) potential, (c) values and (d) aspiration. The general employee population, after screening via the filters, will yield a select group of employees whom the organisation considers as "talent" who will be further distilled into a succession pool slated for its key and leadership positions.

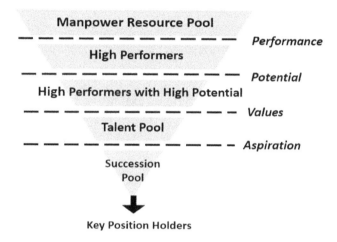

D14.6   All 4 filters are essential. Different organisations will set their own qualifying standard for each filter. The filters must be nuanced to suit the organisation's needs and context. We elaborate more on the 4 filters under the section "The 4 Common Criteria for Talent".

D14.7   Typically, an organisation will start the screening based on *performance*, to be followed by *potential*. This is practical because these 2 factors can be gleaned from the annual rounds of performance appraisals and potential assessments of employees. Next, before an employee from the filtered pool is admitted to the talent pool, his *values* will be scrutinised. Finally, when the organisation reaches the stage of identifying successors for its key and leadership positions, the *aspirations* of the candidates will be looked at.

D14.8   Generally, the "talent" group comprises high-performing and high-potential individuals whom the organisation wants to motivate and retain for its current business needs, as well as develop and groom to be its future leaders. However, there can be nuances to the talent requirements, depending on the type of organisation or the industry in which it operates. Some examples are shared below. Organisations must incorporate the nuanced requirements into their *performance* and *potential* filters so that the right talent pool can be identified.

- In large and established corporates, their "talents" are generally slated for top leadership and C-suite positions. They must be superior in intellectual abilities, business acumen, financial savviness and strategic vision.

- In the case of the public sector, capabilities in public policy conceptualisation, policy efficacy, execution efficiency, governance and fiscal prudence and stakeholder engagement are treasured.

- For organisations in niche industry sectors, their "talents" may be professionals who have specialised skills (such as engineers, researchers, scientists and niche artisans like chefs and designers).

Talent Management (as defined in this Chapter)

D14.9   For this chapter, we use "talent management" to mean an approach or framework (comprising policies, practices and initiatives) that is specially designed and targeted for a select group of employees whom an organisation has identified as its critical and important "talent" (as what we define for this chapter).

D14.10   Talent management encompasses various HR functions and practices aimed at unleashing and maximising the potential of the "talent" group and aligning their skills and competencies with the organisation's objectives and needs. Talent management should adopt a forward-looking lens to ensure that the organisation sustains its success in the future and hence it often integrates succession planning for its future leadership roles.

D14.11   A holistic talent management framework will encompass the following components:

Attraction and Acquisition	Strategic plan to attract and acquire (hire) employees who fit the curated "talent" profile so that they feed the talent pool for the organisation.
Training and Development	Systematic and comprehensive programs and interventions to train and develop the talent and enable them to actualise their full potential.
Rewards and Recognition	Competitive and holistic rewards and recognition program to motivate and retain the talent.

Deployment and Career Roadmaps	Proactive approach in planning and executing career roadmaps for the talent, involving strategic deployments to stretch them, coax their growth and maximise their contribution to the organisation.
Succession Planning	Identifying talent as future successors for the organisation's key/leadership positions, matched to their strengths and career aspirations.
Communication and Engagement	Regular and open communication, credible leadership and meaningful engagement initiatives to create emotional bonding with the employees.

D14.12 As talent management and succession planning (TMSP) require much planning, effort and resources, they are typically adopted in large and established organisations and the focus is on executives/professionals. It is rare for organisations to invest in TMSP for rank-and-file employees or junior executives/professionals for practical reasons. There may be exceptions; employees with certain niche skills (such as master craftsmen) can be regarded as talent assets and warrant being carefully tendered if they give a competitive advantage to their organisations.

Purpose of Talent Management and Succession Planning

D14.13 Organisations do not exist for the sake of developing and taking care of talent. Talent management is not done for altruistic reasons. The organisation invests time, money and energy in developing and looking after talent so that the latter will in turn grow to become their best and correspondingly, contribute at their best to the organisation. It is a mutually beneficial relationship between the organisation and the talent.

D14.14 In specific terms, the organisation and the employees (the talents) benefit in the following ways:

Benefits to the Organisation	Benefits to the Employee
Having a talent pool of capable employees enables the organisation to meet its strategic business and operational needs.	

Developing the talent to become their best enhances organisational capabilities and creates a competitive advantage for the organisation.	Comprehensive training and development opportunities enhance one's competencies and accelerate personal and professional growth.
Rewarding the talent competitively and fairly motivates the talent to pursue excellence and deliver exceptional achievements for the organisation.	Competitive and fair rewards provide motivation to perform.
Succession planning ensures a robust pipeline of committed and capable leaders and expert professionals to meet the future strategic needs of the organisation.	Systematic career charting and advancement opportunities enable one to achieve career aspirations and realise one's full potential.

The 4 Common Criteria for Talent

Performance and Potential: The Difference and Correlation

D14.15   To identify a talent pool, the organisation must invariably use both *performance* and *potential* as criteria (or filters) to segregate its general employee population into the talent and general/normal segments. It is a forgone conclusion that individuals who are high in both performance and potential are the ones who are most likely to succeed in their careers. A "talent" must check these two boxes, period. Organisations certainly would not view a low performer or a low potential as talent.

D14.16   Before we go into the mechanics of using *performance* and *potential* as filters to identify talent, it is useful to have clarity on what *performance* and *potential* mean and emphasise, and appreciate the difference between the two.

Performance versus Potential

D14.17   *What is the difference between "Performance" and "Potential"?*
Put simply, performance is premised on the <u>current</u>, while potential, the <u>future</u>.

Performance

It is a measure of an employee's work output and contributions in his <u>current</u> job role; it is about the actual result which has already been produced or showcased.

Potential

It refers to an employee's capacity, abilities and likelihood to grow and develop and eventually take on a role with higher responsibilities. It entails an assessment of an employee's attributes which can encompass the following: (a) innate cognitive ability or aptitude (manifested in power of analysis, critical thinking and helicopter view), (b) skills and competencies, (c) learning agility, (d) bias for action, (e) growth mindset, (f) leadership qualities, (g) creativity and (h) adaptability and resilience. Assessing an employee's potential is about making a calculated deduction of an employee's ability to scale the corporate ladder and succeed. It is a prediction of the <u>future</u>, albeit based on current assessment or current evidence. As potential assessment is complex, we discuss more under the section "Potential Assessment".

Correlation between Performance and Potential

D14.18 *How do performance and potential correlate? Is a high performer naturally a high potential? Should a low performer presumed to have low potential?*
There is some degree of correlation between performance and potential, but it is not always a tight one. In many instances, one can expect a high performer who has aced his current job to also have the bandwidth and capability to move up to a higher job. Likewise, for a low performer who is struggling in his current job, one would not expect him to have the capability to move higher up to a bigger job. Indeed, these two scenarios are common enough.

D14.19 However, there are exceptions to the performance-potential correlation. The following scenarios may occur:

- *When a High Performer may not be a High Potential*
  A high performer may be delivering excellent results by sheer diligence and familiarity with the current job (say, he has been doing the job for several years). This said employee may already be stretched to his maximum and have neither the bandwidth nor capability to move up to the next rung. Or perhaps the next higher job calls for a different set of competencies from the current job. This is the case for a sales person moving up to become a sales manager, that is, from an individual

contributor role to a managerial role. A high-performing sales person may not have the competencies needed for a sales manager (such as sales planning, market analysis, and training and leading the sales team). This category of employees is labelled as "Solid Performer with low versatility" in the Performance-Potential 3×3 grid that is covered in the next section.

- *When a Low Performer may be a High Potential*
  This scenario is not common but can happen. An employee may be observed to be of high capability (say, he is intelligent, business savvy, eloquent and confident by common standards) but he fails to deliver results in his current job. There may be underlying reasons for his low performance, such as, he is not interested in his current role, or he may be facing some issues/difficulties on a personal front that distracts him from his job. This category of employees is labelled as "Misfit" in the Performance-Potential 3x3 grid that is covered in the next section.

Values Alignment

D14.20   While performance and potential are the mainstay filters for identifying talent, organisations should also look at values alignment. This is important because values alignment underpins an employee's passion for the job and commitment to the organisation. If an employee's values are not aligned with those of the organisation, he will not feel engaged and will be less inclined to go the extra mile for the organisation. Chances are, he will not look towards building a long-term career with the organisation. For talent management to succeed, we need two willing partners. There is no point for the organisation to invest in an employee who has other interests and plans for himself.

Aspiration

D14.21   Aspiration is about one's ambition, dreams and priorities. Some people aspire to rise to the top of the organisation (or the highest that one can go) and lead big teams. Others may aspire to reach excellence in their chosen profession and be recognised as a thought leader or authority on the subject matter; they prefer to guide and mentor others to spread knowledge rather than to manage big teams. There are yet others who aspire to achieve success on both fronts – to lead in management as well as be a subject matter expert.

These nuances in an employee's aspirations are important when the organisation wants to identify successors for its key and leadership positions. Matching the right successors to the right future roles based on their aspirations materially enhances the success of succession planning.

D14.22   Additionally, one would expect high performers with high potential (labelled as "Star Talent" in the Performance-Potential 3×3 grid that is covered in the next section) to be ambitious to climb the corporate ladder, but there may be the occasional exceptions. Someone in this elite group may be content to remain at a rank where he feels comfortable and secure and has the luxury to pursue other life priorities (such as family or other passions outside of work). Such an individual is still a valuable asset to the organisation, although he will not be suitable as a successor for the organisation's key positions at the helm.

How the 4 Criteria Interplay and Impact Career Success

D14.23   All the 4 criteria are essential for a talent to rise to and succeed at the top ranks. If any one of the criteria is missing (or weak in the individual), the individual's likelihood to progress upwards to the top ranks will be materially affected. The ideal talent is one with high performance and high potential and is aligned with the organisation's values and aspires to rise to a key or leadership role in the organisation to deepen his contribution and impact. Some possible scenarios are illustrated below (note: the extent of the presence of each of the 4 criteria is depicted in the length of the respective shaded bar):

Performance	Performance	Performance	Performance
Potential	Potential	Potential	Potential
Values	Values	Values	Values
Aspiration	Aspiration	Aspiration	Aspiration
The Ideal Star Talent	*Disengaged Star*	*Passive Star*	*Engaged Dreamer*
Outstanding capability, aligned and fully engaged with the organisation and aspires to lead at the helm to deepen his impact. *Highly likely to succeed.*	Outstanding capability but does not believe that staying with the organisation is in his best interest. *Not likely to be persuaded.*	Outstanding capability and enjoys staying on but not hungry enough to climb up the ladder. *Will resist being pushed.*	Committed and ambitious but only of average ability. *Not likely to succeed.*

Performance-Potential 3x3 Grid

D14.24 To apply *performance* and *potential* as filters to sieve out a talent pool from the general employee population, a convenient way is to use a Performance-Potential 3x3 grid (with 9 boxes). An example is shown below. Each box denotes a certain profile of employees based on their performance and potential. (The labels used in the boxes such as "Star Talent", "Talent (to push)", "Misfit" and so on are for illustration only; most organisations devise their own labels.)

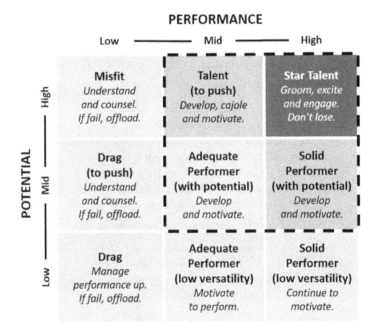

D14.25 *Which of the "boxes" should talent management and succession planning (TMSP) apply to?*
Organisations can decide how broadly (or narrowly) they want to apply their TMSP framework/program. One must bear in mind that TMSP is very resource-intensive and time-consuming and requires a lot of involvement

and attention from the management. This being the case, it is only practical for organisations to judiciously decide where to spend their time and money for TMSP on.

- *Applying TMSP to the elite category only*
  Some organisations would reserve their TMSP only for the elite category which comes with both high performance and high potential (dubbed "Star Talent" in the 3x3 grid). As this select group holds the highest promise to succeed, it makes sense for the organisation to give its special attention to them instead of diluting across wider categories of employees.

- *Extending a differentiated TMSP to immediate peripheral categories*
  On the other hand, there are organisations that prefer to cast the net wider and extend their TMSP to the immediate peripheral groups (dubbed "Talent (to push)" and "Solid Performer (with potential)" in the 3x3 grid). These two peripheral groups somewhat miss being top-notch in either performance or potential. The rationale for netting them into TMSP is the cognisance that performance and potential assessments are based on judgment and therefore subjectivity cannot be avoided. The assessments are not foolproof, and there may be instances where an employee may have missed being placed into the "Star Talent" elite category by a hairline. For this reason, organisations may prefer to include these two peripheral categories into their TMSP program, especially if their resources permit. That said, most organisations will apply a differentiated approach, that is, offer a diluted version of TMSP (aka, TMSP-minus) to these peripheral categories. Some organisations may even extend TMSP-minus to the "Adequate Performer (with potential)" category.

D14.26 How strictly the organisation wants to apply its TMSP or TMSP-minus programs, be it to reserve it for a narrow select talent group or to extend to wider groups of employees, will largely depend on whether it has enough resources to give special attention to these employees. It also depends on what the organisation has packed into its TMSP and TMSP-minus programs. The more comprehensive the TMSP and TMDP-minus are, the more resource-intensive and expensive they will be and hence affect how widely or narrowly the organisation can extend its investment. We further discuss this under the section "Key Talent Program" in the later part of this chapter.

Differentiated Performance and Developmental Interventions

D14.27 The ways to manage and develop employees with different performance x potential (PxP) permutations are necessarily different. This is because each PxP category has its own unique pain points and promise. Interventions must therefore be nuanced to be effective. A brief summary of the intervention approaches for each PxP category is provided below:

Interventions for High Potential	
Star Talent *High Potential x* *High Performance*	• Accelerate development and groom for leadership roles. • Excite with challenging and interesting assignments. • Engage to strengthen alignment and build commitment. • Keep on radar closely. Don't lose.
Talent (to push) *High Potential x* *Mid Performance*	• Motivate, cajole and push to scale up performance. • Provide development opportunities. Test out in other roles that better leverage on employee's strengths. • Pace out assigning higher responsibilities or moving to higher roles; employee must first scale up performance.
Misfit *High Potential x* *Low Performance*	• Engage via critical conversation to understand causes of underperformance. Support employee to overcome difficulties. • Counsel and push employee to improve performance. • Test out other roles that better leverage on employee's strengths and match his interests. • High potential is of no value to the organisation if it is not translated into performance. If underperformance persists, manage out.

Interventions for Medium Potential	
Solid Performer (with potential) *Mid Potential x High Performance*	• Motivate to sustain high performance. • Provide developmental interventions (including job postings and stretch assignments) that expose employee to higher-level thinking and broaden his perspectives. • Provide mentoring and coaching.
Adequate Performer (with potential) *Mid Potential x Mid Performance*	• Motivate to scale up performance. • Provide developmental opportunities to enhance skills and competencies.
Drag (to push) *Mid Potential x Low Performance*	• Engage via critical conversation to understand causes of underperformance. Support employee to overcome difficulties. • Counsel and push employee to improve performance. • Test out other roles that better leverage on employee's strengths and match his interests. • If underperformance persists, manage out.

Interventions for Low Potential	
Solid Performer (low versatility) *Low Potential x High Performance*	• Motivate to sustain high performance. • Engage to sustain morale and commitment. • Provide developmental opportunities to refresh knowledge and skills to maintain currency and safeguard employability. • Keep as dedicated and hardworking soldier.

Adequate Performer (low versatility) *Low Potential x Mid Performance*	• Motivate to sustain or scale up performance. • Provide developmental opportunities to refresh knowledge and skills to maintain currency and safeguard employability.
Drag *Low Potential x Low Performance*	• Engage via critical conversation to understand causes of underperformance. • Counsel and put under Performance Improvement Plan (PIP) to push up performance. • If fail PIP, manage out.

Potential Assessment

D14.28   An employee's potential is based on a complex composite of attributes. "Potential" is also contextual. A person who is viewed as a good or high potential by one organisation may not be viewed the same by another; it all depends on the unique needs of the said organisations. Obviously, every organisation must define its own requirements as to what good/high potential means. The requirements or attributes must take into account the type of industry an organisation operates in, as the attributes required for success will vary. Leadership and people philosophy may also be woven into the requirements.

Defining Attributes for High Potential

D14.29   Since organisations have very much a free hand in defining what good/high potential is, how should they go about doing it? A good place to start is to look at the attributes of its current successful leaders. *What attributes made them successful leaders?*

D14.30   Another important factor to consider is that an organisation should be future-oriented when it defines what potential means. *What kind of operating landscape or challenges will the organisation face in the future? What attributes must its future leaders have to navigate the organisation for success?* After all, the organisation is identifying the key talent whom it will groom to be its future leaders; the time horizon is medium to long-term, so it bears to consider what its future needs will be.

D14.31   Organisations that take their talent management and succession planning (TMSP) seriously will take great care in defining their "high potential" attributes. Potential assessment is used to identify the key talent group for grooming; getting it wrong will mean investing heavy resources in the wrong candidates. Worse, developing the wrong people and putting them into leadership positions will not bode well for the organisation's future.

D14.32   Large and established organisations which have a Human Resource team dedicated for the talent management (TM) function will usually go about their own to engage their senior management personnel on defining "potential". It may begin with the TM team interviewing senior leaders on what attributes they think make a great leader for the organisation, both current and future. The inputs will be collated and presented to the top/ senior management for discussion. Critical conversations will be held (usually facilitated by the TM team) to reach a consensus on the attributes that will define a great leader for the organisation – for the current, medium-term (say, 10 years on) and long-term (say, 15 years on). The attributes so derived will be used for doing potential assessment of high performers. Employees who pass the high performance and high potential filters will become shortlisted as candidates for the organisation's talent management and succession planning (TMSP) program.

D14.33   Some organisations prefer to engage external consultants to help them pin down the definition of "potential". The advantage of using external consultants is that the human dynamics will be better handled (after all, strong leaders have strong opinions), hence more open, candid and fruitful discussions/debates can be had. Experienced consultants may also point out omissions and blind spots. For smaller organisations that do not have their own TM team, engaging consultants to conduct an exercise on defining "potential" should be considered.

Examples of Attributes for High Potential

D14.34   Different organisations will have different definitions for high potential to suit their own context and needs. Although there will be variations and nuances, there are some attributes that are quite common across organisations, notwithstanding the different industry sectors. This is not surprising; a high-potential individual must certainly possess high cognitive ability (as in power of analysis, critical thinking and helicopter view), and additionally, he should have superb leadership qualities to lead and inspire people.

D14.35   The following are examples of how some organisations have defined "potential". Some of the examples are adapted from actual cases.

Example (Singapore Civil Service)
Potential assessment is based on **AIM** attributes.

A   **Analytical and Intellectual Capacity**
Analytical, good judgment, broad perspective

I   **Influence and Collaboration**
Inspire, collaborate, engage

M   **Motivation for Excellence**
Show commitment, take accountability, deliver results

Example (healthcare institution)
Potential assessment is based on **CARE** attributes.

C   **Capacity (HAIR qualities)**
Helicopter view, power of Analysis, Imagination, Sense of Reality

A   **Achievement**
Ambition, resilience

R   **Relationship**
Influence, collaborate, build teams

E   **Ethos**
Integrity, objectivity, moral courage, empathy

> Example (adapted from a global infotech company)
> Potential assessment is based on **Great Leader Model**.
>
> **Business Smart**
> *Know the business, know your business, improve the business*
>
> **Align & Team**
> *Influence, collaborate, work across functions, build relationships*
>
> **Motivate & Champion**
> *Develop others, celebrate success*
>
> **Get Things Done**
> *Move quickly, innovate, adapt, be accountable*
>
> **Killer Communicator**
> *Inspiring, passionate, story teller, stand and deliver*
>
> **Aloha Values**
> *Trust, integrity, character, compassion*

Assessing Potential

D14.36   Assessing (or estimating) the potential of employees is not an easy task; it is not an exact science. It requires keen human observations and judgment. The assessor must have sufficient interactions and dealings with the employee on work matters and gather clues and evidence from various sources, including the following:

> (a) papers and reports prepared by the employee – breadth, depth and clarity
> (b) ideas and proposals from the employee – quality, originality and persuasiveness
> (c) views expressed and questions asked by the employee at meetings and discussions – relevance, insights, sharpness and incisiveness
> (d) how the employee works with other people – collaboration (or competitiveness) and professionalism
> (e) the employee's involvement and contribution to special projects/ assignments – stretchability and versatility
> (f) employee's behaviour under pressure (during crisis or other critical incidents) – composure and decisiveness
> (g) employee's stay during tough times – stamina, resilience and commitment
> (h) employee's interactions with bosses, peers, subordinates and other stakeholders – social presence and confidence, authenticity and trustworthiness

Current Estimated Potential

D14.37   It is appropriate here to make reference to the Current Estimated Potential (CEP) concept. Shell (the multinational oil refining company) is the founder and pioneer of the CEP concept. Many Singapore government-linked organisations and the Singapore Civil Service have adopted or had previously used the CEP as an indicator of an employee's potential.

What is Current Estimated Potential?

D14.38   *Do "Current Estimated Potential" and "Potential" mean the same thing? What is the difference?*

- When we talk about assessing an employee's "potential", it can take on either a shorter-term or longer-term view. A shorter-term view is about assessing whether the employee has what it takes to assume higher responsibilities at the <u>next higher</u> job level. A longer-term view, on the other hand, is about pinpointing the <u>highest</u> job level that an employee is likely able to reach by the end of his career. The term "potential" is therefore an open one; it is up to one to use it in a short- or long-term view.

- "Current Estimated Potential (CEP)" on the other hand, is decidedly used in a long-term view. CEP is an assessment (or prediction) of the <u>highest</u> job grade/level that an employee is potentially able to reach at *the peak of his career*. For example, if an employee is assessed to have a CEP of CEO, it means that he is assessed to have what it takes to eventually reach CEO level of the organisation. Simply put, CEP denotes an employee's peak in his career (where he remains competent) and not just about his suitability or readiness to take on the next higher job role.

Assessing an Employee's CEP

D14.39   The CEP of an employee is arrived at by assessing how an employee scores on those criteria (or attributes) that the organisation views as necessary for scaling the corporate ranks and succeeding. Every organisation will have its own curated criteria suited to its own context and needs. For instance, the criteria for a leadership position in a commercial organisation will necessarily be quite different from that in a public or non-profit organisation.

D14.40 An employee will be assessed based on evidence of his current attributes and projected forward. There are two key points here. First, it is a forward projection, like making an estimation, hence the label "estimated" in CEP. Second, the assessment is based on the employee's current state. Most organisations would continually or periodically review an employee's CEP so as to take in new evidence (if any) of the employee's attributes to keep the assessment current. Hence the label "current" in CEP. To put it simply, an employee's CEP is simply an estimation of his maximum potential at the current review.

D14.41 The first CEP assessment for an employee is usually done after the employee has been in service for about two years in the organisation so as to allow time to gather evidence (or data points) of the employee's attributes.

D14.42 Organisations that subscribe to the CEP concept mostly apply it only to their executives/professionals. Some organisations may narrow it down to only certain job families or specific niche employee groups. Organisations which offer scholarships and management associate schemes invariably put candidates through a stringent selection process to ensure that only those with high potential and values alignment with the organisation get admitted; as scholars and management associates represent the organisation's talent pipeline, they invariably come under the rigour of CEP assessment.

Reassessing and Validating CEP

D14.43 Assessing CEP is not a one-off exercise. As the employee gains work experience and benefits from developmental interventions, he may blossom in his capabilities. An assessor may also get to know an employee more; his assessment may change and become more accurate.

D14.44 Most organisations carry out a reassessment every year or every two years until the employee reaches the age of about 35 or perhaps 40. The assumption is that the person's CEP is likely to stabilise after an adequate number of assessments have been done (each time reviewing any new evidence of his attributes or capabilities).

D14.45 The purpose of doing reassessment of CEP is to validate the accuracy of the earlier assessment or to adjust the CEP accordingly based on new evidence uncovered. In a normal (or calm) situation or familiar environment, it is easier for employees to deliver good results (when one is moving in the same direction as the wind, half of the battle is won). But these same performers may or may not fare well in a crisis or stretch situation. For this reason, organisations should deliberately create "test" situations for a talent. This may come in the following forms: (a) stretch assignments which are more complex and difficult, (b) cross-departmental projects where he works with multiple stakeholders and (c) new job postings where he reports to different supervisors and line heads. The key is to create multiple assessors so that their collective observations and inputs can mitigate bias and improve the accuracy of the employee's CEP assessment. In some situations, an organisation may invest in having selected employees go through assessment centres where the employees will have an independent assessment done by external consultants.

> A financial institution in Malaysia, having acquired a stockbroking firm, decided to have the competencies and potential of the executives and middle managers (from the stockbroking firm) assessed through an assessment centre. The participants underwent a series of intensive exercises and activities under the watchful eyes of the consultant assessors. A report card detailing the proficiency level of each of the competencies assessed, strengths and developmental areas for each participant was prepared. The institution used the findings to determine who should be offboarded or retained to be groomed for leadership positions.

D14.46   As an employee's CEP is continually reassessed in the early years of his service and may be changed (adjusted) as appropriate, for this reason, organisations generally do not inform their employees about their CEPs (at least not officially). CEP information is typically treated as confidential (although some line heads may unofficially hint to their staff). That said, because development and career advancement opportunities are differentiated for different CEP segments, employees may notice and compare the differentiated treatment they receive and thereby "guess" their assigned CEPs.

Differentiated Treatment based on CEP

D14.47   Generally, an employee's assigned CEP will impact him in the following ways:

(a) The pace of career progression for an employee will be differentiated based on his CEP. The higher his CEP, the faster his promotion is charted (the caveat being that he continues to perform well after each promotion). For example, if employee A has a CEP of CEO while employee B has a CEP of Division Head, the pace of promotion for employee A will be faster than that of employee B since employee A will have more ranks to attain before he retires.

(b) Training opportunities will be differentiated in kind based on the employee's CEP. For example, an employee with a CEP of CEO will be slated to attend an advanced management development program at a renowned business school while those with a CEP of departmental head may attend a locally run general management program.

(c) Developmental opportunities in the form of stretch assignments, special projects and job postings will be differentiated according to the developmental needs of the employee. An employee with a higher CEP will necessarily be given more challenging and diverse opportunities to develop and prepare him for his future role. Mentoring and coaching by senior management personnel are also mostly reserved for the select few with high CEP.

Management Involvement and Oversight

D14.48   Organisations that practise the CEP concept invariably pay close attention to their employees who have been assigned high CEP. In many instances, the senior management will invest time to oversee the determination and review of CEPs and decide on which employees should be enrolled or offloaded from its talent management program (sometimes referred to as High Potential scheme) that is reserved for employees who are of the [high performance x high potential] category (referred to as "Star Talent" in paragraph D14.24). The senior management team is also likely to be involved in considering and approving the job postings and promotions of these talents, as well as selecting from among this elite group the potential successors to the organisation's key/leadership positions.

Merits and Demerits of CEP

D14.49   CEP as a concept and tool used for talent management has its supporters and opponents. The CEP assigned to an employee will determine the kind of treatment he gets in terms of training and development opportunities as well as his career progression. For something as "powerful" as CEP, understandably, there are concerns and contentions.

D14.50   The reasons for supporting the use of CEP to guide human resource decisions include the following:

(a) Potential is a predictor of future performance. Investing in people is akin to investing in a business; one would pick the deal that offers a higher chance of success or better return.

(b) Developing employees is a costly affair in terms of time and resources and hence it is untenable to give all employees equal treatment. It is more cost-effective to target an elite group. CEP is the tool to identify the elite group (that is, those with high potential).

(c) Offering the same treatment and development opportunities to all employees may placate some employees but those with high potential may be demotivated by being treated as "average"; they need to be recognised as "special" to feel motivated to stay.

D14.51 Those who disapprove the use of CEP usually cite the following reasons:

(a) CEP estimation is subjective; hence it can be influenced by the bias and perceptions of the assessors. Compared to performance assessment which can be quantified in terms of work results (at least to some extent), CEP estimation is more nebulous. It depends on how detailed or sharp the assessor has been in observing or interacting with the employee over work.

(b) The first CEP assessment is done at the early stage of an employee's career (typically by the end of the second year of service). The contention is whether there are enough data points to make a fair and accurate CEP assessment. Moreover, an employee's CEP may change over time.

(c) It is inequitable to offer differentiated treatment (in terms of job postings, training and development opportunities and pace of promotions) based on the CEP of employees. Better treatment gives high-CEP employees a decisive and early advantage over the rest of their peers; it accelerates their learning and development and thus becomes a self-fulfilling prophecy for them to do well.

(d) The reliance on CEP to do talent management may lead to overlooking individuals who may have untapped potential or who require additional support and development to unlock their potential fully. Late bloomers are disadvantaged in the CEP regime as they will be deprived of the training and development support that they so need to stimulate their growth; they will end up being under-developed or sub-optimised.

(e) With the roll out of the new workplace fairness legislation, using CEP (which is subjectively determined) to chart an employee's development and career progression can be easily challenged and become a target for discriminatory claims.

Measures to Mitigate the Demerits of CEP

D14.52   Organisations that practise CEP are largely cognisant of the contentions (or problems) against the use of CEP to guide talent management. Most of the contentions/problems highlighted can be managed or mitigated to a large extent if the CEP system is designed and administered properly. Organisations can put in specific mitigation measures, including the following:

Contention/Problem	Mitigation Measures
CEP assessment is subjective.	CEP assessments must be moderated upon (much like how performance ratings are moderated by a management panel). The CEP moderation panel should apply rigour in its review to ensure proper calibration and better consistency in standards.
The first CEP assessment is too early; an employee's CEP may change over time.	The organisation must institute the discipline of reviewing an employee's CEP every year or every two years and adjust his CEP (if necessary). Reassessment should take inputs from multiple assessors, which can be arranged via cross-department projects and new job postings for the employee.
Differentiated talent management approach based on CEP feeds a self-fulfilling prophecy. Late bloomers may be disadvantaged under the CEP regime.	At the year/bi-yearly review of an employee's CEP, the reassessment should correlate the employee's CEP with his performance. An employee who is assessed to have a high CEP and given higher-tier training and development opportunities (such as more intensive and diverse training coupled with special assignments and job postings to test his application of learning) but who fails to deliver good performance should be singled out for attention; if there are no extenuating reasons to explain the underperformance, his CEP should be adjusted down. Likewise, for a converse case. If an employee is assigned with a low CEP but gradually shows high performance, his CEP should be double-checked and adjusted up if necessary.

Alternative Approach: Next Level Potential

D14.53   Arguably, the Current Estimated Potential (CEP) regime is not a perfect indicator or a totally equitable basis for developing an employee and managing his career. It is pertinent to note that Shell company and the Singapore Civil Service which have been using CEP for their talent management for many years, have already discarded the use of CEP. On the other hand, many organisations are still searching for a "right" approach to handle the matter of "potential".

D14.54   *How about discarding the use of potential assessment entirely?*
If there is no potential assessment, what is left is only to assess an employee's performance. Without doubt, relying solely on employees' performance in their current roles will be grossly insufficient as the basis to identify the elite group suitable for grooming as successors for the organisation's key/leadership positions. Good performance in a current role/rank does not mean the employee can also perform competently in a higher role/rank. For example, a top sales person may not make a good sales manager/director as the competency requirements are different. That being the case, to entirely discard "potential" and rely solely on "performance" as the talent filter is out of the question.

D14.55   If one is to distil the main discomfort over the use of CEP as a talent filter, it is that CEP assessment is likened to doing a crystal ball forecast about a person's "peak" in his career which may well be some 20 years or more down the road. The time horizon is just too far; the longer the time horizon, the more nebulous the estimate.

D14.56   *If CEP is not used as a talent filter, what is the alternative?*
Instead of using CEP, organisations can consider Next Level Potential (NLP) as an alternative. The NLP of an employee is simply an assessment of whether he can perform competently at the next higher job level/band. After he has progressed to the said higher job level/band, another NLP assessment will be made whether he can perform competently at yet the next higher job level/band. Since the assessment on hand is always about the immediate next higher job level/band, an employee's NLP will be relatively more accurate to assess and predict, compared to the crystal ball forecast of an employee's CEP (his peak level which may materialise only some 20 years or more down the road). The NLP is thus more credible and should see less opposition than the CEP.

D14.57   To operationalise NLP, an organisation may categorise its jobs into, say, 4–5 job levels/bands as shown below. If the organisation has already a job grade/band structure in place, it may just apply the same categorisations. Within each level/band, there can be a few sub-levels. For example, the Executive level/band may be broken down to Executive, Senior Executive and Assistant Manager.

❶ →	❷ →	❸ →	❹
Executive/ Professional	**Manager/ Lead Professional**	**Management/ Master Professional**	**Top Management**
Executive Senior Executive Assistant Manager	Manager Senior Manager Assistant Director Deputy Director	Director Senior Director	Assistant CEO CEO

The above nomenclature is for illustration only. Organisations may use different nomenclature (for example, Vice President may be used instead of Director).

NLP has a Short to Medium Time Horizon

D14.58   An employee with a positive NLP (that is, he has the next level potential) may take, say, anywhere from 5 to 10 years to go from his current job level to the maximum of the next higher job level. For example, if the employee is currently a Manager and assessed with a positive NLP to go to Management level, he may take, say, about 10 years to go from Manager to Senior Director (the maximum of the next level). Another employee who is currently a Deputy Director may take, say, about 5 years to go from Deputy Director to Senior Director. The NLP time horizon is therefore short to medium term. And once an employee has reached the said next level, he will be assessed again in NLP whether he can succeed in yet the next higher level. In essence, NLP is about assessing an employee's potential for the short to medium term on a continual basis.

D14.59   If an employee is assessed with a positive NLP, the organisation has a reasonable time horizon of 5–10 years to test and develop him. The period is long enough for some meaningful developmental interventions such as curated training programs, special/stretch assignments, job postings and mentoring to take place. These serve to develop and prepare the employee for his future role at the next higher level.

Merits of NLP

D14.60   The NLP will attract less criticism compared to the CEP. It has the following merits over the CEP:

(a) NLP assessment which is predicting an employee's ability to scale the next higher level should be more accurate and credible compared to CEP assessment that is crystal ball gazing to an employee's peak;

(b) NLP which rests on a short to medium horizon of 5–10 years gives more focus to planning developmental interventions for the employee than CEP which stretches to a very long term; and

(c) talented and ambitious employees will be kept on their toes because they must continually perform well and demonstrate their capabilities to earn another positive NLP assessment before they can progress further up.

NLP Plus

D14.61   Organisations may consider introducing NLP Plus to augment the NLP. The NLP Plus is an assessment that the employee has the potential to perform competently at two job levels higher than his current level. For example, (using the progression shown in paragraph D14.57, an employee who is currently in Manager/Lead Professional level may show clear signs that he can potentially rise to the Top Management level). NLP Plus should strictly be reserved for employees who show clear and exceptional signs and traits of high potential.

Key Talent Program

D14.62   To recap, at the start of this chapter, we have defined "talent management" to mean an approach or framework (comprising policies, practices and initiatives) that is specially designed and targeted for a select group of employees whom an organisation has identified as its critical and important talent. This is the focus and context for this chapter. Talent management as we refer to in this chapter is not the same as managing the general employee population.

D14.63   Some organisations, in an attempt to communicate and emphasise the intent of their talent management program, give special names to it, such as "key talent program", "star talent program", "high potential scheme" and the like. The message conveyed with these names is that the program/scheme is reserved for a select group of employees who satisfy specific criteria that make them the elite talent group that warrants special attention from the management. For simplicity, for the rest of our discussion under this section, we use the name "Key Talent Program (KTP)". In essence, the KTP is just a special name for what we earlier referred to as talent management and succession planning (TMSP).

D14.64   A key talent program (KTP) (or by whatever equivalent name it is called) invariably holds the elite talent group that will undergo systematic interventions to accelerate their development, motivate and retain them, and groom them as successors for the organisation's key/leadership positions in the future. The KTP must integrate cogently with the other components of human capital management and development (this is covered in the section "Integrating Talent Management and Succession Planning with Other Human Capital Initiatives"). Specifically, the KTP will spell out how these select employees (aka key talent) will receive special attention in terms of training and development and rewards and recognition. Effort is also not spared in engaging them; most organisations closely monitor the resignation rate of employees under the KTP.

Eligibility for Key Talent Program

D14.65   Organisations must define the eligibility criteria for admitting employees into the KTP, which should suit their own unique context and needs and align with the objective of the KTP. For example, an organisation may set these criteria to define its target employees:

(a) a minimum length of service;
(b) a minimum and maximum for the employee's current grade (that is, below the minimum grade, an employee is considered too junior to be admitted into the KTP, while at the maximum grade, an employee should "graduate" out of the KTP);
(c) a threshold performance (a minimum rating averaged over [x] number of years);
(d) a threshold potential that the employee must have (based on CEP, NLP or NLP Plus or any other method that the organisation uses to assess potential); and
(e) aspiration to lead and make a bigger impact on the organisation.

Example (adapted from a global infotech company)

Eligibility Criteria for Key Talent Program (KTP)

- In service for 2 years or more
- Current grade X to Y (Individuals will graduate from the program when they reach grade Y)
- Performance ratings of 4 or better (on a scale of 1–5) over recent 2 years
- *Great Leader* attributes (as per the organisation's Great Leader Model) – business smart, align & team, motivate & champion, get things done, killer communicator and aloha values
- Ability and willingness to move into bigger and broader roles at Vice President level (or professional equivalent) or higher

The management will review the shortlisted candidates. A maximum of 10% of the cohort in grade X to Y may be admitted to the Key Talent Program.

To Tell or Not to Tell the Employee

D14.66   Typically, after the conclusion of the annual performance appraisal, Human Resource (HR) will request line heads to nominate employees whom they assess to be high performers with high potential. Line heads will consult with the respective reporting officers since they have the most interactions with the employees on work matters and can make close observations on their attributes.

D14.67   The nominations from line heads will be collated by HR and tabulated for review by the management. Most organisations convene a panel to do calibration and ensure rigour and consistency in standards. The final candidates endorsed by the panel will be admitted into the key talent program (KTP).

D14.68 *Should the organisation tell or not tell the employee that he is admitted into the KTP?*

Some organisations choose to be transparent about it, while others prefer to keep it confidential. There are pros and cons to telling. Organisations must decide for themselves which way is better for them. A lot depends on the organisation's people culture, whether it is one of collegiality or competitiveness.

Pros of Telling	Cons of Telling
• Builds confidence in the employee • Motivates him to do even better • Employee feels recognised; builds loyalty • Enhances retention of employee	• Employee may become arrogant • Risk of information shared (although supposed to be confidential to the employee only) • Invidious comparisons among employees, causing tension • Other employees may feel demoralised

D14.69 The follow-up under the transparent approach (telling the employees) and confidential approach (not telling the employees) will be somewhat different.

Transparent approach
From an initial shortlist, HR may invite the employees to go through psychometric profiling. Some organisations even put them through an assessment centre. They may also be interviewed by the senior management. The employees know the processes and the outcome of the selection. As there is transparency, HR and the management can openly share about the KTP, but the names of the employees admitted to it will not be publicly shared.

Confidential approach
Some organisations prefer to be discreet. The employees admitted to the KTP are not informed. Their names will not be publicly shared. In fact, the KTP is not openly discussed in the organisation. In reality, however, after a while, the employees on the KTP are likely to guess their status as they are given some "special" treatment such as attending curated leadership programs, assignments to special projects and invitations to events to interact with the senior management. However, there will be no official confirmation from the management.

Developing Employees under the Key Talent Program

D14.70   Employees under the KTP undergo specially curated training and development that aim to accelerate their learning and growth, so as to prepare them for new and higher roles that come with increased complexity and managerial breadth.

D14.71   The common training and developmental activities include the following:

- Milestone and curated executive/management and leadership development programs
- Assignment of stretch performance goals
- Performance feedback and coaching by line head
- Involvement in high-impact project teams, committees and taskforces
- Job rotations, transfers and secondments
- Special postings and appointments
- Acting appointments (or covering for line head at high-stakes meetings)
- Exposure to senior-level meetings, events and platforms
- Mentoring and executive coaching

D14.72   The training and developmental interventions enable the key talent to learn holistically through formal training as well as by doing and experiencing and learning through others. Some organisations deliberately send their key talent for a short attachment in frontline roles so as to humble them and make them more appreciative of the challenges of the frontline "soldiers".

D14.73   Some organisations break down their KTP into different tiers. This is necessary if the organisation has applied some leniency in admitting employees into the KTP. For example (referencing the Performance-Potential 3x3 grid covered in paragraph D14.24), other than admitting employees from the "Star Talent" category, it also admits employees from the immediate peripheral categories of "Talent (to push)" and "Solid Performer (with potential)". If this is the case, the KTP should be differentiated accordingly, that is, a diluted version of the KTP (aka, KTP-minus) should be offered to the peripheral categories. An example of this approach is shown below:

Training and Developmental Activities	KTP	KTP-minus
Milestone executive/management/leadership development programs	●	●
Stretch goals, performance feedback and coaching by line head	●	●
High-impact project teams, committees and taskforces	●	●
Exposure to senior-level meetings, events and platforms	●	●
Job rotations, transfers and secondments to core and strategic functions	●	●
Acting appointments (or covering for line head at high-stakes meetings)	●	
Job shadowing senior management personnel	●	
Mentoring by senior management	●	
Executive coaching	●	
360-degree feedback	●	
Scholarship for Executive MBA or advanced professional equivalent	●	
Individual career roadmap	●	●

Please refer to Chapter D12 "Employee Development" for more elaboration on the design and execution of various developmental activities.

Engaging Key Talent

D14.74 Given the high investment in the key talent, it makes business sense for the organisation to step up its engagement with them, so as to enhance the emotional bonding and build loyalty. Most organisations closely monitor the resignation rate of key talent under the KTP.

D14.75 The engagement is usually done at two levels:

(a) First, Human Resource (HR) would do periodic check-ins with the key talents to ensure that they are benefitting well from the training and developmental interventions. Feedback will be taken in and addressed as appropriate. HR would also monitor that they remain motivated and in high morale.

(b) Second, opportunities will be created for the key talent to interact with senior management personnel. These may include the following:

> • Occasional breakfast/lunch meetings with senior management personnel
> • Serving as secretaries in senior management committees or meetings
> • Assisting a senior management staff in specific projects
> • Senior management personnel conducting small group sharing on, say, overcoming an actual business challenge, how to navigate moral dilemmas in a business environment, how to deal with paradoxical principles/situations, how to stay on top of the game in a VUCA (volatile, uncertain, complex and ambiguous) world

D14.76 Other than creating bonding, the engagement sessions with senior management personnel have developmental elements because their conversations will inevitably touch on experiences, work issues, strategic initiatives and organisational plans. Interactions in a social setting (such as breakfast/lunch meetings) also help the key talents build self-confidence and improve their executive presence. Over time, they will feel comfortable interacting with people in high positions and this will stand them in good stead as they progress up the career ladder.

Management Oversight of Key Talent Program

D14.77 In organisations that have a KTP, the senior management will invest time and attention to it. Often enough, the chief executive officer (CEO) will chair the committee that oversees the review of shortlisted candidates for admission into the KTP, as well as offload any key talents who have not measured up. For succession planning, there is usually a senior-level talent/manpower committee (chaired by the CEO or a designated deputy) which meets quarterly or half-yearly to review the performance, development, job postings and even the well-being of the key talents. The committee will look at issues on succession planning, identify successors and monitor the execution of the succession plan. In some cases, the board of directors may also want to be kept apprised.

D14.78　Such senior management oversight of the KTP sends the message to line heads that the key talents are regarded as "collective assets" of the organisation. Line heads will not be allowed to hog the key talents; this will enable them to be rotated to other roles according to their development plans and career roadmaps as well as in line with organisational needs/objectives.

Succession Planning

The What and Why of Succession Planning

D14.79　Succession planning is a strategic process implemented by organisations to identify, develop and test employees who have the potential, values alignment, commitment and aspiration to fill key leadership positions in the future. The leadership roles comprise both existing positions and new ones that may emerge from the changing needs of the organisation in dealing with challenges and capturing opportunities in the operating landscape.

D14.80　The goal is to ensure that there is a smooth transition of leadership when key executives retire, leave the organisation, or are promoted to higher roles. This will ensure continuity, stability and retention of institutional knowledge and organisational competencies. Also, when new senior roles are created, the talent and succession pool should have credible candidates to take on the challenges, unless the roles are in a new field where expertise and experience can only be found outside of the organisation.

D14.81　Large and established organisations take succession planning seriously. The process and execution are typically driven and overseen by the top leaders and board of directors.

D14.82 Succession planning should be guided by the following principles:

(a) *Future-oriented*
Planning should not be solely based on the current scenario; it must be future-oriented. The leadership team helming the organisation, in terms of its profile and composition, should be continually refined and rejuvenated to meet the evolving needs of the organisation and deal with future challenges and opportunities.

(b) *Alignment*
The end is to build and sustain a capable, resilient and united leadership team to steer the organisation. Successors must resonate with the organisation's values, vision and mission.

(c) *Commitment to develop, groom and retain internal talent*
The organisation must be committed to investing in internal talent with potential and systematically nurture and prepare them to assume senior leadership roles so as to actualise their full potential.

(d) *Open to assimilate new talent*
If there is no available talent from within, the organisation must be proactive and do early sourcing from outside so that the new hires have time to assimilate and be tested.

D14.83 Succession planning is an initiative that takes up heavy management resources. It is also a long game; results may take years to bear fruit. In brief, succession planning involves the following steps:

D14.84   As succession planning is a long-term initiative spanning many years, the organisation must continually monitor the evolving changes in its operating landscape to assess how these may impact its manpower and leadership needs; it calls for a loop back to the starting step of identifying its key mission-critical roles. Additionally, potential successors identified must be tested and if any do not match up, it will call for a review of the succession plan.

Identify and Define Key Mission-Critical Roles

Identify the Critical Roles

D14.85   An organisation must first identify its key mission-critical roles. The following questions may be used to guide the process:

> Q1: *Which are the roles that help chart and steer the organisation's strategic direction?*
> Q2: *Which are the roles that are entrusted with managing a significant proportion of the organisation's resources/assets and are held accountable for giving a good return?*
> Q3: *Which are the roles that spearhead and manage the key operations and processes?*
> Q4: *Which are the roles where mediocrity will greatly impact the organisation's success?*
> Q5: *Which are the roles that require deep institutional and industry knowledge?*

D14.86   The selection of the critical roles depends greatly on the organisation's business needs, how the organisation is run and its people management philosophy. Most organisations will consider the first one or two layers of positions that report to the chief executive officer (the C-1 and C-2 positions) as critical roles; the obvious reason being that these positions would give a "Yes" response to the first 4 filter questions (Q1–Q4). However, this may not always be the case. Some organisations decidedly use the 5th filter question *"which are the roles that require deep institutional and industry knowledge?"* to narrow down their list of critical roles for succession planning. For example, if a C-1 or C-2 position does not particularly require deep institutional and industry knowledge, the organisation may hold the view that these positions can be filled with external talent should they fall vacant. In fact, some organisations may even deem it desirable to inject new external talent when the time calls for it.

Actual Example

Organisation ABC decidedly does <u>not</u> include these senior management positions for succession planning: *director of human resource, director of infotech, director of communications and director of legal.* Director positions relating to corporate support functions, while viewed as senior (and important), are not considered "mission-critical". In comparison, director positions relating to core operational areas are included as critical positions for succession planning.

The organisation holds the view that the talents for specialist corporate support functions are fungible (that is, transferable from industry to industry). While institutional and industry knowledge is good to have, the lack of it is not a showstopper. For this reason, the organisation deems that these positions can be filled with external talent should they fall vacant.

This is not to say that a second officer in these said functions with good potential will not be developed or nurtured. For example, if a deputy director of human resource is of high potential, he will be given training and development opportunities to help him grow. It is just that the organisation will not be devoting high attention to ensure that it lines up a list of potential successors for the director of human resource position.

D14.87 Organisations may also view certain niche specialist/professional roles (at the top level) as mission-critical. Examples are chief engineer, chief data scientist, chief researcher, master designer and master chef. The key is to examine whether the lack of an internal talent pipeline for these niche specialist/professional positions at the top level will hamper the organisation's continual success. If this is the case, the organisation should include these positions in its critical list and devote attention to its succession planning.

D14.88 The list of critical roles is dynamic. As the organisation evolves, expands and adapts to the operating environment, new critical roles may be created, and existing critical roles may be expanded, modified or delisted. The key is to do continual review and not let the list of critical roles become obsolete and irrelevant. It would defeat the purpose of doing succession planning.

Define the Requirements for the Critical Roles

D14.89 Identifying the critical roles is only the first step. The organisation must have clarity on what these critical roles require of the potential successors:

(a) First, look at the current job description as one source of information. It should describe the core functions and accountabilities of the said role, as well as the prerequisites, which must include the core and leadership competencies and other attributes that the jobholder must have.

(b) Next, apply a future lens to the role requirements – *how will the role evolve? What are the future (foreseeable) challenges and accountabilities that this role must tackle?*

(c) Finally, turn the attention to describing the "perfect" successor profile – *what experiences and exposure should the potential successor have so that he can take on the future role competently?*

Example: Requirements of Chief Operation Officer

- Core and leadership competencies and attributes: As per current job description

- Competencies of growing importance in the near and medium to long-term future
  (to be deliberated upon and articulated by the KTP succession planning committee, possibly with involvement from the board of directors)

- Experiences/exposure that a potential successor should have:
  - ▶ worked in at least 3 core divisions
  - ▶ undergone at least 2 overseas postings
  - ▶ managed a significant critical incident or organisational transformation

---

Identify Potential Successors

D14.90   After the critical roles have been identified and their requirements defined, the next step is to scan and match suitable candidates under the KTP as potential successors. The profiles of KTP candidates should be scrutinised for the following:

Evaluating the Profile of a KTP Candidate as Potential Successor
- Academic and professional qualifications
- Number of years and types of work experience (function and geographical coverage)
- Proficiency levels of core and leadership competencies
- Past performance appraisal ratings
- Temperament and energy
- Alignment of values
- Commitment and resilience
- Aspiration

D14.91   Each critical role should preferably have two potential successors, where one is "primary" (that is the prime candidate) and the other "secondary" (that is, the reserve candidate). This is advisable, as although the organisation will do its best to engage and retain the potential successors, it is impossible to guarantee that they will stay, as in a tight labour market, key talents are invariably high targets for poaching by other employers.

D14.92   In the selection of potential successors, organisations may want to consider diversity in terms of gender and other attributes (say, racial, cultural, etc.). It makes business sense as having diversity brings about broader perspectives and makes the leadership team more robust and dynamic. Going for diversity does not mean compromising meritocracy. It only means that where two candidates are almost equal in merit, the one who will add diversity to the leadership team would be accorded an advantage.

Develop and Test the Potential Successors

D14.93   Having identified the critical roles and potential successors, the next step is to develop and test the potential successors. This can be done by assigning them stretch goals, special project work and other assignments as well as job postings meant to get them out of their comfort zones and test their competencies, commitment, adaptability, versatility, resilience and values alignment. Please refer to paragraph D14.71 in the earlier section "Key Talent Program" for the array of developmental activities/interventions that a potential successor can be put through. The planned activities/interventions must be diligently followed through because often, in the flurry of operational demands and sometimes firefighting, for the sake of expediency, potential successors may be diverted to meet urgent manpower needs and in so doing, their curated developmental plans may be put on the backburner or even derailed entirely.

Readiness of Potential Successors

D14.94   The readiness of each potential successor for a critical role must be determined, notwithstanding that the process is somewhat predictive in nature. "Being ready" does not mean that the candidate must be equal in effectiveness to the current incumbent. The current incumbent may have been in the said role for quite some years and likely has attained mastery of it. On the other hand, an appointee who is new to the role will understandably need some time to find his footing. A talented successor should be able to acclimatise quickly once he is on the seat, scale up and carry the baton effectively in his own way.

D14.95 The readiness of a potential successor may be described as follows:

- Ready for succession now
- Ready for succession within 1–3 years
- Ready for succession within 4–5 years
- Ready for succession within 6–8 years

D14.96 The readiness data of potential successors must be reviewed and updated periodically considering each individual's pace of professional and personal growth. At times, the role that a potential successor is slated to fill may change or grow bigger or more complex; such changes will affect the fit and readiness of the said potential successor. If the changes are extreme, it may even call for a change of potential successors for the said role. Needless to say, succession planning is fluid and can be unpredictable.

D14.97 Understandably, potential successors who are deemed to be only ready say, 6 years or later will have to be critically monitored on an ongoing basis. Their readiness may be quickened, or they may be deemed unsuitable after reassessment.

Succession Plan

D14.98 A leadership succession plan is a construct that should list at least the following information:

(a) all the critical roles;
(b) timelines of the planned movements of the current incumbents (movements include contract expiry, retirement, promotion and transfer where the timing may be estimated);
(c) requirements for each critical role; and
(d) names and profiles of potential successors to each critical role, together with the estimated timelines for their readiness.

D14.99 The succession plan serves as a dashboard of sorts to monitor the timelines for the talent pipeline to become successors for the organisation's critical positions. In reality, there is strong likelihood that surprises and disruptions may surface. Gaps may arise from resignations and other reasons for drop-off. The succession plan must also take into account any new candidates admitted to the Key Talent Program (KTP) who may be suitable (or better) potential successors for some critical roles. Continual review of the succession plan is therefore necessary to keep it realistic and current. Most organisations do a yearly or at least a two-yearly review.

D14.100 The succession plan is confidential. In the case of public-listed corporations, it can even be market-sensitive since it involves information on the planned exits of C-suite executives.

Derailers of Succession Planning

D14.101 Succession planning can be disrupted or compromised by various causes, mostly unanticipated. The common causes include the following:

(a) *Reduction, increase or modification of critical roles*
The organisation may shrink its operations due to adverse circumstances. The reverse may also happen; it may expand its operations to capture more business opportunities. The organisation may also undergo major restructuring to align with its evolving strategic focus. All these changes will impact its manpower requirements, including the number of senior critical positions and the composition and profiles of top executives. Potential successors will have to be added or removed, re-validated for suitability and in some cases, reshuffled.

(b) *Failure or delay in preparing successors*
The current incumbent in a critical position may fail to or delay grooming a successor. This may be due to selfish reasons or otherwise (say, procrastination). It is quite common to see a senior incumbent having his contract extended because the right successor has yet to be found or is not yet ready.

(c) *Change in timing of planned succession*
An incumbent in a critical position may decide to leave service earlier or be transferred out earlier or later due to unforeseen operational exigencies. It may also happen that at the time when the timed succession is supposed to take place, the organisation is facing a major crisis. To give confidence to its stakeholders, the organisation may decide to delay the handing over of the baton to the designated successor.

(d) *Successor leaves service or declines appointment*
A designated successor may leave service, or he may feel that he is not ready and therefore decline the position nearing the timed succession.

Mitigating the Derailers

D14.102 All succession plans, no matter how well it has been thought through, will have to be adaptive. Such is the nature of succession planning. That said, the organisation can put in some measures to mitigate the potential derailers as much as possible.

D14.103 Where the derailers are caused by external factors (as in derailer (a) mentioned above), it is challenging and perhaps not cost-effective to put in place onerous preventive or mitigatory measures to cater for unforeseen events which the organisation has little or no control over.

D14.104 In the case of derailers that are "man-made" (as in derailer (b) mentioned above), the organisation must be vigilant and resolute in dealing with them. Succession planning can only be successful if the incumbents of critical positions leave their positions as planned, unless for exceptional reasons. To make the transition more certain, many organisations put their C-suite executives on fixed-term contracts so that they can gracefully relinquish their positions when their contracts end. Many organisations also explicitly put as a key deliverable for the senior executive to identify and groom a successor before his contract expires. The pre-determined timing for the departure of the senior executive gives better certainty to the execution of the succession plan. Additionally, the Retirement and Re-employment Act and the related tripartite guidelines have accorded organisations a large degree of flexibility in re-employing their senior executives after the statutory retirement age so that organisations have the leeway to refresh and rejuvenate their leadership teams at appropriate timings to suit their strategic needs.

D14.105 As for derailer (d), the succession plan should have more than one successor for every critical role. The best insurance is for the succession plan to be robust and to have potential successors who are versatile and fundamentally very strong in core and generic competencies; this way, they may be interchangeable or reshuffled should the need arise.

D14.106 In a situation where the designated successor is not ready to step up and there is no other suitable successor, the organisation may have to delay the departure or transfer out of the incumbent and if that is not possible, to appoint a suitable employee to cover the position while it goes about to find and prepare another successor or recruit an experienced hire from outside as a last resort. Another option is to restructure the said position by removing certain roles and responsibilities to fit the capabilities of the designated successor.

D14.107 When a successor is appointed to assume a critical role, his performance in the initial period (at least for the first year) must be closely monitored. There may be instances where the new appointee may need some mentoring and support (particularly if he has been appointed earlier than planned).

The aim is to help him succeed as far as possible. If the outcome is not good, the organisation must be prepared to acknowledge the "mistake" and take remedial actions quickly. This is important since the performance of incumbents in critical roles has a material impact on the organisation.

Integrating Talent Management and Succession Planning with Other Human Capital Initiatives

D14.108 Talent management and succession planning (TMSP) cannot exist in isolation. It must integrate cogently with the other components of human capital management and development – manpower planning and recruitment, deployment, competency framework, job grade structure, career tracks and career roadmaps, performance management, 360-degree feedback, rewards management, training and development and employee engagement.

D14.109 How the different components of human capital management and development support TMSP is elaborated below:

1. Manpower Planning and Recruitment

Recruiting right helps ensure a continual inflow of quality new hires. If there is not enough talent inventory, it is a non-starter to do TMSP. All else equal, quality new hires make TMSP more cost-effective and impactful. To attract high-quality hires, an organisation should have the following elements in place: (a) strong employee value proposition to attract good candidates, (b) rigorous selection process to select the right candidates and (c) competitive remuneration.

In Singapore, many government agencies and government-linked companies offer scholarships as a strategy to capture top talent. The scholars invariably will be admitted to the key talent program (or equivalent) to be groomed for leadership roles.

Some organisations do not offer scholarships but have a management associate/trainee scheme to hire high-calibre fresh graduates who will be systematically developed and tested, and if they make the cut, will be groomed for future leadership roles.

2. Deployment

Talent must be deployed judiciously. Their deployments (in terms of job postings and special assignments) must achieve dual objectives: (a) to enable the talent to contribute their best to the organisation and (b) to have a developmental purpose to stretch them and broaden their exposure so as to accelerate their professional and personal growth.

3. Competency Framework

Core competencies and leadership competencies and the required proficiency levels provide an objective basis for assessing the performance and potential of the talent, as well as for determining the requirements of key/leadership positions. Please refer to Chapter D9 "Competency Frameworks" for a detailed elaboration on the features and usage of competency frameworks.

4. Job Grade Structure, Career Tracks and Career Roadmaps

A job grade structure is required to provide a basis to determine the rank hierarchy of the talent and the jobs that they perform. Not all talent share the same aspiration to lead big teams and manage people. Some aspire to reach the peak as masters of their professional craft. Career tracks offering both management and specialist roles allow high-calibre talent to actualise their potential according to their aspirations.

Career roadmaps must be planned and executed for the talent so that they can progress systematically to the key/leadership positions that they are slated to eventually assume. Please refer to Chapter D10 "Job Grade Structure and Career Roadmap" for a detailed elaboration of these constructs.

5. Performance Management

The talent will be put through the same performance management framework except that his performance goals and development needs must be given more attention. Performance feedback and coaching and performance critical conversations are essential mechanisms to continually develop the talent. Please refer to Chapters D2, D3 and D4 for a detailed elaboration of the various components of performance management.

6. 360-Degree Feedback

For the select tier of talent who are being groomed for key/leadership roles, their feedback regime may be complemented by 360-degree feedback (from supervisors, peers and subordinates). 360-degree feedback focuses on a person's working style, leadership effectiveness, interpersonal skills and collaboration. It will enable the talent to gain better self-awareness and insights into the impact (both positive and negative) that his working style generates. This will help him take targeted steps to address the negative aspects so that he can become more holistically effective at work. Please refer to Chapter D4 "Performance Appraisal", section "360-Degree Feedback or Reverse Appraisal" for more elaboration.

7. Employee Training and Development

Comprehensive training and development opportunities/interventions must be provided to the talent to enhance their competencies and accelerate their professional and personal growth so as to prepare them systematically for the key/leadership roles that they have been earmarked for. These may include stretch performance goals, assignment to high-impact project teams/committees, job rotations and secondments, special postings and appointments, acting appointments, exposure to senior-level events, leadership development programs, mentoring and executive coaching. Please refer to Chapter D11 "Employee Training" and Chapter D12 "Employee Development" for more elaboration on these interventions.

8. Rewards Management

Competitive remuneration and other rewards must be accorded to the talent commensurate with their contribution and worth so that they stay motivated to perform. Though many organisations and human resource practitioners subscribe to the belief that remuneration, being extrinsic in nature, cannot sustainably motivate talent, paying uncompetitive or unfair salary will certainly demotivate. It is a basic hygiene factor that must be addressed, period.

> **9. Employee Engagement**
>
> It is vital for the organisation to engage its talent to build emotional bonding. Fair and competitive salary and conducive work environment help retain people, but these do not drive commitment or passion. The organisation must share its strategic priorities and goals to foster involvement. It must also pay attention to values alignment to create resonance. Lastly, it must understand the talent's motivational levers and career aspirations so that these can be addressed. It serves to strengthen the talent's alignment with and commitment to the organisation. For details, please refer to Volume E, Chapter E2 "Employee Communication and Engagement".

D14.110 Given that TMSP must be integrated with various components of human capital management and development, it is best to be handled centrally by the corporate Human Resource team with oversight from the top management. The centralised approach gives a vantage point to ensure more seamless integration of the various HR initiatives as well as better alignment with the organisation's strategic goals. If there is no proper integration and alignment, TMSP can become an expensive and time-consuming exercise that is ineffective and wasteful.

Conclusion

D14.111 For talent management to be effective, it must be directed and overseen by the top management. They must regard talent management as a strategic and long-term investment and remain steadfast in their commitment. In times of declining or weak financial performance, the temptation is to roll back investment in acquiring good talent and grooming people for the future. Organisations that have remained unwavering in good and bad times reap benefits; they will have a continual pipeline of capable and committed people as their future leaders.

D14.112 Talent management and succession planning (TMSP) are complicated and sensitive because there are many moving parts involving people. To make them work, the following critical success factors must be observed: (a) high level of unwavering commitment from the top management, (b) holistic and integrated approach of TMSP with other human capital management and development components and (c) accountability and efforts by line heads and Human Resource in recruiting, identifying, developing, managing and engaging talents. TMSP is always a work in progress and can never be perfect. Notwithstanding, it is a strategic investment that an organisation can ill afford not to make; it would be tantamount to leaving its talent management and leadership succession to happen by chance and this is certainly not a wise thing.

Volume A
Employment Management

Chapters

Volume B
Work and Remuneration

Chapters

Volume C
Employee Benefits

Chapters

Volume D
Performance and Development

Chapters

Volume E
Employee Conduct and Relations

Chapters